ESSENTIAL LAWYERING SKILLS

ASPEN COURSEBOOK SERIES

ESSENTIAL LAWYERING SKILLS

Interviewing, Counseling, Negotiation, and Persuasive Fact Analysis

FIFTH EDITION

STEFAN H. KRIEGER
Professor of Law
Hofstra University

RICHARD K. NEUMANN, JR.
Professor of Law
Hofstra University

Wolters Kluwer

Published by Wolters Kluwer in New York.

Wolters Kluwer serves customers worldwide with CCH, Aspen Publishers, and Kluwer Law International products. (www.wolterskluwerlb.com)

To contact Customer Service, e-mail customer.service@wolterskluwer.com, call 1-800-234-1660, fax 1-800-901-9075, or mail correspondence to:

Wolters Kluwer
Attn: Order Department
PO Box 990
Frederick, MD 21705

Printed in the United States of America.

1 2 3 4 5 6 7 8 9 0

ISBN 978-1-4548-3098-6

Krieger, Stefan H., 1946- author.
Essential Lawyering Skills : interviewing, counseling, negotiation, and persuasive fact analysis / Stefan H. Krieger, Professor of Law, Hofstra University; Richard K. Neumann, Jr., Professor of Law, Hofstra University. — Fifth edition.
pages cm
Includes bibliographical references and index.
ISBN 978-1-4548-3098-6 (alk. paper)
1. Practice of law—United States. I. Neumann, Richard K., 1947- author. II. Title.
KF300.E84 2015
347.73'504—dc23

2014045919

About Wolters Kluwer Law & Business

Wolters Kluwer Law & Business is a leading global provider of intelligent information and digital solutions for legal and business professionals in key specialty areas, and respected educational resources for professors and law students. Wolters Kluwer Law & Business connects legal and business professionals as well as those in the education market with timely, specialized authoritative content and information-enabled solutions to support success through productivity, accuracy and mobility.

Serving customers worldwide, Wolters Kluwer Law & Business products include those under the Aspen Publishers, CCH, Kluwer Law International, Loislaw, ftwilliam.com and MediRegs family of products.

CCH products have been a trusted resource since 1913, and are highly regarded resources for legal, securities, antitrust and trade regulation, government contracting, banking, pension, payroll, employment and labor, and healthcare reimbursement and compliance professionals.

Aspen Publishers products provide essential information to attorneys, business professionals and law students. Written by preeminent authorities, the product line offers analytical and practical information in a range of specialty practice areas from securities law and intellectual property to mergers and acquisitions and pension/benefits. Aspen's trusted legal education resources provide professors and students with high-quality, up-to-date and effective resources for successful instruction and study in all areas of the law.

Kluwer Law International products provide the global business community with reliable international legal information in English. Legal practitioners, corporate counsel and business executives around the world rely on Kluwer Law journals, looseleafs, books, and electronic products for comprehensive information in many areas of international legal practice.

Loislaw is a comprehensive online legal research product providing legal content to law firm practitioners of various specializations. Loislaw provides attorneys with the ability to quickly and efficiently find the necessary legal information they need, when and where they need it, by facilitating access to primary law as well as state-specific law, records, forms and treatises.

ftwilliam.com offers employee benefits professionals the highest quality plan documents (retirement, welfare and non-qualified) and government forms (5500/PBGC, 1099 and IRS) software at highly competitive prices.

MediRegs products provide integrated health care compliance content and software solutions for professionals in healthcare, higher education and life sciences, including professionals in accounting, law and consulting.

Wolters Kluwer Law & Business, a division of Wolters Kluwer, is headquartered in New York. Wolters Kluwer is a market-leading global information services company focused on professionals.

For Mary—My Fellow Traveller
And Gary Palm—My Mentor and Friend
S.H.K.

For Deb, Lill, and Alex, with love
R.K.N.Jr

You know more than you think you do.
Benjamin Spock

The lyf so short, the craft so long to lerne.
Chaucer

SUMMARY OF CONTENTS

PART V NEGOTIATION 299

TABLE OF CONTENTS

ACKNOWLEDGMENTS

We are grateful to many people who contributed their thoughts to this book. Among them are Kathleen Beckett, J. Herbie DiFonzo, Deborah A. Ezbitski, Monroe Freedman, Steven D. Jamar, Lawrence W. Kessler, Kathleen H. McManus, Roy Simon, Kathryn E. Stein, Jane Spinak, Ronald Meister, Jane Sovern, Elizabeth Brehm, Heather Canning, Adam Kahn, Evgeny Krasnov, Mirel Fisch, Madelyne Mostiller, Melissa Manna, the anonymous reviewers who examined the manuscript at Aspen's request, and the children at Fellowes Athenaeum, Roxbury, MA, 1970-72. Research assistance was provided by Robin Chadwick, Michelle Chin Que, Brian Bender, Jennifer Goody, Eric Burgos, Dayna Shillet, Shiry Gaash, Richard Soleymanzadeh, Lisa Brabant, Randi Fensterer, Karen Nielson, Jason Parpas, Teresa Staples, Frances Zemel, George Pleasant-Jones, Daniel Rossi, Emily Rothenberg, Michelle McGreal, Silvia Stanciu, Kimberly Kaufman, and Brianne Richards. We are also grateful for research grants provided by Deans Stuart Rabinowitz, David Yellen, Aaron Twerski, Nora Demleitner, and Eric Lane.

Copyright Acknowledgments

Permission to reprint copyrighted excerpts from the following is gratefully acknowledged:

Richard Birke, "Decision Trees—Made Easy." Reprinted by permission of the author.

Agata Szypszak, *Where in the World Is Dr. Detchakandi? A Story of Fact Investigation.* From an article that originally appeared in 6 Clinical L. Rev. 517, 518–529 (2000).

Twentieth Century Fox Film Corporation, a division of Fox Entertainment Group, Inc., *The Simpsons*™, from the episode "Blood Feud," © 1991. Reprinted by permission of Twentieth Century Fox Film Corporation.

Richard C. Wydick, *The Ethics of Witness Coaching.* From an article that originally appeared in 17 Cardozo L. Rev. 1 (1995).

ESSENTIAL LAWYERING SKILLS

PART

I

BECOMING A LAWYER

CHAPTER

1

WHAT THIS BOOK IS ABOUT

This book explains four skills that nearly every lawyer uses, nearly every day. You are much more likely to be an effective lawyer if you are good at interviewing clients and witnesses, analyzing facts to develop persuasive theories, counseling clients, and negotiating. Because these four skills cut across every specialty and field in which a lawyer might work, they are at the core of the practice of law.

In addition, this book stresses a number of themes, which can be grouped under the headings of professionalism, working with and for the client, problem-solving, communications skills, and multicultural skills. Professionalism is a group of characteristics that makes lawyering different from and in many ways more difficult than other lines of work. The attorney-client relationship is, obviously, the heart of lawyering. Problem solving is the art of developing a plan to control events, which is what clients hire lawyers to do. Interviewing, counseling, negotiation, and much of the rest of lawyers' work involves the ability to communicate well orally, and that includes the ability to understand the hidden meanings in what other people say. Multicultural skills add up to the ability to work effectively with people whose cultural norms are different from one's own. These themes are discussed in Chapters 2 through 6.

Lawyers ***interview*** clients and, separately, witnesses. Client interviewing operates on two levels. On one of them, the lawyer finds out what the client knows of the facts. On the other level, the lawyer and client establish and maintain a professional relationship, not just contractually (the client hiring the lawyer) but also personally (developing trust and respect) and strategically (determining the client's goals and other factors that will influence the lawyer's work). Client interviewing is covered in Chapter 8.

Interviewing witnesses is a way of ascertaining what people other than the client know about the facts. Witness interviewing poses special ethical problems and requires special skills. It is covered in Chapter 9.

In both kinds of interviewing, lawyers face problems created by the frailties of human perception and memory. These problems are discussed in Chapter 7.

Persuasive fact analysis is the critical examination of facts—or what appear to be facts—in pretty much the same way that you have learned to analyze judicial decisions, followed by the development of factual theories through which the client's cause can be explained to judges, juries, bureaucrats, or the public. Facts can be organized in three different ways: according to the legal elements in a rule of law, by chronology, or in the form of a story. Fact analysis is covered in Chapters 10 through 17.

Counseling has two aspects. The first is structuring choices so that a client can select from them and make a decision. That includes identifying options and their advantages and disadvantages, predicting each option's likelihood of success. The second is explaining these choices to the client in a way that helps the client select from the options you have identified. Counseling is covered in Chapters 18 through 22.

Negotiating is the process through which two parties attempt to reach an agreement that reflects their interests, rights, and relative power. Some negotiations are by nature adversarial. Some are by nature a form of collaborative problem solving. And some could be either, depending on how the negotiators approach the problem. Negotiation is covered in Chapters 23 through 28.

Ethical concerns are discussed in connection with each of these skills.

Marjorie Shultz and Sheldon Zedeck conducted a research project—which has become known as the "Beyond the LSAT Study"—to develop a law school admissions test that would be more accurate than the LSAT. An admissions test should predict whether an applicant can develop, in law school and through experience, the characteristics that make a lawyer effective. In the first phase of the project, Shultz and Zedeck worked with over 2000 lawyers to learn what those characteristics are, and they identified 26 effectiveness factors. Only a few of them are measured by the LSAT and are taught in law school classroom courses (the kind of courses that teach a part of the law, like Torts, and that use a casebook). The book you are holding in your hands teaches or helps to teach 18 of Shultz and Zedeck's 26 effectiveness factors, some of which are also taught elsewhere in the law school curriculum:

Questioning and Interviewing
Fact Finding
Building Client Relationships and Providing Advice and Counsel
Negotiation Skills
Strategic Planning
Creativity and Innovation

Practical Judgment
Listening
Influencing and Advocating
Speaking
Integrity and Honesty
Analysis and Reasoning
Developing Relationships
Self-Development
Diligence
Passion and Engagement
Able to See the World Through the Eyes of Others
Problem Solving

The eight remaining factors—which are not significantly addressed in this book—are Writing; Researching the Law; Networking and Business Development; Stress Management; Community Involvement and Service; Organizing and Managing Your Own Work; Organizing and Managing Others (Staff and Colleagues); and Evaluation, Development, and Mentoring of Others.

CHAPTER

2

PROFESSIONALISM

§2.1 THE REFLECTIVE PRACTITIONER OF LAW

You go to a doctor and describe the symptoms that bother you. After examining you and perhaps detecting a few symptoms that you had not noticed before, the doctor names a disease, writes a prescription, tells you how many days it should take for the prescription to work, and asks you to telephone by then if it has not. Does the doctor know for certain that you in fact have this disease? Probably not.

The late Donald Schön did the leading research on how professionals in general think. Among many things, he asked doctors to estimate the proportion of their patients who present problems that "are not in the book" in the sense that the doctor needs to "invent and experiment on the spot" to figure out what treatment will work.[1] The estimates he received ranged from 30% to 80%, and he said that the 80% estimate came from "someone whom I regard as a very good doctor."[2]

This is typical of the problems faced by a professional in any field, whether it is medicine or architecture or law. To a layperson, it seems that the distinguishing mark of a professional is knowledge that other people do not have—almost like a sorcerer's secret book of magical formulas. Certainly, professionals do have specialized knowledge. But in professional work there are very few, if any, cookbook answers. Instead, what really distinguishes a professional is *a way of thinking* that enables the professional to solve problems even when a situation is wrapped in a fog of "uncertainty, uniqueness, and conflict."[3]

---

1. Donald A. Schön, *Educating the Reflective Legal Practitioner*, 2 Clinical L. Rev. 231, 239 (1995).
2. *Id.*
3. Donald A. Schön, *Educating the Reflective Practitioner* xi (1987).

People who have not practiced law easily underestimate the amount of uncertainty inherent in nearly every situation presented to a lawyer for solution. The law may be unclear. The facts may be difficult to ascertain. And most often, it is hard to make precise predictions about how judges, juries, administrative officials, adversaries, and opposing parties will react to evidence and arguments. None of that is an excuse for the lawyer to say, "We'll try the first thing that looks good and hope for the best." Professionalism means, among other things, finding a solution that is hidden inside all that uncertainty and conflict.

Schön used the term "reflection-in-action"[4] to describe the process through which professionals unravel problems and solve them. This is not the kind of abstract and academic reflection that you went through when you wrote a term paper in college. Instead, it is a silent dialogue between the professional and the problem to be solved. In that dialogue, the professional uses what is already known in order to learn what is not yet known, through experimentation or some other form of investigation, until a solution is found. (Remember the doctor who does not really know what is making you feel sick. If the medication prescribed works, the doctor has solved the problem. If not, the doctor will experiment with something else.)

The reflective practitioner is one who can reflect *while acting*. To do that well we need "the ability to think about what we are doing while we are doing it, to turn our thought back on itself in the surprising situation."[5] We need to examine our own conduct, self-critically. Effective professionals never stop doing that, no matter how experienced they become.

As Paul Brest has written, "good lawyers bring more to bear on a problem than legal knowledge and lawyering skills. They bring creativity, common sense, practical wisdom, and that most precious of attributes, good judgment."[6] Good lawyers bring as well some characteristics explained in §2.2, such as prudence and a wariness about assumptions.

§2.2 SOME THINGS EFFECTIVE LAWYERS KNOW

Together with the subjects discussed elsewhere in this chapter, in Chapter 3 (clients), in Chapter 4 (legal problem solving), in Chapter 5 (communications skills), and in Chapter 6 (multicultural skills), the ideas mentioned below are among the themes of this book. We will return to them often.

---

4. *Id.* at 22.
5. Schön, *supra* note 1, at 244.
6. Paul Brest, *The Responsibility of Law Schools: Educating Lawyers as Counselors and Problem Solvers*, 58 Law & Contemp. Probs. (Issues 3 & 4) 5, 8 (Summer/Autumn 1995).

§2.2.1 EXCELLENT JUDGMENT IS THE MOST IMPORTANT THING THAT A LAWYER CAN BRING TO ANY SITUATION

Judgment is knowing what to do and say—and what *not* to do or say—to improve a situation or prevent it from getting worse. Professionals *decide what to do*, and excellent judgment is the single most important characteristic that separates good decision-making from bad decision-making. When clients rely on you, they are, more than anything else, relying on your judgment.

Knowledge of the law is not enough. A lawyer who knows the law but lacks good judgment is a lawyer who sounds well informed but makes too many avoidable mistakes.

Judgment is the ability to know what actions and words are most likely to solve problems or, ideally, prevent them. It depends on situation-sense—an instinct for reading between the lines and figuring out what's really going on, without being told explicitly. It operates on several levels at once—the practical, the ethical, and the moral—and it includes "appreciating the hidden complexity in questions that seem easy when they are posed in the abstract."[7]

The phrase *a prudent lawyer* refers to one whose judgment can safely be relied upon. A prudent lawyer foresees risk, makes sure that mistakes do not happen, and, to the extent possible, keeps clients out of trouble.

If you are a novice hiker with a dozen other novice hikers high in the mountains when a sudden and unpredicted blizzard traps all of you in snowdrifts so deep that you can barely walk, good judgment is what you most hope to find in the guide your group hired to lead you through the mountains. As you glance at this guide and feel cold and hunger, you do not want the guide to make foolish decisions that would make a bad situation much worse, such as by taking you through places where your own movements can set off an avalanche. Instead, you want a guide who is calm; thinks carefully before acting but does act decisively; sees, several steps ahead, the consequences of actions; and can quickly understand all the forces and factors, including human nature, that can influence events. You want this person to get you out, and that requires more than knowledge of the geography of the mountains and the rescue policies of the Forest Service. It requires the ability to make decisions for which there is no script and no formula. Should you try to hike out, for example, or wait where you are on the theory that movement expends energy you need to survive in the cold? How much food should you eat each day? You need to eat enough to keep from succumbing to the cold but not so much that you run out of food before help arrives—and no one can predict how long it will take for rescuers to find you. Judgment is the ability to make these decisions well.

Because "it is possible to have knowledge but lack judgment,"[8] knowing the law (or the geography of the mountains) is not enough. Judgment is knowing what to *do*.

---

7. David Luban & Michael Millemann, *Good Judgment: Ethics Teaching in Dark Times*, 9 Geo. J. Leg. Ethics 31, 71 (1995).
8. Mark Neal Aaronson, *We Ask You to Consider Learning about Practical Judgment in Lawyering*, 4 Clinical L. Rev. 247, 262 (1998).

§2.2.2 INTEGRITY IS YOUR MOST VALUABLE ASSET AS A LAWYER

Integrity means

- an honesty so thorough that anyone who knows the lawyer believes and trusts her;
- an instinct for what's right and fair so reliable that others respect the lawyer's moral voice;
- a strong feeling of responsibility for the matters entrusted to the lawyer's care;
- an understanding of appropriateness that prevents the lawyer from crossing over into questionable conduct;
- the strength to resist pressure to do the wrong thing; and
- humility.

A lawyer with integrity treats everyone with respect and empathy, regardless of their station in life.

§2.2.3 A LAWYER'S JOB IS TO FIND A WAY—TO THE EXTENT POSSIBLE—FOR THE CLIENT TO GAIN CONTROL OVER A SITUATION

Often, the situation is already out of control when the lawyer is hired. An obvious example would be any situation in which the client is in conflict with somebody else. To an individual or a small business, few things are as frightening as a situation so out of control that lawyers are being called in. To a large business, it might be more routine, but to the employees of a large business, their careers might be on the line.

At the opposite extreme, things might be happy now, and the client might want to make sure that they stay that way in the future. Here are some examples: The client wants an estate plan that will distribute her assets to her heirs in a way that conforms to her feelings about them. Or the client has agreed to a commercial transaction with someone else and wants that agreement reduced to a written contract in a way that best protects the client. Or the client is a business that wants to know how it can most inexpensively conform to the regulations of the Environmental Protection Agency.

In all these situations, what the client wants from the lawyer is a method of controlling—to the extent possible—what happens. That requires more than knowledge of statutes and case law. It requires the ability to plan ahead, a refusal to place yourself at the mercy of events, decisiveness (the capacity to act under pressure), presence of mind (the capacity to reflect among options while under pressure), and the problem-solving skills explained in Chapter 4.

§2.2.4 EFFECTIVE LAWYERS WORK TO ACHIEVE SPECIFIC GOALS

The client wants something—win this lawsuit, merge with that other company, or stop cattle from overgrazing on publicly owned range land. Whatever the client wants is the overall or ultimate goal. To achieve it, the lawyer must do a number of things along the way—develop evidence that justifies summary judgment, persuade the Antitrust Division of the Justice Department to allow the merger, see whether the ranchers and environmentalists have some interests in common. Those are interim, strategic, or tactical goals. Effective lawyers know exactly what the goals are and focus their work on accomplishing them. They do not work aimlessly on whatever is in the office's file.

§2.2.5 SUCCESS IN THE PRACTICE OF LAW DEPENDS ON EFFICIENT WORK HABITS

Efficiency is getting the best results from a unit of effort, such as a billable hour. It's a ratio between work and gain. A lawyer is more efficient than others if she gets more results from a billable hour or if she gets the same results in less than a billable hour.

The efficient lawyer prospers while the inefficient lawyer works hard without having much to show for it. Many business clients now audit their own law firms' bills to figure out whether the lawyers have used the most cost-effective ways of solving problems. Law firms that fail this scrutiny lose clients. It's difficult to be efficient without working hard, but hard work isn't the same as efficiency. Many inefficient lawyers work long hours without serving their clients well—and they lose clients who figure that out.

Time—including other people's time—is a resource to be used efficiently. A 20-minute conversation with a partner or a client wastes everyone's time if it covers only five minutes of content. The client or partner will assume that the lawyer who has wasted their time uses her own time inefficiently in other respects as well. The client will think about that when deciding whether to pay all or only part of the lawyer's bill. The supervising partner will think about it when deciding whether the lawyer's salary is being used efficiently.

§2.2.6 THOROUGH PREPARATION IS ESSENTIAL

"Winging it" is sloppy and dangerous lawyering. Many lawyering tasks are like icebergs: What the bystander sees (the tip of the iceberg or the visible part of the lawyer's performance) is a tiny fraction of what supports it (the undersea part of the iceberg or the preparation for the performance). In lawyering, the ratio of preparation to performance can easily reach 15 or 20 to 1. It might take 10 hours to prepare for a half-hour counseling session with a client, and it might take 15 hours to prepare for a negotiating meeting that lasts 2 hours. That is why this book devotes entire chapters to preparing to counsel and preparing to negotiate.

In preparation, resourcefulness counts more than brilliance does. Few legal problems are solved by astute insights that no one has thought of before. Most legal problems are solved by diligently learning the details that matter and putting them together into a package that gets results.

§2.2.7 EVERYTHING REVOLVES AROUND FACTS

Law school can mislead you. You are spending so much time learning law and how to analyze law that you might get the impression that factual issues are easy.

They are not easy, and they are not marginal, either. Fact analysis permeates this book because it permeates the practice of law.

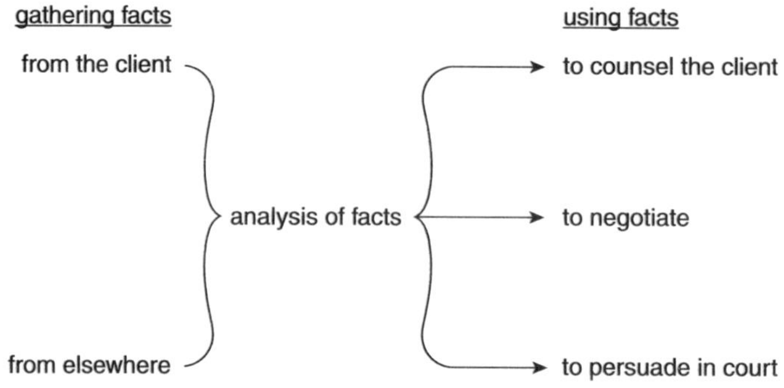

§2.2.8 ASSUMPTIONS CAN SABOTAGE GOOD LAWYERING

You realize that you need to make a decision soon. You also realize that you need to know six things to make this decision. You already know five of them. You have made a guess about the sixth thing, and you are confident that your guess is accurate. You could rely on your guess (make an assumption), or you could devote some effort to finding out what the truth is.

When lawyers make assumptions, they and their clients can get hurt. That is because our guesses turn out to be wrong surprisingly often. It is also because clients hire lawyers for important matters, where mistakes cause real harming.

Not all assumptions are bad. Sometimes, a lawyer will properly make a *temporary* assumption because the truth cannot yet be ascertained and work must proceed in the meantime. Sometimes a lawyer will balance risks and make an assumption because the decision involved is small and the cost of learning the truth is too large. And sometimes a lawyer will have to make an assumption because the truth cannot be learned.

But many of the assumptions you will be tempted to make should not be made. As a general rule, if you do not know whether something is true, find out. And if you must make an assumption, do it explicitly so that you and the people who rely on you know what is happening.

The most dangerous assumptions are the *unconscious* ones—the ones you do not even realize you are making. Suppose that you are chatting with someone in a social situation. Some of the things the other person says are derived from matters that you do not fully know. You might ask a few questions, but for the most part you assume underlying facts without even realizing that you are doing it. You make these assumptions for three reasons. You do not want to appear dumb. You do not want to be a pest, constantly interrupting with questions. And most of the subjects of social conversations are not important enough to merit the kind of thorough exploration that would have to be undertaken if we made no assumptions.

In lawyering, an unconscious assumption is especially dangerous because you do not realize you are making it and therefore cannot control it. You cannot gauge the risk posed by an unconscious assumption, for example, and you cannot commit yourself to learning the truth as soon as possible.

The only way to overcome this problem is to learn to recognize what you do not know and consciously decide what to do about it.

§2.2.9 REPRESENTING CLIENTS IN DISPUTES IS ONLY PART OF WHAT LAWYERS DO—THE REST IS TRANSACTIONAL

Movies and television almost invariably portray lawyers as cross-examining witnesses and making arguments to judges and juries—in other words, litigating. And law school law is taught through cases, or more precisely through judicial opinions that resolve litigation. But many lawyers almost never go near a courtroom. The practice of law is divided into two parts. One is the resolution of disputes, often through litigation. The other is transactional: advising and representing clients in situations where there is no dispute. Sometimes the situation is contractual: two companies have agreed to do business with each other, for example, and the lawyer will turn the agreement into a contract. Sometimes, it involves noncontractual transfers, such as will-drafting and other forms of estate planning. And sometimes it involves advising the client on how to behave to avoid liability of some kind. Some lawyers do only dispute work. Some do only transactional work. And some do both.

Dispute lawyers and transactional lawyers approach legal problems differently and in some respects see the world differently. Most fundamentally, dispute lawyers fight to protect clients who are already in conflict with somebody else. Transactional lawyers plan and draft documents to achieve the client's goals while minimizing the risk of conflict, because conflict could prevent or make more expensive the accomplishment of those goals. Dispute lawyers try to beat the other side through public performances in courtrooms. Or they negotiate settlements in which one side takes something from the other (though perhaps not as much as the taker had hoped to get).

A dispute is what social scientists call a zero-sum game: what one side gains is what the other side loses, averaging out to zero. If a plaintiff gains $100,000, the defendant loses $100,000. (Actually, the average is less than zero because each side has to pay its lawyers and other expenses to resolve the conflict.) Transactional work, however, usually is not a zero-sum game. If two companies do a deal—agree to trade money for goods, services, or other things of value—each of them anticipates becoming better off as a result. If the deal works as planned, it is a win-win situation. The deal lawyer's job is to plan and draft to increase the odds that the deal will work as the client had planned. The lawyers still struggle for control and advantage, but a client who considers a proposed deal a loss can simply walk away and deal with someone else.

§2.2.10 TO BE EFFECTIVE, A LAWYER MUST KNOW HOW—AND WHEN—TO FUNCTION IN INQUIRING MODE AS WELL AS IN PERSUASION MODE

Persuasion mode[9] is the thinking and talking that manipulates a situation. Persuasion is one of the cores of lawyers' work, and the persuasion mode obviously is valuable to lawyers. But it also has disadvantages.

A person in persuasion mode tends to act more or less continually on hidden agendas and strategies, "to minimize self-analysis and to reserve it for private moments when it will not weaken instrumental effectiveness,"[10] to argue in ways that are subtle but "needlessly stylized and hyperbolic,"[11] and to treat others often as objects and as types, rather than as individually unique. When a person in persuasion mode listens, it is less out of curiosity than out of a search for ammunition that can be used to gain or maintain control. Persuasion-mode behavior is profitable in situations where the struggle is for control rather than insight, and where the "self-sealing properties of persuasion-mode habits"[12] minimize tentativeness, doubt, and perplexity over the unknowable and gray areas of life.

Persuasion-mode behavior can be destructive in other ways as well. Unrestrained persuasion-mode behavior produces over-simplified reasoning, self-serving speech, and a reduced loyalty to truth. "Persuasion-mode habits predispose lawyers to take evaluative stands automatically" so that they "make statements that, on reflection, they know to be false."[13] "It causes one to impute rather than explore others' ends, shut off rather than encourage legitimate objection, . . . and accumulate rather than share decision-making authority."[14] Other people see it as manipulative and controlling.

> [T]he persuasion mode is not always associated with bad, unpleasant, aggressive behavior. The mode is just as often a low-visibility, indirect, and even cordial method of manipulating others. . . . The persuasion mode is used among friends as well as enemies and people feel good about it as often as they feel resentful. . . . [T]he true test of persuasion-mode behavior is in what it seeks to accomplish (e.g., victory rather than understanding or uncoerced agreement) and by what strategies (e.g., private, unilateral, competitive, and self-sealing actions rather than public, bilateral, cooperative, and self-reflective ones).[15]

---

9. Lawyers do not use the term *persuasion mode*. Persuasion-mode behavior was first described by Chris Argyris & Donald Schön, *Theory in Practice: Increasing Professional Effectiveness* (1974), although Argyris and Schön used different terminology to describe it. Robert Condlin was the first to discuss it in the legal literature. See Condlin, *The Moral Failure of Clinical Legal Education* in *The Good Lawyer: Lawyers' Roles and Lawyers' Ethics* 318 (D. Luban ed. 1983) [hereinafter Condlin, *Moral Failure*] and Condlin, *Socrates' New Clothes: Substituting Persuasion For Learning in Clinical Practice Instruction*, 40 Md. L. Rev. 223 (1981) [hereinafter Condlin, *Socrates' New Clothes*]. Schön later explored the subject in further detail. See Donald Schön, *Educating the Reflective Practitioner* (1987).
10. Condlin, *Moral Failure, supra* note 9, at 330.
11. *Id.* at 326.
12. *Id.*
13. *Id.*
14. *Id.* at 329.
15. *Id.* at 328.

Even when accompanied by pleasantness and charm, persuasion-mode behavior is recognized by others, who often react defensively.

The opposite pattern of behavior might be called the inquiring mode: open-ended curiosity and an interest in exploring things regardless of the consequences. A person in inquiring mode is not trying to accomplish anything except learn. The following illustrates the difference. In each column, a lawyer is asking questions.

Persuasion Mode

Q: Didn't your company's lab tests show that this tire disintegrates at 90 miles per hour?

Q: And didn't your company advertise this tire as suitable for use on police cars?

Q: Police sometimes have to chase criminals at high speeds, don't they?

(Are you persuaded that the tire manufacturer did something wrong?)

Inquiring Mode

Q: Could you tell me everything you know about how this tire was tested in the lab?

Q: What were the results of those tests?

Q: What did the advertisements say about using the tire on police cars?

Q: Where were the advertisements placed?

Q: How was the decision made to advertise the tire that way?

Q: Could you tell me everything you know about the stresses tires are subjected to when used on police cars?

(Would you learn more from the answers to these questions than from the answers to the questions in the persuasion mode column?)

Although the answers are omitted here, you can easily imagine what they might look like. The answers to the persuasion-mode questions will typically be short and perhaps defensive. (At trial, that might persuade a fact-finder to agree with the lawyer.) The answers to the inquiring-mode questions will typically be much longer and include far more information. From the answers to the inquiring-mode questions, you would know much more about what *really* happened than you would from the answers to the persuasion-mode questions.

The persuasion mode and the inquiring mode both have their uses in the practice of law. To be an effective lawyer, you need to know how to function well in both modes. The problem is that many lawyers are so locked into persuasion mode that they do not know when or how to switch into inquiring mode.

In the skills covered in this book, the inquiring mode is more valuable than you might think. Most—but not all—of what a lawyer does in interviewing and counseling is best done in inquiring mode. In those and similar situations, the very qualities many lawyers use to project forcefulness can inhibit open-ended inquiry.

Negotiation, on the other hand, is often primarily persuasion. But even in negotiation, there are times when it is best to stop trying to persuade and instead to switch into the inquiring mode.

§2.2.11 NUMBERS MATTER

A great deal of what lawyers do involves reallocating money. In counseling, you develop a list of options from which the client will choose. If money is a significant part of the decision, each option can be valued in money terms. Suppose that Option A offers a 50% chance of getting $100,000, while Option B offers a 75% chance of getting $50,000. If you dislike numbers, you might describe the options only in words and never do the math. But that would be an incomplete job of counseling. Without the numbers, the client cannot decide. (By the way, the expected value of Option A is $50,000 because the client has a 50% expectation of getting $100,000, and the expected value of Option B is $37,500 because the client has a 75% expectation of getting $50,000. For why, see §20.3.2.)

In negotiation, you might be taken advantage of if you are bargaining about money and if the other lawyer is much better at numbers than you are. Suppose you represent a plaintiff and have reached a tentative agreement with the defendant that will produce $500,000 for your client. The defendant's lawyer proposes that the money be paid out in five annual installments of $500,000. Why should you consider resisting this proposal? Money paid out over time is worth less than the same amount paid in one lump sum. Wherever the money is, it can grow because it can earn interest. While the defendant keeps some of the money, it earns interest for the defendant and not for your client. This is called the time value of money. See §§20.3.2 and 24.6.

Except in a few fields where money is usually not the focus, an effective lawyer knows how to work out the numbers and how to present and explain numbers to other people.

§2.2.12 TAXES MATTER

Whenever money changes hands, the transaction might have tax consequences, and you cannot counsel or negotiate without knowing what those consequences are.

Suppose you represent a plaintiff who has pleaded claims of wrongful discharge and battery. The defendant offers to settle by paying an amount of money that your client finds satisfactory, and the defendant prefers to pay the money entirely as back pay. He would rather be thought of as someone who fires an employee illegally than as someone who swings a tire iron at an employee while screaming "You're fired." "It's a good amount of money," your client tells you. "Does it matter whether we call it back pay or damages for battery?"

"Yes," you reply. "It does matter. The $100,000 they are offering is worth only $65,000 to you because you'll pay federal and state income tax on it. But $100,000 in damages for battery is $100,000 because it's not taxed." If you fail to tell your client that, you have committed malpractice. And when you do say it, your client will probably send you back to tell the defendant that the money will be acceptable only as damages for battery. See §20.3.2.

You don't need to know the tax code from end to end. Instead, you need to know how tax law affects the issues you deal with frequently. A personal injury lawyer would know how tort recoveries are taxed. If you're inexperienced in the type of transaction you're doing, you should be able to recognize *potential* tax issues and know when to get answers from a lawyer who specializes in tax.

§2.2.13 OVERLAWYERING CAN BE AS DAMAGING AS UNDERLAWYERING

Underlawyering is doing a cursory or half-hearted job. Overlawyering is making an issue out of everything, whether it really matters or not.

Business people use the term "deal killers" to refer to lawyers who regularly overlawyer. Suppose that Dynamo Electric, Inc., a chain of retail stores, wants to rent a warehouse to store household appliances such as refrigerators and stereos. The most suitable warehouse is owned by Belinsky Properties, Inc. Dynamo talks to Belinsky, and they agree on how much rent Belinsky will receive and how many years Dynamo will occupy the building. Because a lease must be drawn up, each company calls in its lawyers. The lawyers start by arguing with each other over who will bear the risk of loss to Dynamo's merchandise if the warehouse burns down. This is a useful argument. Lawyers are paid to identify potential problems like that and then make sure that harm is minimized.

But we are long past the point of diminishing returns when Belinsky's lawyer demands that Dynamo post a bond to indemnify Belinsky in case Belinsky is ever named as a defendant in a products liability suit concerning an appliance stored in the warehouse by Dynamo. When the clients learn of this, Dynamo will think that if Belinsky is this unreasonable now, things will only get worse later. So Dynamo will instead rent a different warehouse from Franken & Partners. And Belinsky will want to know what went wrong.

"It isn't that the lawyers are actually trying to kill the deal. They just want to . . . dot the 'i's [and] cross the 't's . . . And they love to 'one-up' the other party's lawyers; in this game, being the last one to add a clause gains them great face."[16] This can get so bad that "some business people . . . never allow[] their own lawyer to talk to someone else's without supervision—the goal is to keep the lawyers from arguing back and forth until the contract is [too] long and the deal is dead."[17] "Friends who practice law in Canada have commented that 'The American lawyers do seem to try and squeeze every drop out of a deal.'"[18] From the client's point of view, the last few drops are rarely cost-efficient: they cost too much in legal fees, in deal-killing risk, and in damage to the ongoing relationship between the parties (if there is one).

Focus on what is really needed to accomplish the client's goals. Provide just the right amount of lawyering to do that—not more and not less.

16. Nicholas Carroll, *Dancing with Lawyers: How to Take Charge and Get Results* 60 (1992).
17. *Id.* at 61.
18. *Id.* at 60.

§2.2.14 FOR MOST LAWYERS, IT'S A STRUGGLE TO LEAD A BALANCED LIFE, BUT IT'S A STRUGGLE YOU CAN WIN

A study by Lawrence Krieger and Kennon Sheldon[19] of thousands of lawyers showed that happiness—both in a job and generally—is most strongly correlated with the extent to which a lawyer has autonomy, such as the freedom to choose how to do one's work; competence; relatedness, such as meaningful interaction with clients, colleagues, friends, and family; and internally motivated fulfillment, such as enjoyment in doing one's work and awareness that the work furthers one's values. Happiness comes in part from how you experience a job and in part from the life you lead away from the job. A healthy relationship between a job and the rest of life is called *balance*.

Your family and the other people you care about are *not* less important than lawyering. Each day that you do not spend time with them is a day you cannot recover later, no matter how much you might want to. Do some things that have nothing to do with law—sports, cooking for the pleasure of it, gardening, something artistic or spiritual. Not only will they refresh you, but they will also help you become a happier and more complete person.

Integrity plays a special role in this. It is a professional asset (§2.2.2) and it is also one of the keys to happiness generally. If you know that you have acted with integrity, you can have more respect for yourself and know that you have truly earned the love, affection, and respect of others.[20]

§2.3 PROFESSIONALISM IS A WAY OF BEING

Becoming a professional is a long and gradual process, beginning in law school and continuing for years afterward. Throughout that time, you make choices about the kind of professional you'll be. Some of those choices are made in many small steps—so many and so small that you might not realize that they add up to important decisions. You have been making these choices since the first day of law school when teachers began to pressure you to speak and listen—and to read and eventually write—with more precision than had ever been expected of you before. If you met that challenge, you've made some choices about the kind of lawyer you want to be, and you have probably become stronger for it and learned to see many things around you with greater clarity.

As you become a professional—an effective problem-solver, with excellent judgment and integrity, who communicates precisely, produces high-quality work reliably and efficiently, and accomplishes client goals with a minimum of supervision—you're becoming a different person. In their path-breaking lawyering

---

19. Lawrence S. Krieger & Kennon M. Sheldon, *What Makes Lawyers Happy? Transcending the Anecdotes with Data from 6200 Lawyers*, 83 G.W. L. Rev. ___ (2015 forthcoming).

20. If the subject of balance resonates with you, we recommend that you read a book by Steven Keeva: *Transforming Practices: Finding Joy and Satisfaction in the Legal Life* (1999), as well as two articles by Patrick J. Schiltz, previously a law school teacher and now a federal judge: *Legal Ethics in Decline: The Elite Law Firm, the Elite Law School, and the Moral Formation of the Novice Attorney*, 82 Minn. L. Rev. 705 (1998), and *On Being a Happy, Healthy, and Ethical Member of an Unhappy, Unhealthy, and Unethical Profession*, 52 Vand. L. Rev. 871 (1999).

skills textbook, Gary Bellow and Bea Moulton began with this quote from Coles' biography of Erik Erikson:

> In this life we prepare for things, for moments and events and situations. . . . We worry about things, think about injustices, read what Tolstoi or Ruskin . . . has to say. . . . Then, all of a sudden, the issue is not whether we agree with what we have heard and read and studied. . . . The issue is *us*, and what we have become.[21]

This is true for every lawyer, doctor, therapist, architect or other professional. It's not just that a professional knows things that other people don't know or can use that knowledge. It's also that a professional thinks differently and sees the world differently. This issue is every one of us—what kind of lawyer each has become or is becoming.

We are what we do. The *manner* in which we win a victory becomes a fact that affects the situation that follows, the client's appreciation of it, and—ultimately, after many such victories—the kind of people we are. Victories won by bullying and deceit leave a residue that is very different from victories won with integrity.

---

21. Gary Bellow & Bea Moulton, *The Lawyering Process: Materials for Clinical Instruction in Advocacy* 1 (1978), quoting from Robert Coles, *Erik H. Erikson, The Growth of His Work* 39 (1970).

CHAPTER 3

LAWYERING FOR AND WITH THE CLIENT

§3.1 CLIENT-CENTERED LAWYERING

One lawyer had this to say about legal representation:

> I represent people, not cases. . . . [W]hen I did criminal defense work[, c]lients came to me with more than just their criminal case. Their families were on welfare, or they'd lose their job if they couldn't make bail. There are drug problems which affect whole families. . . . One time, my client came to court with her three-year-old child, and the judge rolled her up into jail on some technicality. We [later] got her out on a writ, but I couldn't leave the child there [in the courtroom], so I took her with me.
>
> You've got to go the whole nine yards for your clients. If you don't, you're really not meeting their needs. I had a poor client with a big products liability case. She had almost no clothes and had never been in a courthouse, so we went out and bought her a whole wardrobe for trial. When we won big, we [counseled her to] put money in trust for the kids, and buy a nice home but pay in cash so you don't have monthly payments. Otherwise, the money could have been gone in a year. . . .
>
> I don't want to take over their lives or force them to do something they don't want, but I never want to abandon my clients at the courthouse door. I guess that

> means getting emotionally involved in your clients' lives. . . . [T]hat's a price I'll gladly pay to try to help the *person*, not just the case.[1]

A client is not an item of work. You probably dislike it when a doctor treats you as a case of flu rather than as a human being who has the flu. And the problem is more than unpleasantness: a doctor who treats you as a human being with symptoms of the flu might spend enough time with you to learn that you also have other symptoms, and that you therefore do not have the flu, but instead another disease, which should be treated differently. You can imagine much of how a client experiences an interview with a lawyer simply by remembering how you have experienced contact with doctors.

The opposite of treating the client as an item of work is "client-centered lawyering," a phrase that originated in a ground-breaking book by David Binder and Susan Price.[2] It means focusing our efforts around what the client hopes for (rather than what we think the client needs) and treating the client as an effective collaborator (rather than as a helpless person we will rescue). We have no special wisdom about what clients should want, and each client has to live with the results of our work long after the case has faded into the back of our memory. Clients are not helpless, and even if they were, only rarely could we rescue them. A better view is this: the client is a capable person who has hired us to help the client accomplish a particular goal.

The client who is not experienced at hiring lawyers is very different from the client (usually a business person) who hires lawyers routinely. The inexperienced client may have more anxiety and may understand less about how lawyers work. The experienced client may have more sharply defined goals and may think of hiring the lawyer as bringing in a specialist to perform an already defined task.

And the client who wants help with a dispute (suing over an auto accident, for example) can be very different from the client who wants assistance completing a transaction (typically, negotiating a contract). If the transaction is important, the transactional client might be experiencing some stress, which might be replaced with happiness if the transaction is successful. But a dispute client has a greater chance of feeling stress, trauma, and anger.

§3.2 THE CLIENT AS A COLLEAGUE AND COLLABORATOR

Consider two scenes in two different lawyers' offices. In one, the lawyer sits behind a large desk, and the client sits in a chair on the opposite side of the desk. When the client speaks, it is to supply facts the lawyer has asked for. When the lawyer speaks, it is to provide professional advice and judgment. This is often

---

1. An anonymous lawyer quoted at Richard A. Zitrin & Carol M. Langford, *Legal Ethics in the Practice of Law* 230 (1995).

2. David A. Binder & Susan M. Price, *Legal Interviewing and Counseling: A Client-Centered Approach* (1977). A more recent version is David A. Binder, Paul B. Bergman, Susan M. Price & Paul R. Trembley, *Lawyers as Counselors: A Client-Centered Approach* (2d ed. 2004).

called the traditional model of the attorney-client relationship: the passive client protected by the powerful professional.

In the second scene, the lawyer and client sit together, perhaps at a conference table. They brainstorm, go over documents, and talk about which of several possible strategies would best accomplish the client's goals—and in doing so, they are both active. This has been called the participatory model of the attorney-client relationship: the lawyer assumes that she does not have all the answers, and the client is enlisted to supply an added measure of creativity and an often superior knowledge of the facts.

Most clients today want lawyers who know how to use the participatory model, although a significant minority still prefer the traditional model. The reverse was probably true 40 or 50 years ago. Some clients who still prefer the traditional model do so because they feel reassured turning things over to a trusted authority figure.

A client who prefers the traditional model might reduce anxiety by turning a problem over to a professional, thinking about it as little as possible while the professional works on it, and then following the professional's instructions. That client might trust more easily a professional who resembles an authority figure.

But a client who prefers the participatory model might reduce anxiety by becoming actively involved in solving a problem. That client might more easily trust a professional who is openly accessible and has a problem-solving style that the client understands and respects.

In a pioneering study, Douglas Rosenthal studied a number of personal injury cases to determine whether—personal preferences aside—one model produces better solutions than the other.[3] Rosenthal examined a number of personal injury cases, categorized the plaintiff's attorney-client relationship in each case as either traditional or participatory, and compared the result in each case with an independent evaluation of what the plaintiff's claim was worth. On average, the participatory plaintiff's lawyers got better results. The gap between the participatory and the traditional results was not huge, and Rosenthal's sample was relatively small. But since then, the impression has become widespread that participatory relationships with clients produce better and more satisfying results than traditional relationships do.

Why does the participatory model seem to work better and to satisfy more clients and lawyers? First, because lawyers are human, they make mistakes, and an actively involved client will catch at least some of those mistakes before they cause harm. Many clients can understand more of how to solve their problems than some lawyers give them credit for, and most clients know at least as much or even more about their own needs than a lawyer will. (For both of these reasons, the lawyer and client working together will come up with more and better solutions than the lawyer working alone.) Third, "[t]he participatory model promotes the dignity of clients as citizens" because it "makes the client a doer, responsible for his choices."[4] Fourth, it reduces the client's anxiety because the client is not kept in the dark about what is happening. Fifth, it protects "the integrity of professionals by

---

3. Douglas E. Rosenthal, *Lawyer and Client: Who's in Charge?* (1974).
4. *Id.* at 168.

liberating them from . . . the burdens imposed [by a] paternal role" and from client suspicion caused by client ignorance.[5] And sixth, it "invites personal contact in a society becoming increasingly impersonal."[6]

The participatory model also carries some burdens. Some clients may find their anxiety increased if they have to think about their problems; they would rather hire a professional and forget about it.[7] A lawyer with an emotional need to be "paternalistic and dominating" will be frustrated and unhappy in participatory relationships with clients. "Lawyers, and perhaps most professionals, seem to have two human needs in disproportionately great measure: the desire to control their environment and aggressive (and competitive) feelings."[8] On the other hand, a dominating but subtle lawyer might manipulate a client into thinking the relationship is participatory when in fact it is not. (Over time, many clients in this situation can figure out that they have been manipulated, although that might not happen until some time after the lawyer has finished the work.) Finally, the participatory model is more expensive.[9] It takes more time, and time is money. And it also takes more effort, in the form of "energy, intelligence, and judgment" from the client and, from the lawyer, "patience and tolerance built on recognition of an obligation to earn the client's cooperation."[10]

In today's law practice environment, a lawyer will be more effective at getting the desired results and satisfy more clients if the lawyer *usually* develops participatory relationships but can nevertheless work within a traditional relationship with those clients who would find a participatory relationship stressful. This book assumes that participatory lawyering is the norm and that traditional lawyering is now the exception.

How can you tell one type of client from another? It usually does no good to ask in the initial interview, "Would you rather have a traditional or a participatory relationship?" Only a rare client would be able to answer that question well, even if you were to explain what the terms mean. A better method is to start on a participatory basis and switch to a traditional relationship if you learn along the way that the client would be happier that way.

Are some types of clients more likely to prefer one type of relationship to the other? It is a commonly held view that, with exceptions, the more educated a client is, the more likely the client will feel comfortable working with a professional.[11] If that is true, a well-educated client might readily acclimate to (or even demand) a participatory relationship, while a less-educated client might prefer a more traditional one. But this question is a minefield in which generalizations can be both true and outrageously false at the same time. Every poverty lawyer can describe wonderful participatory relationships with clients who had little formal education. And Rosenthal found some very well-educated clients who preferred a traditional relationship.[12] A busy and well-educated client might have little time to spare for

---

5. *Id.* at 169.
6. *Id.* at 170.
7. *Id.*
8. *Id.* at 172–173.
9. *Id.* at 176.
10. *Id.* at 15.
11. *Id.* at 184.
12. *Id.* at 171.

a participatory relationship. Where the client might want involvement but not full participation in decision-making, the lawyer should differentiate between those situations where the client would want to be consulted (or must by law be consulted) and those where the client would prefer that the lawyer simply exercise her expertise.

§3.3 WHO DECIDES WHAT

The law of agency, professional responsibility, malpractice, and constitutional criminal procedure provide that certain decisions are reserved to the client and may not be made by the lawyer. The law of agency matters because the client is a principal whose agent is the lawyer. If the lawyer makes decisions reserved to the client, the lawyer can be disciplined under the rules of professional responsibility, or held liable in malpractice, or both.

The client defines the goals of the representation. The client decides whether to accept an adversary's offer of a negotiated settlement,[13] although the client can preauthorize acceptance of an offer meeting a particular description ("if they'll pay anything over $60,000, I'll take it, but don't stop negotiating until you've gotten them as high above that figure as you think you can"). In a criminal case, the client decides whether to plead guilty or not guilty, "whether to waive jury trial and whether the client will testify."[14] But the client makes all these decisions—which are momentous ones—only after the lawyer has counseled by explaining the alternatives and their advantages, costs, and risks.

Traditionally, the lawyer has decided "technical, legal, and tactical matters,"[15] such as where to sue, what theory of the case to rely on, what evidence to submit and witnesses to call, and what arguments to make. The case law allows the lawyer to make these decisions unilaterally, without consulting the client or even over the client's objections. But if you do such a thing, the case law will not stop the client from firing you and telling every other potential client in North America never to hire you. Moreover, the Model Rules of Professional Conduct require not only that a lawyer "abide by a client's decisions concerning the objectives of representation [but also] *consult with the client as to the means by which they are to be pursued*."[16] And the Model Rules suggest that the lawyer should defer to the client when technical and tactical decisions raise "such questions as the expense to be incurred and concern for third persons who might be adversely affected."[17]

In the participatory model of lawyer-client relations, some of these decisions are made jointly by the lawyer and client: in a surprisingly large number of instances, the client has valuable insights on technical and tactical questions such as where to sue, what theory of the case to rely on, what evidence to introduce and witnesses to call, and what arguments to make. Depending on the client and the

---

13. Rule 1.2(a) of the Model Rules of Professional Conduct.
14. *Id.*
15. Comment to Rule 1.2(a).
16. Rule 1.2(a) (emphasis added).
17. Comment to Rule 1.2(a).

circumstances, some of those decisions are more effectively made jointly by the lawyer and client, working together. Sometimes this involves a full counseling session as described in Chapter 21. Sometimes it involves a phone call in which the lawyer describes a technical or tactical action the lawyer is considering—making a particular motion, for example—and asks the client whether the client sees any problems in doing so.

What kinds of problems might the client see? The three most typical are (1) the client has information that changes things, (2) the proposed action would cause difficulties for the client or for someone the client would like to avoid harming, and (3) the client might be reluctant to pay for the proposed action. Let's take each in turn.

Suppose the motion would seek an order compelling the other side to turn over certain documents. Some lawyers would consider such a thing so hyper-technical that they would never consult a client about it. It is true that if the lawyer were to call the client, the latter would often say, in a tentative voice, something like "Sounds O.K. to me." But clients appreciate the courtesy of being told, and Model Rule 1.4(a) requires that you "keep the client reasonably informed about the status of a matter." And every once in a while the conversation might lead to very different results:

Lawyer: [after describing the motion] I just wanted to mention it to you in case you have any thoughts on it.

Client: Let's back up a minute. Would you describe the documents again?

Lawyer: [does so]

Client: I think I might have seen those documents, and I think they don't say what you're hoping they say.

Lawyer: Since your memory is unclear, maybe the safe thing to do is make the motion anyway and see what they look like when and if we get them.

Client: I think I know somebody who has a copy of them.

Lawyer: A complete copy?

Client: I think so. I'll call him as soon as we get off the phone.

This conversation could change everything in the lawyer's plans.

A lawyer is like an elephant in a china shop. The elephant might not want to break china, but any inadvertent move on his or her part might shatter something precious. There are plenty of ways in which a lawyer, using routine methods of representation, might accidentally damage the client or someone the client wants to avoid harming. A prudent lawyer behaves like an elephant who wants to be able to leave the china shop without having broken anything unnecessarily. Frequent consultation with the client is one of the ways in which effective lawyers assure that.

Clients worry constantly about the cost of legal work. Some lawyers are oblivious to that. Others try carefully to deal with their clients' concerns. If the client is being billed by the hour, the discovery enforcement motion discussed above would cost the client money in lawyer billing time. When a large corporation hires outside litigation counsel, it might initially impose a budget and later want to know things such as how this motion would affect the budget. Even without a budget, the client is entitled to ask how much the motion will cost, what it will probably accomplish, and whether the probable benefit is worth the cost. A lawyer who can answer those questions intelligently, precisely, and nondefensively can earn the loyalty of clients, so that they become repeat customers. A lawyer who cannot do that well risks losing clients to the first kind of lawyer.

To summarize: The client should, of course, decide questions that the law gives the client the right to decide. And even for questions that by law a lawyer can decide unilaterally, you should consult with the client anyway if there is a possibility that the client might be able to add information or ideas or if the client might have preferences about how the question is handled. If in doubt, err on the side of consulting with the client. Not only does consultation improve the odds of getting good results, but it reduces the chances of friction between lawyer and client. Lawyers who often consult with clients seem to have fewer ethics complaints and malpractice actions brought against them. And if the client has preferences on a technical or tactical question that by law the lawyer can decide unilaterally, follow the client's preferences.

The boss is the one who gets to hire and fire. The client hires and can fire the lawyer, not the other way around.

§3.4 WHAT CLIENTS *DISLIKE* IN A LAWYER

Charles Dickens' novel *Bleak House*[18] concerns, among other things, a lawsuit to divide up an estate. The suit has "become so complicated that no man alive knows what it means."[19]

All the parties to the suit are oppressed by it. One of them complains, "We are always appearing, and disappearing, and swearing, and interrogating, and filing, and cross-filing, and arguing, and sealing, and motioning, and referring, and reporting. . . . Law finds it can't do this, Equity finds it can't do that; neither can so much as say it can't do anything, without this solicitor instructing and this counsel appearing for A, and that solicitor instructing and that counsel appearing for B; and so on through the whole alphabet."[20] The same person exclaims, "The Lawyers have twisted [the lawsuit] into such a state of bedevilment that the original merits of the case have long since disappeared from the face of the earth."[21]

Finally, nearly 800 pages later, the lawyers declare that the suit is over because the estate is now empty, everything in it having been spent on lawyers' fees.[22]

---

18. Charles Dickens, *Bleak House* (1st ed. 1853) (page numbers in the next few footnotes are to the Penguin 1971 edition edited by Norman Page).
19. *Id.* at 52.
20. *Id.* at 145–146.
21. *Id.* at 145.
22. *Id.* at 920–924.

This is the subliminal fear of everyone with a problem that might have something to do with the law—that if you hire a lawyer, you will have two problems. The first will be the original problem, and the second will be the lawyer.

Clients intensely dislike lawyers who make promises they cannot keep, brag, speak in legal jargon, are pompous and patronizing, and talk too much and listen too little. Clients hate having to fight to get their lawyers' attention. When you and a client are talking together, an interrupting knock on your office door or telephone call demeans the client. Making a client wait is a form of disrespect. Clients "who are made to drive across town and wait with children in a crowded room while their attorney is an hour late for their brief interview may not know whether their attorney is technically knowledgeable, but they certainly understand how little [the attorney] cares about their needs. . . ."[23]

Corporations have general counsel departments made up of in-house lawyers. A general counsel will hire law firms for work better done outside the corporation. Huge national and international law firms earn their revenues primarily by doing this work. A general counsel is thus both a lawyer, advising the corporation as an in-house employee, and a client, retaining outside lawyers as needed. A survey of corporate general counsels asked, "What is the one thing your outside counsel does that just drives you crazy?" More than half the answers can be categorized as bad communication—not keeping the client informed, not listening to clients and focusing on client needs, communicating arrogance, making decisions without getting client authorization or even informing the client, and giving vague and unclear advice.[24] These are among the factors that cause corporate general counsel to replace their outside law firms.[25]

Some of the characteristics that lawyers consider indicia of competence are actually considered by clients to be indicia of *incompetence*. For example, the English legal profession is divided into barristers and solicitors, and a study of solicitors quotes this client:

> I went to [her] because of her reputation and expertise. . . . She listens for part of what I have to say, and then interrupts, saying something like "OK, I've got the picture, what we'll do is. . . ." and she hasn't really got the picture, she's only got half the picture. I think it's partly because she so busy, and also because she's simply not used to giving clients a voice. . . . I am about to change to another solicitor.[26]

Many lawyers on both sides of the Atlantic would assume that this solicitor is a decisive professional who gets results because she determines quickly what to do. But on the same evidence, the client is ready to fire her.

Studies have shown that lawyers who communicate infrequently or badly with their clients have more fee disputes with clients, are sued more often for malpractice, and are complained about more often to bar disciplinary authorities. A study

---

23. Martin J. Solomon, *Client Relations: Ethics and Economics*, 23 Ariz. St. L.J. 155, 175 (1991).
24. Clark D. Cunningham, *What Do Clients Want from Their Lawyers?*, 2013 J. Disp. Resol. 143, 144 (reporting a 2005 study by the BTI Consulting Group).
27. *Id.*
26. *Id.* at 148 (quoting Hilary Sommerlad, *English Perspectives on Quality: The Client-Led Model of Quality—A Third Way?*, 33 U.B.C. L. Rev. 491, 509–510 (2000)).

showed that how doctors talk to patients is the strongest predictor of how frequently the doctors will be sued for malpractice.[27] Those who take the time and effort to deal with the patient's thoughts and feelings get sued less than doctors who don't, regardless of the number and severity of the mistakes the doctors make in diagnosis and treatment. Rule 1.4(a) of the Model Rules of Professional Conduct provides that "[a] lawyer shall keep the client reasonably informed about the status of the matter [and] promptly comply with reasonable requests for information." The less clients know about what is happening, the more anxious and unhappy they are.

Many lawyers don't explain to their clients what will happen in court. Clients arrive at court baffled by what people there are doing, why they are doing it, and what the consequences can be. Clients describe feeling like furniture—even though they actually are the most important people in the courtroom. They experience the court system as a bureaucracy that cares nothing about the burdens that litigation imposes on them, and they often feel as though their own lawyers are part of that bureaucracy.

Clients especially hate not knowing how much their lawyers will cost. Corporations can impose budgets on lawyers. But human clients usually cannot. In the billable hour system, lawyers do things they have not explained to their clients; send bills to their clients demanding to be paid; and then do more things their clients do not understand and send more bills. As in *Bleak House*, this sometimes seems to many clients to have no end. Clients become all the more outraged if they fear that a lawyer will lose commitment unless paid promptly and without complaint.

§3.5 WHAT CLIENTS *LIKE* IN A LAWYER

Obviously a client will appreciate a lawyer who does none of the things clients hate. And obviously every client wants a lawyer who wins a lawsuit or in some other way produces a good result.

But getting results is not the most important factor clients typically use in judging their lawyers. The most important factor is how a client *experiences* working with the lawyer. As Clark Cunningham points out, "[m]any lawyers equate client satisfaction with the outcome achieved; however, studies over the past three decades in three different countries have produced impressive evidence that clients evaluate their lawyers' competence more in terms of the *process experienced* by them in the representation than the outcome."[28]

Clients prefer lawyers who truly hear and understand. *One of the most powerful forces in life is validation from being heard and understood.* Partly this is a function of the lawyer's listening skills. But mostly it is a function of empathy—seeing the world through the client's eyes.

Clients want their lawyers to talk with respect and in plain language. Again, English clients describing their solicitors:

---

27. Malcolm Gladwell, *Blink: The Power of Thinking without Thinking* 39–43 (2005).
28. Cunningham, *supra* note 24, at 146 (italics added).

> "She talked to me, as a person, with respect."
>
> "I can have a chat with her, I trust her . . . [she's] much better than other solicitors I've had. . . . The other solicitor—I was just a file for him, but for her I'm a real person and that comes across in court."
>
> "[My current solicitor is] very easy to talk to—some solicitors can be intimidating."[29]

Most of what clients like is a good human being—with emotional intelligence, maturity, and integrity—who can do high-quality legal work. That is the lawyer they want to hire.

§3.6 HOW TO WORK BETTER WITH CLIENTS

When answering client questions, do not just give an answer that makes sense to you. Give an answer that makes sense to the client, and make sure that the client understands what you've said. Ineffective lawyers toss out quick answers to client questions and then move on to something else, as though the client's worries are marginal to the lawyer's work. Clients notice that, although they might not say anything about it at the time. Clients do not want to fight with their lawyers, but when they reach a point of dissatisfaction, they quietly take their business elsewhere.

When communicating with clients, talk and write in plain English. If you have to use a term of art, explain its meaning without condescending. Use concrete, precise language and not vague generalities. Behave in ways that encourage clients both to tell you things that you need to know and to ask questions about things that make the client anxious. More than anything else, that means be a good listener.

When a client calls, if you cannot come to the telephone immediately, return the call within hours or, if you are in court or its equivalent, have another lawyer or a paraprofessional do so. A law office should be accessible and responsive, not a bureaucracy.

Introduce the client to the people in your office who will do work on the client's behalf, including secretaries. If it's not obvious, explain to the client the role each person will play.

Unless a client would prefer otherwise or there are special reasons not to, send copies to the client of all court papers and your correspondence with other people concerning the client. And whenever a document would not be self-explanatory to a layperson, tell the client why it exists and what it means.

Get to know the client so that you can understand what the client really needs from you. How risk-averse is the client, for instance? The client will have to live with what you do long after you drop out of the picture. If the client is a business,

29. *Id.* at 149–150 (quoting Hilary Sommerlad, *English Perspectives on Quality: The Client-Led Model of Quality—A Third Way?*, 33 U.B.C. L. Rev. 491, 503–505 (2000)).

get to know the business as well as the industry in which it operates. For example, you cannot possibly do good general legal work for a symphony orchestra unless you are familiar with things like how grants are obtained from foundations, where the market for classical music recordings is headed, and perhaps even what second violinists are typically paid.

How can you learn about your client's business and industry without embarrassing yourself? You can go to a library and read books on the industry. You can read the relevant trade magazines; every industry has at least one. And you can read articles in the general press, which you can find through an Internet search. You can also visit the client's place of business to get a feel for it physically and organizationally. And you should read as much as you can on your client's website.

Large corporations hire law firms to solve problems that are usually quantifiable in money terms. From the client's point of view, this might be a pure business transaction without any emotional content whatsoever, and the only concerns are results and efficiency. But individuals and small businesses go to lawyers for two reasons. The first is to solve a problem, which might be quantifiable in money terms. The second is for relief from fear and pain. These clients consider it your responsibility to deal with both, and if you want clients to recommend you to their friends and neighbors, you will need to be able to deal with both.

In the end, clients are loyal if you

1. get results;
2. do so efficiently, in both time and cost;
3. reduce their anxiety and frustration while they await results; and
4. are considerate, likeably human, and in other ways a pleasure to work with.

§3.7 CONFIDENTIALITY

The duty to keep a client's confidences secret is one of the central obligations of ethics law.

In most states, the obligation is defined by Rule 1.6 of the Model Rules of Professional Conduct: "A lawyer shall not reveal information relating the representation of a client." Rule 1.6 provides several exceptions. Some of them have been controversial, and in your state's version of Rule 1.6 the exceptions might differ from the ones presented here. The most recent ABA version of Rule 1.6 sets out the following exceptions (in the words of Rule 1.6):

- the client gives informed consent
- the disclosure is impliedly authorized in order to carry out the representation
- the lawyer reasonably believes [disclosure] necessary . . .
    - to prevent reasonably certain death or substantial bodily harm;
    - to prevent the client from committing a crime or fraud that is reasonably certain to result in substantial injury to the financial interests or property of another and in furtherance of which the client has used or is using the lawyer's services;

- to prevent, mitigate or rectify substantial injury to the financial interests or property of another that is reasonably certain to result or has resulted from the client's commission of a crime or fraud in furtherance of which the client has used the lawyer's services;
- to secure legal advice about the lawyer's compliance with these Rules;
- to establish a claim or defense on behalf of the lawyer in a controversy between the lawyer and the client, to establish a defense to a criminal charge or civil claim against the lawyer based upon conduct in which the client was involved, or to respond to allegations in any proceeding concerning the lawyer's representation of the client; or
- to comply with other law or a court order.

Rule 3.3 provides two additional exceptions. First, under Rule 3.3(a)(3), if the client testifies falsely and refuses to confess the falsity to the court, the lawyer must take "reasonable remedial measures, including, if necessary, disclosure to the tribunal." Where the client is a criminal defendant, somewhat different principles might govern because of the client's constitutional right to decide whether to testify. The Comment to Rule 3.3 notes that jurisdictions differ on how they handle this problem. Second, Rule 3.3(b) provides that if the client "intends to engage, is engaging or has engaged in criminal or fraudulent conduct related to the proceeding"—such as bribing a witness—the lawyer again must take "reasonable remedial measures, including, if necessary, disclosure to the tribunal."

These ethical duties are separate from the evidentiary attorney-client privilege, which prohibits an attorney or an attorney's employee from testifying to communications from a client made for the purpose of obtaining legal advice when the client has treated the communications as confidential and has not waived the privilege.

CHAPTER

4

LAWYERING AS PROBLEM SOLVING

Lawyers solve existing problems and prevent future problems. That's what clients want and need. And truly top-notch lawyers—the most effective and capable ones you can find—don't really "practice law." They're problem solvers and problem preventers, and law is just one of their tools.

§4.1 DIAGNOSIS, PREDICTION, AND STRATEGY ARE INTERTWINED IN PROFESSIONAL WORK

Professionals *diagnose* what's happening now or has happened in the past, *predict* what will happen in the future, and create and implement *strategies* to influence events.

A lawyer diagnoses by figuring out why events are happening or have happened. Why is the client more upset over a small problem than a big one? Why exactly is Norcomm, Inc., not making deliveries on time? In a negotiation, why is the other side unable to see why your proposal is good for both sides?

A lawyer predicts by prophesying how other people will react to events. If the client sues, who will win? How will the other side respond to a negotiation offer you are contemplating making?

A lawyer strategizes by developing a plan for solving a problem. When you counsel a client, you will offer several plans as options from which the client can choose. When you prepare to negotiate, you will develop a strategy for getting the other side to agree, as much as possible, to what your client wants.

Suppose the client is a developer who has signed a contract to buy a farm on which he had intended to build tract homes. Before the transaction could be completed, two things have happened. First, the local government has declared a five-year building moratorium because explosive development has outstripped the government's capacity to provide tap water and to process sewage. Second, the client has begun to suffer health problems; his family has persuaded him to go into semi-retirement; and he is entertaining the thought that, rather than develop the land for housing, he would like to live in the farmhouse and hire neighboring farmers to farm the land. The problem is that the contract includes the fields but not the farmhouse. The client has offered to buy the farmhouse as well, but the owners have refused. They do not care much about living in the farmhouse themselves. They believe its value will go up substantially in the future, and they simply want to sell it later rather than now. So the client would like to get out of this contract and maybe buy some other farm.

In a client interview and afterward, you diagnose by learning the facts and figuring out how they affect the client legally, financially, and emotionally. To make your diagnosis concrete, you predict how people and courts will treat the client in the future. Based on the law, your prediction might be this: *The contract is enforceable. If we sue for a court order rescinding it, we'll probably lose. If the client refuses to complete the purchase as required in the contract, and if the sellers sue for breach, they'll probably win, and the client will have to pay whatever damages they can prove.*

Don't give up yet. Instead, develop strategies to protect the client despite his weak position in contract law. With the client, choose the best one based on predictions of each strategy's likelihood of success and on the client's preferred style of addressing the problem. An effective strategy could involve converting conflict into an inclusive solution that satisfies everyone's needs. The developer's lawyer might say to her client:

> We could fight them in a lawsuit. But we'll probably lose, and your litigation expenses, including attorney's fees, would be at least $15,000 and could go as high as $120,000, and you'd have to pay them damages when you lose.
>
> But they don't seem to realize that this transaction is badly structured from their point of view. If you and they go ahead with the deal as it is now structured, they will pay a lot more tax than they need to. We can offer to renegotiate the whole deal to eliminate their unnecessary tax exposure, on condition that they agree to sell you the farmhouse at a reasonable price. If that works, it would satisfy your preference for solving this problem quickly and with as little conflict as possible.

As you implement the chosen strategy, unexpected things can happen. If the unexpected events are harmful, you will diagnose what is going wrong and restrategize by modifying the strategy or adopting a new one.

> When I called their lawyer and offered to renegotiate, the sellers blew a gasket and made a lot of threats about suing us. I've been trying to figure out why they would react this way. They seemed to be thinking that we were trying to take advantage of them, which makes no sense if they really understood the tax consequences. The sellers refused to meet with us and sent word back through the lawyer that our choice was to go through with the deal as is or get sued for damages.

I asked around, and the sellers do not have a reputation for being suspicious by nature. So I wondered just how much they really knew about taxes in this kind of transaction. I sent a letter to their lawyer offering to pay for a consultation with any tax advisor they chose. We would not be present, and the only condition would be that the tax advisor be given a copy of the contract before meeting with the sellers. Because this was an offer in negotiation, their attorney was ethically obligated to inform them of it.

It turns out that they had been doing their own taxes for years and had no idea what a mess they were about to get into. When a neutral tax advisor explained it to them, they realized that it made good financial sense to sell you the farmhouse now through a restructured deal that puts them in a better tax situation.

This lawyer's diagnosis of what was going wrong allowed her to restrategize and solve the problem.

Problem prevention is problem solving in advance. Effective lawyers develop the skill of foreseeing risk—predicting now that a problem will arise in the future if something is not done now to prevent it, or at least reduce its harm if it does occur. Some risks are remote. They are so unlikely that effort and client money would be wasted dealing with them now. Accurately assessing the odds of a problem occurring is predictive thinking. For many lawyers, much of any day's work is preventing future problems as well as solving current ones.

For conciseness, this book uses the term *problem solving* to cover both solving existing problems and preventing future ones.

§4.2 HOW PROFESSIONALS DIAGNOSE, PREDICT, AND STRATEGIZE

The six steps of diagnosis, prediction, and strategy track the creative process.[1]

1. ***Recognizing a problem and defining it.*** Something starts to go at least vaguely wrong. It takes an eye for trouble to notice this early, while something might be done about it, and to bring it into focus. Consider what happened when the farmland sellers refused to renegotiate the contract. The developer's lawyer could have given up at that point, accomplishing nothing for her client. But she didn't give up. She considered their refusal to be a solvable problem rather than an unchangeable fact. A lawyer who's good at problem recognition is a lawyer who looks for problems rather than hiding from them, avoids guessing, doesn't make unnecessary assumptions, and hates to be at the mercy of events.

2. ***Preparing: gathering and evaluating information and raw materials.*** This includes discovering relevant law and facts in a fairly open-ended manner aided by an aggressive curiosity.

1. See Teresa H. Amabile, *Creativity in Context: Update to the Social Psychology of Creativity* 119 (1996); John S. Dacey & Kathleen H. Lennon, *Understanding Creativity: The Interplay of Biological, Psychological, and Social Factors* 82–83, 173 (1998).

3. ***Generating a range of options: hypotheses or potential solutions.*** If you are diagnosing, imagine potential explanations for the events in question. If you are predicting, imagine potential prophesies of the future. The potential diagnoses and prophesies are hypotheses. If you are strategizing, imagine potential solutions, which would be plans for influencing events. *The more hypotheses or solutions you can generate here, the larger is the field from which you can choose later.* In this stage, you aren't verifying or judging each hypothesis or solution—that's the next step. Here, you are only listing possibilities.

4. ***Evaluating options: hypotheses or potential solutions.*** If you're diagnosing, test each possible explanation to see whether it accurately tells you why things are happening. If you're predicting, test each potential prophesy to estimate how likely it is to happen. If you're strategizing, test each plan for effectiveness: how well would it achieve the client's goals, at what cost, and with what risks? In all three activities, look for concrete, clarifying facts, evidence, and law.

   What would *confirm* that an explanation is accurate (if diagnosing), that a prophesy is likely to happen (if predicting), or that a plan will influence events (if developing a strategy)? Also look for *negative proof* that could eliminate options. What information would show that a diagnosis is inaccurate or that a prophecy is unlikely or that a strategy will probably fail? Ask yourself questions like these: *If my hypothesis is true, what else must also be true (or false)? If my strategy will work, what facts, evidence, or law would already exist (or not)?*

   For example, if irrational suspicion of other people caused the farmland sellers to doubt the buyer's motives, they would probably have reputations in the local community based on similar incidents in the past. The buyer's lawyer investigated and found that they had no such reputation, which eliminated the irrationality hypothesis. Therefore, their suspicion might have been a rational reaction to what they believed to be the facts.

   The buyer's lawyer then hypothesized that the sellers reacted as they did out of misunderstanding about their own tax situation (a diagnosis) and that if they discovered the truth, they might change their minds (both a prophecy and a strategy). The lawyer tested the diagnosis, prophecy, and strategy by offering to pay for disinterested tax advice. When the sellers learned how much tax they would have to pay unless the deal was restructured, the diagnosis was confirmed. When they agreed to renegotiate, the prophecy was confirmed. When the renegotiation enabled the buyer to purchase the farmhouse, the strategy became effective.

5. ***Deciding.*** Choose the most accurate diagnosis, the most likely prediction, or the most effective strategy.

6. ***Acting.*** If the decision is a diagnosis or a prediction, report it to whoever who needs to know (the client, for example) or use it yourself for whatever purpose you had. If the decision is selection of a strategy, implement it.

In practice, the six stages are not segmented as neatly as they appear here.

The thinking process can be recursive. There is a lot of circling back. As you evaluate hypotheses, for example, you might realize that you need to know some things you don't already know. So you go back into preparation to learn about those things and then return to evaluation. On the way, you might generate some other potential solutions. Or when you act on a solution, it might fail, and then you return to option evaluation or even to option generation for another solution.

Preparing and generating options often happen at the same time. That can also be true of evaluating options and deciding how to proceed. And "the mind may be unconsciously incubating on one aspect" of a problem while "consciously . . . preparing for or verifying another aspect."[2] Ideas often surface into consciousness "unexpectedly, with surprising suddenness."[3] Professional work is an uneven mixture of "sudden bursts of insight and tiring efforts at execution."[4]

Don't be satisfied with the first reasonable hypothesis or solution you come up with. "In high-pressure situations, . . . most people seem to latch onto the first plausible idea they get and push it as far as they can."[5] Clients need better than that. Work through the process of problem solving *professionally*.

Generating and evaluating options pose the greatest challenges for students—in part because they require contrary skills. To generate the largest number of possible solutions or hypotheses, look under the surface of facts and law for deeper possibilities and meaning. Deactivate your skepticism. (You'll activate it again during the evaluation stage.) For now, think without inhibition.

All ideas have flaws. And many of those flaws can be fixed—later. Ideas that might turn out to be good arrive together with ideas that might turn out to be wrong or even silly. If you criticize ideas as they arrive, they'll stop coming—all of them, the good as well as the bad—before you can understand their potential. *(Ideas fear rejection. If you were an idea, would you appear in the mind of a person eager to reject you?)* It is too easy to dismiss as foolish an incomplete hypothesis or solution that could become a better one if you let it stay long enough for you to work out its faults.

The skepticism on which evaluation depends is prized throughout the practice of law. It is taught in law school, and lawyers tend to be verbally aggressive. But a lawyer who is "more adept at criticizing ideas than at creating them"[6] will, for that reason alone, be a less effective problem solver. If you or someone else makes snap criticisms of your ideas as soon as they arrive, your idea option generation will be paralyzed. In any profession, hyper-criticism is dangerous because it shuts down the flow of ideas. When you see a lawyer, a student, or a teacher doing it, consider the damage it can cause. While generating ideas, don't be afraid of embarrassing yourself. Lon Fuller, the great Contracts scholar, wrote that creative thinking stops when you ask yourself "anxiously at every turn that most inhibitive of questions, '*What will other people think?*'"[7]

---

2. Graham Wallas, *The Art of Thought* 81–82 (1926).
3. Teresa H. Amabile, *The Social Psychology of Creativity* 85 (1983).
4. Vera John-Steiner, *Notebooks of the Mind: Explorations of Thinking* 79 (1985).
5. John S. Dacey & Kathleen H. Lennon, *Understanding Creativity: The Interplay of Biological, Psychological, and Social Factors* (1998).
6. Paul Brest & Linda Krieger, *On Teaching Professional Judgment*, 69 Wash. L. Rev. 527, 541 (1994).
7. Lon Fuller, *On Teaching Law*, 3 Stan. L. Rev. 35, 43 (1950) (emphasis in original).

Evaluating options, on the other hand, requires the qualities that would cripple option generation: rigorous skepticism, a pragmatic sense of the realistic, a precise ability to calculate risk, and a fear that an idea might truly be foolish. Turn these qualities off while generating hypotheses and solutions. Turn them back on once you have assembled a full range of options and are ready to start evaluating them. During option generation, you will do best if you think freely and tolerate some intellectual chaos. But during evaluation, become a completely different kind of person, viewing things with the cold realism of one who must take responsibility for success or failure.

Evaluating options also depends on something that's not taught in most large law school classes: an accurate feel for how clients, judges, and juries make decisions and for how clients, judges, juries, witnesses, and opposing parties and their lawyers will react to things you do. Evaluating options requires a good intuition about people and situations to balance the analytical reasoning that law school has helped you develop. Analytical reasoning is useful up to a point. But it's not more valuable than emotional intelligence, especially the understanding of human nature that comes from empathy.[8] Good problem solving involves *all* of you, not just the logically analytical part.

Without the problem-solving process explained here, professional work is reduced to bureaucratic routine—doing one task at a time, thinking about the next task only after the preceding one is completed, and never seeing the big picture or addressing the entirety of a client's problems. That would be lawyering without much conscious attempt to predict how actions will influence events.

This book sometimes uses interchangeably the terms *strategies* and *solutions* as choices. But not all choices are potential solutions. Where the client has suffered a loss and the law and facts are all against the client, doing nothing is one of the choices, and sometimes it is the only realistic one. But it does not solve the client's problem.

Unless the circumstances are urgent, do not rush to make decisions. Premature judgment will cut off the earlier stages before they've done their work. The first good idea you come up with typically isn't the best idea you can find. And if you decide too soon, you might select an inferior option, the flaws of which take time to appear.

§4.3 THINKING DIVERGENTLY AS WELL AS CONVERGENTLY

Convergent thinking narrows an inquiry to find (converge onto) the single right answer. Divergent thinking is the opposite: It entails broadening the inquiry by thinking in several directions at once to find more answers (or hypotheses or strategies). Here's the difference:[9]

---

8. See Howard Gardner, *Multiple Intelligences* (2006); Daniel Goleman, *Emotional Intelligence* (2006).
9. See Malcolm Gladwell, *Outliers* 86–89 (2008).

Convergent exam question:

Which of the following is commonly used in the manufacture of bricks?

(a) cooled lava

(b) clay

(c) fossil oil

(d) synthetic oil.

Correct answer: (b).

Divergent exam question:

In three minutes, think of as many uses for a brick as you can.

Some possible answers: to build steps, a walkway, or a garden border; to use as siding on a house exterior; to use as a paperweight on a desk; to hold down newspapers left by the curb for recycling; to throw at windows and break them; to circle a campfire so it doesn't spread while you sleep in a tent; to hold down the corners of the tent in a wind; to hide a secret message on a piece of paper folded underneath the brick; to throw at an opponent in a duel instead of shooting with a pistol; to block car wheels to keep the car from rolling away; to put in the trunk of a rear-wheel-drive car so it gets better traction in snow; to help weigh down a dead body to be thrown into a lake or stream; etc.

The more uses, the more uninhibited your divergent thinking. If you came up with only a few uses, don't be discouraged. It's not your fault. For most students, education to this point has taught convergent thinking almost exclusively, largely omitting divergent thinking. Many students, when given an exercise like this, ask something like, "Are we allowed to think like that? Isn't the most important thing to know the one right answer?" The answers are *yes* (you're allowed to think like that) and *no* (knowing the one right answer is not the most important thing).

You already know how to think convergently. It got you through college and into law school. Convergent thinking is measured in every standardized test, including the SAT, ACT, and LSAT. Every multiple-choice question in a course exam can be answered only through convergent thinking, and that's also true of most issues in law school essay exams. To gain basic and essential knowledge, you've had to learn correct answers (negligence is the sum of duty, breach, injury, and proximate cause) and to separate what's correct from what isn't (breach of contract isn't a tort). But if education were to stop there, it would be unrealistic and incomplete. A professional eventually begins to think divergently.

Generating options is divergent thinking. You start in one place (the problem), and you diverge—go out—in a number of directions. When lawyers solve real problems in the real world, they think divergently to come up with options.

Then lawyers think convergently to eliminate options that are impractical or aren't supported by the law or the facts. Evaluating options is convergent thinking.

Effective professionals thus think divergently as well as divergently. And for many professionals, the opportunity to think divergently can introduce elements of play into professional work. All the research into creativity—*all* of the research—shows that in virtually every occupation, the top performers are unable to separate play from work and wouldn't want to anyway. Work is not inherently dreary.[10]

Creativity is not an innate and mysterious personality trait possessed only by people in the arts. And it's not an all-or-nothing characteristic, which you either have or do not have. Empirical research has repeatedly shown that most people are creative, at least in small ways, although some people are substantially more creative than that.[11] Painting the ceiling of the Sistine Chapel involves creativity. And so does coming up with a good recipe for apple pie.

Creativity isn't particularly correlated to academic success. Some students who have received disappointing grades over the years are creative in ways not measured by exams. And some students who earn high grades are less naturally creative and have to work harder than others at developing a creative process of their own.

§4.4 AVOIDING COGNITIVE ILLUSIONS

A *cognitive illusion*—also called a *cognitive bias*—is a pattern of thought that causes someone to reason unrealistically.[12] Here's an example:

> In researching what classes he wanted to take for his third year, [Frank] had examined the course catalogue and looked up the student evaluation results for all the classes and professors in which he was interested. Having done an exhaustive review of all the possibilities, Frank completed his registration form and got on line at the Registrar's office to turn it in. While on line, he got into a conversation with a student from his first-year section, not his friend or someone he knew well, but an acquaintance. They compared their registration lists to see what they were going to take, and the other student commented that he had heard that a professor teaching a course Frank was signing up for was a real bore and that the course sounded a lot better than it really was. This surprised Frank, because he

10. See Mihaly Csikszentmihalyi, *Beyond Boredom and Anxiety: Experiencing Flow in Work and Play* (2000); Mihaly Csikszentmihalyi, *Flow: The Psychology of Optimal Experience* (2008); *Optimal Experience: Psychological Studies of Flow in Consciousness* (Mihaly Csikszentmihalyi & Isabella Selega Csikszentmihalyi, eds. 1988).

11. The research is summarized at Raymond S. Nickerson, "Enhancing Creativity" in *Handbook of Creativity* 392, 399 (Robert J. Sternberg ed. 1999).

12. Daniel Kahneman received a Nobel Prize for pioneering the research into cognitive illusions, biases, and heuristics. His collaborator, Amos Tversky, died earlier and could not share the Nobel. Their publications greatly exceed the number that could be cited here.

> had looked up the course evaluations, and the students in the classes the previous few years had given the professor above average reviews. Nevertheless, Frank . . . changed his registration form right there on line to substitute a different course.
>
> [Frank was later asked why he did this.] . . . did he have any particular reason to trust the other student's opinion (no, he did not really know the student very well); did he change his mind because the opinion expressed related to something that would not be captured on an evaluation, such as whether the teacher was a tough grader (no, it was based purely on the "boring" comment, which was one of the subjects covered in the evaluations); had the spontaneous hearsay opinion confirmed anything else he'd heard about the professor (no, in fact all he knew about the professor was the generally positive commentary from the published evaluations). Having done exhaustive research into course evaluations, Frank had accumulated dozens, if not hundreds, of student evaluations of the professor that convinced him that the course was worth taking. But all that research got pushed aside on the hearsay opinion offered by a student that Frank did not even know very well.[13]

Frank might have acted on any of several cognitive illusions or biases, and without asking him further questions, it's hard to say which persuaded him.

Frank might have acted on a false assumption that anecdotal evidence trumps empirical evidence. The anecdotal evidence here amounted to rumor from a student Frank did not know to be reliable. The empirical evidence that Frank himself had studied was impressive. But people often do what Frank did because empirical evidence seems cold and distant while anecdotal evidence is more immediate and vivid, though often unreliable.

Another cognitive illusion is the false assumption that the most recent information we are offered (or the first we are offered) is more valid than other information. People are often persuaded by *when* they get information, although its quality has no relationship to when it is delivered, which may be merely coincidental.

Much research appears to show that many of the mistakes made by doctors are caused by their own cognitive illusions.[14] Although the legal profession has not been studied in the same way, it seems likely that cognitive illusions cause a significant proportion of lawyers' mistakes as well. "Most physicians are not aware of their cognitive mistakes."[15] Probably, most lawyers aren't either. As you diagnose, predict, and strategize, examine your own thinking to make sure that you aren't being influenced by any of the following:

Availability bias is "the tendency to judge the likelihood of an event by the ease with which relevant examples come to mind."[16] This is part of why Frank rejected his own empirical evidence after someone told him an anecdote.

---

13. Joseph W. Rand, *Understanding Why Good Lawyers Go Bad: Using Case Studies in Teaching Cognitive Bias in Legal Decision-Making,* 9 Clinical L. Rev. 731, 751–752 (2003). See also Ian Weinstein, *Don't Believe Everything You Think: Cognitive Bias in Legal Decision-Making,* 9 Clinical L. Rev. 793 (2003).
14. Jerome Groopman, *How Doctors Think* (2007).
15. *Id.* at 277.
16. *Id.* at 64.

Suppose that last month Judge Patel sentenced one of your clients to the maximum penalty available for the crime of which the client was convicted. You will appear before Judge Patel again tomorrow with Lusardi, another client who has been charged with the same type of crime. Lusardi asks you to predict what will happen if he pleads guilty. Will Judge Patel again impose the maximum sentence, or something close to it? You're tempted to predict exactly that because you saw her do it only last month. And many lawyers would be tempted to make the same prediction.

But what do you really know? Suppose that in the past 12 months Judge Patel has sentenced 100 defendants for this type of crime. Of that data, you know only one percent—your client from last month. It's possible that Judge Patel sentenced every one of the other 99 defendants to the maximum, which would give her a 100% maximum-sentence rate for this crime. It's also possible that your client from last month was the *only* one sentenced to the maximum, and that Judge Patel was remarkably lenient with each of the other 99. If that's true, she sentences to the maximum only one percent of the time—not 100%.

You don't know any of this. All you know is what you saw last month. You're tempted to say to Lusardi, "You're looking at something like the maximum sentence, which is what she did to one of my clients last month." No. Don't say that. If you do, you will have been seduced by an illusion caused by availability. One example was available—an anecdote, really—and it biased you so that you did not investigate further. You assumed that the anecdote was representative of everything.

To avoid availability bias, refuse to be seduced by an example and instead investigate the whole picture. Find out what Judge Patel did in *many* of the cases where a defendant was convicted of this crime. You might not be able to find out what she did in all of them. But learn enough so that you can estimate what the pattern is. For example, find some lawyers who are in her courtroom often and ask them. Even a court clerk has better information than you have right now from your one experience.

Availability bias can even cut a professional off from what the professional already knows. Doctors can be influenced by "the last bad experience."[17] A doctor might have prescribed a routine treatment hundreds of times without a problem. But if that treatment caused trouble yesterday, the doctor might now hesitate to do what had always worked before. Why is yesterday's experience so influential? It is only one event among hundreds, but it outranks all the others because it is the most recent—and thus the most available.

Anchoring bias chains you to an idea simply because that idea is present. "Anchoring is a shortcut in thinking where a person doesn't consider multiple possibilities but quickly and firmly latches on to a single one."[18] Anchoring can happen even after you have considered several possibilities. You might have chosen one option after careful thought. But you are now anchored to it if you no longer entertain the possibility that it might be wrong. An anchored mind is no longer free to explore.

---

17. *Id.* at 188 (quoting E. James Potchen). See *id.* at 287.
18. *Id.* at 65.

Confirmation bias causes you to focus on information that confirms your preconceptions while ignoring information that challenges them. You discover what you expect or want to discover, and not much else. Many people get locked into this loop once they form an opinion.

Suppose that when you first meet your client, you become convinced that he's not guilty of the crime. The story he tells is utterly convincing, and the witnesses against him are inherently incredible. You know that they have testified in other cases, and that no judge or jury has ever believed them. Now you have a preconception—that your client is innocent—and you're at risk for confirmation bias. If you brush off evidence that might challenge your preconception, you will make mistakes.

The future could turn out to be very different. The prosecutor might know the witnesses are liars and won't use them. The prosecutor might instead have far better evidence that you don't know about—perhaps a recording of your client admitting to a friend that he committed the crime. If you're subject to confirmation bias, you might learn of this recording for the first time when it's too late for you to do anything about it.

You can limit confirmation bias by waiting before forming an opinion. Once you have formed an opinion, you can discipline yourself to look for disconfirming as well as confirming information. You can enjoy undermining your own opinions as much as confirming them.

Search satisficing or ***satisfaction of search*** is the tendency to stop searching for explanations once you've found one.

But the explanation you found might not be the right explanation or the best one. It's nothing more than the *first* one you found. If you call off the search because you've found an explanation, you won't know about the other explanations because your mind closed up tightly as soon as you found one. You assumed there were no others. The one you found might not be the best one or even an accurate one. Some of the others may be so much better that the one you found initially might turn out to be awful in comparison.

Confidence illusions frequently infect professionals conscious of their own expertise. Many confident experts diagnose the present and predict the future—and turn out to be flat-out wrong. Predictions by confident experts in the stock market, for example, are wrong more often than they're right. Cable news commentators confidently make predictions that are interesting at the time but often later turn out to be untrue. Even nonexperts overestimate their own abilities. Most drivers believe they have above-average driving skills, which is mathematically impossible.[19]

A confidence illusion can lead you to think you know something when you are actually only guessing. Because of the illusion, you don't realize that you are guessing—and that causes mistakes.

---

19. Tom Vanderbilt, *Traffic: Why We Drive the Way We Do (and What It Says About Us)* (2009).

§4.5 THE INCLUSIVE SOLUTION

In an influential book titled *In a Different Voice*, Carol Gilligan differentiates between the ethic of justice and the ethic of care, illustrated through the responses of two children to a hypothetical that poses a moral problem.[20] Jake and Amy are 11 years old and, in interviews, have been asked to state their opinions on Heinz's dilemma: Heinz's wife is ill, and her life can be saved only with a drug that costs more money than Heinz and his wife have. The local druggist refuses to lower his price. Jake and Amy have been asked whether Heinz should steal the drug. Jake answers yes because

> a human life is worth more than money. . . . [*Why is life worth more than money?*] Because the druggist can get a thousand dollars later from rich people with cancer, but Heinz can't get his wife again. . . . [If Heinz is caught], the judge would probably think it was the right thing to do.[21]

Jake says that Heinz's dilemma is "a math problem with humans."[22]

Jake reasons exactly the way students are taught to think in law school, through a hierarchy of principles. Some principles are more important than—and therefore trump—other principles. Jake "spots the legal issues of excuse and justification, balances the rights, and reaches a decision, while considering implicitly, if not explicitly, the precedential effect of his decision."[23] This sounds as close as an 11-year-old can get to legal analysis. It's also not the best way to solve a real-life problem.

Amy says that Heinz should not steal the drug:

> I think there might be other ways besides stealing it, like if he could borrow the money . . . , but he really shouldn't steal the drug—but his wife shouldn't die, either. [*Why shouldn't he steal the drug?*] If he stole the drug, he might save his wife then, but if he did, he might have to go to jail, and then his wife might get sicker again, and he couldn't get more of the drug. . . . So they should really just talk it out and find some other way to make the money.[24]

In the rest of her response, Amy focuses on the relationships between Heinz and his wife and between them and the druggist. In Gilligan's words:

> Amy envisions the wife's continuing need for her husband and the husband's continuing concern for his wife and seeks to respond to the druggist's need in a way that would sustain rather than sever connection. . . . Since Amy's moral judgment is grounded in the belief that, "if somebody has something that would keep somebody alive, then it's not right not to give it to them," she considers the

---

20. Carol Gilligan, *In a Different Voice* 25–37 (1982).
21. *Id.* at 26.
22. *Id.*
23. Carrie Menkel-Meadow, *Portia in a Different Voice: Speculations on a Women's Lawyering Process*, 1 Berkeley Women's L.J. 39, 45–46 (1985).
24. Gilligan, *supra* note 20, at 28.

> problem in the dilemma to arise not from the druggist's assertion of rights but from his failure of response.[25]

Jake "speaks about equality, reciprocity, fairness, rights," while Amy "speaks about connection, not hurting, care, and response."[26] Amy "fights the hypo" and "wants to know more facts: Have Heinz and the druggist explored other possibilities, like a loan or credit transaction? Why couldn't Heinz and the druggist simply sit down and talk it out so that the druggist would come to see the importance of Heinz's wife's life?[27]

Don't dismiss Amy's thinking as naive. Jake might do better in a law school classroom. But Amy would make a better lawyer because she's the more effective problem solver. Jake has responded to what he believes to be a question about hierarchical logic, which would determine who wins and who loses. Amy wants to find a way for nobody to lose. She's searching for a *solution* rather than a way of scoring who's more right.

Amy is close to finding the decisive event. She wants to help the druggist understand, in his heart, the wife's desperate situation or, if that doesn't work, to persuade other people to help. What Jake heard as a question about hierarchical score-keeping, Amy heard as a question about solving a problem. When she "fights the hypo," it's because she's perceptive enough to recognize that the problem does not necessarily require a decision about whose rights are more important. She resists the restrictions imposed by the interviewer, and her solution generation is richer because she tries to break out of the interviewer's preconceptions.

Here's an example in which one lawyer reasons like Jake and fails, while a second lawyer reasons like Amy and succeeds:

> [A] lawyer who came to my office . . . presented this problem to me as an attorney for a local bank. Where the signature card required *A*, *B*, and *C* to sign, and *C* refused because of a disagreement with *B*, what kind of court order would permit the bank to release the funds? Since any court proceeding is relatively involved and expensive (and also since I had not the faintest idea what kind of an order could be obtained), I suggested that we broaden the problem definition to, "In what ways might we obtain the release of the funds?" [That led to] an effective method of convincing C to sign the withdrawal slip. *What turned out to be the best solution had simply not occurred to the [first] attorney because he had limited himself to the narrow "court order" definition of the problem.*[28]

Amy's solution evaluation is more realistic than Jake's because she looks for what Gilligan calls "the inclusive solution"[29]—the one that solves the problem by satisfying the needs of everyone involved. Her focus on relationships helps her realize that Heinz isn't really free of his dilemma until the druggist is as well.

---

25. *Id.* at 28.
26. Remarks by Gilligan in *Feminist Discourse, Moral Values, and the Law—A Conversation*, 34 Buff. L. Rev. 11, 44 (1985).
27. Menkel-Meadow, *supra* note 23, at 46.
28. Gordon MacLeod, *Creative Problem-Solving—For Lawyers?!*, 16 J. Legal Educ. 198, 201 (1963) (emphasis added).
29. Remarks by Gilligan, *supra* note 26, at 45.

Perhaps with some oversimplification, the end of Amy and Jake's reasoning—as seen on the evening news—would be Amy's announcement of the kind of fund-raising that touches everyone's heart and wallet, while Jake desperately tries to persuade a judge and jury not to send his client to prison.

In the farmhouse problem at the beginning of this chapter, the lawyer's solution was inclusive. It solved her client's problem and eliminated conflict by simultaneously solving a problem that the sellers didn't realize they had. The most satisfying solutions are the ones that leave no losers.

§4.6 DEVELOPING A PROBLEM-SOLVING STYLE

It will take years to develop a problem-solving style that makes the best use of your strengths and limits the effect of your weaknesses. But here are some suggestions.

Learn from experience. When you look back on a professional situation that turned out in a disappointing way, critique your own work. Did you fail to recognize places where you could have made an important decision that might have altered the result? Was your preparation so cursory that you did not have all the information you needed? Or, conversely, was it so unnecessarily exhaustive that you didn't have time to do other things? Was there an hypothesis or solution that you became aware of too late because your generation was weak? Did you evaluate hypotheses or solutions accurately? When you decided, did you forget or ignore some of your evaluation? Or did other factors sneak in and influence the result? Looking at the big picture, how could you have done better?

In postmortems of your work, a supervising lawyer or a teacher might ask you a litany of questions about strategy:

- What was your goal?
- What was your strategy?
- What other possible strategies did you consider and reject?
- For each rejected strategy, why was it inferior to the one you did choose?
- What led you to believe that the strategy you chose would actually achieve the ultimate goal?
- Did you do all the things necessary to execute the strategy you chose?
- Did you do anything that impeded that strategy?
- If the goal was not achieved, why not?
- If the goal was achieved, did your strategy *cause* that? Or was it caused by something else, such as an adversary's mistake?

Supervisors and teachers ask these questions because a lawyer's job is to make desired things happen. The supervisor or teacher will be trying to make sure that your planning is free of thinking that inhibits strategy, such as overlooking opportunities, relying on unrealistic assumptions, or engaging in wishful thinking. *Analyze both your successes and your mistakes—and learn from all of them.*

If you're willing to be self-reflective, and if you scrutinize your own planning work with some regularity, you might notice some patterns. You can figure out which parts of the process come naturally to you and which parts you need to improve. Do you sometimes fail to notice opportunities to transform a situation? If so, you might try to improve your problem-recognition skills by disciplining yourself to look for those opportunities. Does important information seem to enter the picture too late to help you? During preparation, you might become more aggressive about figuring out exactly what you do not yet know and then filling those gaps. Does your idea-generation seem unproductive? Your well-developed critical and convergent thinking skills might be shutting down your imagination. Do you generate a large list of hypotheses and solutions but then tend to choose one with a fatal flaw in it? Perhaps those same critical thinking skills aren't helping you at the time when you really need them: while evaluating and deciding.

Discover your strengths as well. What have you done effectively? If you understand your strengths, you know what you can capitalize on.

Treat the entire problem as an integrated whole. Step back far enough to see the big picture—the whole forest instead of only the individual trees—and keep that big picture in mind as you think about each smaller portion of the problem.

Sometimes all of a problem's aspects fit together into a single problem solvable through a strategy that addresses everything—if only the lawyer can see the entire problem as an integrated whole. Try to cultivate "peripheral vision": the "ability to see what is going on in the total environment, to understand how things connect. Lawyers with well-developed peripheral vision can be awesome in their ability to look at problems from many different perspectives, to see not only what is presented, but what is not presented."[30]

Identify the few things that really matter. An effective problem-solver identifies the very few things—facts, pieces of evidence, aspects of law or policy—that are most likely to affect the way a client's situation is resolved. Of hundreds of relevant facts or points of law, in most instances only a very few—perhaps two or three or four—will in the end affect results. Strategic vision begins with the ability to predict which few things will determine the result.

Identify the decisive event (or events). Effective strategies almost never consist of throwing everything at the other side and then awaiting further developments. The best strategies are based on accurate predictions that a particular kind of future event (or a small number of events) will cause a desired result—if only that event could be made to happen. You might think of it as the *decisive event* because its occurrence would effectively solve the problem.

Once the event is selected, strategic planning concentrates on causing it to occur. Organize your work to cause the decisive event or events by planning backward—from the future to the present—identifying the things that must be done to make the decisive event happen. Neustadt and May called this "backward mapping."[31]

---

30. Sallyanne Payton, *Is Thinking Like a Lawyer Enough?*, 18 U. Mich. J.L. Reform 233, 241 (1985).
31. Richard E. Neustadt & Ernest R. May, Thinking in Time: The Uses of History for Decision-Makers 255 (1986).

For example, in the farmhouse problem earlier in this chapter, the decisive event was persuading the sellers that it would be to their own advantage to sell the farmhouse now rather than later. The law would neither force them to sell nor allow the client to escape the existing contract to buy the surrounding farmland, which the client now did not want without the farmhouse. From that insight, the lawyer mapped backward.

What would persuade the sellers that they would be better off selling the farmhouse now? Their reason for wanting to wait was financial. They assumed that the farmhouse would be worth more later. Their assumption created the client's problem. What might prove that assumption to be wrong or show it to be irrelevant? This line of questions led to the tax considerations. Treat the decisive event as a goal and then think from that goal back to where you are you so you can figure out what to *start* doing.

Don't just throw effort at the problem. Concentrate your work on whatever will most likely resolve the situation on desirable terms. Effort is wasted if diffused on other things. This is simple efficiency.

Although predictions, of decisive events and everything else, turn out to be inaccurate more often than you would like, your problem-solving effectiveness will be measured in part by your ability to choose a decisive event wisely and to organize and concentrate effort to cause that event to happen. Often the decisive event can't be recognized until well after you've begun work, but once it becomes identifiable, effort is wasted unless directed at it.

Develop one or more back-up strategies, if possible, in case the original strategy proves ineffective as a whole. You can identify alternative decisive events and strategize to cause them, in case they should become needed.

Because life is random, even chaotic, you'll never fully be in complete control of a situation. Problem solving depends in part on the ability to integrate the unexpected into an *evolving* plan—to capitalize on accidents rather than be victimized by them. Sometimes a lawyer doesn't so much cause events as she *shepherds* facts and circumstances so that they travel in the direction of the decisive event. Sometimes, the lawyer doesn't even try to cause the decisive event. The event might be occurring anyway, independently of the lawyer's efforts—but without decisive effect unless the lawyer adds to it or alters it in some way. The lawyer's contribution is to recognize the event's potential and do things that endow it with its decisive quality.

Don't be afraid to take calculated risks. Recognize risks and decide when to take them and when to avoid them. Many problems can't be solved without risk taking. A calculated risk is one you take after weighing possible benefits and the odds of achieving them against potential harms and the odds of suffering them.

A lawyer with a low tolerance for risk may reject strategies with substantial risk elements, even when the client's goals can't fully be accomplished without risk taking. Conversely, some lawyers have an exaggerated view of their own abilities and fall into high-risk strategies without calculating potential benefits and harms. If you take risks unwisely, you'll create additional problems and probably won't solve the one problem you're trying to solve.

Help your mind wander. Many professionals find that they have their best ideas when traveling to or from the office, showering, doing the dishes, or jogging. What these have in common is that the professional is doing something mechanical, freeing the mind to wander. It can help to keep a pad and pencil handy while doors are open in your mind.

Resist the temptation to act on nonstrategic motivations. Act only after understanding how, in the situation at hand, your actions really will influence events. An action isn't strategic if its hidden function is to satisfy the lawyer's own emotional needs—for example, to hide fear, to create a reassuring illusion of doing something, to avoid admitting the error of earlier actions, to vent anger, or simply to reflect the lawyer's personality. What feels good isn't the same as what's strategically wise. Act only on the basis of evidence that the action will probably cause the desired result.

Most lawyers have some personal trait that, if left uncontrolled, will in one way or another obstruct problem solving. An example is the confrontational personality that confuses, hostility, voice-raising, and table-pounding with problem solving. Sometimes, a staged display of anger is strategically appropriate to communicate that the other side's actions are unacceptable. But just as often it can be counterproductive. Lawyers who automatically seek self-fulfillment through confrontation are usually not thinking through the process of problem solving. The express-train roar of a confrontational lawyer at full throttle is often the equivalent of "strategic bluster"[32] that camouflages the confrontational lawyer's own anxiety and perplexity.

When you're attacked by a confrontational lawyer, you may have advantages. It might not feel that way, especially if you're a young professional verbally ambushed by an intimidating and more experienced practitioner. But consider what's really going on. Loud, bellicose talk often means either of two things: the talker knows he's in a weak position or he's too confrontational to be a good strategist. (The older lawyer may have other advantages, however, such as a more thorough knowledge of your client's industry.) If you are yourself a confrontational person, you can probably improve your own strategic skills if you learn to control that part of your personality.

Good strategy results from calm reflection.

32. Michael Sherry, *The Slide to Total Air War*, The New Republic, Dec. 16, 1981, at 20, 23.

CHAPTER 5

COMMUNICATIONS SKILLS

§5.1 WHY COMMUNICATION THROUGH THE SPOKEN WORD IS A CORE LAWYERLY SKILL

Most of what lawyer do involves communication. You have already had a substantial dose of written lawyerly communication. The first year of law school is devoted in part to developing your ability to interpret statutes and judicial opinions (and thus receive written communication). The first-year Legal Writing course develops your ability to communicate arguments in writing. This book focuses, among other things, on *oral* communication.

You might think that oral communication will not present any particular challenges. After all, you and everyone you know have been talking for as long as you can remember. But that is exactly why learning to communicate orally at a professional level is deceptively difficult. It looks familiar, but habits that have worked before often do not work in a law office. At the same time, you might be afraid to do some things you know how to do conversationally because you think they do not belong in a law office.

For example, you might be in the habit of saying "O.K." when you mean "I've heard what you just said," like this:

You: How can I get to Magnolia Street?

Friend: Walk two blocks in that direction. The first street is Jena but keep going. The second street is Cadiz. Turn right there. Then walk four blocks to Magnolia. If you get to Clara Street, you've gone too far.

You: O.K.

You've heard something complicated, but you think you understand it, so you say O.K. Now, in a client interview:

Client: I worked for Intercontinental Airlines. When the company went under, I lost my job. And I lost my pension. It was invested in company stock, which is now worthless. I don't have any money to live on. I've applied for hundreds of other jobs and haven't gotten so much as an interview. I think it's because nobody wants to hire a pilot who's 54 years old. My car has been repossessed, and my landlord has threatened to evict me because I haven't been able to pay the rent.

You: O.K.

Here, your client will believe that you think that the tragedy that has befallen her is O.K., even though all you meant to communicate was "I hear you." (About half of all law students make this mistake in their initial client interviews.) What your client needs from you is something that you already know how to give but might think inappropriate in a law office: *empathy*, as you would give a friend who tells you something tragic:

Client: [*same as above*]

You: Oh, my. That's terrible.

How can you decide what is the right thing to say? How can you avoid saying the wrong thing? The rest of this book helps you learn effective and appropriate oral communication in the three most important interactive tasks lawyers do outside the courtroom: interviewing, counseling, and negotiation.

How you say something has an enormous effect on the way people respond. In part, it's the words you use. Two words that seem to convey approximately the same idea may actually have two separate meanings with a precise difference between them ("curious" and "nosy," for example). Or they might mean the same thing, but with different connotations (such as "dirty" and "filthy"). Senior lawyers greatly value the ability to communicate orally. When law firm hiring partners were surveyed about the skills they expected new law school graduates to have mastered before they start work, 91% of them mentioned oral communication.[1]

1. Bryant Garth & Joanne Martin, *Law Schools and the Construction of Competence*, 43 J. Legal Educ. 469, 490 (1993).

§5.2 EIGHT ORAL COMMUNICATION SKILLS

The skills explained below are among the themes of this book. We return to them in later chapters.

§5.2.1 LISTENING

"Listening," says playwright and actor Anna Deavere Smith, "is not just hearing what someone tells you word for word. You have to listen with a heart. . . . It is very hard work."[2] "Listening," adds Nance Guilmartin, "isn't just about being quiet. It's about listening to what people say, what they don't say, and what they mean. . . . Listening is about hearing with our eyes, our ears, and our heart. . . ."[3] Listening includes *figuring out the person who is speaking.* What matters to her as a person? How does she see the world? If you do not ask yourself these questions, you will not understand the full meaning behind the words.

Some lawyers talk too much and listen too little. Here is an example. The client has been in the lawyer's office for less than five minutes and is now beginning to explain why he is there:

Client: I was walking down the street and found a big envelope.

Lawyer: What did it look like?

Client: Tan colored, eight-and-a-half by eleven inches. It was lying right there on the pavement. It looked full of something, so I picked it up.

Lawyer: Have you ever done this before?

Client: No.

Lawyer: What did you do after you picked it up?

Client: I looked inside and saw money. I looked around for somebody who might have dropped it.

Lawyer: You want to know whether you can keep the money?

Client: Oh, no.

The following is better. The lawyer learns much more just by listening.

Client: I was walking down the street and found a big envelope. It was lying right there on the pavement. It looked full of something, so I picked it up. There was a lot of money in it but no name or address on it.

---

2. Karen W. Arenson, *The Fine Art of Listening: Anna Deavere Smith Helps N.Y.U. Law Students Look Beyond the Legal Questions*, N.Y. Times, Jan. 13, 2002, Educ. Life at 34, 35.
3. Nance Guilmartin, *Healing Conversations* xx (2002).

> I looked around for somebody who might have dropped it, but nobody seemed to be looking for something. I waited about 15 minutes, but nothing happened. I was late for a dentist appointment, so I left. At home that night, I counted the money. It was $10,000 exactly. I read the newspapers carefully for a week to see if anybody was reported to have lost the money, and nobody was. I'd like to donate it to the West Side Home for Orphans. Can I legally do that?

The ability to listen well is as important in the practice of law as the ability to talk well. The popular image of a lawyer is of a person talking—to juries, to judges, to adversaries, to reporters. But in the end, the lawyer who knows how to listen has a tremendous advantage. Knowledge can be power, and in the practice of law one of the most important means of gaining knowledge is to listen carefully and precisely.

Some lawyers find it hard to listen because they cannot stop talking for very long. Some people talk out of nervousness, to prevent uncomfortable silences, no matter how brief. Some people like to hold forth and be the center of attention. And some lawyers talk when they should be listening because they feel that talking helps them control whatever situation they happen to be in.

But listening is not passivity. It is hard work and a skill that can be learned. It includes "active listening": encouraging the other person to talk and occasionally asking the other person to clarify something that is confusing or to add details to something that would otherwise be sketchy. In a sense, it even includes listening with your eyes: what is the other person telling you through attire, facial expression, or body position, for example? (Active listening is explained in §8.1.2.)

You can listen more effectively if you ask yourself these questions while the other person is talking:

What words—exactly—am I hearing, and what do those words mean?

What do the speaker's words imply (hint at)?

What do the speaker's tone of voice and body language (facial expression, posture, etc.) imply?

Why is the speaker saying or implying these things?

What is the speaker *not* saying or implying that other people in her situation often communicate? Why?

§5.2.2 EMPATHIZING

> Empathy is feeling what another person feels. Sympathy is more common and less valuable than empathy. "If you are sympathetic to others, your heart goes out to them, and you feel compassion, but these are *your* feelings. You don't know what *they're* feeling. . . . If you are empathetic to others, you are not merely feeling sorry for them but are projecting yourself into their hearts, as though you are sensing what it's like to be in their shoes."[4]

---

4. Tim Sanders, *The Likeability Factor* 117 (2005).

A struggling rock musician recalled two conversations about his difficulties. The first was with a successful performer named Timmy, the brother of a friend.

> My band had played only fifteen shows in the previous year, and even those had been sparsely attended. Regardless of how much we practiced and promoted our shows, we couldn't generate a dedicated following.
>
> When I told this to Timmy, he simply shrugged his shoulders and said, "Let me tell you about my experience. If you rock, the crowds will double every week and someone will offer you a deal. No way I'd do fifteen gigs without having a big crowd. You're in a real bad place there."
>
> To this day I still remember how terrible I felt after that conversation.
>
> In contrast, a week later I met a musician named Joe, the bass player in a successful local reggae band. I shared my problems with Joe, too. Although he was also successful, Joe, trying hard to understand how I felt, blurted out *how uncomfortable he knew it must be to stand in front of those small crowds. . . .* Was there anything he could do to help?
>
> For years I basked in the glow of his kindness. . . .[5]

Empathy is invaluable in interviewing, counseling, and negotiating. Empathy helps you find out who your clients really are and what they are really feeling, and once they sense true empathy from you, they will tell you more and trust you. At the same time, empathy from a lawyer often helps a client feel stronger and more capable of dealing with the problems the client has brought to the lawyer. Even in negotiation, empathy can be helpful, although only in carefully chosen spots. Empathy at the right moment can sometimes break the stalemate of confrontation and move the discussion toward mutual understanding.

But the empathy has to be authentic. If you try to pretend to be empathetic, people will sense that it is not genuine and feel uncomfortable.

§5.2.3 ASKING QUESTIONS

One of the marks of an effective person—in law and in almost any part of life—is the ability to ask the right question in the most productive way. A good question is artistic. It cuts through a mountain of debris to find hidden treasure. An effective lawyer asks good questions constantly. The questions are put to clients, witnesses (in and out of court), colleagues, opposing lawyers, and government employees.

What can you do to ask questions well? Later, when we cover interviewing (Chapters 7 through 9) and negotiation (Chapters 23 through 28), we examine question-asking skills in more detail. Here are some basic concepts:

Ask for all the important information. Good questions seek things of value, things that really do need to be known. Some people can fill an hour with marginal questions. Others can learn everything in five minutes.

---

5. *Id.* at 121 (emphasis added).

When asking questions, use the words that are most likely to produce valuable information. Some words help find information and encourage answers, while other words confuse, cloud memory, or provoke resistance.

Ask at the right time and in the right context. Sometimes other questions have to be asked first, and often the person being asked has to be put into a mood to be helpful.

Know when to ask narrow questions and when to ask broad questions. A narrow question asks for specific information ("What time did your plane arrive?"). A broad question asks for general information and often invites the person answering the question to decide what to emphasize ("How was your flight?").

If you need to know something specific, a narrow question is the fastest way to find out. If you're not sure what's important, a broad question can produce a lot of information, which you can then begin to sort out. Often (but not always), it is more effective to start with broad questions and then work toward narrow ones. Section 8.3.2 explains why.

Know when to ask leading questions and when to ask nonleading questions. A leading question not only suggests the answer; it also creates pressure to provide that answer.

"You've just returned from Bermuda, haven't you?" is a leading question. You can expect the questioner to be surprised—and maybe unhappy—if you answer no.

"Have you been to Bermuda lately?" is a narrow nonleading question. It's narrow because it asks for specific information. It's nonleading because the wording implies that the questioner would be satisfied with either yes or no, as long as it is truthful.

"Tell me about any trips you might have taken recently" is a broad nonleading question. It's broad because it asks about traveling in general and not just Bermuda. It's nonleading because, again, the wording implies that the questioner would be happy with any truthful answer.

Leading questions are useful in only two situations. The first is where you think you know the answer and are using the question only to raise a topic so you can then ask other questions to learn things you do not already know:

> "You've just returned from Bermuda, haven't you?" [*a leading question*]
> "Yes."
> "What is it like to visit Bermuda at this time of year?" [*a broad nonleading question*]

The second situation is where you are trying to pin something down or extract a factual concession:

> "You've just returned from Bermuda, haven't you?" [*a leading question*]
> "Yes."
> "And while you were in Bermuda, you explored the possibility of avoiding U.S. taxes by incorporating off-shore, didn't you?" [*another leading question*]

Be patient. Patience, as Henry Aaron said, is "the art of waiting."[6] Some lawyers do not know how to wait. If they do not get an instantaneous answer to a question, they ask another one immediately. The other person might have been thinking about the first question and about to give an interesting and useful answer, but the second question cut that off. Because of impatience, the lawyer might never learn the answer to the first question.

Let silence help you. You ask a question and hear nothing in response. Actually, you do hear something. You hear the silence of the other person deciding how to answer. Listen to the silence, and wait. If you dislike silence, the other person might, too. And the other person's dislike of silence might cause her to produce lots of information. Be patient.

Listen carefully to answers and ask thorough lines of questions. You ask a question on Topic A and get some of the information you asked for. If you imitate the interviewers you see on television, you will ignore the missing information and ask an unrelated question on Topic B. But if you are a good lawyer, you will *not* go on to Topic B without asking all the follow-up questions necessary to get all the information you need on Topic A. Find out everything. Not just a lot of things. *Everything.*

§5.2.4 FINDING AND TELLING STORIES

A story has characters and a plot, like a novel or a movie.

Through their actions, the characters reveal what kind of people they are. We, the audience, decide to like them or dislike them. If we like them, we get upset when they suffer, and we want things to get better. If we are judges or jurors, we might hope to be able to decide in their favor. We like characters who are honest, caring, careful, hard-working, not selfish, and so on. We dislike characters who have the opposite qualities, especially if they have harmed characters we like (and if we are judges or jurors, we might enjoy making the bad characters pay).

A story also reveals *why* events happened, especially how harm was caused. For example, one character is suffering.

Is it because her own carelessness put her in a dangerous situation or because some other character's carelessness did that? In one kind of compelling story, we can see that the bad characters caused the good characters to suffer—and we want to do something about it. In another kind of compelling story, the bad characters are pretending that the good characters hurt them—and we want to make sure the bad characters don't get away with it. This seems like an oversimplification, but trials are contests between competing stories. And as we will see in §8.3.1, the party with the most compelling story usually wins.

In addition to characters and a plot that reveals the characters' nature, an effective story *makes the audience want to act.* And lawyers tell stories to audiences that have the *power* to act. In the courtroom, the audience includes

---

6. Henry Aaron with Lonnie Wheeler, *If I Had a Hammer: The Hank Aaron Story* 236 (paperback ed. 1992). (Aaron hit 755 home runs in part by waiting for the right pitch.) See also Stefan H. Krieger, *A Time to Keep Silent and a Time to Speak: The Functions of Silence in the Lawyering Process*, 80 Or. L. Rev. 199, 240–242 (2001) (on "using silences to promote gathering of information").

judges and juries. Inside and outside the courtroom, the audience includes, among others, the lawyer who is your adversary—the lawyer who represents the opposing party. In negotiation, you tell the story to that lawyer in hopes that she will foresee that the courtroom audience will be persuaded by your story and therefore offer you concessions to prevent the courtroom audience from deciding in your favor.

Effective lawyers have two clusters of story skills. The first are *story-finding* skills. You interview the client and witnesses and have located a number of documents and other pieces of evidence. Out of this, you have identified exactly 1000 facts. Now in this forest of facts, you have to *find the story*. Which facts reveal what kind of person your client is? Which facts reveal what kind of people the other characters are? Which facts show how harm was caused? Do these few facts coalesce into a plot? You do not invent the story. That would be lying. You find it in the facts. Section 13.7 explains how.

The second cluster of skills involves *telling* the story. If you are telling the story yourself (as in negotiation), what words will express it in a way that makes it most persuasive? If you are telling it through evidence in the courtroom, what questions put to witnesses, for example, will cause them to bring out the story in the most compelling way?

§5.2.5 PAINTING A PICTURE

When you paint a picture, you use words to create a scene in the listener's mind. The listener will have to use a little imagination to see the scene, but the more details you provide and the more vivid your words, the easier it will be for the listener to see the scene. Story finding and storytelling are usually thought of as a litigator's skills. But painting a picture is useful both in conflict resolution (such as litigation) and in transactional work (such as contract negotiation).

In counseling, to help a client understand the consequences of a particular option, you might paint this picture, which should be frightening to the client:

> The second option is to refuse the prosecution's offer of a plea bargain and go to trial. The government has video from a hidden camera, of what looks like you accepting a bribe. In the video, you can be heard saying that in exchange for the $20,000 in the briefcase you are being given, you will prevent enforcement of the air pollution statutes at the factory owned by the person giving you the money. The factory is the only source of industrial air pollution in the city. The prosecution will not be able to get into evidence the fact that the city has one of the highest lung cancer rates in the country. But the jurors all live here, and they will all know about the cancer rate because it's been reported in the newspapers often. Our motion for a change in venue has been denied. . . .

As you read this, do you imagine a picture of the jurors in the courtroom watching the video? In your mind, are you already seeing their frowns and grim faces?

In negotiation, you might paint this picture, which the other side, a manufacturer of electronics gadgets, might find intriguing:

> As you know, my client has developed a patent-protected device that silences automobile security alarms within a range of 400 feet.
>
> Although people install these things in their cars, studies show that car thieves are not deterred by them. Nearly every time you hear a car alarm, it has been set off accidentally by electrical malfunction, by a thunderclap, by another car tapping the alarmed car while parking, or even by somebody leaning against the alarmed car. Everybody knows that. So when a car alarm goes off, nobody thinks a car is being stolen. The only thing the alarm accomplishes is to annoy neighbors.
>
> If we can agree on a price, my client would license this device to you exclusively. You would be the only manufacturer in the world selling a product that could be used to stop this ear-shattering racket.
>
> Suppose you live near a parking lot or a street with a lot of parked cars. Every once in a while, one of these alarms goes off in the middle of the night. You were asleep but suddenly you sit bolt upright in bed. If the alarm doesn't turn itself off in a minute or two, you'll listen to it for a long time and won't be able to go back to sleep. Even if it does turn itself off quickly, you will not be rested the next day because rest is accomplished only with uninterrupted sleep.
>
> This doesn't have to happen. Before you get into bed in the first place, you turn on my client's device. Then you go to sleep confident that you will sleep through the night. Our market surveys suggest that to get this benefit people are willing to pay . . .

From this, are you able to imagine a television commercial for the product?

§5.2.6 GIVING INFORMATION

Sometimes lawyers give complete information precisely, and sometimes they don't. For example, your client has over ten years built a business from something that operated out of his garage into an enterprise that employs 1000 people and earns $200 million a year. He is now selling the business, and you are involved in negotiating the sale. The buyer's representatives ask what your client plans to do after the sale. If you want to provide a lot of information, you could say:

> He enjoys building up a company from nothing. That's his thrill. And the only business he knows is manufacturing the product he's making now. He's had a few ideas in the last two years for revolutionary changes in the product that would make everything now on the market obsolete. But he hasn't developed them through this company because he knew he was going to sell it and start over. He has talked informally with investment bankers to get a new company up and running. He's written a business plan already, and the bankers are eager to lend the money, although nothing will be agreed to until after he has taken six months off to travel around the world.

This is very informative. In some situations, it would be exactly the right thing to say. But here, it tells the other side so much that they might walk away from this deal because they will not want to compete with your client's new company. If you want to give the *smallest* amount of information possible, you could answer by speaking incompletely or ambiguously or both:

> He's explored some business ideas, but nothing is certain yet except that he and his family will take a trip around the world for the next six months. They'll go

> to Paris, Prague, Kenya—the sort of places where you can relax and get away from an exhausting business life. He was telling me the other day about plans to visit the Studio Ghibli museum in Japan. He's an entrepreneur by nature. He'll get into something when he gets back.

Here, the details about the trip are a smokescreen. In the negotiation chapters of this book, we explore the ethical rules governing an answer like this one. The buyer asked generally what the seller's post-sale plans are without saying why he wants to know, and the ambiguous answer above contains no untruthful statements. If the buyer wants to know whether the seller will compete in the same market, he has to ask that question directly and listen carefully to the answer.

Two kinds of skills are involved here. The first is knowing *when* to speak completely and precisely and when to speak incompletely or ambiguously. The second is knowing *how* to speak in those ways.

§5.2.7 IMPLYING THROUGH TONE OF VOICE AND BODY LANGUAGE

Some things are not communicated very clearly or naturally in words. Suppose that a client is a charming and witty person whose presence you enjoy. If you say that to the client, both of you might feel uncomfortable. But if you smile and speak in a friendly tone whenever you see the client, the message gets across much more naturally. (This should not stop you from using words to compliment the client on qualities that are more directly related to your collaboration with the client. If the client is realistic, reasonable, creative, or perceptive when you work together, it is not inappropriate to mention those things.)

Suppose that in negotiation your adversary has just made a proposal that seems to ignore everything you have said about your client's needs. You will make things worse if you say, "You blockhead! Didn't you understand anything I've told you about my client?" That would introduce pointless interpersonal conflict. And you have concluded that words alone are not getting through to this adversary. You might say, "For the reasons I've explained before, that will not satisfy any of my client's needs," while using a tone of voice and perhaps a facial expression to suggest that the negotiation will fail unless the adversary becomes more responsive.

When are tone of voice and body language better than words? Sometimes, words will make one or both people uncomfortable (as with the charming and witty client). And sometimes, words that convey all you feel will make it hard for the other person to change behavior (as with the negotiating adversary who has not been listening to you). Tone of voice and body language can be used to imply where explicitly saying something would cause additional problems.

§5.2.8 MAKING ARGUMENTS

A lawyer's argument is not bickering. An argument is a group of ideas expressed logically to convince a listener to do a particular thing or to adopt a particular belief.

For good reasons, we list making arguments last among oral communication skills. One of the signs of *in*effectiveness in a lawyer is a tendency to make arguments in situations where it would be more productive to do the things we've listed above: listen, empathize, ask questions, find or tell a story, paint a picture, give information, or imply through tone of voice or body language.

Nobody really knows why ineffective lawyers do this. It might be because argument is one of the first communication tools, oral or written, taught in law school, which might leave students with the impression that arguing is the essence of lawyering. Or it might be because the stereotype of lawyers as arguers attracts to the profession people who like to argue.

Certainly, every lawyer needs to know how to make good arguments. There are plenty of times when the only way, or the most effective way, to get what the client wants is through argument. But a threshold skill is knowing when to argue and when to do something else instead. In the negotiation chapters of this book, we help you develop that skill.

§5.3 THE TELEPHONE, EMAIL, AND TEXTING

Each of these three media—the telephone, email, and texting—has different uses and can be dangerous unless you are careful. Law students and newly graduated lawyers who don't understand this can get into trouble very quickly.

The telephone. You might be in the habit of avoiding voice mail so you can avoid conversation with whoever left a message. But in law practice people leave messages *because they need to converse with you.* And you have professional obligations to converse with them. If you ignore voice mail from clients, they will hate you for reasons explained in Chapter 3. Clients may fire you over this, and they are more likely to refuse to pay your bill or file ethics complaints or sue for malpractice, rather than forgive you, if you make other mistakes. To a client, a lawyer who ignores voice mail, or email, is guilty until proven innocent. If you ignore messages from other lawyers, they will assume that you are an amateur. Failure to respond to a message shows disrespect for the person who left it.

Respond to every voice mail on the same day the caller left a message or, at the latest, early in the next morning. If it is impossible for you to return the call within that time, have someone else in your office do it. That person should apologize on your behalf and find out whether the caller's needs can be addressed by someone else in your office who can be available immediately. If the caller needs to speak with you specifically, the person who responds from your office should find a time when you and the caller are both free to talk. This will be an appointment to speak by telephone, and you must treat it the same way you would treat an appointment for the caller to visit you in your office.

Never leave a substantive message by voice mail. Imagine the recipient checking her voice mail on a speaker phone while someone else is in the room. Assume that could happen with any message you leave.

Never discuss a confidential matter by telephone in a public place. Find a quiet location where no one can hear what you say.

Email. Do not use email as a substitute for conversation. *Lawyers make their living conversing. Voice conversations are the most central part of a lawyer's* *job*. It's impossible to interview, counsel, or persuade entirely or even primarily by email. Those things happen in conversation. Email plays only a supporting role. Use it to convey information or send attached documents or for uncomplicated question-and-answer exchanges that have little emotional content. A particularly good use is to provide information that the recipient would want to think about in preparation for a voice conversation.

Email has no tone of voice or body language. When you converse with someone, you communicate through tone of voice as well as through words. If you and the other person are in the same room, you also communicate through body language. Conversation is a warm medium because the other person can hear your tone and perhaps see what your body communicates.

Email is a cold medium. It's just words. The same words can sound friendly in the repartee of conversation but come across as innuendo or even insulting in an email. Your tone of voice and body language, which tell the other person you are being friendly, are not in the email. Never use email to communicate when emotions are important either to you or to the recipient. Even if your wording is so perfect that it cannot be misunderstood—a rare achievement—email is *cold.*

Assume that anything sent by email can be read eventually by the wrong people unless you take strong steps to prevent that.

Email is forever. You might delete it from your system, and the recipient might do the same—but it will continue to live on your server and on the recipient's server or in the cloud through backup systems. Killing it is impossible. Anybody with access to the servers or the backup can read it. And anybody who reads it can forward it or even put it on a website. Some lawyers have seen email they wrote carelessly go viral on the Internet.

Unless you are absolutely certain that the recipient will keep it confidential, never put anything in an email that you would not want the world to see. Email systems autofill familiar addresses after you type the first few letters. This convenience is an invitation to disaster. If you are not paying attention and inadvertently send confidential client information to someone who shouldn't have it, you may have waived the attorney-client privilege. Law office email systems attach a boilerplate disclaimer to every email. The disclaimer is useful, but it might not save you if your own carelessness has sent the information to the wrong person.

You must teach your client to be as careful as you are in this respect. If your client accidentally sends confidential information to the wrong person, that might be an even more clear-cut waiver of the attorney-client privilege. And make sure your client uses a personal email account and not an employer's account. An employer has both the right and the ability to get into its own accounts and read anything sent through them. If the client's employer reads confidential information there and tells the world about it, the privilege has almost certainly been waived. It won't matter who sent the email, you or the client.

You—and your client—should check every email's address and any attachments just before sending. This is the last opportunity to prevent the disaster of the wrong person receiving confidential information. Even laying aside waivers of the attorney-client privilege, will a client trust you after receiving, as an attachment, another client's confidential document? Will a supervisor think you are a careful lawyer after reading attachments that have nothing to do with the email you sent?

Make sure that the subject line tells the recipient exactly what your message concerns, especially when the recipient is another lawyer. Some lawyers receive hundreds of emails per day. Many of those will be deleted without being read. Unless your subject line states exactly what you are writing about, your email may be deleted inadvertently with all the rest.

Email systems are designed for sending, not writing. You can compose simple messages in your email system. But when you are composing a longer message or one requiring delicate wording, you might find it easier to write in a word processing program such as Word or WordPerfect and then copy and paste what you have written there into the email. This can also be safer. It is impossible to send an unfinished message accidentally from a word processing program.

Read every message carefully before sending it. If you make any changes, read it again before sending. If you make more changes, read it a third time before sending. Is everything *exactly* what you want the recipient to read? Once you click on the send button, you cannot recall the message.

Don't send angry emails. Email is forever, and when your message is read long in the future and far from the incident that has provoked you, angry words can look petty. Send stern messages instead. A stern message sets out boundaries of what you consider acceptable and gives objective reasons for them. Write in a way that makes you seem reasonable to *anybody* who reads your message.

Avoid sending email from your phone except for short messages and for housekeeping such as asking the recipient to call or scheduling a meeting or telling the recipient that a court date has been changed. Every email risk is multiplied from a cell phone.

Texting. In almost every respect, texting is worse than email. An appropriate text might be, "Please call me right away. The other side has contacted us." But it can be foolish to send a text telling the client that the other side has made a settlement offer. It's too easy for that message to be read by the wrong person.

Never send substantive messages by text. Use texting only for housekeeping—scheduling appointments, telling the recipient to check her email, and so forth.

Never use textisms such as *b4*, *ttyl*, or *brb*. Communicate like a professional.

CHAPTER 6

MULTICULTURAL LAWYERING

§6.1 HOW CULTURE MATTERS IN LAWYERING

A lawyer can be effective only if the lawyer understands cultural differences and knows how to recognize and deal with them. You will deal with people from widely varied cultures, regardless of the type of legal work you do. Different cultures are entitled to respect on their own terms and without stereotyping.

A culture is a body of values, customs, and ways of looking at the world shared by a group of people. A culture can be based on any of the following:

- ethnicity or race
- gender
- age
- locality or geography
- religion
- nationality or immigrant status
- disability
- sexual orientation
- income, education, or both
- occupation or the organization in which one works

Obviously, many people have sensibilities shaped by more than one culture.

If you ignore the differences among cultures—or if you think of people in cultural stereotypes—you will alienate clients, witnesses, other lawyers, and judges and juries. You will also cut yourself off from a great deal of information, simply because different cultures communicate in different ways.

Working with people of diverse backgrounds is a skill—actually a cluster of skills.

§6.2 HOW CULTURAL DIFFERENCES CAN MATTER IN LAWYERING

Here are some ways in which cultures can differ and how that can affect how you do your job as a lawyer.

Are events viewed differently by people from different cultural contexts? A police car is following another car. The police car's siren and flashing lights go on, and both cars pull over to the side of the road. A police officer steps out and walks toward the other car. The officer plans to issue a traffic ticket and believes he is just doing his job. At least some of the police officer's expectations might arise from the organizational culture prevailing in the police department. If the driver is from a culture that does not have a troubled history with the police, the driver expects merely the unpleasant experience of receiving a traffic ticket. But what is about to happen could be perceived very differently by the driver if that person is from a culture in which contact with the police sometimes creates risks not shared by the majority U.S. culture. Either driver might be surprised by what happens when the police officer reaches the car and begins a conversation. But the cultural norms and expectations of all three of these people will affect what they say and do and how they remember the event afterward.

How is conflict viewed? In the majority U.S. culture, conflict is considered socially acceptable and even socially useful. That does not mean that every person in the majority culture enjoys conflict. Many people do not, and they will avoid conflict if they can. But conflict is not considered disgraceful in the United States. It's honorable to complain when something goes wrong. And U.S. law resolves disagreements through procedures that might be more adversarial and contentious than in any other country. Even lawyers in other common law countries are sometimes shocked by the way American lawyers behave in the courtroom.

In some other countries, however, conflict is considered disgraceful. In some cultures, anyone involved in open and public conflict is thought to have done something shameful. People in these cultures may often simply suffer a loss rather than complain officially about the person who caused the loss, especially if that person has a higher status or power of some kind. The world is not divided into conflict-tolerant cultures and conflict-intolerant cultures. Instead, cultures have a broad range of attitudes toward conflict, from those that honor conflict (such as the majority U.S. culture) to those that dishonor it, with many cultures somewhere in between. And in some cultures certain types of conflict are acceptable while others are not.

If you counsel a client whose cultural assumptions about conflict are different from yours, you might create a set of options that are entirely inappropriate for the client unless you take the cultural differences into account. And if you negotiate confrontationally against someone who views conflict as a disgrace, you might make agreement impossible.

Is hierarchy valued? Participatory relationships between professionals and their clients (see Chapter 3) reduce hierarchy although they don't eliminate it. Participatory relations do not always seem natural in cultures where authority figures are deferred to in ways that most Americans are no longer accustomed to. It might be difficult for a lawyer to create a participatory relationship with a client from a culture where hierarchy is valued. The client might view the lawyer as an authority figure who must be given respect and deference. See §26.1.2.

Is formality valued? The majority U.S. culture is, by world standards, unusually informal. In business situations, for example, we quickly get on a first-name basis. In some cultures, this can be taken as a show of disrespect for the person whose first name you have started using. In those cultures, informality can imply that you do not take seriously the person you're talking to or the subject you're talking about. See §26.1.2.

How much do personal relationships matter? In some cultures, two business people will do a deal just because each expects to make money from the transaction. Nothing else really matters. If, after "running the numbers," each side is confident of making a profit, the deal is turned over to lawyers, who draft a long contract intended to govern the behavior of the parties in every detail. This is typical in the United States, where the contract is the entire transaction, and anything not provided for in the written contract is usually considered not part of the deal.

In other cultures, business people will spend a great deal of time getting to know each other as human beings before either mentions even the possibility of doing a deal together. Each will want a great deal of confidence that the other can be trusted. If they do agree on a transaction, the contract might be two or three pages long, specifying little. After it is signed, it will be filed away and probably never looked at again. This is typical in Latin America and many parts of Asia, where *the relationship* is the core of the deal, and later problems and confusions will be resolved through the relationship, which would be damaged by referring to the contract.

This kind of cultural difference has obvious ramifications in international business transactions. But it also matters in the everyday practice of law. For several cultures inside the United States, personal relationships are much more important than they are to the majority U.S. culture. A person from a culture where personal relationships are highly valued can experience the majority U.S. culture as cold and impersonal, which can be important if that person is a client or a lawyer in a case you are working on.

How acceptable is it to show emotion or to talk about emotion? In some cultures, it is not acceptable to discuss emotions about personal matters except with family or long-time friends in the privacy of the home. And in many cultures, including several in the United States, people do not talk about their emotions as spontaneously as many Americans do. A client might be suffering emotionally even if the client, for cultural reasons, does not talk about it in an interview. And some clients might be made uncomfortable if their lawyer tries to express empathy too overtly. In some cultures, empathy is best expressed by subtle changes in tone of voice or facial expression rather than in words.

How much is typically said in words, and how much is left to implication or context? In the majority U.S. culture, a relatively high proportion of what one communicates is expressed in words. In some other cultures, this is considered unsubtle or bluntly rude. In some cultures, words are carefully chosen to imply messages that are not explicitly spoken. When a person from one of these cultures deals with a person from the majority U.S. culture, the potential for misunderstandings is large. For example, the person from the majority U.S. culture might not hear the other person's implications and might become impatient, wrongly assuming that the other person is uncommunicative.

The difference is one of contexting. A low-context culture (such as the majority U.S. culture) communicates primarily through words, leaving little to be implied from the context in which the words are spoken. In a low-context culture, things that have not been spoken are probably not meant. A high-context culture communicates less in words and more by implying meaning from the context. In a high-context culture, what is *not* spoken may be as meaningful as—or more meaningful than—what is spoken. See §26.1.2.

For lawyers, there is a paradox here. In negotiation, you will have to communicate some things without saying them bluntly in words. If you say them bluntly in words, your adversary will use them against you. If you imply them, or let the context imply them, your adversary can get the message but not in a form that can be used against you. Thus, in one part of their work—negotiation—American lawyers, who otherwise may be among the wordiest and most blunt people on earth, communicate a great deal through implication and context. You will have to learn how to do that in negotiation.

What does body language communicate? There are many ways in which body language that seems natural in one culture may convey inappropriate messages in another culture. For example, one of the authors of this book grew up in a part of the United States where two groups of minority cultures coexist with the majority U.S. culture. In one of these groups, if you fail to look into another person's eyes while talking to them, you show disrespect. For many people in the other group of minority cultures, the opposite is true: to look into another person's eyes is to show *disrespect*. In the majority U.S. culture, looking into another person's eyes while talking is optional: you can do it or not do it, with no implication concerning respect.

Which is more important, the individual or the group? In the majority culture in the United States, individuals are expected to make their own decisions based on what's best for them. In some other cultures, an individual might decide on the basis of what's best for a group—the family or the community, for example. In still other cultures, a group reaches a consensus and decides for the individual, usually on the basis of the group's needs. If you are counseling a client from a culture where group needs or group decision-making prevail over individual needs or individual decision-making, you can be helpful to the client only if you take that into account.

§6.3 WHY YOU SHOULD CARE ABOUT MULTICULTURAL LAWYERING

For three reasons, you should care about multicultural lawyering:

First, it is the right thing to do. If we really do center on the client, then we also should be able to respect the cultural, racial, ethnic, and gender differences that exist between us and our clients. That means that we recognize the differences and adapt to them rather than assume that the client will adapt to us. For example, we learn to listen for meaning that, in the client's culture, might be implied, even if in our own it would be expressed if intended at all. And we adapt to differences sincerely because insincerity is condescension.

Second, it's in your own self-interest to care. It's good business to respect the cultural and gender differences between yourself and your clients. A very large amount of a lawyer's work comes through recommendations by satisfied clients, and clients whose differences have been respected sincerely are that much more likely to recommend.

Third, the world is a more interesting place when we become open to cultural differences and the ways in which people from other backgrounds live and perceive what happens around them.

§6.4 THE RISKS OF STEREOTYPING

Stereotyping occurs when cultural characteristics are oversimplified and exaggerated and then, in that oversimplified and exaggerated form, applied to everyone who shares something of that culture. The following is stereotyping: "White Anglo-Saxon Protestants dislike emotion." The combined effect of the oversimplification, the exaggeration, and the false assumption that all persons who share the culture are alike is to trivialize, marginalize, patronize, and insult.

The opposite of stereotyping is showing respect for a culture by trying to understand it and all its complexities. Respect includes genuine curiosity and a willingness to accept the culture on its own terms rather than judging it. Respect also includes an understanding that people who share a culture might individually have different relationships to it. One person might feel immersed in her culture and its values and customs. Another person might have a much more detached relationship with her culture, adopting some aspects of it, rejecting others, and not caring or knowing about still others. Respect for another culture includes recognition of individual differences within that culture.

If you stereotype other cultures, people in those cultures can often quickly sense how you are thinking. The stereotyping will prevent you from having constructive working relationships with them. Genuine respect for a culture, on the other hand, can make it much easier for you to work with people in that culture.

§6.5 MULTICULTURAL SKILLS

What skills do you need to work with people of diverse cultural backgrounds?

You cannot memorize—in advance—every detail about every culture you might deal with professionally. There are far too many cultures for that to be possible. Instead, develop *an instinct for situations where another person's cultural assumptions may be very different from yours*. Learn to look for indications of cultural difference. And then try to figure out what would be the appropriate way for you to respond.

If you cannot memorize every detail about every culture, how can you be informed? First, learn about the other cultures that are most commonly found in the area where you will practice law. Learn not only some of their customs and values but also how people in those other cultures view your culture and the world in general. Second, when you foresee a situation in which you can do a better job if you take another person's culture into account, think carefully about what behavior on your part would be appropriate. Think also about what behavior you should avoid either because it would be stereotyping or because it might accidentally give offense in other ways. Third, if you make a cross-cultural mistake—if you create a problem because you did not understand how your behavior would be seen by people in the other culture—apologize promptly. Often, the best apologies are short and simply note that you were unaware of the cultural difference.

The most important thing is to be curious and open-minded about how other people think and act and why they think and act that way. A generous frame of mind on your part and a genuine liking for other people—and their differences—go a long way in this respect. So do flexibility, empathy, patience, and a reluctance to see things judgmentally.

It helps, also, to understand how your own culture "shapes [your] attitudes, values, biases, and assumptions about lawyering" and about social interaction and life generally.[1] How is your culture different from the other cultures you know? This is not the same as asking how those cultures are different from yours. When you ask how other cultures are different from yours, you treat your culture as normal and look for abnormalities elsewhere. Turn it around. Take another culture as normal and ask how your culture differs from that norm. More concretely, how do people in that other culture view your culture? If they were meeting you for the first time, what would they anticipate finding culturally in you?

If you ask people from other cultures, the answers may surprise you. For example, when Americans visit an office and are offered a chair, they are easily willing to move that chair to "adjust the distance" between themselves and the person with whom they are speaking, for example, or to get closer to or farther from a table. This seems so natural to us that we assume anyone in the world would do it. But in some cultures it creates discomfort and disturbs the settled order of things, and an American entering an office is considered rambunctious.[2]

---

1. Carwina Weng, *Multicultural Lawyering: Teaching Psychology to Develop Cultural Self-Awareness*, 11 Clinical L. Rev. 369, 398 (2005).
2. Edward T. Hall, *The Hidden Dimension* 137 (1969).

After living for five years on their reservations in northeastern Arizona, Ned Hall realized that Navajos and Hopis "believed that whites were crazy, although they didn't tell us that. We were always hurrying to get someplace [even though] that place would still be there whenever we arrived. Whites had a kind of devil inside who seemed to drive them unmercifully. The devil's name was Time."[3]

§6.6 DO MEN AND WOMEN PRACTICE LAW DIFFERENTLY?

DEBORAH TANNEN, *TALKING 9 TO 5*
124–125 (1994)

Mona Harrington writes of three women who left large law firms to start their own "alternative" firm specializing in commercial litigation. They determined to do things differently from the way things were done in the large firms where they had worked before—both in managing their relationships with each other and in doing work for their clients.

In terms of interoffice relations, in the women's firm all partners make decisions together at meetings, have offices equal in size, and divide money earned equally among them, regardless of who brought in the client or who worked on the case. In terms of their working styles, the women told Harrington that they represent clients not by being as aggressive and confrontational as possible, but by listening, observing, and better "reading" opponents. One pointed out that in taking depositions, they get better results by adopting a "quiet, sympathetic approach," charming witnesses into forgetting that the attorney deposing them is their adversary, than by grilling witnesses and attacking them.

Yet when interviewed by the press about their approach, these same women do not mention their different styles, not even to explain how well they work. Just the opposite, they stress that they are "tough" litigators and seasoned veterans of traditionally contentious legal settings. . . .

MONA HARRINGTON, *WOMEN LAWYERS:*
REWRITING THE RULES
186–187 (1994)

[Describing the same law firm:]

. . . Many men as well as women employ a quiet style, my interviewees agree, and some women litigators are vigorously aggressive. But they agree that on a stylistic continuum from quiet subtlety to loud antagonism, there is a gender breakdown at the extremes—quiet women, loud men—with an overlap in the middle where you find the counterexamples in both sexes. Still, adds one [partner in the firm], ". . . We've been in situations where the two lawyers are women and the judge is a woman. Then the court works differently. There's less dueling going on. People don't have their swords out. . . . It's not a pissing contest. It's more getting to the heart of whatever it is they're supposed to be doing. . . ." . . .

3. Edward T. Hall, *An Anthropology of Everyday Life: An Autobiography* 218 (1992).

Says another, "We've had clients tell us that they thought [that before hiring us they had been] spending a lot of money on [their prior attorneys'] male ego, men showing off, wasting time. A lot of bluster and showmanship is not necessarily in the client's best interest."

So why don't these women market themselves as different—subtle, psychologically astute, sensible, time-saving, wise? Why [do they talk to the media] about being tough? . . . Because, they tell me, there is no available language to describe the alternative qualities credibly within the necessarily adversarial tradition of litigation. The risk is too great that to describe themselves as different in this context is to convey that they are soft, weak, second-class, not to be trusted. One of the women says of the model of difference they've described, "I don't think there's ever been a language to talk about these things. You just have to *be* it, and develop a reputation" [based on getting results for clients].

DEBORAH TANNEN, *YOU JUST DON'T UNDERSTAND: WOMEN AND MEN IN CONVERSATION* *14–17, 49–50 (1990)*

Some men hear any statement about women and men, coming from a woman, as an accusation . . .

But it is not only men who bridle at statements about women and men. Some women fear, with justification, that any observation of gender differences will be heard as implying that it is women who are different—different from the standard, which is whatever men are. The male is seen as normative, the female as departing from the norm. And it is only a short step—maybe an inevitable one—from "different" to "worse." . . .

Pretending that women and men are the same hurts women, because the ways they are treated are based on the norms of men. It also hurts men who, with good intentions, speak to women as they would to men, and they are nonplussed when their words don't work as they expected, or even spark resentment and anger. . . .

. . . There *are* gender differences in ways of speaking, and we need to identify and understand them . . .

Eve had a lump removed from her breast. Shortly after the operation, talking to her sister, she said that she found it upsetting to have been cut into, and that looking at the stitches was distressing because they left a seam that had changed the contour of her breast. Her sister said, "I know. When I had my operation I felt the same way." Eve made the same observation to her friend Karen, who said, "I know. It's like your body has been violated." But when she told her husband, Mark, how she felt, he said, "You can have plastic surgery to cover up the scar and restore the shape of your breast."

Eve had been comforted by her sister and her friend, but she was not comforted by Mark's comment. Quite the contrary, it upset her more. Not only didn't she hear what she wanted, that he understood her feelings, but, far worse, she felt he was asking her to undergo more surgery just when she was telling him how much this operation had upset her. "I'm not having any more surgery!" she protested. "I'm sorry you don't like the way it looks." Mark was hurt and puzzled. "I don't care," he protested. "It doesn't bother me at all." She asked, "Then why are you telling me to have plastic surgery?" He answered, "Because you were saying you were upset about the way it looked."

Eve felt like a heel: Mark had been wonderfully supportive and concerned throughout her surgery. . . . He thought he was reassuring her that she needn't feel bad about her scar because there was something she could do about it. She heard his suggestion that she do something about the scar as evidence that he was bothered by it. Furthermore, whereas she wanted reassurance that it was normal to feel bad in her situation, his telling her that the problem could easily be fixed implied she had no right to feel bad about it.

Eve wanted the gift of understanding, but Mark gave her the gift of advice. . . .

Lawyers have to be able to give both. Clients hire lawyers for advice and for other forms of problem solving, but many clients also expect understanding. And even if the client does not expect it, advice offered with understanding is easier to accept than advice offered without it.

This might involve speaking in two dialects almost simultaneously. Tannen points out that "because boys and girls grow up in what are essentially different cultures, . . . talk between women and men is cross-cultural communication."[4]

DEBORAH TANNEN, *YOU JUST DON'T UNDERSTAND: WOMEN AND MEN IN CONVERSATION* *297–298(1990)*

. . . The biggest mistake is believing there is one right way to listen, to talk, to have a conversation. . . . Nothing hurts more than being told your intentions are bad when you know they are good, or being told you are doing something wrong when you know you're just doing it your way.

. . . Understanding style differences for what they are takes the sting out of them.

If you understand gender differences in . . . conversational style, you may not be able to prevent disagreements from arising, but you stand a better chance of preventing them from spiraling out of control.

---

4. Deborah Tannen, *You Just Don't Understand: Women and Men in Conversation* 18 (1990).

PART

II

INTERVIEWING

CHAPTER

7

OBSERVATION, MEMORY, FACTS, AND EVIDENCE

§7.1 THE DIFFERENCES BETWEEN FACTS, INFERENCES, AND EVIDENCE

A fact is what actually happened (for example, "at the moment the car left the road, it was traveling at 82.4 miles per hour").

A factual inference is not a fact. It is a conclusion derived from facts ("the car was speeding" or "the car left the road because of its speed").

Evidence is proof of a fact ("the state trooper testified that her radar device measured the car's speed as 82.4 miles per hour"). Put another way, evidence is the source of our knowledge that a fact really is true.

Some evidence is testimonial, and other evidence is tangible. Testimony is what witnesses say in court, on the witness stand, after taking an oath to tell the truth. Tangible evidence is evidence you can put your hand on. Examples are the murder weapon, the contract signed by the parties, and the videos on which people are recorded saying things they later regret.

Another way to divide evidence is into direct evidence and circumstantial evidence. Direct evidence proves a fact without the need for inference. A witness's testimony that she saw the defendant get into a car at a certain time and place is direct evidence that the defendant got into the car at that time and place.

Circumstantial evidence proves a fact through inference. If a witness testifies that he saw a car leave the road and hit a tree, that she got to the car a minute or two after it hit the tree, and that she found the defendant behind the wheel, that is circumstantial evidence that the defendant was driving the car just before it left the road. (It's strong circumstantial evidence, but it's not direct evidence unless the witness saw the defendant driving as the car left the road.)

Some of the most persuasive cases are built mostly on circumstantial evidence. Suppose you buy an over-the-counter medication intended to open up your sinuses, suppress your cough, and in other ways relieve you of the symptoms of a cold. You leave the store carrying a small box wrapped in sealed cellophane bearing the manufacturer's trademark. Inside the box is a bottle, the top of which is wrapped in a plastic band that also bears the manufacturer's trademark and can be removed only with scissors. After you have removed all this packaging, you open the bottle and find, in addition to the medicine, an animal's decayed remains.

If you are inclined to sue, how much can you prove through eyewitnesses? You will testify that you bought the product and removed the packaging. It would be helpful, though not absolutely necessary, if somebody who was with you at the time could testify to corroborate that. The packaging and its contents will be tangible evidence. Beyond that, everything is circumstantial. You will probably never find an eyewitness from the factory who saw how the animal part got into the medication you bought. But you might not need that witness because the circumstantial inferences from the other evidence tend to show that it probably got into the package before it left the factory.

When you interview clients and witnesses, you have to think in terms of evidence. Judges and juries make their decisions based on the evidence because they can know about a fact only through its proof. For this reason, lawyers develop an evidentiary instinct: *when someone mentions a fact, a lawyer wants to know what the evidence for it is.*

Admissible evidence is evidence that a court will consider. If evidence is inadmissible, it might be probative of something, but the law will ignore it. The rules on admissibility are so complex that virtually the entire law school course called Evidence is devoted to teaching them.

Although witness interviewing (covered in Chapter 9) is in many ways different from interviewing clients, nearly all clients are themselves witnesses to at least some of the facts at issue, and clients often do testify if their cases go to trial. In the chapter you are reading now, when we mention witnesses, we mean anybody, including clients, who observed relevant events and might testify about them at trial. In Chapter 9, we use the word to mean only those witnesses who are not also your client.

§7.2 THE MYTHS

> Imagination *and* Memory *are but one thing, which for divers considerations hath divers names.*
>
> Thomas Hobbes

> *[W]ithout corroboration, there is absolutely no way to know whether somebody's memory is a real memory or a product of suggestion.*
>
> Elizabeth Loftus

For over a century, teachers have been illustrating the frailties of eyewitnesses by staging crimes in the classroom. One of the first of these experiments happened in Berlin in 1901:

> [A] professor of criminal law . . . was lecturing to his class when a student suddenly shouted an objection to his line of argument. Another student countered angrily, and the two exchanged insults. Fists were clenched, threats made. . . . Then the first student drew a gun, the second rushed at him, and the professor recklessly interposed himself between them. A struggle, a blast—then pandemonium.
>
> Whereupon the two putative antagonists disengaged and returned to their seats. The professor swiftly restored order, explaining to his students that the incident had been staged, and for a purpose. He asked the students, as eyewitnesses, to describe exactly what they had seen. Some were to write down their account on the spot, some a day or a week later; a few even had to depose their observations under cross-examination. The results were dismal. The most accurate witness got twenty-six per cent of the significant details wrong; others up to eighty per cent. Words were put in people's mouths. Actions were described that had never taken place. Events that *had* taken place disappeared from memory.[1]

Much of our trust in the ability of witnesses to observe and remember accurately is based on myth. Because of that, a lawyer's ability to "know" the facts is much more limited than you might suppose. Experienced lawyers sense this intuitively, even if they are unaware of the psychological research described in this chapter. In a moment of candor, such a lawyer might tell you that it is easier to prove something than to know that it is true.

MONROE H. FREEDMAN & ABBE SMITH, *UNDERSTANDING LAWYERS' ETHICS* *196–201 (2010)*

A common misconception about memory is that it is a process of reproducing or retrieving stored information in the manner of a videotape or computer. In fact, memory is much more a process of reconstruction. . . . "According to the cliche, memory fades. In fact, it grows."* Although the initial perception may fade, "every time we recall an event we must reconstruct the memory, and so each time it is changed—colored by succeeding events, increased understanding, a new context, suggestions by others, other people's recollections."** . . .

We are not talking about dishonesty. A witness may reconstruct events "without being in the least aware that he is either supplementing or falsifying the

---

1. Atul Gawande, *Investigations Under Suspicion: The Fugitive Science of Criminal Justice*, The New Yorker, Jan. 8, 2001, at 50.

* Elizabeth Loftus, *Memory* 169 (1980).

** *Id.*

data of perception. Yet, in almost all cases, he is certainly doing the first, and in many cases he is demonstrably doing the second."*

An interesting illustration of the tendency to eliminate ambiguities by imaginative reconstruction was provided in the Senate Watergate hearings. John Dean, who had been President Nixon's White House Counsel, was testifying about a meeting with Herbert Kalmbach, who had been Nixon's private attorney. Dean had no incentive whatsoever to lie about that particular incident; indeed, it was extremely important to him to state the facts with as much exactness as possible.

Dean testified that he had met Kalmbach in the coffee shop of the Mayflower Hotel in Washington, D.C., and that they had gone directly upstairs to Kalmbach's room in the same hotel. Dean was pressed several times on this point, in a way that implied that his questioners had reason to believe that he was not telling the truth as to whether the meeting had taken place at all. Each time, Dean confidently reaffirmed his clear recollection about the incident. Finally, it was revealed that the Mayflower Hotel's register showed that Kalmbach had not been staying at the hotel at the time in question. Dean nevertheless remained certain of the occurrence, putting forth the unlikely theory that Kalmbach had used a false name in registering.

The difficulty was cleared up when someone realized that there is a Mayflower Doughnut Coffee Shop in the Statler Hilton Hotel in Washington—and Kalmbach had been registered at the Statler, under his own name, on the day in question. Thus, Dean's basic story was corroborated. Without realizing it, however, Dean had inaccurately resolved the ambiguity created by the coincidence of the two names by confidently "remembering" the wrong (but more logical) hotel, and by inventing the use of an alias by Kalmbach. He had done so, moreover, in a way that was "subjectively accurate" even though "objectively false."

John Dean is not unusual in this regard. . . . This is true even when the material to be memorized is short and simple, and when the witness knows that he will be asked to describe it later. . . .

[Similar effects] can result from interest or prejudice. A classic example of prejudice is the study in which subjects were shown an illustration of a scene in a subway car, including an African-American man wearing a jacket and tie and a white man dressed in work clothes and holding a razor in his hand. In an experiment in which people serially described the picture to each other (as in the game "telephone"), the razor "tended to migrate" from the white man's hand to that of the African-American man. . . .

Another important aspect of constructive remembering is the witness's "readiness to respond and his self-confidence when in fact he ought to be cautious and hedge his statements."** In an experiment relating to the ability to remember faces, . . . the person who unconsciously invented more detail than any other in the test group was "completely confident throughout."*** In another case, . . . "it was precisely concerning his [unconscious] inventions that the subject was most pleased and most certain."****

---

* Frederick C. Bartlett, *Remembering: A Study in Experimental and Social Psychology* 14 (1967).
** George Alexander Talland, *Disorders of Memory and Learning* 19 (1968).
*** Bartlett, *Remembering*, at 78.
**** *Id.*

Everyone has had difficulties like John Dean's—pressed to remember an event; trying to figure out how that event would have occurred; treating that speculation as though it were a memory; finally becoming confident that the recollection is a 100% accurate memory even though it actually isn't a memory and is instead the mind inventing the past. For most people, this occurs regularly. Usually it doesn't cause much harm. But when law is involved, the consequences can be disastrous.

In recent years, DNA tests have been able to tell with absolute certainty from whom something like a hair or a spot of blood came. A surprising number of criminal convictions that occurred before DNA tests were developed have been vacated after DNA testing established that the defendant could not possibly have committed the crime. Eyewitnesses misidentified the defendant in 76% of the first 250 cases in which convictions had to be vacated because DNA evidence later proved that the defendant, by then in prison, could not have committed the crime. "Almost all the eyewitnesses in these trials expressed complete confidence at trial that they had identified the attacker."[2] In one case, a defendant had been convicted based on the testimony of five eyewitnesses. He was on death row awaiting execution when DNA testing showed that what the five witnesses had testified to was impossible.

Another study located 340 prisoners who had been convicted were but were later exonerated for various reasons. Nearly all of them had been sentenced to death or to long terms of imprisonment. In 64% of these cases, "at least one eyewitness misidentified the defendant," and in the overwhelming majority of those instances, the eyewitness appears to have been honestly mistaken (and not lying).[3] A different set of data—maintained by the Innocence Project, affiliated with the Benjamin N. Cardozo School of Law at Yeshiva University—shows that more than three-quarters of 258 prisoners exonerated by DNA evidence had been "convicted on the strength of eyewitness identifications."[4] The studies "have consistently shown that mistaken eyewitness identification is responsible for more of these wrongful convictions than all other causes combined."[5] Although juries instinctively treat eyewitness testimony as the gold standard of proof, "eyewitness identification . . . is among the least reliable forms of evidence."[6]

---

2. Brandon L. Garrett, *Convicting the Innocent* 63 (2011). See Elizabeth F. Loftus & James M. Doyle, *Eyewitness Testimony: Civil and Criminal* 1 (3d ed. 1997). The Department of Justice's study has been published as *Convicted by Juries, Exonerated by Science: Case Studies in the Use of DNA Evidence to Establish Innocence After Trial* (1996). See also Brian L. Cutler & Steven D. Penrod, *Mistaken Identification: The Eyewitness, Psychology, and the Law* (1995); Daniel L. Schacter, *The Seven Sins of Memory: How the Mind Forgets and Remembers* (2001); Daniel L. Schecter, *Searching for Memory: The Brain, the Mind, and the Past* (1996).
3. Samuel R. Gross et al., *Exonerations in the United States 1989 through 2003*, 95 J. Crim. L. & Criminology 523, 542 (2005).
4. James C. McKinley, Jr., *Cleared, and Pondering the Value of 27 Years*, N.Y. Times, Aug. 13, 2010, at A12.
5. Gary L. Wells, Mark Small, Steven Penrod, Roy S. Malpass, Solomon M. Fulero & C.A. Brimacombe, *Eyewitness Identification Procedures: Recommendations for Lineups and Photospreads*, 22 L. & Human Behavior 603, 605 (1998).
6. *Id.*

Experiments by social scientists illustrate the same thing. One experiment included two sets of subjects. Some acted as witnesses and others as jurors. Witnesses to a theft identified the thief from an array of photos. The theft had been staged, at the direction of the researchers, and the witnesses did not know in advance that it would happen. (The researchers, of course, knew who the "thief" was—which is what allows the experiment to reveal what it does.) In simulated trials, the second set of subjects—the jurors—observed cross-examinations of the witnesses and decided whether to believe the witnesses' identifications of the "thief." The jurors were divided into panels, and each panel observed one witness's cross-examination. About 80% of the jurors believed the witness they saw cross-examined, but they "were just as likely to believe a witness who had made an incorrect identification as one who had made a correct identification."[7]

In another experiment, researchers

> made a video of two teams of basketball players, one team in white shirts and the other in black, each player in constant motion as two basketballs are passed back and forth. Observers were asked to count the number of passes completed by members of the white team. After about forty-five seconds, a woman in a gorilla suit walks into the middle of the group, stands in front of the camera, beats her chest vigorously, and then walks away. "Fifty per cent of the people missed the gorilla," [said one researcher]. "We'd get the most striking reactions. We'd ask people, 'Did you see anyone walk across the screen?' They'd say no. Anything at all? No. Eventually, we'd ask them, 'Did you notice the gorilla?' And they'd say, 'The *what*?'"[8]

Why are fact-finders eager to believe eyewitnesses? There seem to be two reasons. First, "in most of our life experience truly precise memory is not demanded of us. We often do not catch the mistakes of memory that we make, leading us to believe that our memory is more accurate than it actually is. Since people trust their own memories more than they should, they then trust the memories of others."[9]

Second, people are persuaded by stories, as we explained in §5.2.4. Documents, fingerprints, DNA, murder weapons, and other tangible evidence usually do not tell stories, although they provide ingredients out of which a story can be constructed. Eyewitnesses, on the other hand, tell stories from the beginning to the end, explaining who did what when, and adding enough detail to make the story seem real.[10]

---

7. Elizabeth F. Loftus & James M. Doyle, *Eyewitness Testimony: Civil and Criminal* 2-3 (3d ed. 1997).
8. Malcolm Gladwell, *Wrong Turn: How the Fight to Make America's Highways Safer Went Off Course*, The New Yorker, June 11, 2001, at 50, 54.
9. *Id.* at 6.
10. *Id.* at 5.

§7.3 WHAT SCIENCE KNOWS ABOUT OBSERVATION AND MEMORY

Elizabeth Loftus has studied extensively "the extraordinary malleability of memory,"[11] and her book *Eyewitness Testimony*[12] is the leading work in the field. According to her and others' research, the following appear to be the major factors affecting the extent to which an eyewitness accurately observes an event, retains the observation in memory, and later retrieves it.

§7.3.1 WHAT AFFECTS OBSERVATION

The length of time the witness was exposed to the event. If a witness has more time, the witness will observe more. It also takes time to begin observing. If you are preoccupied with something else, it takes at least a short while for you to shift your attention and begin to observe an event that is just starting to unfold. Some events are so short that they are over before you can focus on them.

The extent to which the event in question stood out from (or blended with) its surroundings. Suppose you are traveling on a municipal bus that stops every four or five blocks so passengers can get on or off. You are on the bus for half an hour, during which you see a continual stream of people dressed in everyday clothing going to or from jobs, schools, shopping, and so on. About halfway through the trip, Batman and Catwoman get on the bus, ride for five minutes, and then leave. At the end of the ride, you are asked to describe, in as much detail as possible, everybody you saw. About whom would you have noticed more: Batman and Catwoman or the elderly couple who sat across from you near the end of the trip?

Whether conditions or simultaneous events helped or interfered with observation. How far was the witness from the event? Was the lighting good or bad? Did anything make it hard or easy for the witness to hear the event? Are the witness's hearing and eyesight good or bad? Did anything happen that would have distracted the witness?

What the witness was doing at the time of the event. Was the witness's purpose to observe the event? Or was the witness engrossed in some other activity that was interrupted by the event? Did the event cause the witness to do something (such as run away) that would have interfered with observation?

Whether the witness is by nature a careful observer in general or a careful observer of the type of event that is at issue. Some people often notice a lot of what goes on around them, and others tend to be oblivious. Sometimes, training or experience can heighten an ability to observe because the witness knows what to look for. A structural engineer who watches a bridge collapse might notice things that other witnesses miss. And sometimes much larger factors can make someone

---

11. *Id.* at 54.
12. First published in 1979. Citations in this chapter are to the third edition (1997), expanded with a coauthor.

a good or a bad observer of a particular kind of event. During the Second World War, Eric Newby escaped from a prisoner-of-war camp in Italy and tried for many months to disguise himself as an Italian to blend into his surroundings. Although he was at times stopped by German soldiers, they did not recognize him as an Englishman. After carefully studying his identity documents, which had been skillfully forged, the Germans would let him go each time. Their observational skills were bureaucratic—limited to official documents—and they did not observe anything else about him. But Italians could tell just by looking at Newby that he was not whoever he was pretending to be at any given time. Invariably, something about whatever clothing he was wearing would turn out to be inappropriate to the role he was trying to play.[13]

Whether the witness was under stress at the time of the event. A moderate amount of stress has been found to make you more observant, but a greater amount of stress has the opposite effect, making you much *less* observant.

The event itself might stress the witness (violence being an example). It is commonly believed that dramatic events increase a witness's ability to observe. The opposite is true. Dramatic events are often quick and unexpected, which means that witnesses are unprepared to observe. And any event that seriously stresses a witness sharply diminishes the ability to observe carefully. During a robbery, for example, victims and bystanders are usually not taking note of everything about which the police will later be curious; they are just trying to survive. The same thing happens during auto crashes. But later, when lawyers, police, insurance companies, judges, and juries expect reliable information from those present during a stressful event, the witnesses feel compelled to become more reliable than they really are, which means that at least some of what they say is creative reconstruction.

A witness can, of course, be stressed by things completely unrelated to the event. A witness who is worried about career, family, or health might be a poor observer of things done by strangers in plain view.

The witness's own self-interest, expectations, and preconceptions. Often, people see what they want or expect to see.

A witness's observations might be colored by the witness's own self-interest. Experiments have shown that if witnesses are given an incentive, even a small one, to see or not see a particular thing, they honestly see and remember that which they have an incentive to see and remember. Sometimes, the incentive can be extraneous (people the witness cares about will be better off if the witness saw and remembers X rather than Y). Sometimes, especially when the witness is a party to the dispute, it is self-contained (the witness will personally profit from a favorable memory). And very often it is simple self-flattery:

> People . . . tend to see themselves as more honest or more creative than the average person. When they work on a joint task, they tend to overestimate their

13. See Eric Newby, *When the Snow Comes, They Will Take You Away* (1984).

> own contribution to the task. . . . People remember themselves as having . . . received higher pay for work [than they actually did], purchased fewer alcoholic beverages, contributed more to charity, taken more airplane trips, and raised smarter than average children.[14]

Usually, little or none of this is conscious lying to get a reward or avoid a penalty. The witness honestly remembers observing whatever was in the witness's own self-interest to remember.

Or a witness might "see" something because it conforms to the way the witness assumes the world works. Suppose an airliner develops mechanical problems moments before take-off, and the flight is canceled. A line of anxious passengers forms at the check-in counter, each passenger hoping to make other travel arrangements that will not spoil a vacation or ruin a business meeting. A shouting match begins between one of the passengers and the airline employee working behind the counter, and airport police forcibly take the passenger away. Witnesses who believe that airline employees have difficult jobs will tend to see, hear, and remember details that suggest that the passenger started the argument and abused the airline employee and perhaps the police as well. Witnesses who have the opposite assumptions, perhaps having been treated badly by airlines in the past, will tend to see, hear, and remember details that suggest that the airline employee started the argument and abused the passenger, who was then mistreated by police. These preconceptions are what Chapter 10 refers to as *schemas*. Even when a video recording of such a scene is shown to jurors (converting the jurors into witnesses), the same thing can happen. Photographs, film, or video recordings cannot prevent this because our preconceptions shade not only our memory of what we have seen; they also shade what we see from the moment we first see it.

§7.3.2 WHAT AFFECTS RETENTION IN MEMORY

The amount of time that has passed since the event. Memory fades fast after observation. Can you remember where you were and what you did exactly one year ago today? If you are like most people, your memory about the day started fading before the day was over, and, unless something especially memorable happened, those memories were completely gone within a few weeks afterward.

The extent to which the witness has had past experience with aspects of the event. This is particularly important when the witness identifies a defendant in a criminal case. From the research, Loftus concludes that an eyewitness identification of a criminal defendant not already well known to the witness is—scientifically—virtually worthless. We can remember a face that we have seen many times before because we are remembering not just a face but also a person about whom we know other things as well. But it is extremely difficult to remember accurately a face we have seen only once.

---

14. Loftus & Doyle, *supra* note 5, at 61–62.

Whether the memory has blended with other memories so that an aspect of one event becomes part of the memory of another. This is called "unconscious transference." It is particularly dangerous in identification testimony. Eyewitnesses have been known to identify as criminals people they saw shortly before or after the crime or even at the same place on a different day.

Contamination of the memory caused by the conduct of other people. Suppose you witness a crime. The police give you a dozen photos to look at and say, "We think the perpetrator might be one of these people." They do not say the perpetrator *is* one of these people, but you are trying to be a good witness. If you say that none of the photos looks familiar to you, you are not helping to identify the criminal. There is a pronounced risk here that unconsciously you will try too hard to see similarities that do not naturally stand out to you. And if you do not do that at first, the police might inadvertently encourage you to. Suppose you look up and say, "I'm not seeing anyone familiar here," and the police say, "Take another look." Will you feel like a failure if you cannot "find" the perpetrator? Suppose you do identify someone and the police look pleased. Will you take that to mean that you are "right"? Two kinds of contamination are going on here. The police are giving you, by implication, new information (that they have reasons of their own to believe that one of the photos represents the true criminal). And their reaction confirms your guess, which encourages you to transmute it into a *confident* memory. The police might not have meant to do any of that, but this scene illustrates how other people—including lawyers asking questions in an interview—can contaminate memory.

Contamination of the memory caused by the witness's own conduct. You do not need the police to contaminate your memory. You can do it yourself, unassisted. Suppose you are asked what you saw. You give lots of details, trying to be a good witness. Some of the details are not entirely accurate, but once you say them, they become frozen in your memory. Saying them locks them in, even if they are wrong. You will probably not say to yourself afterward that you are afraid you might be mistaken about some of the details. Instead, you will become more confident about all of the details, and the fact that you have lots of details helps you become more confident.

§7.3.3 WHAT AFFECTS RETRIEVAL FROM MEMORY

How questions are asked can alter memory:

> [E]ven "straightforward questions of fact" may significantly affect what a witness remembers, and leading or loaded questions can be particularly powerful in inducing good faith errors in memory. Illustrative is a study that showed that witnesses' estimates of the speed of an automobile involved in an accident varied in accordance with the verb used by the interviewer in asking the question. For example, when the question was phrased in terms of one car "contacting" the other, the speed averaged 31.8 miles per hour. The speed of the car increased in the

> witnesses' memory, however, as the verb was modified: "hit" (34.0 mph), "bumped" (38.1 mph), "collided" (39.3 mph), and "smashed" (40.8 mph).[15]

Here is another example:

> [S]killed trial lawyers know that once a witness accepts a version of the story, that version can "harden" and become the reality so far as that witness is concerned. An English barrister of long experience used the following hypothetical piece of witness interview to illustrate the point:
>
> *Q:* When Bloggs came into the pub, did he have a knife in his hand?
> *A:* I don't remember.
> *Q:* Did you see him clearly?
> *A:* Yes.
> *Q:* Do people in that neighborhood often walk into pubs with knives in their hands?
> *A:* No, certainly not.
> *Q:* If you had seen Bloggs with a knife in his hand, would you remember that?
> *A:* Yes, of course.
> *Q:* And you don't remember any knife.
> *A:* No, I don't remember any knife.

During the days or months between the interview and the trial, the story can harden, and what started as "I don't remember" may come out like this at trial:

> *Q:* When Bloggs came into the pub, did he have a knife in his hand?
> *A:* No, he did not.[16]

§7.4 HOW COURTS TREAT OBSERVATION AND MEMORY

When you interview in preparation for litigation, you need to understand what will happen to observations and memory in the courtroom. At trial, a lawyer who calls on a witness to give evidence might try to bolster the testimony by asking questions that would show the witness to be reliable according to some of the factors listed in §7.3. On cross-examination, the opposing lawyer might ask questions that would show the witness to be *un*reliable according to other factors listed in §7.3. Otherwise, law and science follow different paths when evaluating eyewitness testimony.

First, the lawyers do not have to ask these questions, and many times they do not. "Repeated surveys of defenders, prosecutors and judges indicate that many (as

---

15. Monroe H. Freedman & Abbe Smith, *Understanding Lawyers' Ethics* 210 (3d ed. 2004).
16. Richard C. Wydick, *The Ethics of Witness Coaching*, 17 Cardozo L. Rev. 1, 11–12 (1995).

to some respects, most) lawyers are ignorant" of the scientific research on eyewitness testimony.[17] There are some exceptions. In criminal procedure, for example, the law has been aware of the risks that testimony might be contaminated if a witness is asked in a suggestive manner to identify an accused.[18]

Second, even if the lawyers do ask these questions, the fact-finder—the jury or, in a bench trial, the judge—is free to discount the answers. To many fact-finders, "there is almost nothing more convincing than a live human being who takes the stand, points a finger at the defendant, and says, 'That's the one!'?"[19]

Third, juries are instructed to use their own common sense and experience in life when evaluating evidence. This encourages them to subscribe to fallacies that science has shown to have no basis in fact. The most common is the fallacy that a confident witness is a reliable witness. The research shows that confident witnesses can be wrong just as easily as tentative witnesses can be.[20] In fact, tentativeness may be a sign that the witness is aware of the limits of her own knowledge, a humility that can be more trustworthy than misplaced confidence. But many fact-finders appear to consider the witness's confidence to be solid proof of the witness's reliability.[21]

The next most common fallacy appears to be the one of detail. Fact-finders are impressed by witnesses who can remember many details, whether or not the details are directly relevant to the factual issues. But "a witness's memory for details about peripheral matters may not be related at all to the witness's accuracy about central aspects."[22] In fact, a witness who can remember an endless supply of details about everything might be a witness with an active *reconstructive* imagination.

Juries are at times even specifically instructed by judges to act on particular assumptions that science has shown to be wrong. For example, in criminal cases juries are often instructed that they may take into account the confidence with which a witness makes an identification. Even the Supreme Court has approved such an instruction.[23]

Only in unusual circumstances do judges allow juries to hear expert testimony to the effect that most of the "common sense" about eyewitnesses is myth.[24] In the overwhelming majority of the cases in which a party offers such expert testimony, it is excluded.

---

17. Loftus & Doyle, *supra* note 5, at 8.
18. 2 Wayne R. LaFave, Jerold H. Israel & Nancy L. King, *Criminal Procedure* 630–636, 666–689 (1999).
19. Elizabeth F. Loftus, *Eyewitness Testimony* 19 (1st ed. 1979).
20. Loftus & Doyle, *supra* note 5, at 66–67.
21. Loftus & Doyle, *supra* note 5, at 2–4.
22. Loftus & Doyle, *supra* note 5, at 4.
23. *Neil v. Biggers*, 409 U.S. 188 (1972). At least one state has decided otherwise. *Commonwealth v. Santoli*, 424 Mass. 837, 680 N.E.2d 1116 (1997).
24. See *Commonwealth v. Santoli*, 424 Mass. 837, 680 N.E.2d 1116 (1997), and the cases cited there.

§7.5 THE PROBLEM OF STATES OF MIND

The law's conception of states of mind leads to two problems in trying to learn the facts and prove them.

The first is that it is much harder to remember what you *thought* at any given time in the past than it is to remember what you saw, heard, or did. Your hopes, desires, and fears are so fluid that you have no solid base to start from when trying to remember them later, unless you found a way to make a record of them in something you said or wrote at the time. And because your past thoughts are so fluid, you may, every time you try to remember them, reinvent them to conform to what you would have liked them to have been in retrospect.

The second problem is that the law's state-of-mind formulas—intent, willfulness, maliciousness, voluntariness, and so on—do not fit the patterns in which people normally think. If you doubt this, stop someone who is about to jaywalk and ask whether that person intends to commit comparative negligence or assume the risk of another's carelessness. Even after you explain those terms, the person you have stopped will think you are a nut, even though once she sets foot in the street, the law will probably judge her to have had at least one of those states of mind. Here is another example:

> A young man and a young woman decide to get married. Each has $1,000. They decide to begin a business with those funds, and the young woman gives her money to the young man for that purpose. Was the intention to form a joint venture or a partnership? Did they intend that the young man be an agent or a trustee? Was the transaction a gift or a loan? Most likely, the young couple's state of mind did not conform to any of the modes of "intention" that the law might look for. Thus, if the couple should subsequently visit a tax attorney and discover that it is in their interest that the transaction be viewed as a gift, they might well "remember" that to have been their intention. On the other hand, should their engagement be broken and the young woman consult an attorney for the purpose of recovering her money, she might well "remember," after proper counseling, that it had been her intention to make a loan.[25]

This couple are not lying when they give these answers to their lawyers. People do what they feel like doing, and afterward the law has to put a label on what they thought at the time they acted. As a rule to guide courts' decision-making, the label may work, but it often does not represent precisely what people were really thinking. That is why the jaywalker will think you're peculiar if you ask about an intention to assume risk or commit a form of negligence.

State of mind usually has to be proved through circumstantial evidence. And the law is usually satisfied with whatever the circumstantial evidence shows. Suppose the couple in the example above decide that they want to have the transaction considered a gift. It's honest for their lawyer to figure out what circumstantial evidence might prove a donative intent (an intent to make a gift) and then ask whether that evidence exists. If it does, it's also honest for the lawyer

---

25. Monroe H. Freedman, *Lawyers' Ethics in an Adversary System* 70 (1975).

to introduce that evidence in court to prove a donative intent, even though the couple have only the vaguest idea of what they had been thinking at the time of the transaction.

But it would be dishonest—potentially a crime—for the lawyer or the couple to manufacture false evidence, such as a back-dated letter from the woman to the man saying, "Please accept this gift."

§7.6 HOW TO EXPLORE MEMORY ACCURATELY IN AN INTERVIEW

Traditionally, lawyers have interviewed by asking for a narrative ("please tell me what happened, from beginning to end"), and afterward asking follow-up questions designed to clarify or fill gaps in the narrative ("let's go back to what happened after the accident—how long did it take the ambulance to arrive?").

That is not a bad approach. But it can be improved with modifications that some researchers have called "cognitive interviewing." Cognitive interviewing helps the witness to remember by using any or all of four techniques. The most important is suggesting that the witness reconstruct the scene and relive the event in the witness's own mind before narrating it to the interviewer.

Near the beginning of the discussion, you should ask the witness to include all the details the witness can recall (even those that seem irrelevant); to avoid guessing; and if the witness infers anything, to label it as an inference rather than the witness's direct observation. Most people are not this careful and precise about facts, and most witnesses will need gentle reminders from you about these requests at strategic points during the interview ("Do you remember seeing that event yourself? Or are you inferring that it probably happened because of the other things you did see?").

RICHARD C. WYDICK, *THE ETHICS OF WITNESS COACHING* 17 *CARDOZO* L. REV. 1 (1995)

[P]sychologists Edward Geiselman, Ronald Fisher, and their colleagues [have developed] a package of interview techniques that they call the "cognitive interview." . . .

Technique One: Reinstate Context

[A witness remembers best when immersed in an environment substantially similar to the one that surrounded the event to be remembered.] The witness need not return physically to the scene; returning in one's mind is generally enough. Thus, Geiselman and Fisher recommend giving the witness an instruction something like this: "First, try to reinstate in your mind the context surrounding the incident. Think about what the room looked like and where you were sitting in the room. Think about how you were feeling at the time and think about your reactions to the incident."

Technique Two: Tell Everything

. . . Geiselman and Fisher urge witnesses to lower their standards for relevance and to report every scrap they can remember, even if it seems incomplete or irrelevant. The hope is that incomplete or irrelevant scraps of memory might cue other material that could prove useful.

Technique Three: Recall the Event in Different Orders

[T]his technique recognizes that information can be stored in memory according to a variety of patterns, and that one pattern of access may be more effective than others. Geiselman and Fisher recommend instructing the witness in the following manner:

> [I]t is natural to go through the incident from beginning to end, and that is probably what you should do first. However, many people can come up with more information if they also go through the events in reverse order. Or, you might start with the thing that impressed you the most and then go from there, proceeding both forward and backward in time.

Technique Four: Change Perspectives

The fourth technique likewise seeks to open a variety of retrieval paths. After the witness explains what she perceived from her perspective, she should be instructed something like this:

> [Now] try to adopt the perspective of others who were present during the incident. For example, try to place yourself in [X's] role and think about what she must have seen.

[Structuring the Fact-Gathering]
. . . In a cognitive interview . . . , the witness should do most of the talking and hard thinking, while the interviewer should be mostly listening, gently guiding, and probing when necessary. [Getting the facts from the interviewee is a process that can be broken down into three stages.]

Introductory Stage

In the introductory stage, the interviewer should first seek to put the witness at ease. If the witness shows unusual stress, one way to do that is to begin with easy questions to get background information about the witness. Next, the interviewer should seek to build rapport with the witness and should explain the witness's central role in the interview. The witness plays the central role because the witness is the one who knows what the facts are! In a cognitive interview (unlike many ordinary interviews), the witness should do most of the talking and hard thinking, while the interviewer should be mostly listening, gently guiding, and probing when necessary. Finally, the interviewer should explain to the witness the four basic memory enhancing techniques, and encourage their use during the interview.

Open-Ended Narration Stage

In the open-ended narration stage, the interviewer asks the witness one or more broad, open-ended questions that are designed to elicit from the witness a narrative about the entire event. For example, "Tell me in your own words whatever you can remember about the [meeting]. Tell me everything you can in as much detail as you can." Despite the request for details, at this stage the interviewer should be listening, not for details, but for the overall pattern of the witness's memory about the event. This is not an information gathering stage—it is a planning stage, in which the interviewer should be designing the best way to probe the witness's memory.

Probing Stage

The probing stage is the main information gathering stage of a cognitive interview. The interviewer directs the witness's attention back to each significant topic the witness mentioned in the open-ended narration, patiently taking each topic separately and exhausting the witness's memory about that topic before moving on to the next. The interviewer should begin each topic with an open-ended question that asks the witness to give a detailed narrative of everything the witness can remember about it. For example, "You told me earlier that the thin man in the blue suit mentioned something about 'cutthroat bidding.' Tell me everything you remember about that, in as much detail as you can." The interviewer must not interrupt the witness's answer, and must not move to a different topic until the witness's memory about the first topic is exhausted. If the first open-ended question fails to produce the needed detail, the interviewer can follow up with a narrower but still open-ended question, such as, "Tell me what he said about 'cutthroat bidding'." If that does not work, the interviewer can resort to a closed-ended (leading) question, such as, "Did he say that 'cutthroat bidding' is bad for the industry?"

Review Stage

In the review stage, the interviewer should repeat in the witness's presence all of the relevant pieces of information the witness has provided. This has two purposes. First, it gives the witness and interviewer a chance to make sure the interviewer has understood correctly, and second, it gives the witness an additional chance to search for forgotten details. . . .

Practical Suggestions for Cognitive Interviews

. . . The single most important skill an interviewer can learn is not to interrupt the witness in the middle of a narrative response. When the witness says something worth pursuing, the interviewer should make a note of it and come back to it later. Even if the witness pauses for several moments during the narrative, the interviewer should keep quiet, or perhaps use a gesture, to encourage the witness to continue.

Some interviewers insist on demonstrating dominance during the interview. That can be a big mistake because the witness is the one holding all the memories. . . .

One of the four basic memory enhancing devices urges the witness not to edit out material that seems incomplete or irrelevant. Another urges the witness to consider the event from the perspectives of other people. Some witnesses misinterpret these suggestions as an invitation to guess or fabricate. The interviewer should expressly caution the witness not to guess or fabricate.

The interviewer should avoid skipping from topic to topic during the probing stage of the interview. How many times have we seen some television lawyer interviewing the witness in his office like this:

Q: How tall was he?
A: Oh, average, maybe six feet or so.
Q: What color car did you say he had?
A: Puce. It was a puce Cadillac coupe.
Q: Puce, eh. Any tatoos, scars, or other marks on his face or body?

This interview style makes for fast-paced television, but it wastes the witness's mental effort. It takes effort to summon up the mental image of the car. Instead of skipping to tatoos, scars and marks, a real life interviewer should stay with the car image until the witness cannot summon up any more about it. . . .

In a police department, about half the detectives were trained to interview cognitively. Afterward, researchers studied tape recordings of real witnesses in real cases conducted by these detectives and compared them to similar recordings of interviews conducted in other real cases by the detectives who had not been trained to interview cognitively. "The results were dramatic. The detectives who used the cognitive interview obtained significantly more information."[26]

26. Loftus & Doyle, *supra* note 5, at 73.

CHAPTER

8

INTERVIEWING THE CLIENT

§8.1 CLIENT INTERVIEWING AS PROBLEM SOLVING

Lawyers conduct two kinds of interviews. Client interviewing is covered in this chapter. Witness interviewing is covered in Chapter 9.

Client interviewing is hard work for two reasons. The first is the intellectual challenge of beginning a diagnosis of the client's problem while, at the same time, carefully discovering the client's goals and the facts known to the client. The second is the emotional challenge of establishing a bond of trust and helping a person who may be under substantial stress.

If you're a very rational person, you might ignore the emotionally charged atmosphere of the interview, much to the frustration of the client. If you are more astute about emotions than about ideas, you might give a client an emotionally satisfying interview while leaving big holes in your development of the facts. If you are at one or the other of these extremes, you can improve your interviewing by becoming more rounded. Students at one of the extremes often gain a lot of insight about themselves from critiques of their first interviews.

An allied problem is the question of control. The professions in general are attractive careers in part because they offer opportunities to control one's environment. Aggressiveness and competitiveness are useful in performing many of the tasks in a professional's work life (such as trying cases in court). The urge and ability to control can help a lawyer keep an interview focused, but, if not carefully managed, they can also smother a client's communicativeness. Many lawyers find that they must turn their control impulses on themselves, exercising more control over their own behavior than over that of the client. But even this can go too far. Spontaneous warmth and empathy are powerful professional tools.

§8.1.1 YOUR PURPOSES IN INTERVIEWING CLIENTS

Client representation usually starts with an interview. A person who wants legal advice or advocacy calls to make an appointment. The secretary finds a convenient time and, to help the lawyer prepare, asks what the subject of the interview will be. The person calling says, "I want a new will drawn" or "I've just been sued" or "I signed a contract to buy a house and now the owner won't sell." At the time of the appointment, that person and the lawyer sit down and talk. If the visitor likes the lawyer and is willing to pay for what the lawyer might do, the visitor becomes a client of the lawyer.

During that conversation, the lawyer learns what problem the client wants solved and the client's goals in getting it solved; learns, factually, what the client knows about the problem; and tries to get to know the client as a human being and gives the client a reciprocal opportunity. Then or later, the lawyer and client also negotiate the retainer—the contract through which the client hires the lawyer—but here we focus on other aspects of the interview, especially fact-gathering.

These, then, are the lawyer's purposes in interviewing a client:

1. *To form an attorney-client relationship.* That happens on three levels. One is personal, in that you and the client come to understand each other as people. To satisfy the client's needs, you have to understand the client as a person and how the problem matters in the client's way of thinking. If you and the client are to work together in the participatory relationship described in Chapter 3, you need to know each other fairly well. And the client cannot trust you without a solid feeling for the person you are. The second level is educational, in that you explain to the client (if the client does not already know) things like attorney-client confidentiality (see §3.6) and the role the client would or could play in solving the problem. The third is contractual, in that the client agrees to hire you and pay your fees and expenses in exchange for your doing the work you promise to do.

2. *To learn the client's goals.* What does the client want or need to have done? Does the client have any feelings about the various methods of accomplishing those goals ("I don't want to sue unless there is no other way of getting them to stop dumping raw sewage in the river").

3. *To learn as much as the client knows about the facts.* This usually takes up most of the interview.

4. *To reduce the client's anxiety without being unrealistic.* On a rational level, clients come to lawyers because they want problems solved. But on an emotional level, they come to get relief from anxiety. Even the client who is not in a dispute with anybody and wants something positive done, such as drafting a will, feels a reduction in anxiety when you are able to say—if you can honestly and

prudently say it:—"I think we can structure your estate so that almost nothing would be taken in estate taxes and virtually everything would go to your heirs. It would take some work, but I think we can do it." Most of the time, you cannot offer even this much assurance in an initial interview because there are too many variables and, at the time of the interview, too many unknowns. When first meeting a client, you are almost never in a position to say, "If we sue your former employer, I think we will win." You need to do an exhaustive factual investigation before you can say something like that responsibly.

Most of the time, clients in initial interviews experience a significant degree of relief from anxiety simply from the knowledge that a capable, concerned, and likeable lawyer is committed to doing whatever is possible to solve the problem. When you help a client gain that feeling, you are reducing anxiety without being unrealistic.

§8.1.2 ACTIVE LISTENING AND OTHER INTERVIEWING DYNAMICS

What is really going on in a client interview? Here are the otherwise hidden dynamics:

Inhibitors. What might inhibit a client from telling you everything the client thinks and remembers?

The interview itself might be traumatic for the client. It can be embarrassing to confess that a problem is out of control. And the details of the client's problem are often very personal and may make the client look inadequate or reprehensible, even when the client might in the end be legally in the right.

The client might be afraid of telling you things that she thinks might undermine her case. You are part of the legal system, and most inexperienced clients do not realize that you can help only if you know the bad as well as the good.

Traditionally, lawyers are seen as authority figures. A client might feel some of the same inhibitions talking to a lawyer that a student feels when meeting privately with a teacher. And this can lead to etiquette barriers: deference to an authority figure may deter a client from challenging you when the client does not understand what you are saying or when the client believes that you are wrong.

The client might feel inhibited by cultural, social, age, or dialect barriers.

Finally, the client's memory is subject to all of the problems described in Chapter 7.

Facilitators. What might help a client tell you as much as possible?

You can build a relationship in which the client feels comfortable and trusts easily. And you can show empathy and respect rather than distance. (See §5.2.2.)

You can encourage communication with nonverbal communication and active listening, and you can set up your office in a way that clients find welcoming (see the next few paragraphs).

You can ask clear and well-organized questions (see §8.3.2).

Nonverbal communication. You are used to "reading" people based on their posture, facial expression, eye contact, and the like. Some of the messages you receive that way are inaccurate, but body language appears to tell us enough about another person's feelings that we take it for granted. A person who looks us firmly in the eye while talking to us seems to be taking us seriously. Someone who leans back in a chair with arms crossed looks bored or impatient, while a person who sits up straight with arms uncrossed appears to want to hear what is being said. When someone nods vertically while we are speaking, we think that means agreement, or at least "I hear you and accept the importance of what you say."

When does body language give us inaccurate messages? Sometimes, it is simple accident. A person might be very interested in what we have to say but lean back lazily because of fatigue. Sometimes, it is because body language means different things in different cultures.

Sometimes, a client's body language tells you something about the client's feelings. Sometimes, it does not. But you can use your own body language to show your interest in and respect for the client.

Active listening. The ability to listen well is as important in the practice of law as the ability to talk well (see Chapter 5). Some lawyers just want to get to the heart of the matter and quickly move on to other work, but they are in such a hurry that they leap onto the first important thing they hear, even if it is not in fact the heart of the matter. Instead, relax, let the client tell the story, and listen patiently and carefully.

Passive listening is just sitting there, hearing what is being said, and thinking about it. That is fine as long as the client does a good job of telling the story and is confident that you care.

Active listening, on the other hand, is a way of encouraging talk without asking questions. It also reassures a client that what the client is saying has an effect on you. In active listening, you participate in the conversation by reflecting back what you hear.

Compare these three examples:

1. lawyer listens *passively.*

Client: I wanted to buy a very reliable car with a manual transmission and a sunroof. The car has to be reliable. I can't spare the time to take it into the shop any more than necessary. You can't get a sunroof and a manual transmission from Toyota. You can at Honda, but the dealer didn't have any cars in stock. I had to special order it. I gave them a $5000 deposit. Two months later, they called to tell me the car had arrived. But it had an automatic transmission and no sunroof. I told them that wasn't the car I ordered. They refused to return the deposit and said I had to accept the car. I don't want it. A sunroof helps cool off the car quickly, and in the winter it lets in light and makes the car feel roomier. And a manual transmission makes the car more fun to drive.

2. lawyer listens *actively.*

Client: I wanted to buy a very reliable car with a manual transmission and a sunroof. The car has to be reliable. I can't spare the time to take it into the shop any more than necessary. You can't get a sunroof and a manual transmission from Toyota. You can at Honda, but the dealer didn't have any cars in stock. I had to special order it. I gave them a $5000 deposit. Two months later, they called to tell me the car had arrived. But it had an automatic transmission and no sunroof.

Lawyer: Really?

Client: I was astounded. I told them that wasn't the car I ordered. They refused to return the deposit and said I had to accept the car!

Lawyer: You must have been pretty upset.

Client: Absolutely. I don't want the car. A sunroof helps cool off the car quickly, and in the winter it lets in light and makes the car feel roomier.

Lawyer: They are nice.

Client: And a manual transmission makes the car more fun to drive.

3. lawyer listens *with a tin ear.*

Client: I wanted to buy a very reliable car with a manual transmission and a sunroof. The car has to be reliable. I can't spare the time to take it into the shop any more than necessary. You can't get a sunroof and a manual transmission from Toyota. You can at Honda, but the dealer didn't have any cars in stock. I had to special order it. I gave them a $5000 deposit. Two months later, they called to tell me the car had arrived. But it had an automatic transmission and no sunroof. I told them that wasn't the car I ordered.

Lawyer: Did you sign a contract with them that specified that the car had to have a sunroof and a manual transmission?

Client: I didn't sign anything except the $5000 check. They refused to return the deposit and said I had to accept the car.

Lawyer: Is the car defective in some way, or is it just not the car you want?

Client: I don't want it. It's not what I ordered, and I shouldn't have to accept it. I want a sunroof and a manual transmission. A sunroof helps cool off the car quickly, and in the winter it lets in light and makes the car feel roomier. A manual transmission makes the car more fun to drive.

In the first example, the client tells the story without any reaction from the lawyer. At some point, most clients would become uncomfortable in such a situation, and eventually the client would stop talking.

In the second example, the lawyer's interjections show understanding and empathy and encourage the client to continue. But notice that the lawyer waits before saying anything. That is because clients "will reveal critical material as soon as they have the opportunity to speak,"[1] and in the first few moments of a client's narrative the lawyer should stay out of the way and let the client talk. Here, the first time the lawyer interjects is the first time that simple courtesy would demand an acknowledgement of the client's predicament. Before that point, it is often better to confine active listening to nonverbal support, such as nods and eye contact.

In the third example, the lawyer asks relevant questions but seems not to have heard any of the emotional content in the client's story, leaving the client with the feeling that the lawyer is unsympathetic. The lawyer asks the questions prematurely. They could have been asked later. When asked here, they get in the way of the client's telling the story. To the client, the lawyer's inability to hear all the client says suggests that the lawyer is not likely to be helpful.

An office arrangement comfortable for clients. Consider the furniture arrangement that would help you open up to a lawyer if you were a client. Some people are perfectly willing to talk over a desk to a lawyer. Other people would want something less formal, perhaps two chairs with a small table to the side (all of which can be in the same room as the desk). We believe most clients are more at ease if you are not behind a big desk, which is both a physical barrier and a symbol of your authority. Sitting *with* the client—rather than across from the client—communicates in a subtle way that you are open to the kind of participatory relationship described in Chapter 3.

Your office should also communicate professionalism. An office that is a mess, with papers piled everywhere, suggests that the lawyer's work is out of control. Some lawyers say that they "know where everything is." Clients instinctively doubt that.

Taking notes. Clients are not bothered by your note-taking, although the client might appreciate it if you were to ask, "Do you mind if I take notes?" If you become too wrapped up in note-taking, however, it can be hard to listen (and certainly hard to maintain eye contact). The most effective practice is to take minimal notes while the client is telling the story, perhaps writing down only topics you want to go back to later, and then to take a complete set of notes while you are asking questions after the client has told you the story.

The most important dynamic in the room. "What clients want more than anything is to be understood, both for who they are and what they have suffered."[2]

---

1. Gay Gellhorn, *Law and Language: An Empirically-Based Model for the Opening Moments of Client Interviews*, 4 Clinical L. Rev. 321, 344 (1998).
2. Anthony I. DeWitt, *Therapeutic Communication as a Tool for Case Theming,* 29 Am. J. Trial Adv. 395, 404 (2005).

§8.2 ORGANIZING THE INTERVIEW

You can do a better interview if you prepare before the interview begins, as described below in §8.2.1. The interview itself can be broken down into five parts.

1. A brief opening part in which the lawyer and client become acquainted and get down to business (see §8.2.2).
2. An information-gathering part (see §8.2.3)—usually the longest part of the interview—in which you learn everything the client knows about the facts; if you are using cognitive interviewing techniques, this part of the interview is subdivided into the stages described in §7.6:
   a. an open-ended narration stage (the client tells the story);
   b. a probing stage (you ask detailed questions);
   c. a review stage (you describe the story as you understand it and the client makes corrections and additions).
3. A goal-identification part, in which you learn exactly what the client wants to accomplish in resolving the problem at hand (see §8.2.4).
4. A preliminary strategy part, in which you might discuss with the client—usually only tentatively—some possible strategies for handling the problem; in a dispute situation, this usually includes some consideration of possible theories in support of the client's position (see §8.2.5).
5. A closing phase in which you and the client agree on what will happen after the interview (see §8.2.6).

In practice, these parts usually overlap. For example, some theory-testing and strategizing (part 4) might happen during information-gathering (part 2). Or the client might volunteer clearly stated goals (part 3) in the first moments of the interview (part 1). Overlap is fine as long as it does not interfere with your own interviewing purposes (see §8.1.1).

§8.2.1 PREPARING

You might have spoken with the client briefly over the telephone when the client made the appointment. Otherwise, in a well-run office the secretary will have asked the client the nature of the problem the client is bringing to you. Some clients decline to say, but most of the time, you will have beforehand at least a vague sense of why the client wants to see you.

Unless you know well the field of law that seems to be involved, take a look at the most obviously relevant parts of the law before the client arrives. If the client says she was arrested for burglary, read the burglary statute and browse through the annotations. If the client wants you to help negotiate a franchise agreement with McDonald's, look through a practitioner's book that explains how franchising works in the fast-food industry.

The interview is more productive if the client brings the papers that are relevant to the problem. Whoever in your office speaks to the client when making the appointment should ask the client to do that. But clients are not good at judging relevance. Try to be specific. If the client is threatened with mortgage foreclosure, the client should be asked to bring the documents that created the mortgage, all statements sent by the bank that holds the mortgage, records from the checking account used to make mortgage payments in the past, any official-looking notices sent by the bank or a sheriff or a lawyer, and anything else the client has that seems to be related to this mortgage.

§8.2.2 BEGINNING THE INTERVIEW

In some parts of the country, "visiting"—comfortable chat for a while on topics other than legal problems—typically precedes getting down to business. In other regions, no more than two or three sentences might be exchanged first, and they might be limited to questions like whether the client would like some coffee.

When it is time to turn to business, the lawyer says something like:

> "How can I help?"
> "Let's talk about what brings you here today."
> "My secretary tells me the bank has threatened to foreclose on your mortgage. You're probably worried. Where shall we begin?"

Soon afterward, the client will probably say something that means a great deal emotionally to her or him. Some examples:

> "I've come into some money and would like to set up a trust for my granddaughter, to help her pay for college and graduate school."
> "I've just been served with legal papers. The bank is foreclosing on our mortgage and taking our home away from us."

Too often, when clients say these things lawyers just ask, "Tell me more," and start taking notes. That may be a sign of the law-trained mind at work, ever quick to find the legally significant facts. But clients rightfully dislike it. If given a choice, most clients would rather not hire "a lawyer." They want a genuine human being who is good at doing the work lawyers do. If you were to hear either of the statements above in a social setting, you would express pleasure at the first or dismay at the second because empathy and active listening are social skills that you already knew something about before you came to law school. Do the same for the client in the office—sincerely.

But do not leap in here with questions. Give the client a full opportunity to tell you whatever the client wants to talk about before you start structuring the interview. There are two reasons. First, many clients want to make sure from the beginning that you hear certain things about which the client feels deeply. If you obstruct this, you will seem remote, even bureaucratic, to the client. Second, many clients will pour out a torrent of information as soon as you ask them what has brought them into your office. If you listen to this torrent carefully, you may learn a lot of facts in a short period of time. You may also learn a lot about the client as a person and about how the client views the problem.

If the client is inexperienced at hiring lawyers, you will need to explain attorney-client confidentiality (see §3.6). But the best time to do so is probably not in the very beginning. It seems awkward and distancing there, and clients are eager to tell you the purpose of their visit anyway. A better time is in the information-gathering part of the interview, after the client has told you the story and before you start asking detailed questions discussed below in §8.2.3. Most clients will tell you the basic story at the beginning regardless of whether they understand confidentiality. It is when they begin to answer your questions later that confidentiality encourages clients to be more open with you.

Use the client's name during the interview ("Good morning, Ms. Blount"). Saying the client's name at appropriate points in the conversation shortens the psychological distance between you and the client because it implies that you recognize the client as a person rather than as an item of work. Which name you say—the client's first or last name—depends on your personality, your guess about the client's preference, and local customs. If you live in an area where immediate informality is expected, it may be acceptable to call the client by first name unless the client is so much older than you that, out of respect, you should use the client's last name until the client invites you to switch to first names. But in most parts of the country, the safest practice for a young lawyer is to start on a last-name basis with nearly all clients and wait to see whether you and the client will feel comfortable switching to first names.

§8.2.3 INFORMATION GATHERING

After the client has explained why you are being consulted, the information-gathering part of the interview begins. If it is important for you to learn the details of past events, this is where you use the cognitive interviewing techniques described in §7.6.

Not all clients, however, need cognitive interviews. That is especially true in transactional work. When a client wants you to draft a will or help negotiate a contract, you will need to learn many facts, but usually you do not need to worry about the client's memory of past events. Much of the information you need is about current conditions. To draft a will, for example, you need a list of the client's assets, a list of the client's potential heirs, and so on. In situations like this, start by asking the client to tell you everything the client thinks you will need to know. After the client has done that, start asking detailed questions to get the rest of the information you will need.

If, on the other hand, you are using cognitive interviewing techniques, the information-gathering part of the interview is subdivided into three stages:

a. an open-ended narration stage in which the client is asked to describe everything the client remembers about the facts at issue;
b. a probing stage in which you go back over the client's story and ask questions to fill in gaps and clarify ambiguities;
c. a review stage in which you reiterate the most important parts of the story as you understand them to give the client an opportunity to correct misunderstandings and to supply additional information.

Before inviting the client to narrate the story, recreate the context and ask the client to describe everything she remembers about the incidents at issue, regardless of relevancy (see §7.6). Say something like this:

Lawyer: I need to learn everything you can remember about what happened inside the store. Let's go back to the point where you got out of your car in the parking lot. Take a few minutes and return in your own mind to that moment. Think about what you were seeing and hearing at the time, as you were walking through the parking lot toward the store. Don't rush this. I can wait until you're ready. And when you are ready, tell me everything you remember—even if it does not seem to be related to the store manager's accusation about shoplifting.

If the client has trouble producing a complete and coherent story, you might ask her to recall the event in a sequence other than chronological, perhaps starting with the thing that impressed the client the most, or you might ask the client to change perspectives and assess what others present might have seen or heard (see §7.6).

While listening to the story, take two kinds of notes. Write down what you are being told, and make a list of topics to go back to later for clarification or to fill in gaps. You can use two pads of paper to do this. Or you can use one pad, drawing a vertical line on each page to separate the two kinds of notes.

After the client has told the story, you can start asking questions. This is the second stage of the cognitive part of the interview. Get a clear chronological view of events from beginning to end, as well as a firm grip on the precise details of the story. For example, exactly when and where did each event happen? See §8.3.1 for what to ask about and §8.3.2 for how to formulate and organize questions.

You can introduce the review stage by saying something like this:

Lawyer: I think I've got a clear picture now. Let me tell you my understanding of what happened. If I've got anything wrong, please correct me. And if you remember anything else as I go along, please interrupt me to point it out.

Then briefly summarize the relevant parts of the story.

Regardless of whether you are using cognitive interviewing techniques, the time to bring up attorney-client confidentiality is when you start asking questions. How should you explain confidentiality? It is not accurate to say, "Everything you tell me is confidential." There are important exceptions to that statement (see §3.6). Most clients, however, do not want to hear a lecture on all the exceptions. A middle course is better:

Lawyer: Before we go further, I should explain that the law requires me to keep confidential what you tell me. There are some exceptions, some situations where I may or must tell someone else something you tell me, but for the most part I am not allowed to tell anybody other than the people who work with me representing you.

You can explain the exceptions if the client asks about them or if one of them is obviously relevant.

Do not label the problem until you have heard all the facts. A client who starts by telling you about a dispute with a landlord might have defamation and assault claims instead of a violation of the lease or of the residential rental statutes.

§8.2.4 ASCERTAINING THE CLIENT'S GOALS

From the client's point of view, what would be a successful outcome?

If the client wants help in facilitating a transaction, the client will want the transaction to take a certain shape. For example, the client might want to buy a thousand t-shirts with pictures of Radiohead, but only if they can be delivered two days before next month's concert and will cost no more than $6.50 wholesale each, preferably less. And the client will not want the lawyer to kill the deal by overlawyering (see §2.2).

If the client wants help in resolving a dispute, the desired outcome may vary. The client might want compensation for a loss (money damages, for example) or prevention of a loss (not paying the other side damages, not going to jail, not letting the other side do some threatened harm out of court) or vindication (such as a judgment declaring that the client was right and the other side wrong).

Depending on the situation, the client might want or need results very quickly. And most clients also want economy: they want to keep their own expenses (including your fees) to a minimum or at least within a specified budget.

Goals often conflict. A client who wants a large problem solved immediately on a small budget might have to decide which goals are most or least important. If the client has to compromise on something, will the client spend more, wait longer, or accept less than complete justice?

Whether the problem is transactional or a dispute, the client might want comfort and understanding. Some clients are not under stress or would prefer to keep their emotional distance from lawyers. But most stressed clients at least want empathy.

Most clients do not volunteer all of their goals in an interview. Some clients know what their goals are and assume that they should be obvious to the lawyer. The goals might *seem* obvious to the lawyer, but because assumptions are dangerous, it is best to get a clear statement from the client. And some clients have not thought through the situation enough to be sure what their goals are. They need help from the lawyer in figuring that out.

Helping the client identify goals requires patience and careful listening, often for messages that are not literally being expressed in the client's words. "Find[ing] out what the customer wants [is something that l]awyers are famous for [doing badly]. They snap out the questions, scribble on a pad, and start telling you what you're going to do."[3] Here is an example of what might happen when lawyers do not take the time to do this carefully:

> Two law students under the supervision of a law professor represented M. Dujon Johnson on a misdemeanor charge. . . . The lawyers[4] investigated the case thoroughly, interviewed their client, developed a theory of the case, and represented Mr. Johnson aggressively. When the case came to trial the prosecutor asked the judge to dismiss the case, a victory for the defense. The client was furious. . . .

---

3. Nicholas Carroll, *Dancing with Lawyers: How to Take Charge and Get Results* 5 (1992).

4. For conciseness, the author of the article from which this excerpt is taken uses the term "the lawyers" to refer to the team made up of the professor and the law students, who were practicing in a law school legal clinic. Because clinic students are not members of the bar, they may not hold themselves out as lawyers, however.

> Johnson . . . had been arrested by two state troopers when he pulled into a service station at night [and t]he troopers called out, "Hey, yo," to Johnson, an African American undergraduate. They ordered him out of the car and asked him to submit to a pat-down search. When Johnson refused, claiming that such a search would violate his constitutional rights, the troopers arrested him for disorderly conduct, searched him, pressed his face on the hood of the car while handcuffing him, and took him to jail.
>
> [When they first interviewed him,] the lawyers did not ask Johnson what his goals were. If they had, they would have learned that he wanted more than simply to be cleared of a misdemeanor charge. As he said later, "I would like to have my reputation restored, and my dignity."
>
> . . . If [the lawyers had inquired more thoroughly], they would have learned that he wanted a public trial. They would have learned that, at . . . arraignment, the prosecutor had offered to dismiss his case if he would pay court costs of fifty dollars, and he had refused. The trial itself was the relief Johnson sought. Without discussing it with their client, the lawyers filed a motion to suppress evidence that, if successful, would have drastically shortened the trial. . . .
>
> . . . [A]fter his case had been dismissed, Johnson said the lawyers had been "patronizing" . . . [that] he was always the "secondary person[," and] that they had treated him like a child.[5]

Here, the client understood what his goals were, but the professionals representing him did not. Another client might have only a vague sense of goals, and one of the lawyer's tasks is to work with the client to clarify them.

For example, after being served with an eviction notice, a client might have come to the lawyer just because that seems like the right thing to do when confronted with confusing and intimidating legal papers. But the problem may be a deeper one. The client might have lost a job, and the client's family might be disintegrating under financial pressures. There are two reasons why you should care. First, there may be legal issues inside the deeper problem (abusive discharge? child custody?). And second, even if there are no legal issues other than the eviction proceeding, the lawyer, as a disinterested observer, is still in a position to offer valuable advice that the client cannot easily find elsewhere (see §3.1).

Here are some questions that help clarify the client's goals:

> *"If you could imagine the best outcome we can reasonably hope for, what would that be?"* You want a list of the things the client wants to accomplish.
>
> *"If we achieve that best outcome, how will it affect you?"* Or *"how will it affect your family?"* Or *"how will it affect your business?"* These tell you why the client has the goals listed in response to the first question. If the goals the client has initially cannot be accomplished, you and the client can try to develop other goals that have as nearly as possible the same effect.

---

5. Alex J. Hurder, *Negotiating the Lawyer-Client Relationship: A Search for Equality and Collaboration*, 44 Buff. L. Rev. 71, 71–73 (1996) (summarizing Clark D. Cunningham, *The Lawyer as Translator, Representation as Text: Towards an Ethnography of Legal Discourse*, 77 Cornell L. Rev. 1298 (1992)). (Johnson asked that Cunningham use his real name.)

"*What possible bad outcomes are you worried about?*" And "*Are there any other things that you want to make sure do not happen?*" You want to know what the client wants to prevent.

"*If any of those negative things were to happen, how would each of them affect you?*" (*Or "your family?" Or "your business?"*) These tell you why the bad outcomes must be prevented.

§8.2.5 CONSIDERING A STRATEGY DURING THE INTERVIEW

During an initial client interview, you will not know enough to start making clear plans for solving the problem. You will probably need to investigate the facts and read the law, and you will certainly need to think over the problem. But you and the client can do some brainstorming, starting the process of generating solutions (see §4.1.2). And you can learn something about the ones that are generated by asking the client for relevant information (including the client's feelings). For example:

Lawyer: So the Santiagos do not seem to regret signing a contract to buy your house. In fact, they seem eager to move in. I get the sense that the only real problem from their point of view is that they can't get a mortgage because the house has a zoning violation. Am I missing something?

Client: No. The only complaint I hear from them is about that.

Lawyer: One way of handling that is to ask the local zoning board to issue a variance. That could take at least two or three months. Do the Santiagos seem to want the house enough to wait that long?

Client: They like the house a lot. And I think they're worried about having to sue to get their deposit back.

Lawyer: Do they have a strong need to move into a house—any house—as soon as possible?

Client: I don't think so. They're living in a rental now, and they haven't given their landlord notice that they're moving out.

Lawyer: I can't predict at this point whether the zoning board would issue a variance. I'd have to look at exactly what this violation is and then see what your zoning board has done in similar cases in the past. But there is one thing I know right now: if any of your neighbors object, the board might not issue a variance. Do you think we'd have a problem there?

Client: We're on good terms with our neighbors, and none of them has ever complained about our backyard deck, which seems to be what the violation is all about.

Lawyer: To get the Santiagos to agree to a delay, we might have to say that you will not return their deposit unless ordered to do so by a court. In other words, we'd be saying that if they won't wait, they'll have to sue to get their money back. Would you be comfortable taking that position?

Client: I don't mind saying it. But if they actually do sue us, I think I'd rather give them the money and find another buyer. A court fight doesn't seem like the fastest way to get our house sold.

Lawyer: That's certainly a reasonable way to look at it.

This is a transactional situation that could evolve into a dispute. In addition to some important details, the lawyer learns here that the client prefers to keep the situation transactional and will walk away from the deal to avoid litigation.

In a more typical dispute situation, where litigation is likely, strategizing includes finding the client's persuasive story—finding a way of looking at the facts that will seem most persuasive to a fact-finder. Lawyers call such a way of looking at the facts a factual theory. In an initial client interview, you are not in a position to develop the theory fully. As with strategies generally, you need to do a factual investigation and read the law first. The most you can do in an initial client interview is to come up with some tentative theories and test them against what the client knows of the facts.

In Chapters 10–17, we will examine in detail how to develop a theory and what makes one persuasive. For now, however, it is enough to understand two things about effective theories. First, if you will have the burden of proof, your theory must satisfy the elements of the legal tests that make up your burden. If the other side will have the burden of proof, your theory must prevent the other side from satisfying at least some elements of the legal test the other side must prove. Second, a persuasive theory is based on solid evidence and the inferences people will typically draw from that evidence. In court, ambiguous evidence and debatable inferences are usually resolved in whatever way is most consistent with the evidence that cannot be questioned.

§8.2.6 CLOSING

Assuming that the client wants to hire you and that you want to be hired, two agreements conclude the interview.

One is an agreement that the client is in fact hiring you to do the work discussed in the interview. If the client has not made clear that is happening, you can ask a simple question like this: "Now that we've talked about it, would you like me to defend you in this lawsuit?" Some clients will say yes or no on the spot. Others will want to think about it after the interview. If you are hired, that should be formalized through a written retainer (see §8.4.5).

The other agreement concerns what each party will do—and not do—next. Here is a typical example: the client will provide copy of the lease by the end of today; the lawyer will check the law on constructive eviction and call the client tomorrow; in the meantime, the client will not speak to the landlord and will tell anybody who makes demands to call the lawyer. In agreeing on what to do next, consider the following:

1. The client should not do anything to make the situation worse. Agree specifically on what the client will not do. This could involve restraints that might seem unnatural or abnormal to the client. Most clients do not realize that anything they say to an adverse party might escalate conflict, or that anything they say to anybody other than you might be later testified to by the other person, perhaps not accurately. In addition, it is part of a lawyer's job to bear some of the pressure that would otherwise be inflicted on the client. If people have been demanding that the client do something that the client does not want to do, the client should now start telling them to communicate only through you.
2. You should make a realistic and clear commitment of what you will do in the immediate future, together with a schedule for when you will do it. Clients feel much better if you set a schedule for accomplishing certain tasks, keep to the schedule, and report back to the client on what you have accomplished. Otherwise, a client has no idea whether you are working diligently or are ignoring the problem.
3. The client should commit to provide specific things that you need (information, documents) to do your share of the work, and there should be a schedule for this, too. (Paying your retainer is included; see §8.4.6.) Some tasks—for example, asking the Internal Revenue Service for copies of prior tax returns—are things that you and the client are each capable of doing. If the client does some or most of them, the client can avoid paying what it would cost for you to do them.

The end of the interview should provide the client with a sense of closure—a feeling that a problem has been handed over to a professional who will do whatever can be done to solve it. Some clients get closure from the mutual agreements described above. Others may appreciate a comment from you that shows that you understand what this problem means for the client and are concerned about it on a human level.

Explain to the client how best to contact you. That is most easily done by giving the client your business card, which will include your phone number and your email address. You might explain your habits in returning phone calls and email. For example, if you are in court a lot and tend to respond late in the day, explain that to the client and add that if the client needs a faster response she should tell your office's secretary or paralegal that the client is calling about something urgent.

What if you do not want to be hired to do this particular work? Make absolutely clear that you are not in a position to take it on. If you think another lawyer would do a good job and would want the work, you might make a referral.

If you are not hired—whether by your choice or the prospective client's—it's wise to document that with a follow-up letter to the client in which you thank the client for the interview and reiterate that you have not been hired. Lawyers call this a "nonengagement letter." Some clients do not hear a soft no when a lawyer refuses their case. If such a client were not to seek another lawyer, and some bad thing were to happen (such as the expiration of a statute of limitations), you want it on record that you are not this person's lawyer. A typical nonengagement letter warns the would-be client of a statute of limitations or whatever other deadline might compromise rights if ignored.

§8.3 QUESTIONS

Remember that one of the marks of an effective professional is the ability to ask useful questions in a productive way (see §5.2). In a client interview, you need to know what to ask about and how to organize and formulate questions.

§8.3.1 WHAT TO ASK ABOUT

During the information-gathering part of the interview (§8.2.3), be sure to explore the following:

Ask for the raw facts and the client's source of knowledge. Do not ask whether the other driver's car was exceeding the speed limit (a conclusion). Ask how fast it was going and how the client knows that. At trial, the client can testify only to the client's estimate of the car's speed in miles per hour. And that can happen only after the client has laid a foundation by testifying that he has a source of knowledge that the law of evidence recognizes as sufficient. If all you know is that the client thinks the car was speeding, you have no idea what the client will testify to at trial, or even whether the client will be allowed to testify on that point. If the client says he does not know the car's actual speed, but that a friend told him the car had been traveling at about 60 miles per hour, the client will not be allowed to testify to that unless the friend's statement fits within one of the exceptions to the hearsay rule. The friend's name goes on your list of witnesses to interview.

Ask for all the details. If the client says, "Ling told me about that last week," do not go on to the next topic. Ask when this conversation happened—not just the day, but also the time. Where did it happen? Who else was present? What else was discussed? How long did the conversation last? How did it start? How did it end? What words did Ling use, and what did the witness and anybody else present say? You are going to need these details to prepare your case. Because in nonprofessional life vagueness and approximation are usually enough, young lawyers are too casual about these things. Experienced lawyers know that in representing clients only precision works.

Ask about everything the client saw, heard, and said. You need to be able to see and hear in your own mind the scene in which the events described by the client occurred. Do not assume anything. If the events happened at the busiest intersection in town, do not assume that cars were whizzing past while the client was standing on the sidewalk. If the cars actually matter, ask. You might be surprised to learn that the street was torn up for construction and all the traffic routed elsewhere. Ask about *any detail* that might matter.

If a diagram would help you understand what happened, ask the client to draw one. That can be particularly important if the position of people and things in a scene is important.

Make sure you learn all the basic information as well: the client's full name, age, address, all telephone numbers, occupation and job title, employer, job site, and work hours. Get similar information for the client's spouse, as well as the ages of and some details on any children. For each witness or other person with a role in the problem, get as much identifying information as the client can provide.

Ask whatever questions are needed to prevent The Three Disasters. The Three Disasters are (1) accepting a client who creates a conflict of interest, (2) missing a statute of limitations or other deadline that extinguishes or compromises the client's rights, and (3) not taking emergency action to protect a client who is threatened with immediate harm. If you allow any of them to happen, you may commit malpractice and may also be punished for unethical conduct.

A lawyer or a law firm has a conflict of interest where the interests of one client conflict with those of another client, a former client, or the lawyer or law firm.[6] A well-run law office will have a conflicts database so that, if you suspect a conflict, you can quickly find out whether the office represents or has represented a conflicting party. Once a new client has begun to reveal confidential information to you, the damage might be uncontainable, and you or the firm might have to withdraw from representing either client or both. (There are exceptions, which are complicated and explored in the course on Professional Responsibility or Legal Ethics.)

Suppose a client has suffered a wrong and seems to be entitled to a remedy in court. Suppose also that during the interview you don't bother to pin down the date on which the statute of limitations would have begun to run, and after the interview you don't bother to read the statute. And suppose the statutory period expires tomorrow. You have accepted a client and allowed the client's rights to be extinguished. The client still has a remedy, but now it is against you in a malpractice lawsuit. Although the statute of limitations, because of its inflexibility, is the most dramatic example, other deadlines can have similar effects. For example, if the client has been sued by somebody else, when was the client served with the summons and complaint, and when does the time to answer the complaint expire?

Suppose the client has been served with a notice of eviction, and the notice says that the sheriff will evict the client tomorrow. Are there facts that could lead a court to grant an emergency order temporarily restraining the sheriff from putting all your client's belongings on the sidewalk? The only way to find out is to ask pertinent questions during the interview so that, if there are grounds, you can start drafting a request for court relief immediately.

Ask about pieces of paper. Ask whether there are any pieces of paper, not already mentioned by the client, that might be related to the problem. Avoid using lawyer jargon. Do not ask about "documents." Is a memo a document? You might say yes, but many clients would think no. If relevant pieces of paper exist, ask where they are and who has possession of them. Ask whether the client has *signed* any papers connected to the problem. In a dispute situation, ask whether the client

6. See Rules 1.7, 1.8, 1.9, 1.10, and 1.11 of the Model Rules of Professional Conduct.

has *received* any pieces of paper from a court, a lawyer, or a government agency. Many clients will not understand if you ask whether they have been "served with papers."

In a dispute situation, ask all the questions needed to find the story in the facts. In the movie *Amistad*, Africans who have been brought to Connecticut against their will in 1839 sue to gain their freedom. Slave traders claim they own the Africans, who in turn claim they were kidnapped. At a critical point in the movie, one of the Africans' supporters (played by Morgan Freeman) seeks the advice of a former President, John Quincy Adams (played by Anthony Hopkins). The case is going badly for the Africans, and the Morgan Freeman character wants to know how to handle it better. Adams says "Well, when I was an attorney a long time ago . . . , I realized after much trial and error that in a courtroom whoever tells the best story wins. In an unlawyer-like fashion, I give you that scrap of wisdom free of charge."

That is the first of two great insights in the conversation between these two characters. Then, Adams explains how, although the Morgan Freeman character *knows the facts* about the Africans, he has not yet discovered their story. The second great insight is that *you can know the facts but miss the story*. Inside a mass of facts—hundreds of events and circumstances—is a story that touches your heart and makes an audience—the judge and jury—hope that one person gets better treatment in the future and another person gets worse. The story does not leap out of the facts. You have to *find* it. Ask questions that reveal the story you need to represent this client well.

For more on how to do this effectively, go back to §5.2.4 and reread the material on finding and telling stories. We return to this skill in later chapters as well.

In a dispute situation, ask questions that would reveal what arguments the other side might make. There are two sides to every dispute, and you cannot prepare without knowing what the other side will claim. But you will learn little if you ask in a way that seems threatening to the client. For example, if your client has been charged with a crime, do not ask whether she is guilty. Ask what the police and the complaining witness will say about her. Before doing that, explain in detail why you can be a good advocate only if you know in advance what the other side will claim.

In a dispute situation, explore for other evidence. For example, ask who else saw or heard any of the things the client describes. Ask who else might know of aspects of the dispute that the client does not know about.

In a dispute situation, evaluate the client's value as a witness in court. Is this client likely to tell the story in a way that can influence a fact-finder? Is the client credible and likely to earn the fact-finder's respect? Are there any doubts about the client's honesty or ability to observe and remember accurately?

In a dispute situation, ask whether the client has talked with anybody else about the subjects you are asking about. Those people might help corroborate what your client is telling you. Or they might end up testifying against your client at trial, saying that your client made statements that hurt her case.

In a transactional situation, learn the posture of the deal so far. What is the present state of discussions between the client and the other party? What has already been agreed to? What issues have not yet been resolved? What obstacles does the client see to wrapping up the agreement? How much does the other party want or need this transaction? Is either party in a hurry?

In a transactional situation, learn the parties' interests. What is the big picture? What about this transaction is most important to the client? To the other party? (In other words, what is each party trying to accomplish?) How will the deal operate financially? Where will the profit be made? How does the client envision, on a practical level, the transaction will operate once agreement is complete? How does the transaction fit into the client's larger plans for the future? Is the transaction part of a long-term relationship—or a hoped-for long-term relationship—between the parties? In agreeing to this deal, is the client relying on factual assumptions about which the other party has or should have superior knowledge? (If so, the client can be protected by drafting the contract so that the other party represents and warrants the truthfulness of those facts.) Is there a risk that the transaction might violate the law? Can the transaction be structured to minimize the client's tax? In drafting the agreement, what potential future difficulties should be provided for in advance? (The most obvious example would be breach: how should the agreement define breach, and what consequences would follow breach?) Are there any other ways that the agreement can be drafted to protect the client? What provisions does the client want in the drafted agreement?

In addition, for each type of agreement, there's a laundry list of issues that a prudent lawyer would typically resolve in drafting. If you rent an apartment, look at your lease; it probably reflects the residential lease version of such a list from the landlord's point of view. What do you need to know in order to handle the laundry-list issues?

Ask whether the client has talked about this problem with another lawyer. If you are the seventh lawyer the client has consulted about this problem, there is a reason why the other six lawyers have not done what the client wanted. It might be a reason that should not influence you. But most of the time the other lawyers are not presently working for the client because the case is meritless or the client tends to sabotage a lawyer's work.

§8.3.2 ORGANIZING AND FORMULATING QUESTIONS

Organizing questions. When you start exploring various aspects of the problem in detail, try to take up each topic separately. Too much skipping around confuses you and the client.

On each topic, start with broad questions ("tell me what happened the night the reactor melted down") and gradually work your way toward narrow ones ("just before you ran from the control panel, what number on that dial was the needle pointing to?"). Broad questions usually produce the largest amount of information, especially information that you have not anticipated. A versatile broad question is "What happened next?" Narrow questions produce details to fill in gaps left after the broad questions have been asked.

Move gradually from broad questions to narrow ones. If you jump too quickly to the narrow ones, you will miss a lot of information because it is the general questions that show you what to explore. Here's an example of what can go wrong:

Lawyer: What happened next? [*a broad question*]

Client: The store manager grabbed me and took me to a back room, where they opened my shopping bag and accused me of shoplifting. They were really abusive and embarrassed me in front of everybody in the store.

Lawyer: Did they touch you? [*a narrow question, asked before the client has finished answering the broad one*]

Client: Yeah, the manager grabbed me by the arm and practically dragged me to that back room. And when I tried to leave, a big security guy stood in front of the door, took me by the shoulders and sat me back down.

Lawyer: How many people heard them call you a shoplifter? [*another narrow question*]

Client: Maybe a dozen or so. They looked at me as though I was disgusting.

Lawyer: Do you know any of them by name? [*yet another narrow question*]

Client: Oh, yeah. A couple of them belong to the PTA at my children's school. Another is the receptionist in my doctor's office.

Here, the lawyer is constructing a case against store personnel for assault, false imprisonment, and defamation. What the lawyer does not know is that the police came and arrested the client, who is scheduled for trial next week. The lawyer missed this by going too fast to narrow questions. If the lawyer had not done that, the following might have occurred:

Client: The store manager grabbed me and took me to a back room, where they opened my shopping bag and accused me of shoplifting. They were really abusive and embarrassed me in front of everybody in the store.

Lawyer: Oh, my. That must have been very upsetting. Let's start from the point where the store manager first approached you. Please take a few minutes and remember everything that happened. Then, after you've finished running it through your mind, tell me everything you remember.

[*a period of silence*]

Client: O.K. I was standing at the dairy counter. The manager walked up from my left and grabbed me by the arm and said, "I saw you put something in your bag." I said, "What?" or something like that. And he pulled me to that back room, closed the door, and told me to sit down. [*As the client describes the scene in detail, we learn that the police arrived and arrested the client.*]

Here, the lawyer asked the client to recreate the context, and then let the client tell the whole story before beginning to probe (see §7.6).

Ask broad questions until you are not getting useful information any more. Then go back and ask narrow questions about the facts the client did not cover. While the client is answering the broad questions, you can note on a pad the topics you will explore later by means of narrow questions.

Formulating questions. Phrase your questions carefully. Remember that how you say something has an enormous effect on how people respond (see §2.2). A good question does not confuse, does not provoke resistance, and does not help distort memory (see Chapter 7).

Ask one question at a time. If you ask two at a time, only one of them will be answered.

Lawyer: How much did Consolidated bid on this project? Were they the low bidder, or was somebody else?

Client: I think somebody else submitted the lowest bid, a company in Milwaukee that later had trouble posting a performance bond.

Did we learn how much Consolidated bid?

A leading question is one that suggests its own answer ("When the store manager took you into the back room, he locked the door, didn't he?"). A leading question puts some pressure on the person answering it to give the answer the question suggests ("Yes, he locked the door"). The question implies one or both of two things. One is that the questioner expects that answer because the questioner already thinks or knows that it is true. The other is that the questioner *wants* that answer (for example, to help prove something, such as false imprisonment).

Because of the malleability of memory (see Chapter 7), leading questions have the potential to cause inaccurate answers. If a leading question—or any type of question—in an interview causes a client to "remember" things more favorably to the client's case, and if the client is later to testify to that "memory" at trial, the leading question creates an ethical problem (see §8.4.1). (At trial, a lawyer is normally not allowed to ask a leading question of the lawyer's own witness on direct examination. But leading questions are permitted when a lawyer cross-examines the other side's witnesses, who can be expected to resist attempts to influence their memories.)

Leading questions, however, can be useful when the client might be fabricating (see §8.4.3) and for the review stage of cognitive interviewing (see §§7.6 and 8.2.3).

At times, you can probe for information without using questions at all. For example, active listening or body language indicating that you are particularly interested in what the client is saying can encourage the client to go into the facts in greater detail (see §8.1.2).

§8.4 SPECIAL PROBLEMS IN CLIENT INTERVIEWING

You may face problems of ethics (§8.4.1), information that the client considers private or too unpleasant to discuss (§8.4.2), a possibility that the client is not being honest with you (§8.4.3), pressure from the client to make a prediction before you have had an opportunity to research the law and investigate the facts (§8.4.4), or negotiating a fee agreement with the client (§8.4.5).

§8.4.1 ETHICS IN CLIENT INTERVIEWING

First and foremost, you and those who work for you are obligated to keep confidential that which the client tells you, with the exceptions noted in §3.6.

In addition, you may not "falsify evidence [or] counsel or assist a witness to testify falsely."[7] If your client will become a party to litigation, your client will probably become a witness. Thus, you may not suggest that your client testify falsely or that your client falsify evidence. Nor may you help your client do either of those things. Falsifying evidence and suborning perjury are also crimes. And "many jurisdictions make[] it an offense to destroy material for purpose of impairing its availability in a pending proceeding or one whose commencement can be foreseen."[8] Even those that do not make it a crime may impose sanctions, including dismissal or claim preclusion on those who fail to preserve evidence crucial to an adversary's case.

Perhaps the best known ethical dilemma in client interviewing is called the *Anatomy of a Murder* problem, after the novel[9] and movie of the same name. There, a lawyer interviews his client, who is accused of murder. Before asking the client for the facts in detail, the lawyer gives the client a lecture explaining all the defenses to a murder charge. After listening to this, the client describes facts that would support a defense of temporary insanity. We are left with the impression that if the client had not heard the lecture, he would have told a different story—that the lawyer essentially told the client what the client would have to say in order to escape conviction.

Lawyers are not allowed to help create false testimony. But clients are entitled to know the law and to get that knowledge from their lawyers. How can you observe both of these principles while interviewing clients? The best approach is to interview for facts first and to explain the law afterward. The reasons are partly ethical and partly practical. In the novel and the film, the client invents a story and wins at trial. That is harder to do in the real world than it is in fiction. There are

---

7. Rule 3.4(b) of the Model Rules of Professional Conduct.
8. Comment to Model Rule 3.4.
9. Robert Traver, *Anatomy of a Murder* (1958).

always other witnesses and evidence and facts, some of them incontrovertible. Not many clients are clever and lucky enough to be able to invent stories that are either consistent with or more believable than everything else the fact-finder will be exposed to at trial. Much of the time, you can do a better job of advocacy if the client does not invent a story.

If the client is an organization, you have some special obligations. You do not represent the organization's officers or employees, even though they are the people you normally deal with. This can be difficult in a situation where the people with whom the lawyer is dealing fear damage to their careers. Rule 1.13(f) of the Model Rules of Professional Conduct requires that, when dealing with officers or employees whose "interests are adverse" to those of a client organization, you make it clear that you represent the organization and not them. The Rule's Comment adds that you "should advise . . . that [you] cannot represent such [a person,] that such person may wish to obtain independent representation[, and] that discussion between the lawyer for the organization and the individual may not be privileged." The evidentiary attorney-client privilege and the ethical duty of confidentiality belong to the client (the organization) and not to the client's officers or employees. In fact, the lawyer is obligated to tell responsible people elsewhere in the organization whatever the officers or employees tell the lawyer.

§8.4.2 HANDLING PRIVATE OR EMBARRASSING MATERIAL

If you suspect that the client will be reluctant to talk about some things because they seem embarrassing or especially private, you might wait until the end of the interview to explore them or even wait until a subsequent interview. Give the client time to appreciate that you are a person of discretion who can be entrusted with the kind of information that the client might not even be willing to tell friends about.

When you do raise the topic, begin by saying that you need to ask about something that the client might not find it easy to talk about; that you apologize for having to do so; and that you can do a good job for the client only if you ask these questions. Explain why you need to know, and remind the client of the rules on confidentiality. Then ask, respectfully but precisely.

Sometimes it helps to reverse the normal sequence of beginning with broad questions and moving toward narrow ones. Instead, start with carefully chosen narrow questions that take the client well into the subject. Then ask general questions, such as "Please tell me all about it."

§8.4.3 WHEN THE CLIENT IS DISTRAUGHT

Sometimes clients bring an enormous amount of emotional pain with them into a lawyer's office. The situation that has compelled them to seek legal assistance may be one of the most distressing things that has ever happened to them. You have just met this person. What can you do about the pain?

First, do not make superficial comments such as "Everything will be all right" or "I know how you feel." Everything will not be all right. And unless you have suffered something very similar to what the client is suffering, you do not really know how the client feels.

Second, listen, patiently and attentively, to the client's description of the most painful parts of the situation. Listen with care to anything the client says about the emotional aspect. You might be one of the few people to whom the client confides this. Try to understand, and let your tone and body language imply that you consider the emotional aspect important and are trying to understand. The fact that you are trying to understand may be a comfort to the client. Other people might not be trying to understand. You may not be able to understand fully, but your listening in a caring way may mean a great deal to the client.

Third, although you cannot honestly guarantee to solve the problem, your commitment to do the best you can may introduce hope.

§8.4.4 HANDLING POSSIBLE CLIENT FABRICATION

When you suspect falsity, the cause might be unconscious reconstruction of memory, semiconscious fudging, or conscious lying. Most clients try to tell you the truth as they understand it, which means that when the client is wrong, there is a good chance that something other than lying is involved.

Unconscious reconstruction of memory. Chapter 7 explains why this can happen, and §7.6 explains what to do about it. We are all capable of unconsciously reconstructing memory. When a client does it, that does not mean the client is a bad person.

Semiconscious fudging. Some people try to bolster their positions by putting a spin on objective facts. If something occurred three times, a person like this might say it happened "many" times (if more is better) or "barely at all" (if less is better). This can become so habitual that the person might not be fully conscious of individual exaggerations. But it is conscious in the sense that the person can stop doing it if she really wants to. When you find someone doing this, it means that even though the person might be wonderful in other ways, she is not always a reliable reporter of facts. The best thing to do is to press hard for precise answers.

Client: It happened many times.

Lawyer: How many times—exactly—did it happen?

Client: I don't know—a lot.

Lawyer: Let's list each time you can remember. On what date did the first one happen?

Client: Right after that blizzard we had last February. [*Client gives details.*]

Lawyer: When was the next time?

You have to ask these precise questions anyway with every person you interview. But with one who is fudging, you have to be firm and determined. Do not give in to a fog of vague generalities spoken by the client.

Conscious lying. Here the client deliberately tells you something that is not true. Some clients do this because they are fundamentally manipulative. But others might be generally honest people who are in desperate or embarrassing situations, are lying reluctantly, and naively do not understand that it is in their own best interests to tell you nothing but the truth.

You probably don't know for sure that the client is lying. If you become annoyed or accusatory, you may damage the attorney-client relationship irretrievably. But you do need to know the truth from the client. The best way to get that is to show the client that it is in her own interest to tell you the truth and that other people—a judge and jury, for example—will not believe what she is telling you. If you say that you do not believe the client, you are accusing the client, and the client will fight back.

Start by giving the client a motivation to tell you the truth. Explain how you can do a good job only if you know everything—including the unfavorable facts—from the beginning. You might give one or two illustrations of how disaster can happen if you learn of an unfavorable fact for the first time in the courtroom when there is no longer time to prepare. Choose illustrations that are similar to the situation the client is in.

Say that your first loyalty is to the client, and summarize the rules on attorney-client confidentiality. Do all of this before you turn to the lie you suspect you are being told.

If the client seems manipulative, you can use leading questions to box the client into a corner. Think this through very carefully. You do not want to humiliate the client, and you are not absolutely certain the client is lying.

You might explain how opposing counsel will cross-examine at trial. Tell the client that you will give a demonstration of what that will be like. Start from what is undeniably true and conduct a determined but polite cross-examination, showing the client how a disinterested fact-finder is not likely to believe what the client is saying, given how inconsistent it is with what is undeniably true. Do this in such a way that the client can begin to tell you the truth without losing dignity.

Alternatively, you can ask questions—some of them leading—based on the assumption that the truth is something other than what the client has said. Do not point out the difference between your assumption and what the client said. If the client answers the questions consistently with your assumption, you have begun to establish the truth without a confrontation.

If the client seems to be a generally honest person who might be lying out of desperation or embarrassment combined with naivete about your role as an advocate, you might use some of the same techniques. But remember that this client does not really want to lie. You can probably be more gentle than you would with a manipulative client.

§8.4.5 WHEN THE CLIENT WANTS A PREDICTION ON THE SPOT

Clients often want the lawyer to predict immediately whether the client will win or lose. In nearly all instances, you cannot make that prediction. You might have to check the law or investigate the facts, or both. And you need to think about it. Predicting hastily raises the risk of error.

But clients want assurance. What can you give them? Usually, it's enough to explain what work you will do, what issues you need to research, and what facts you need to investigate. You can add that you take the problem very seriously and want to do something about it ("I want to try to find a way to get you compensation for this injury"). Choosing a time by which you will have an answer also helps.

Some lawyers feel comfortable saying something noncommittal about what they are thinking. For example, "I'm hopeful, although I'm also worried about what the harbor master will say about the docking arrangements." Or: "It might be difficult to win unless we can find witnesses who saw the other boat exceeding the speed limit; I want to work on that right away." If these comments accurately summarize the lawyer's reaction, it seems fair to share them with the client. They are explicitly tentative and point to what the lawyer sees are the variables. It would also be prudent to tell the client that the whole situation can change based on other facts that you do not know about yet.

§8.4.6 NEGOTIATING A FEE AGREEMENT

There are four different ways for a client to pay for a lawyer's services.

The client can pay an hourly rate. In a firm, the rate will differ according to the status and experience of the lawyer (senior partner, junior partner, senior associate, junior associate). If two or more lawyers are assigned to the case, the client will be billed at different rates depending on who did what. The advantage of an hourly rate is that the client pays for exactly the amount of effort the lawyer expends. The disadvantage to the client is that the total cost of the work can only be guessed at when the client hires the lawyer. The disadvantage to the lawyer is that she needs to fill out detailed time sheets and have office staff convert them to detailed bills.

Or the client can pay a flat fee for specified work, such as $850 for an uncomplicated will. The client knows from the beginning how much the job will cost, and the lawyer does not need to keep detailed time records. But flat fees are appropriate only for very routine work where the lawyer can predict in advance how much effort the task will take.

Or the client can pay a contingency fee. Typically, the lawyer would be paid a percentage, such as 33%, of any money recovered on behalf of the client. If the client recovers nothing, the lawyer gets nothing. A contingency fee makes justice theoretically available to a client who wants to sue for money damages but cannot afford an hourly fee. In nondamages cases, a contingency fee is impractical, and in criminal and domestic relations cases, it is illegal.[10] Contingency fees are sometimes abused by lawyers, and in many states they are strictly regulated by statute or court rule.

Or the client can pay a percentage of the value of a transaction. To probate an estate, for example, a lawyer might in some situations charge a percentage of the value of the estate.

Usually, the lawyer suggests the type of fee that makes most sense from the lawyer's point of view, and the client either agrees or tries to persuade the lawyer to charge another kind of fee. Whatever the type, a fee is unethical unless "reasonable" according to the rules of ethics.[11] In addition to the fee, the client usually pays certain expenses, such as photocopying, messenger services, court reporter fees, and the like.

---

10. Model Rule 1.5(d).
11. Criteria for "reasonableness" are set out in Model Rule 1.5(a).

The appropriate time to negotiate the fee is usually in the closing part of the interview (see §8.2.6). Earlier, you do not know enough about how much work will be involved, and the client is usually not yet ready to hire you formally. The fee agreement should explicitly define the services you will provide.

Lawyers cost more—often much more—than clients want to pay, and fees generate more conflict between lawyers and clients than almost any other issue. For that reason, in a well-run law office all fee agreements are reduced to writing, usually through an engagement letter, which the lawyer sends or gives to the client. When the client countersigns it, the engagement letter becomes the contract through which the client hires the lawyer and agrees to pay the fee. A thorough engagement letter will describe the work the lawyer is to do, specify the fee and how it will be billed and paid, and so forth.

If the client is ready to hire you on the spot and wants you to start work immediately, you can ask your secretary to word-process an engagement letter quickly so the client can sign it before leaving. Otherwise, the engagement letter can be mailed to the client.

Except when the client will pay a contingency fee, lawyers usually ask for a retainer, which is a payment in advance for the first part of the lawyer's work. The retainer should be large enough to assure the lawyer that the client is serious about paying for the lawyer's work. Retainers of $2,000, $5,000, or $10,000 are common for the typical work that an individual or a family might ask a lawyer to do. Business retainers might be larger.

A careful lawyer usually will not do any work until after the client has signed an engagement letter and paid a retainer.

Many—but not all—lawyers do not charge for the initial client interview.

CHAPTER 9

INTERVIEWING WITNESSES

§9.1 HOW WITNESS INTERVIEWING IS DIFFERENT FROM CLIENT INTERVIEWING

A witness will be one of three kinds. A friendly witness wants your client to win and is willing to help. A neutral witness does not care who wins; a neutral witness either does not want to get involved or is willing to testify at trial out of a sense of obligation to the system of justice. (What makes the witness neutral is not caring who wins. What the witness observed and remembers, however, usually does help one party and hurt the other.) A hostile witness wants your client to lose—or at least wants the other side to win—and is willing to say and do things that hurt you. As we shall see, each of these kinds of witnesses needs to be handled differently.

Witness interviewing can be both easier and harder than client interviewing. It is easier because your main goal is to develop information and evidence. You are not, for example, building a professional relationship with a client or helping a client deal with a stressful situation. Witness interviewing can be harder if the witness is neutral or hostile. Out of self-interest, a client will usually tell you what you need to know. A neutral or hostile witness will not do so unless you can provide sufficient motivation.

In witness interviewing, you will use and experience many of the dynamics and techniques explained in Chapter 8. But, as we shall see, you often will follow an organization very different from the one set out in §8.2—especially when the witness will give you very little time and you need to get to the most important material almost immediately.

The three big problems of witness interviewing are

1. handling yourself ethically in a situation fraught with temptations (see §§9.2 and 9.5);
2. getting neutral and hostile witnesses to cooperate with you (see §9.3); and
3. finding out everything the witness knows (see §9.4).

§9.2 HANDLING YOURSELF ETHICALLY

Imagine that you have never been to law school and do not know much about lawyers. You see an event that becomes an issue in litigation, and a lawyer comes to see you and asks you questions about what you saw. The lawyer does not seem to like some of the details you are describing, and she implies subtly that you should say things at least slightly differently. You have a vague impression that justice is based on truth, but you are feeling pressured to say something different from the truth. This is the first time you have dealt directly with a lawyer. What are you likely to think of lawyers as a class of people?

Of all the things lawyers do to alienate the public, manipulating witnesses is high on the list. In fact, the pretrial "preparation of witnesses . . . is a practice that, more than almost anything else, gives trial lawyers their reputation as purveyors of falsehoods."[1]

In many countries outside the common law family, lawyers are actually forbidden to talk to witnesses before trial. The rules in those countries are strict, and they exist to prevent lawyers from manipulating evidence. In Germany, for example, a lawyer "virtually never [has] out-of-court contact with a witness,"[2] because, under the German rules of ethics, a lawyer "may interview witnesses out of court only when it is justified by special circumstances. He has to avoid even the appearance of influencing the witness and is, in principle, not allowed to take written statements."[3] And "German judges are given to marked and explicit doubts about the reliability of the testimony of witnesses who previously have discussed the case with counsel."[4]

When speaking with witnesses, what ethical rules will govern you as an American lawyer? In representing a client, you are not allowed to do any of the following:

- "communicate about the subject of the representation with a person [you know] to be represented by another lawyer in the matter, unless [you have] the consent of the other lawyer or [are] authorized to do so by law or a court order"[5]

---

1. David J. Luban, *Lawyers and Justice: An Ethical Study* 96 (1988).
2. John H. Langbein, *The German Advantage in Civil Procedure,* 52 U. Chi. L. Rev. 823, 834 (1985).
3. Dietrich Rueschemeyer, *Lawyers and Their Society: A Comparative Study of the Legal Professions in Germany and in the United States* 143 (1973). See also David J. Luban, *Lawyers and Justice: An Ethical Study* 96–97 (1988).
4. Benjamin Kaplan, Arthur T. von Mehren & Rudolf Schaefer, *Phases of German Civil Procedure,* 71 Harv. L. Rev. 1193, 1201 (1958).
5. Rule 4.2 of Model Rules of Professional Conduct.

- "make a false statement of material fact or law"[6]
- "state or imply [to a person not represented by counsel] that [you, as an attorney, are] disinterested"[7]
- "give legal advice to an unrepresented person, other than the advice to secure counsel if [you] know or reasonably should know" that there is "a reasonable possibility" of a conflict of interest between the unrepresented person and your client[8]
- "use means that have no substantial purpose other than to embarrass, delay, or burden a third person, or use methods of obtaining evidence that violate the legal rights of such a person"[9]

And regardless of whether you are representing a client, you may not:

- "engage in conduct involving dishonesty, fraud, deceit or misrepresentation"[10]
- "engage in conduct that is prejudicial to the administration of justice"[11]
- "request a person other than a client to refrain from voluntarily giving relevant information to another party unless: (1) the person is a relative or an employee or other agent of a client; and (2) the lawyer reasonably believes that the person's interests will not be adversely affected by refraining from giving such information"[12]
- "falsify evidence, counsel or assist a witness to testify falsely, or offer an inducement to a witness that is prohibited by law"[13]

The Comment to Model Rule 3.4 notes that "many jurisdictions make[] it an offense to destroy material for purpose of impairing its availability in a pending proceeding or one whose commencement can be foreseen. Falsifying evidence is also generally a criminal offense. [But] it is not improper to pay a witness's expenses or to compensate an expert witness on terms permitted by law." An expert witness may be compensated for services rendered, but not through a contingent fee. And a subpoenaed occurrence witness (an eyewitness to an auto accident, for example) may be paid only the statutory witness fee (typically $12 or $15 a day), plus travel expenses to the courthouse.

Lying is not only unethical; it also backfires tactically. If you lie to a witness, the odds are high that opposing counsel will learn of it and find ways to tell the judge and jury about it over and over again, greatly diminishing and perhaps destroying your value to your client as an advocate.

---

6. Model Rule 4.1(c).
7. Model Rule 4.3. "When the lawyer knows or reasonably should know that the unrepresented person misunderstands the lawyer's role in the matter, the lawyer shall make reasonable efforts to correct the misunderstanding." *Id.*
8. Model Rule 4.3.
9. Model Rule 4.4(c).
10. Model Rule 8.4(c).
11. Model Rule 8.4(d).
12. Model Rule 3.4(f).
13. Model Rule 3.4(b).

RICHARD C. WYDICK, *THE ETHICS OF WITNESS COACHING* *17 CARDOZO L. REV. 1 (1995)*

The standard wisdom about the ethics of witness coaching can be briefly stated something like this:

First, a lawyer may discuss the case with the witnesses before they testify. A lawyer in our common law adversary system has an ethical and legal duty to investigate the facts of the case, and the investigation typically requires the lawyer to talk with the witnesses—the people who know what happened on the occasion in question. . . .

Second, when a lawyer discusses the case with a witness, the lawyer must not try to bend the witness's story or put words in the witness's mouth. As an old New York disciplinary case puts it: "[The lawyer's] duty is to extract the facts from the witness, not to pour them into him; to learn what the witness does know, not to teach him what he ought to know."

Third, a lawyer can be disciplined by the bar for counseling or assisting a witness to testify falsely or for knowingly offering testimony that the lawyer knows is false. . . .

This Article divides witness coaching into three grades, as follows:

Grade One witness coaching is where the lawyer knowingly and overtly induces a witness to testify to something the lawyer knows is false. "Overtly" is used to mean that the lawyer's conduct is "openly" or "on its face" an inducement to testify falsely. Grade One witness coaching obviously interferes with the court's truth-seeking function and corrodes the morals of both the witness and the lawyer. . . .

Grade Two witness coaching is the same as Grade One, except that the lawyer acts covertly. Thus, Grade Two is where the lawyer knowingly but covertly induces a witness to testify to something the lawyer knows is false. "Covertly" is used to mean that the lawyer's inducement is masked. It is transmitted by implication. Grade Two witness coaching is no less harmful to the court's truth-seeking function than Grade One, nor less morally corrosive, nor less in breach of the lawyer disciplinary rules and perjury statutes. . . .

Grade Three witness coaching is where the lawyer does not knowingly induce the witness to testify to something the lawyer knows is false, but the lawyer's conversation with the witness nevertheless alters the witness's story. Given the malleable nature of human memory, Grade Three witness coaching is very hard to avoid. It lacks the element of corruption that Grades One and Two have, but it does alter a witness's story and can thus interfere with the court's truth-seeking function. Therefore, this Article argues, when a lawyer's conversation with a witness serves a proper purpose, such as refreshing the witness's memory, the lawyer should nonetheless conduct the conversation in the manner that is least likely to produce inaccurate testimony. . . .

Grade One Witness Coaching

In this Article, "witness coaching" means conduct by a lawyer that alters a witness's story about the events in question. . . .

Example One

As an example of overt inducement, suppose that lawyer L represents plaintiff P in a tort suit against defendant D. Suppose it is important in the case to know how far apart P and D were standing at the time in question. If the distance was 100 yards or less, that will help P's case, but if it was more than 100 yards, that will help D's case. Further, suppose that L knows that the distance was about 150 yards; she knows this from an unquestionably reliable source that is privileged and therefore unavailable to D. Finally, suppose that the following conversation takes place the first time L interviews eyewitness W, who is P's best friend and is therefore quite cooperative:

Q: At the time in question, were you standing where you could see both P and D?

A: Yes.

Q: Let me be frank. In this lawsuit it would be very helpful to P if the distance between P and D were less than 100 yards. Could you help us out on that?

A: Oh, I'm quite sure it was less than 100 yards.

L's inducement appears at lines 4–6. It is overt because one can read L's statement and fairly conclude that L is offering W a way to benefit his friend P by giving testimony that L knows is false. The inducement is not as blatant as an offer to give W a new car if he testifies favorably, or to break his legs if he testifies unfavorably, but the inducement is obvious enough from the face of L's statement to be called overt. . . .

A lie affects the liar personally in several ways. First, Professor [Sissela] Bok says, the liar knows that he lied, and that knowledge can destroy his integrity.[*] Second, after the lie, the liar must be more cautious of the people he deceived; they could discover the deception, and their discovery could ruin him. Third, lies seldom come as singles:

> It is easy, a wit observed, to tell a lie, but hard to tell only one. . . . More and more lies may come to be needed; the liar always has more mending to do. And the strains on him become greater each time—many have noted that it takes an excellent memory to keep one's untruths in good repair and disentangled. The sheer energy the liar has to devote to shoring them up is energy the honest man can dispose of freely. . . .[**]

Professor Bok's arguments apply equally to the lawyer who induces the witness to lie. In some ways the corruptor's conduct is worse than the corruptee's, and in some periods of English history, a suborner of perjury could be punished more severely than the perjurer.

---

* Sissela Bok, *Lying: Moral Choice in Public and Private Life* 24 (1978).

** *Id.* at 25.

Grade Two Witness Coaching

Grade Two witness coaching is similar to Grade One, except that the lawyer acts covertly rather than overtly. Thus, Grade Two witness coaching is where the lawyer knowingly but covertly induces a witness to testify to something that the lawyer knows is false. . . .

As used here, "covert" inducement means that the lawyer's inducement is masked. It is transmitted by implication. To use the common image, the lawyer sends the witness a message "between the lines" about how to tell the story. If the witness understands the message and wants to cooperate, he alters the story accordingly. . . .

Grade Two witness coaching is no less harmful than Grade One to the court's truth-seeking function, nor to the morals of the lawyer and witness, nor is it any less serious a violation of disciplinary rules or subornation of perjury statutes. . . .

[Now] let us suppose that plaintiff P has sued defendant D Company for millions of dollars on some civil claim, the nature of which need not concern us. One of the issues in the case involves a certain meeting between representatives of P and D Company. P asserts that at the meeting, Ms. E (a high-ranking executive of D Company) made statements X, Y, and Z. If Ms. E did make any one or all of those statements, it will benefit P's case and harm D Company's defense.

Two representatives of P were present at the meeting. D Company was represented by Ms. E, who took along her assistants Mr. A and Ms. B. Nobody else was present, and nobody else has personal knowledge of what was said at the meeting.

Suppose that lawyer L is interviewing Mr. A for the first time to find out what A remembers about the meeting. Suppose, further, that L does not know what was said at the meeting. L would . . . like to develop evidence that Ms. E did not say X, Y, or Z at the meeting. Suppose that the critical part of the interview goes like this:

Q: At the meeting, did Ms. E say X?

A: No, I am quite certain she didn't.

Q: Did she say Y at the meeting?

A: Again, I am quite certain that she did not.

Q: At the meeting, did Ms. E say Z?

A: Well, you know, as to Z, yes, I think she may very well have said Z.

Q: O.K. now, I need to make sure that I understand correctly what you are telling me. You are absolutely certain that E did not say X, is that right?

A: Yes, that's right.

Q: And you are absolutely certain that E did not say Y, is that right?

A: Yes, that's right.

Q: And as to Z, you say "I think," but you aren't certain?
Am I correct in believing that you simply do not know
one way or the other as to Z?

A: Yes, I guess that's right.

Q: So you remember for certain that she did not say X, and
you remember for certain that she did not say Y, but you
do not remember one way or the other about Z, is that
right?

A: Right.

What is happening on lines 15–17? . . . [L]awyer L is . . . making a statement that he knows is false, and he is doing it blatantly, so that A will be alert to the covert message. L's statement is false because it butchers what A said on lines 6–7. There A said he thinks that E "may very well have said Z." On lines 15–17, L turns that into a statement that A does "not know one way or the other" about Z.

Bearing in mind that A is an employee of D Company and that Ms. E is A's immediate superior, what is likely to be the covert message in lines 15–17? Isn't it something like this: "Look, A, I am trying to defend your employer, D Company, and to keep your boss, E, out of trouble—please don't tell me that E may have said Z at the meeting!" On line 18, A acquiesces in L's false paraphrase, and lines 18–23 show A agreeing to L's further refinement, a statement that A does not remember about Z one way or the other. Thus L transforms A's perhaps uncertain memory that E "may well have said" Z into a lack of memory about Z. That is an example of Grade Two witness coaching. It is unethical, and it is bad tactics as well.

What should L have done differently? Bearing in mind that this is L's first interview with A, shouldn't L be trying to find out what E really said at the meeting? Doesn't L need to know that information in order to advise D Company about whether and how to defend the case?

Focus again on A's statement on lines 6–7: "Well, you know, as to Z, yes, I think she may very well have said Z." Notice that A opens with "well," a clue that A may be uncomfortable with what he is about to say. Notice also that A says he is "quite certain" about X and Y, but he uses waffle words about Z, saying that he "thinks" Ms. E "may very well have said Z." Lawyer L should have used a series of non-leading questions to find out why A is uncomfortable and is waffling. Perhaps A simply does not like being the bearer of bad news. On the other hand, perhaps A is sincerely uncertain about statement Z. If so, why? Perhaps he could not hear well during that part of the meeting, or perhaps something has distorted his memory of that part of the meeting? Lawyer L should be trying to answer questions such as those, rather than trying to alter A's story to fit L's preconceived pattern of the case. . . .

Grade Three Witness Coaching

Grade Three witness coaching is where the lawyer does not knowingly induce the witness to testify to something the lawyer knows is false, but the lawyer's conversation with the witness nevertheless alters the witness's story. Unlike Grades One and Two, Grade Three witness coaching is not grounds for lawyer discipline or criminal prosecution for subornation of perjury. Grade Three witness coaching lacks the element of corruption that Grades One and Two have. It does, however, alter the witness's story, and can thus interfere with the court's truth-seeking function.

[P]sychologists who study human memory . . . conclude that [it] is highly malleable, that a small difference in the content of an interviewer's questions can make a big difference in the witness's story, and that new information incorporated into an interviewer's questions can mislead a witness into remembering things that he did not perceive. If those psychologists are right, then the quality of testimony is at risk when even the most ethical and prudent lawyer interviews and prepares a witness.

[But] the adversary system benefits from allowing lawyers to interview witnesses and to prepare them to testify. . . . What is needed now is a method of analysis that will give a lawyer reasonable latitude when interviewing and preparing a witness, yet will minimize the risk to the quality of the witness's testimony. . . .

The method of analysis proposed below covers all three grades of witness coaching. A lawyer can use the following steps to test the propriety of her next question or statement in an interview or preparation session with a witness:

Step One: Will my next question or statement overtly tell this witness that I want him to testify to something I know is false? If so, I could be disciplined or criminally sanctioned. If not, then—

Step Two: Will my next question or statement send a covert message to this witness that I want him to testify to something I know is false? If so, I could be disciplined or criminally sanctioned. If not, then—

Step Three: Is there a legitimate reason for my next question or statement to this witness? If there is no legitimate reason, then I should not ask the question or make the statement. If there is a legitimate reason, then—

Step Four: Am I asking the question or making the statement in the manner that is least likely to harm the quality of the witness's testimony? If not, then I should change my approach.

Non-Suggestive Interviewing

How can a lawyer get past Step Four of the proposed method of analysis when interviewing a problem witness—for example, a witness who perceived but has now forgotten; a witness who perceived but is now mistaken; or a witness who perceived and remembers but is now quaking with uncertainty? . . .

The psychologists have some recommendations that can reduce lawyers' need for the old remedies. Their recommendations must be prefaced, however, with a realistic warning from two experienced trial lawyers: every witness is different, and "no one method works successfully with all witnesses."

1. *Recall first, then recognition:* Suppose that a witness observes some detailed event such as a car crash or a price-fixing meeting. If she is later asked to state all the details she can remember about it, she might come up with only forty-five percent of the details, but she will be quite accurate about the ones she remembers. Psychologists call that kind of remembering "recall." If, instead, she were given a series of specific questions asking whether she saw this or that detail, she might be able to answer sixty-five percent of the questions with confidence, but her accuracy rate would be lower. Psychologists call that kind of remembering "recognition." Recognition produces more details but less accuracy; recall produces more accuracy but fewer details. A lawyer who needs both accuracy and details should therefore draw on both recall and recognition, and most psychologists recommend using recall first, then recognition. That is, the lawyer should open the topic with a broad question that calls for a narrative answer. (For example, "Please tell me everything you can remember about the meeting that afternoon.") After the witness has recalled all that she can, the lawyer should then ask her some narrow, specific questions that draw on her power of recognition. (For example, "At the meeting, did anybody use the term 'cutthroat bidding'?")

2. *Neutral Questions:* Small differences in the wording of questions can make large differences in a witness's responses. One well-known study concerns the two articles "a" and "the." If a witness is asked, "Did you see the thin man in the blue suit?" he will be more likely to answer affirmatively than if he had been asked, "Did you see a thin man in a blue suit?" One explanation is that "the" tips off the witness that the questioner thinks such a man was present, whereas "a" keeps the questioner in a more neutral position.

In another study of wording differences, two equivalent groups of people were asked about headaches. One group was asked, "Do you get headaches frequently, and, if so, how often?" That group reported an average of 2.2 headaches per week. The second group was asked, "Do you get headaches occasionally, and, if so, how often?" That group reported an average of 0.7 headaches per week.

Experiments of this sort suggest that a lawyer should use care in wording interview questions and should, where possible, use neutral words instead of words that reveal the lawyer's beliefs, value judgments, attitudes, desires, or expectations.

3. *Ordering of Questions:* Assume for the sake of argument that there is some kind of connection between the way we humans store information in memory and the way we retrieve it from memory. . . .

Psychologists Valerie and Peter Morris tested this hypothesis by showing a group of subjects a television clip in which the main event was an exciting chase scene. Then each person wrote out a narrative account of what he or she had seen. After that, the people were divided into four groups, and the groups were asked a set of specific questions about what they had seen. All groups were asked the same questions, but the order of the questions differed. One group got their questions in time sequence, that is, the order in which the events happened in the television clip. The second group got theirs in random order. The third group received all the questions about the main characters at the beginning, with the rest of the questions in time sequence at the end. The fourth group got all the questions about the main event (the chase) at the beginning, with the rest in time sequence at the end. In the

Morris study, the highest proportion of correct answers came from the time sequence group, with the main character group as a close second. . . .

When a lawyer starts interviewing a witness, the lawyer's mind is likely to be focused on the "main event," meaning the nucleus of facts that the lawyer hopes this witness can supply. The Morris study suggests that the lawyer's point of focus may not be the best point around which to organize the witness interview. The lawyer may do better to organize the interview on whatever pattern the witness is likely to have used when storing the information in memory.

§9.3 GETTING COOPERATION FROM NEUTRAL AND HOSTILE WITNESSES

Many *neutral* witnesses do not want to talk to you because you will create inconvenience, if not trouble, for them. They have other, more pressing things to do. Or they do not want to get caught in the middle between disputing parties. Or they suspect that if a lawyer does not like what they say, that lawyer will abuse them in court.

Hostile witnesses want you and your client to lose, and they do not want to talk to you. They like the opposing party. Or they dislike your client. Or, on principle, they think that the merits of the dispute are against your client.

How can you get neutral and hostile witnesses to talk to you? Consider your goals.

Your primary goal is to learn as much as you can from the witness. That can be done best in inquiring mode rather than persuasion mode (see §2.2.9). You will learn more if your mind is open and receptive. An additional benefit is that witnesses will trust you more easily if they think that you have an open mind.

A second goal is to make a lasting good impression. There is a fair chance that you will have to deal with this witness again, and the witness may treat you better in the courtroom if the witness has experienced you as a reasonable and fair-minded person. And sometimes hostile witnesses over time become less hostile.

One of the worst things you can do is alienate a neutral witness. Fact-finders trust neutral witnesses more quickly than they trust partisan witnesses, and a neutral witness who distrusts you can create problems for you. Neutral witnesses are sometimes more accommodating to the side of the first reasonable, friendly, and fair-minded interviewer with whom they have contact. If a neutral witness has contact with an alienating interviewer from each side, the witness may retreat from the controversy. If both interviewers make favorable impressions, the first to arrive may have an advantage.

A third goal might be to point out the witness's inconsistencies in a principled way that allows the witness to revise memory without feeling manipulated. Again, you will get more cooperation by being reasonable, fair, and open-minded than you will by trying to trick or push the witness around (§9.4 explains how).

A fourth goal might be to preserve evidence. The most common way of doing that is by writing out on the spot an account of what the witness has told you and then asking the witness to sign it (again, §9.4 explains how). Witnesses are more likely to sign if they believe that you are not trying to trick them.

Remember that what you say and how you say it will have an enormous effect on how people respond to you. Here, the first few moments of the conversation are crucial. If you cannot begin to motivate the witness with your *first few sentences*, the witness might terminate the conversation before you can get much further.

Every witness is different, and you will do better with a style that fits your personality, but here is one way to open a conversation with a witness who probably does not want to talk to you:

> Hi, Mr. Trecewski. I'm Maria Hernandez, a lawyer for Tri-City Bus Lines. I'm sorry to bother you, but I'm trying to figure out what happened last Thursday night when the bus hit the store on the corner. Could you explain it to me? I'm trying to learn exactly what happened, and the only way I can do that is to talk to the people who saw it first-hand.

What makes this opening better than some others? First, the lawyer shows respect for the witness. She calls him by name and apologizes for taking his time. Second, her words show her to be open-minded ("I'm trying to figure out what happened. . . . Could you explain it to me? I'm trying to learn exactly what happened. . . ."). Third, without seeming to be unprofessional or undignified, she impliedly puts herself in the inferior position of ignorance and asks whether he will share his superior knowledge ("the only way I can do that is to talk to the people who saw it first-hand"), which many people find it hard to resist.

If you can say something like this in a likeable way, many witnesses will tell you more than they otherwise would. Do not try to be a tough lawyer. People are more helpful to those they like, and this is a good time to show the parts of your personality that others find most likeable, if that is not inappropriate to the occasion. For some young lawyers, their earnest and sincere side is what works. For any lawyer, it might be cheerfulness and warmth.

Go to the witness's home (or workplace if necessary) and conduct the interview there. Unlike friendly witnesses, those who are neutral or hostile will not usually come to your office. Do not call ahead to say you will be coming. You will probably be told not to. Just go at a time when the witness is likely to be there. You will be imposing, but from the witness's point of view, anything you do will be an imposition anyway.

As soon as they meet resistance, some lawyers start threatening ("if you don't talk to me now, we'll have to depose you under oath in our offices before a court reporter"). This hardly ever works. Once you have threatened somebody, they will not usually cooperate, and threats are very hard to retract. Instead, threats breed counter-threats and further confrontation. And this kind of threat is hollow. A deposition is likely to be as inconvenient for you as for the witness and expensive for your client as well.

If a witness refuses to speak to you and you feel a deposition is necessary, apologize for subpoenaing the witness. Do not apologize profusely, but do it more than once. If the witness feels that you are being vindictive, you will get less information at the deposition than otherwise.

Some lawyers give little speeches about the justice of their client's cause and how the witness should want to help the client. Witnesses react to these speeches the way that most people react to speeches given by sales people. It's a good idea to humanize your client and the risks and suffering that are or could harm your client. But a sales speech is a clumsy way to do it. Instead, think of three or four things about your client that might have a sympathetic effect on this witness and mention those things—one at a time—at points in the conversation where they are germane. If you try too hard, the witness will become defensive.

Do not promise—or even imply a promise—that if the witness talks to you now, the witness need not be subpoenaed to testify at trial. You cannot guarantee that. The witness might tell you things that you need to put into evidence, and you cannot prevent opposing counsel from subpoenaing the witness.

§9.4 FINDING OUT EVERYTHING THE WITNESS KNOWS

Remember what you learned in Chapter 7 about observation and memory. Remember also the value of listening and of carefully wording questions and other things you say (see §5.2).

Interview the witness as soon as possible. The more quickly you can interview the witness, the smaller the risk that the witness's memory will be degraded by the passage of time or contaminated by the comments or questions of other people.

Before you begin, decide what you need to know. You can begin to figure out what is relevant by making a list of all the things that each party would have to prove at trial. What parts of either party's burden of proof might the witness be able to testify to, one way or the other (see Chapter 13)? Then go through the story the client has told you and the story you think the opposing party is likely to tell at trial. What can the witness add, corroborate, or contradict?

Corroboration is often neglected by inexperienced lawyers. Ask yourself: If what your client says is true, what else might naturally also be true? Suppose the client "claims she was defrauded in the door-to-door sale of a food freezer plan. She understood the salesman to say that she was leasing the freezer and could cancel at any time."[14] The company refuses now to let her do that.

> If the client's story were true, what else would be true? The following possibilities come immediately to mind: (i) the freezer, not the food plan, would be the money-maker for the company; (ii) the salesman might have . . . made similar representations to other purchasers; (iii) there may be . . . written instructions to salesmen on the sales "pitch;" (iv) complaints about similar practices may be on file with better business or consumer protection agencies; (v) the salesman may have been under some particular pressure to make sales at the time he visited [the] client.[15]

---

14. Gary Bellow & Bea Moulton, The Lawyering Process: Materials for Clinical Instruction in Advocacy 321 (1978).
15. *Id.*

What witnesses might be able to tell you whether each of these hypotheses is accurate? What will you ask those witnesses?

Conversely, if what the other side is saying is true, what else might naturally also be true? Carry it a step further. If what the other side is saying is true, what else *inevitably must* be true? If event B nearly always follows event A, and if the other side claims A happened, you should be very interested in B. If B did not happen, that can help you prove that A did not happen either. But if B did happen, then at least you have been forewarned about what your problems are. You need to know the unfavorable facts as well as the favorable ones. A hostile witness who tells you about the weaknesses in your case is doing you a favor, for which you can be grateful rather than annoyed.

Before you begin, sequence the topics you will ask about. If the witness is neutral or hostile, do not begin by asking questions that might offend the witness. Give yourself time to build rapport first. In fact, you might want to begin by asking questions that will help you build rapport, especially questions that the witness might really want to answer. If you think the witness might terminate the interview before you are finished—and that is not unusual with hostile witnesses—ask those questions to which you most need the answers as early as you can without alienating the witness.

On the other hand, if the witness is friendly, you can sequence the questions in whatever order produces the most information.

Isolate the witness during the interview. Do not allow the witness's friends or family or other witnesses to be present while you and the witness are talking. There are three reasons. First, in front of other people the witness might try to say things to earn or retain their respect or might avoid saying things that would lose their respect. Second, other people can be a distraction, and you want the witness to focus on the information you need to know. Third, other people might interject comments of their own, contaminating the witness's memory.

Build a relationship with the witness. You will have to deal with this person again. Find the things that are likeable in the witness so that when you express empathy, it is sincere. And give the witness an opportunity to like you. Even friendly witnesses do better if you are a good human being rather than a question-asking machine. And the witness might deserve some empathy. The witness might have seen a frightful event, might feel caught in the middle between warring parties, and probably has been or will be inconvenienced.

To the extent you can, conduct a cognitive interview. See §7.6. You will have the most difficulty doing this with a hostile witness who wants to stop talking to you soon.

Ask for the raw facts and the witness's source of knowledge. Do not ask for conclusions, and do not accept conclusions as answers. Find out whether the witness has the kind of knowledge that the rules of evidence require if the witness is to testify at trial. (See §8.3.1.)

Ask for all the details. You need them from witnesses just as much as you needed them from the client (see §8.3.1). Also, ask for the details that will help you find the witness many months later—for example, if you later need to subpoena the witness to testify.

Ask whether the witness has talked with anybody else about the subjects you are asking about. Sometimes the answer will surprise you. The witness might say that she has talked to your client, and that your client said some things that disappoint you. Or the witness might say that she has talked to opposing counsel and then tell you some very interesting things about that conversation.

If the witness is hostile, find out why. If the witness testifies at trial and is still hostile then, you may be able to use the hostility and its cause to impeach the testimony.

Be careful about friendly witnesses. When a witness who likes your client says things that will help you in court, that might be good news or it might be bad news. Friendly witnesses sometimes exaggerate, and exaggerations can wilt under cross-examination at trial, hurting your case. Near the beginning of the interview, tell a friendly witness that you need to know everything the witness knows, even the things that reflect badly on your client. And explain why the witness should be very precise with the facts.

If you decide to ask the witness to change the story, do it in a principled way. Suppose the witness says he drove past Maureen's Grocery at 5:05 p.m. You believe—and hope—that the time was closer to 5:15. The witness was driving home from his job and would have punched out a time card before leaving. The distance from the witness's place of work to Maureen's is two miles, over suburban streets with stop lights.

Lawyer: What time do you usually clock out?

Witness: As soon after five o'clock as possible. I'm sorry, but I'm a clock watcher. When it hits 4:59, I'm out of my chair, putting on my coat.

Lawyer: What happens if you clock out before five?

Witness: They dock your pay.

Lawyer: When's the last time they did that?

Witness: Not lately.

Lawyer: One thing puzzles me. It's two miles to Maureen's, with lots of traffic lights. How could you walk to your car and drive that distance in five minutes or less? Time is a hard thing for most people to judge. Could you be mistaken about the time?

Witness: It's possible.

Lawyer: How could we pin it down?

Witness:	I don't know.
Lawyer:	Is there any way to know for sure what time you clocked out that day?
Witness:	I could ask the bookkeeper.
Lawyer:	Tomorrow, on the way home, could you time yourself and see how long it takes you to get from the time clock to Maureen's?
Witness:	Yeah.
Lawyer:	It would be important to notice whether the traffic tomorrow is like the traffic on that day.

Why might this work? First, when the lawyer points to the inconsistency, the witness is offered a rationale that saves face ("Time is a hard thing for most people to judge"). Second, the lawyer proposes an objective method of determining what the facts should be. The lawyer has accepted the possibility that the witness might have clocked out early or in some other way gotten to Maureen's by 5:05 p.m., and that helps the lawyer maintain credibility while challenging the witness. Third, the lawyer prepared for this interview by measuring the distance from the job to Maureen's. And fourth, the witness seems open-minded about the possibility of being wrong.

On the other hand, if you decide* not *to ask the witness to change the story, carefully note all the self-impeaching things the witness says, but do not point them out to the witness. If the witness says things that will be hard for a factfinder to believe, and if you think you will not be able to change the witness's mind, do not even try. If you try and fail, a stubborn witness will be forewarned of the weaknesses in the witness's story, and by the time of trial the witness will have come up with reasons why they are not weaknesses after all. When you cross-examine at trial, you will have lost the advantage of surprise.

Instead of challenging a stubborn witness, silently note the self-impeaching things the witness is saying. Suppose the witness who drove past Maureen's Grocery (see above) has been stubborn instead of open-minded, and the lawyer has figured that out early in the interview:

Lawyer:	What time did you drive past Maureen's Grocery?
Witness:	Five minutes after five in the afternoon.
Lawyer:	Where were you traveling from and to?
Witness:	I was going home from work.
Lawyer:	Where do you work?
Witness:	Donatelli's Sheet Metal, over on Aurora Boulevard.
Lawyer	Do they make you punch out on a time clock?
Witness:	Yeah.
[Lawyer thinks:	*"Good. We'll be able to prove when this guy left work."]*

Lawyer:	What time do you usually clock out?
Witness:	As soon after five o'clock as possible. I'm sorry, but I'm a clock watcher. When it hits 4:59, I'm out of my chair and putting on my coat.
[Lawyer thinks:	*"This is wonderful. Donatelli's is two miles from Maureen's. And he thinks he drove that in five minutes or less."]*
Lawyer:	What happens if you clock out before five?
Witness:	They dock your pay.
Lawyer:	When's the last time they did that?
Witness:	Not lately.
[Lawyer thinks:	*"OK. I'll subpoena Donatelli's clock-out records for that day, and I'll have an investigator drive the route at five o'clock and see how long it takes. If this guy testifies to the 5:05 time at trial, I'll impeach him with the clock-out records and the investigator will testify to how long it took."]*

Evaluate the witness's value in court. See §8.3.1.

At the end, ask whether the witness knows anything else about the case that you have not asked about. You cannot think of everything, and some witnesses will tell you what you missed.

Take a written statement on the spot. While the witness is explaining the story, listen carefully. You might make a few written notes, but concentrate on listening and on asking whatever questions are needed to clarify the story.

After you have heard everything, tell the witness that you would like to write everything out because you do not want to get anything wrong. Write out the statement in pen. At the top of the first page, write something like this:

> Statement of Alan Trecewski, 996 Fortenbaugh Lane, Waynesboro, taken by Maria Hernandez, attorney for Tri-City Bus Lines, on February 2, 1999.

Include the identity of your client here so that the witness cannot later claim that you misrepresented whom you are working for.

Then write out what the witness has told you. Include the evidentiary foundation (how the witness knows these things), as well as all the details the witness can remember.

Read aloud each sentence as you write it and watch the witness for nods of agreement or some form of objection. If the witness seems unhappy with the way you have worded something, cross it out and substitute whatever words the witness prefers. When you are finished, count the pages and then write on each page its number and the total ("page 4 of 7," for example). Then write something like this on the last page:

I read this seven-page statement on February 2, 2015, and it is accurate.

Ask the witness to read the statement and to point out anything that should be changed. When the witness is finished, ask the witness to initial every cross-out and change, to initial each page, and to sign on the last page. After the witness is finished, look at every page to make sure that the witness did not miss anything that should be initialed. Finally, offer to mail the witness a photocopy of the statement if the witness wants one, or to photocopy it on the spot if a copier is handy.

A friendly witness will almost always do all of this for you. A neutral or hostile witness might, too, if you have built a good relationship. Do not be surprised, however, if a neutral or hostile witness cuts you off at some point. The witness might, for example, read the statement but refuse to initial or sign it. But go as far along in this process as the witness will let you.

If the witness refuses to sign and initial the statement, ask the witness whether the statement is true. If the witness says yes, write on the last page that the witness has read the statement, has told you the statement is accurate, but prefers not to sign it. Then you sign.

You want this statement for two reasons. The first is that psychologically it freezes the witness's recollection: the next time the witness is asked, by opposing counsel or anybody else, the witness's memory will tend to resemble the statement as written. If opposing counsel or somebody else tries to manipulate the witness's memory, the statement will help prevent that. The second reason is to provide a means of impeachment if the witness testifies differently at trial.

§9.5 HANDLING YOURSELF ETHICALLY (REVISITED)—WHO SHOULD INTERVIEW THE WITNESS?

You cannot function as both an advocate and a witness in the same trial, which means that, with very limited exceptions, you are not permitted to represent a client at a trial where you are "likely to be a necessary witness."[16] If the witness testifies to a different story at trial, you may need to impeach the witness by putting into evidence whatever the witness told you.

On cross-examination, you could ask the witness if she or he made a contrary statement to you, but if the witness says no and if the witness did not sign a statement, then the only way to impeach is for you to testify about the interview. If you have a written statement signed by the witness, you can, on cross-examination, ask the witness if the signature on the last page and all the initials were made by the witness, but you would still have to testify if the witness denies the signature or invents a tale about how you tricked the witness into signing the statement.

How can you prevent these problems? There are several steps you can take, none of them completely satisfactory.

16. Rule 3.7 of the Model Rules of Professional Conduct.

1. ***Hire an investigator to do the interviewing instead.*** If you need to impeach at trial, the investigator can testify. And some witnesses will feel less threatened when approached by an investigator than if approached by a lawyer. But using an investigator has two disadvantages. First, the investigator might not do a complete job, being less familiar than you with both the case and the law. Second, you must supervise the investigator closely to make sure that the investigator does not violate any of the ethical rules discussed at §9.2. If the investigator violates any of them, you might be held personally accountable.[17]
2. ***Ask another lawyer in your firm or organization to interview the witness.*** This might not be better than using an investigator. Although the other lawyer would have a better sense of the legal context and the ethical rules, don't count on finding a colleague with time to spare whenever you need to interview a neutral or hostile witness. And in some states, local rules might limit the colleague's testimony in a trial where you are acting as an advocate.
3. ***Interview the witness yourself, but take along an audio recording device.*** That might enable you to impeach the witness at trial without testifying yourself. But many witnesses would be frightened into silence under these circumstances.
4. ***Interview the witness yourself but take along with you a nonlawyer from your firm.*** If you need to impeach at trial, the nonlawyer can testify to what the witness told you. During the interview, the nonlawyer can be put in the role of assisting you. But many witnesses will be at least somewhat inhibited if confronted by two people rather than one. For that reason, the best nonlawyer to take with you is someone who is very reliable but appears completely unthreatening.
5. ***Interview the witness yourself, alone, and hope that the witness will sign a statement.*** If your hopes are frustrated, the judge has some discretion to let you testify, but typically you will not be allowed to.

What do most lawyers do? Audio recorders are very rarely used. Sending another lawyer in the firm is most typically done where one lawyer (usually a partner) is going to do all the courtroom work and another lawyer (usually an associate) is helping the courtroom lawyer prepare and therefore is already familiar with the case and available to interview witnesses.

Otherwise, lawyers choose among the remaining three options—sending an investigator, taking a nonlawyer, or interviewing alone—depending on the resources available and the nature of the witness. If the witness is friendly, most lawyers are quite comfortable interviewing the witness alone. If a lawyer distrusts a witness, the lawyer might send an investigator or take a nonlawyer.

---

17. Model Rule 5.3.

PART

III

PERSUASIVE FACT ANALYSIS

CHAPTER

10

HOW WE ORGANIZE AND THINK ABOUT FACTS

§10.1 FACTS IN THE LAWYERING PROCESS

Throughout the representation of a client, you deal with facts. When a client comes into the office for an interview—regardless of whether she wants to recover for injury in an accident, to defend a claim on a contract, to purchase some real property, or to plan her estate—the client provides you with facts, not a list of legal theories. In preparing a case, you will often devote far more time to fact investigation than to legal research. During most negotiations, lawyers focus as much (if not more) of their attention on the facts of the case as they do on the applicable law. At trial, witnesses testify in regard to the facts as they know them, lawyers address the facts in opening statements and closing arguments, and also argue about the facts in pretrial and trial motions. In every appeal, briefs will be introduced by a "statement of the facts," and oral arguments will often center on disputes as to findings of fact. And even in the transactional context—the drafting of a will or a contract, for example—you must investigate and assemble facts in a form that represents the client's "story."

Unfortunately, we spend very little time in law school addressing issues of how to investigate, organize, and present facts. As Kim Lane Scheppele notes, we take the position that "[l]aw is what needs to be interpreted, but facts are simply true or false. Theories of interpretation are overwhelmingly about how to read legal texts, and the various strategies of interpretation provide orienting rules in understanding these texts. . . . Understanding the facts drops out as an uninteresting or unchallenging or irrelevant part of the process."[1] Once in practice, lawyers are expected to develop "on the job" the skills for investigating facts, organizing the facts discovered, and designing persuasive factual theories.

This chapter and Chapters 11 through 17 introduce methods for understanding, interpreting, and investigating the facts in a case. These chapters discuss the nature of facts, models for organizing facts, methods for investigating facts, and strategies for responding to the facts presented by your adversary. We will look to research in the areas of cognitive psychology, cultural anthropology, linguistics, literary criticism, and even film theory to explore issues of fact interpretation. This is not a text on evidence law. Throughout your development of a factual theory, you will, of course, have to consider the constraints of evidentiary and other procedural rules of the forum on your final presentation. But putting most procedural issues aside, these chapters will focus on the character and use of facts in the lawyering process.

§10.2 SCHEMAS AND THE PROCESSING OF INFORMATION

A "fact," the dictionary says, is "what . . . really happened."[2] As we all know from common experience, however, that definition is not quite so simple. Two people can see the same event but have two entirely different accounts of "what really happened." And the same person can witness an occurrence, relate one version of the story on one day but a few weeks later embellish the details of "what really happened," leave out other details, and give a very different account of the event. Moreover, a person can tell a story of "what really happened" to a group of people, and each member of the group can come away differing in his or her own retelling of the tale.

These different versions of "what really happened," cognitive scientists tell us, result from the manner in which we process and organize information.[3] We are constantly bombarded by stimuli from our environment. Our perception and

---

1. Kim Lane Scheppele, *Facing Facts in Legal Interpretation,* 30 Representations 42, 43–44 (1990) (footnote omitted).
2. *American College Dictionary* 431 (1964).
3. The following sources were consulted in writing this section and can be referred to for further reading on the subject of schemas: W. Lance Bennett & Martha S. Feldman, *Reconstructing Reality in the Courtroom: Justice and Judgment in American Culture* (1981); Susan Engel, *Context Is Everything: The Nature of Memory* 28–29 (1999) (describing research showing that babies begin to develop schemas by the time they are 10 months old); Hendall Haven, *Story Proof: The Science Behind the Startling Power of Story* (2007); Mark Cammack, *In Search of the Post-Positivist Jury,* 70 Ind. L.J. 405 (1995); Gerald P. Lopez, *Lay Lawyering,* 32 UCLA L. Rev. 1 (1984); Jean M. Mandler & Nancy S. Johnson, *Remembrance of Things Passed: Story Structure and Recall,* 9 Cognitive Psychol. 111 (1977); Albert J. Moore, *Trial By Schema: Cognitive Filters in the Courtroom,* 37 UCLA L. Rev. 273 (1989); Kim Lane Scheppele, *Forward: Telling Stories,* 87 Mich. L. Rev. 2073 (1989); Richard K. Sherwin, *The Narrative Construction of Legal Reality,* 18 Vt. L. Rev. 681 (1994).

recall of these "facts" are filtered and organized through "schemas," "mental blueprints that we carry around in our heads for quick assessments" of what we think should be happening in a particular situation.[4] When we witness an event, we process the "facts" we perceive by using our "schemas."

When, on Halloween night, for example, a masked and costumed child rings your doorbell with a brown bag in his hand, you assume, based on your prior experiences, that he is trick or treating and that you should place some candy or other goodie in the bag. If you had no experience with Halloween, you might assume that the child is attempting to rob you, has a mental illness and needs shelter for the night, or is soliciting for some exotic religious cult. Our perception of that incident is not merely a passive procedure by which all the data are merely input into our brains. Rather, it is a constructive process in which we filter and organize information according to previously developed cognitive structures.

Schemas serve a number of functions in the perception and recall of information. In regard to perception, they help us give meaning to information we see and hear and direct us to those significant facts to which we should pay attention. They help us keep track of the infinite number of details thrown at us in a given situation. In this way, they "give meaning to [our] every circumstance by reducing the complexity of all that exists. In order that something might be understood, most reality is disregarded."[5] When we go to a restaurant, for example, and a person comes to our table with a pad and pencil, we do not expect that the person is going to ask for an autograph or take dictation, but without giving the situation a second thought, we anticipate that the person will take our order.

In terms of recall, schemas help us draw inferences about what happened in the past. If we cannot remember a particular part or the details of an event, we can reconstruct that portion based on schemas of what we infer should have occurred in that situation. If, for example, an employee had an argument with her boss and cannot remember everything that the boss said to her, she will fill in the details of the conversation based on her schema of the personality of her boss and past experiences with him.

There are several types of schemas. "Script" schemas concern events, such as a baseball game, a doctor's visit, or the administering of the LSAT exam, in which a particular sequence of causally related events is expected to occur. When we go to a restaurant, for example, we expect to be seated, to be given a menu, to have our order taken, and to be served. "Role" schemas relate to occupations, social roles, or social groups. Each of us, for instance, has a schema about doctors, lawyers, sanitary workers, New Yorkers, Texans, stock brokers, landlords, and tenants. Finally, "person" schemas concern different personality types. Our inference about how Homer Simpson will react during church services is quite different from the response we would expect from Ned Flanders.

Obviously, we all do not have the same schemas. Some develop from the region or culture in which we live. Others evolve from the ethnic, racial, religious, or social group to which we belong. And still others depend on our individual prior

---

4. Sherwin, *supra* note 3, at 700. The cognitive structures we refer to as "schemas" have also been termed "frames," "scripts," and "stock stories."
5. Lopez, *supra* note 3, at 19.

experiences and observations about the way situations occur and persons behave. Whatever their source, one individual's schemas may be very different from another's and, as a result, their versions of "what really happened" in a particular circumstance may vary broadly.

In the context of representation of a client, the concept of schemas is very important to fact analysis. The information your client reports to you is based upon her perception of the events—based on her own schemas. The same, of course, is true of your adversary's version. This does not mean that one side is necessarily lying and the other is telling the truth. Rather, it is the result of the fact that we all perceive and organize information based on individual schemas. As Kim Lane Scheppele observes in the context of trial decision-making:

> Judges and jurors are not witnesses to the events at issue; they are witnesses to stories about the events. And when litigants come to court with different stories, some are accepted and become "the facts of the case" and others are rejected and cast aside. Some of what is cast aside may indeed be false (and some of what is accepted may be too). But some of the rejected stories may be accurate versions of events that grow from experiences different from the experiences of those who are doing the choosing.[6]

The findings of fact of "what really happened" in a case can, therefore, hinge to a certain degree on the schemas of the different witnesses and those of the fact-finder. Even given the same legal standards, it is possible in a given case that the decision might differ depending on the different schemas of the witnesses presented and the particular judges or jurors.

In the transactional context, too—negotiating a contract, for example—"what is really happening" can vary depending on the schemas of the parties. In a negotiation between a manufacturer and a distributor for the sale of goods, for example, the perception of events by parties who have had a longstanding, amicable relationship may be very different from those of parties who have had no previous dealings and who feel that they have been burned in recent, similar transactions.

§10.3 DIFFERENT MODES OF THINKING ABOUT FACTS

Another helpful contribution of psychologists to lawyers' understanding of the fact-finding process is the notion that people have two very different modes of thinking about facts. As James White describes,

> We all know how to talk about war and can carry on the arguments for and against a particular one, balancing costs and benefits, rights and wrongs. But when the story of a single wartime death is told—how it happens and what it means to the victim, to his family, to the killer—it fills the mind, and who can then go on to justify a war with words and reasons? You have perhaps seen conversations come

6. Scheppele, *supra* note 3, at 2082–2083.

to an end at such a point, one side consumed by the story, the other resisting it as irrelevant or emotional, neither satisfied with his response.[7]

Jerome Bruner contends that people use these two modes of thought—paradigmatic and narrative—in ordering their experience.[8] Fact-finders—judges, jurors, agency officials—are not first-hand observers of the events at issue. They must reconstruct reality—"what really happened"—based on the testimony of witnesses and arguments presented by the lawyers. Based on these presentations, they come to their own conclusions about what really happened. The distinction between paradigmatic and narrative thought is helpful in understanding how fact-finders engage in this reconstruction process.

The paradigmatic mode of thought "attempts to fulfill the ideal of a formal, mathematical system of description and explanation."[9] This type of thought is the domain of mathematics, logic, and science, in which abstract principles guide the search for truth. Using this mode of thought, we approach a problem as if it is a mathematical proof: given certain general propositions, if the requisite facts exist, then a particular conclusion is required. Treating issues like algebra problems, we search for the "truth" in a given situation.

Legal argument is primarily framed in terms of paradigmatic thinking. Statutes, case law, or administrative regulations provide an organizing structure for finding the "truth" in a given case. They set forth the necessary elements for a claim or defense, and the lawyers prove their claims by presenting facts in support of the required elements. In a jury trial, jurors are given instructions as to these elements and are directed to structure their decision-making according to those instructions. Appellate judges use this same rational approach to justify their decisions. They identify the legal elements applicable to the case, review the trial court record to marshal the facts establishing each of the elements, and then determine whether the relevant legal standards have been met. The general rules and principles derived in the context of the facts of that particular appeal are later applied by decision-makers in subsequent cases.

But thinking is not limited to this paradigmatic mode. While paradigmatic thinking addresses primarily the rational part of ourselves, narrative thinking attempts to speak not only to our rational side, but also to the "emotional,

---

7. James B. White, *The Legal Imagination* 865 (1973).
8. Jerome Bruner, *Actual Minds, Possible Worlds* 11–43 (1986). Besides this text, the following sources were consulted in writing this section and can be referred to for further reading on the subject of different modes of thinking and legal decision-making: Anthony G. Amsterdam & Jerome Bruner, *Minding the Law* (2000); Bennett & Feldman, *supra* note 3; Bernard S. Jackson, *Narrative Theories and Legal Discourse*, in *Narrative in Culture* 23, 24 (Cristopher Nash ed. 1990); Philip N. Meyer, *Storytelling for Lawyers* (2014); Janice Schuetz & Kathryn H. Snedaker, *Communication and Litigation: Case Studies of Famous Trials* 96–97 (1988); Cammack, *supra* note 3; Reid Hastie, *The Role of "Stories" in Civil Jury Judgments*, 32 U. Mich. J.L. Reform 227 (1999); Lopez, *supra* note 3, at 22; Nancy Pennington & Reid Hastie, *A Cognitive Theory of Juror Decision Making: The Story Model*, 13 Cardozo L. Rev. 519 (1991); Scheppele, *supra* note 1, at 42; Richard K. Sherwin, *Law Frames: Historical Truth and Narrative Necessity in a Criminal Case*, 47 Stan. L. Rev. 39 (1994); David Dante Troutt, *Screws, Koon, and Routine Aberrations: The Use of Fictional Narratives in Federal Police Brutality Prosecutions*, 74 N.Y.U. L. Rev. 18 (1999); Steven L. Winter, *The Cognitive Dimension of the Agon Between Legal Power and Narrative Meaning*, 87 Mich. L. Rev. 2225, 2228, 2259–2260 (1989).
9. Bruner, *supra* note 8, at 12.

irrational, mystical, needing, loving, [and] hating" parts of ourselves.[10] It does this by structuring facts in the context of stories. Unlike paradigmatic thinking, which applies general principles to the facts to ascertain the "truth" in a situation, narrative thinking places the facts in the context of a particular story to provide "meaning" for that situation.

A story presents the facts as a causal chain of events describing the development of a situation, its climax, and eventually its outcome. It does not, however, merely relate a sequence of events. By focusing on specific details and ignoring others, by highlighting certain tensions between the characters and the circumstances in which they find themselves, by arranging events in a certain order, or by using particular language or symbols, a story attempts to endow the facts with a given meaning. "A circumstance that [might] resist[] reduction into some authoritative and unambiguous proposition [in a paradigmatic formula] may be persuasively expressed in all its complexity in a well-told story."[11]

Psychologists tell us that narrative thinking pervades our whole life. Like schemas, stories serve a "screening function." When we witness an event, they help us organize the large amounts of information we perceive. We filter out details that we consider extraneous and include others that we consider essential.

> Narrative . . . differs from purely logical [thinking] in that it takes for granted that the puzzling problems with which it deals do not have a single "right" solution—one and only one answer that is logically permissible. It takes for granted, too, that a set of contested events can be organized into alternative narratives and that a choice between them may depend upon perspective, circumstances, interpretive frameworks.[12]

When we are involved in or witness an automobile accident, for example, we focus on certain aspects of the event and the parties and ignore others, structuring a story for ourselves of "what is really happening." Likewise, when we later recall the accident, our recollection is in story form, attempting to give meaning to the myriad facts which we previously observed. Then, when we recount the accident to someone else, we tell it in story form, emphasizing those features that we consider important to the listener but ignoring others that we view as irrelevant. And finally, a listener hearing the story reconstructs it according to the listener's own point of view. At any of these stages—perception, recall, recounting, or listening—different participants or observers may develop radically different stories, depending upon their vantage points, personal interests, emotional states, or individual schemas. Each of those persons may experience a situation differently and give it different meaning.

Besides their screening function, stories provide a means for understanding the "Troubles" that people encounter in their lives. When people strive to attain certain goals, they sometimes face unexpected dangers and obstacles along the way. Stories help the participants in these events and onlookers to create meaning from these situations. Depending on the spin we give the facts, the version of the

---

10. Lopez, *supra* note 3, at 34–35.
11. *Id.* at 29.
12. Amsterdam & Bruner, *supra* note 8, at 141.

story can range from comedic to tragic. "It is through narratives that we come to see people [coping with their Troubles] as heroes, villains, tricksters, stooges (and so forth) and that we come to see situations as victories, humiliations, career opportunities, tests of character, menaces to dignity (and so forth)."[13]

This distinction between paradigmatic and narrative thinking has much significance for lawyers' representation of clients. The legal process entails both modes of thought. Obviously, much legal work requires paradigmatic thinking. Lawyers, judges, and jurors all are constrained somewhat by the requirements of established legal doctrine and attempt to fit the facts presented into the applicable legal formulas. Often, we hear judges and jurors complain that they had no option in a case other than to render a particular decision because of the "requirements of the law." They feel that their decisions are compelled by the legal requirements.

But since all legal problems are at base human problems, and narrative thinking is part of our nature, storytelling is also an essential part of legal decision-making. The primary sources of facts are witnesses who observed or participated in certain events. They engaged in narrative thinking during their observations of the relevant events to give those circumstances meaning, concentrating only on the information they considered significant and filtering out the rest. And, at trial, despite the admonition "to tell the whole truth," as witnesses they recount these stories, again focusing on those details they now consider important and downplaying others. Even when documentary or other recorded evidence is offered, it is presented in the context of an overall story.

As the witnesses tell their stories, fact-finders (judges, jurors, administrative officials) construct their own story about "what really happened." Cognitive scientists tell us, for example, that jurors do not merely tape record the testimony in their heads throughout the trial in order to plug it into legal formulas at the conclusion of the trial or hearing. Rather, they impose a narrative story organization on the evidence as it is presented. They attempt to find their own meaning from the differing, and perhaps inconsistent, stories they hear from the witnesses, focusing on certain aspects of the evidence, ignoring others. They strive to provide meaning to the Trouble that is the focus of the case. When they ultimately make their decision, they try to determine not only whether a specific event occurred, but also whether it could have occurred in the context of the story they have developed in their minds. As the Supreme Court has observed,

> Unlike an abstract premise, whose force depends on going precisely to a particular step in a course of reasoning, a piece of evidence may address any number of separate elements, striking hard just because it shows so much at once; the account of a shooting that establishes capacity and causation may tell just as much about the triggerman's motive and intent. Evidence thus has force beyond any linear scheme of reasoning, and as its pieces come together a narrative gains momentum, with power not only to support conclusions but to sustain the willingness of jurors to draw the inferences, whatever they may be, necessary to reach an honest verdict. This persuasive power of the concrete and particular is often essential to the capacity of jurors to satisfy the obligations that the law places on them. A

---

13. *Id.* at 46.

> syllogism is not a story, and a naked proposition in a courtroom may be no match for the robust evidence that would be used to prove it.[14]

For a lawyer, the concept of narrative thinking "means that, within certain limits, disputants have some escape from . . . the reality of the dispute."[15] In other words, the decision in a case may result as much (or more) from the nature of the stories presented by the parties as it does from the "truth" or "falsity" of a story. An experienced lawyer knows that sometimes it is easier to "prove" something through persuasion than to know whether it is true.

Indeed, one study of responses to storytelling starkly confirms this point. In this study, 85 college students were each asked to compose stories about themselves or what they had done and to tell their stories to the remaining students. Half were directed to tell false stories. The other half were instructed to tell true stories. The audience members were then told to record their evaluations of the truth or falsity of each story told. The results of this study showed that the assessments of the truth of the different stories were not related to the actual truth or falsity of the story. Instead, the researchers found that the believability of stories was correlated with the storyteller's ability to craft a well-structured story.[16] Accordingly, even if you present a wealth of evidence in support of your case, you may not convince the decision-maker if you fail to present a believable story. Conversely, even if you have only limited evidence, you might succeed if you can construct a persuasive story.

You need, therefore, to understand how narratives are constructed. As lawyers tell stories—to adversaries, judges, jurors, or agency officials—these audiences develop their own story of "what really happened" based on their own schemas and notions of what is supposed to happen in certain situations. Accordingly, in constructing a story—to present in a negotiation or at trial—you need to be aware of what makes a story meaningful for your audience so that you can attempt to influence the listener's reconstruction of the story.

Our job then as lawyers is not only to assemble the relevant legal doctrine in support of our clients' cases but also to construct the facts in the case in terms of the audience's narrative thinking. We will not gain an understanding of that thinking by browsing in law libraries. Rather, we will discover it by watching television shows, films, and YouTube videos; listening to podcasts and popular music; reading blogs and mainstream publications, such as *Us Weekly and USA Today*; online social networking; and paying close attention to the "stock stories" reflected in our daily conversations and banter. "As in politics and advertising, effective lawyering requires a familiarity and facility with commonly shared

---

14. *Old Chief v. United States*, 519 U.S. 172, 187, 189 (1997); see also *Wiggins v. Smith*, 539 U.S. 510, 537 (2003) (holding that a defense attorney provided constitutionally ineffective representation to his client in the sentencing phase of a death penalty case because he showed only one mitigating factor—the fact that the defendant had no prior convictions—and failed to present the defendant's "powerful mitigating narrative" of an "excruciating life history").
15. Bennett & Feldman, *supra* note 3, at 33. *See also* Amsterdam & Bruner, *supra* note 8, at 111; Janet Malcolm, *The Crime of Sheila McGough* 26 (1999) ("all attorneys know . . . truth is a nuisance in trial work. The truth is messy, incoherent, aimless, boring, absurd. The truth does not make a good story; that's why we have art."). Obviously, these insights raise some important ethical issues. See *infra* §13.8.
16. Bennett & Feldman, *supra* note 3, at 69–83.

meaning-making tools as well as commonly shared meanings. In short, lawyers must know what's in our popular culture toolkits."[17]

While many lawyers have the intuitive ability to identify the appropriate "narrative frame" for a given case, others of us were not born with that facility and must learn the craft of narrative design.

Chapters 11, 12, and 13 explain how lawyers can use these insights from cognitive psychology—schemas, paradigmatic thinking, and narrative thinking—to organize facts persuasively through three different methods of organizing the facts: the legal elements model (Chapter 11), the chronological model (Chapter 12), and the story model (Chapter 13). Each model addresses different approaches people use in processing facts and can help you test the persuasiveness of facts you unearth in investigating a case. Chapter 14 explains how to select the model best suited for presentation to a given audience.

---

17. Richard K. Sherwin, *When Law Goes Pop: The Vanishing Line between Law and Popular Culture* 25–26 (2000). As Jerome Bruner notes, "A novelist friend of mine spent months in Naples, getting a feel for its sights and smells while preparing to write a novel set there. A litigating attorney might do well to steep herself in novels and plays about the matter at hand before devising a strategy for her case." Jerome Bruner, *Making Stories: Law, Literature, Life* 13 (2002).

CHAPTER

11

THE LEGAL ELEMENTS MODEL OF ORGANIZING FACTS

As you learned in §10.3, much legal decision-making requires a paradigmatic mode of thought. From cases, statutes, or regulations, lawyers and judges extract general propositions (legal rules) which they attempt to apply to the facts of a given case. The facts are significant only in so far as they support a legal claim or defense.

One model that lawyers use in organizing the facts is to focus on legal rules that will be applied to those facts. The process of organizing facts in the context of legal rules has three stages. First, you identify the legal elements for a claim or defense. The elements identify the facts the plaintiff must prove to establish a prima facie case (or that the defendant must establish to support an affirmative defense or counterclaim). You already know how to discover which elements are required for a particular cause of action or defense by carefully reading and interpreting relevant case law, statutes, or regulations. For a common law breach of contract claim, for example, the elements would be (1) offer, (2) acceptance, (3) consideration, (4) breach, and (5) damages. For an accusation in a criminal case of first degree assault, the elements might be (1) intent, (2) to cause serious physical injury, (3) to another person, (4) causes such injury to such person or to a third person, and (5) by means of a deadly weapon or a dangerous instrument.

After identifying the applicable elements, restate the elements as "factual propositions."[1] In other words, express each element in the context of the facts of the case. Court decisions and statutes generally provide what must be proved, for instance, in any contract case or first degree assault action to establish a prima facie case. Factual propositions identify what evidence must be presented by the plaintiff or prosecutor to establish that element. They also assist the defendant's lawyer in determining the elements to admit or contest. Finally, factual propositions express what findings the decision-maker must ultimately make in order for the plaintiff or prosecutor to prevail.

Finally, under the legal elements model, you need to marshal the facts discovered in support of each factual proposition to determine if a prima facie case can be established. For the plaintiff or prosecution, identify each item of evidence (e.g., testimony of the client, testimony of a third party, admission by the opposing party, or document) you can present at trial to prove each factual proposition. For the defendant, identify those factual propositions that you will admit in your pleadings and then marshal the evidence challenging each of the contested factual propositions.

To illustrate the use of this model, let us assume that we represent a tenant in a case who has come to our office complaining about the conditions in her apartment. Here are excerpts from the June 20, 1996, initial interview memo of the client:

> Susan Ransom is a 28-year-old mother of two children (ages two and four). She lives on the second floor of 289 Hudson Street; the first floor is an upholstery store. Her apartment and the store are the only units in the building. She moved into the apartment on January 5, 1996, with her husband, Keith Ransom. In February, Mr. and Mrs. Ransom separated, and he no longer lives in the apartment. She has a written lease with the landlord, Samuel Dusak, and pays $650.00 a month rent.
>
> Ever since she moved into the apartment, she has had problems. During the third or fourth week of January, she didn't have enough heat because the furnace was not functioning properly. She called Mr. Dusak, but it took him until the beginning of February to send out a plumber. Even then, throughout the winter, the temperature would drop into the low fifties in her apartment at night. Her children came down with bronchitis, and she has doctor bills for $250.00.
>
> In late February, after a large snowstorm, the roof began leaking in her bedroom. Now, every time it rains, there is a downpour in her bedroom. She is unable to sleep in the bedroom and sleeps on the couch in the living room. She has called Mr. Dusak, who sent a roofer out in April. Mr. Dusak says the leak has been fixed, but in a heavy storm, there's still a problem.
>
> In late March, she began having a roach problem. She tried using Raid but to no avail. Finally, she called Mr. Dusak around April 12, who yelled at her that he had never previously had a roach problem in that apartment and that she must be the cause of it. On April 19 at 8:00 in the morning, an exterminator arrived at the apartment unannounced, but Ms. Ransom was leaving for work and told him to call back to make an appointment. He never came back. She did not call Mr. Dusak again about this problem because she did not want to be yelled at again.

---

1. See Albert J. Moore et al., *Trial Advocacy: Inferences, Arguments, and Techniques* 10–22 (1996).

The whole apartment is now infested with roaches. She called the Health Department on May 6, which sent out an inspector, Tom Daniels.

Ms. Ransom brought a number of documents to the interview. She has a lease for the term January 1, 1996 to December 31, 1997 for 289 Hudson Street which is signed by Samuel Dusak, landlord, and Keith Ransom, tenant, and dated December 15, 1995. She also has rent receipts for January through June 1996 acknowledging payment of rent by Susan Ransom. She also brought to the interview a letter dated April 22, 1996 from Samuel Dusak to her which states, in part:

> In regard to your complaint about roach infestation, I sent an exterminator to your apartment on April 19. He told me that you refused to allow him to exterminate the apartment. I cannot help you with your problem unless you cooperate. Please call me immediately so we can reschedule the appointment. I should also note that the exterminator told me that he noticed open boxes of food on the drain board. As I told you on the phone, unless you keep your apartment clean, you will not get rid of the roaches.

Finally, Ms. Ransom brought us a report from the Health Department, signed by Tom Daniels and dated May 8, 1996, which states that he inspected 289 Hudson on May 6, and that he found moderate swarming of roaches in the kitchen and a few roaches in other areas of the apartment.

In our state, the applicable statute provides:[2]

Property Code §500

(a) In every written or oral lease for residential premises, the landlord shall be deemed to warrant to the tenant that the premises so leased are fit for human habitation.

(b) Any landlord who violates the warranty provided in paragraph (a) shall be liable to the tenant for actual damages caused by the violation, and, if the violation was knowing, for punitive damages.

(c) When any violation of the warranty described in paragraph (a) has been caused by the misconduct of the tenant or persons under his or her control or direction, the landlord shall not be liable for that violation.[3]

With this background, you can organize the facts in a legal elements chart. This and the other charts in this book reflect the kind of thinking used by effective lawyers in preparing cases. While experienced lawyers might not take the time to write down their thinking in a chart format, we suggest that you do so until you know thoroughly how to use the analytical process involved.

---

2. After our interview with the client, we would, of course, consider all the possible claims Ms. Ransom might have against Mr. Dusak. For purposes of this discussion, however, we will limit our analysis to a breach of warranty of habitability claim.
3. See N.Y. Real Prop. Law §235-b (McKinney 2006).

Under the legal elements model for organizing facts, we first identify the elements for a cause of action under the statute. It is also helpful to identify the source of the element (the statutory provision or court case) for later reference in any legal memorandum or brief and for assessment of the sufficiency of your proof (see §15.1). Reading the statute word-by-word, we discover the elements that are listed in Chart 11A for a breach of the warranty of habitability.

CHART 11A SOURCES OF LEGAL ELEMENTS

	Elements	Source
1	Written or oral lease	Property Code §500(a)
2	Residential premises	Property Code §500(a)
3	Premises unfit for human habitation by the occupants	Property Code §500(a)
4	Actual damages to tenant caused by the violation	Property Code §500(b)
5	Violation was knowing	Property Code §500(b)

The number of elements identified for a cause of action is not fixed in stone. In Ms. Ransom's case, for example, a lawyer might divide element 1 into two alternative subelements—written lease or oral lease—or element 4 into two separate elements—actual damages and causation. As you use this model, you will determine what level of precision is necessary for you to organize the facts. It is important, however, to try to identify as narrowly as possible each operative proposition that will require proof at trial and to limit each element to a single proposition.

Then, we need to state the generic legal elements as factual propositions applicable specifically to our client's case. This is done in Chart 11B.

CHART 11B LEGAL ELEMENTS → FACTUAL PROPOSITIONS

	Elements	Factual Propositions
1	Written or oral lease	Ms. Ransom has a written lease for 289 Hudson Street.
2	Residential premises	The apartment on the second floor of 289 Hudson Street is a residential premises.
3	Premises unfit for human habitation by the occupants	The premises at 289 Hudson Street are and have been unfit for human habitation because of the lack of sufficient heat, the leak in the bedroom, and roach infestation.
4	Actual damages to tenant caused by the violation	The lack of heat, the leak in the bedroom, and the roach infestation at 289 Hudson Street caused Ms. Ransom to pay rent for

CHART 11B CONTINUED

	Elements	Factual Propositions
		an apartment she could not fully use and to pay medical bills for illness caused by the conditions.
5	Violation was knowing	Mr. Dusak knew of the lack of heat, the leak in the bedroom, and roach infestation, yet failed to remedy these problems.

As you can see, the factual propositions provide a segue between the generic elements required in a breach of warranty of habitability case and the evidence that must be presented if this case goes to trial.

Now that we have identified the specific factual propositions which must be proven to establish a breach of warranty of habitability, we can start to organize the facts in Ms. Ransom's case. The "facts" will be contained in client interview memos, witness statements, police reports, hospital records, depositions, answers to interrogatories, or any other documents or statements you unearth in your fact investigation.

As with the legal elements, it is a good idea to identify the sources of the facts for later assessment of their credibility (see §15.2). This organization is shown in Chart 11C.

CHART 11C RANSOM LEGAL ELEMENTS CHART

	Factual Propositions	Facts	Source
1	Ms. Ransom has a written lease for 289 Hudson Street.	Ms. Ransom has a written lease with Mr. Dusak.	6/20/96 Client Interview Memo
		On 12/15/95, Dusak, as landlord, signed lease for 289 Hudson Street with Keith Ransom, as tenant.	Lease
		Mr. Dusak acknowledged rent payments by Ms. Ransom.	Rent receipts acknowledging payment by Ms. Ransom
2	The apartment on the second floor of 289 Hudson St. is a residential premises.	Ms. Ransom lives on the second floor of 289 Hudson Street with her two children.	6/20/96 Client Interview Memo

CHART 11C CONTINUED

	Factual Propositions	Facts	Source
3	The premises at 289 Hudson Street are and have been unfit for human habitation because of the lack of sufficient heat, the leak in the bedroom, and roach infestation.	*Lack of Sufficient Heat* During the third or fourth week of January, the apartment did not have enough heat because the furnace was not functioning properly. Ms. Ransom called Mr. Dusak, but it took him until the beginning of February to send out a plumber. Even then, throughout the winter, the temperature would drop into the low fifties in her apartment at night.	6/20/96 Client Interview Memo
		Leak in Bedroom In late February, after a large snowstorm, her bedroom roof began leaking. Now, every time it rains, there's a downpour in her bedroom. Ms. Ransom is unable to sleep in the bedroom and sleeps on the couch in the living room. She called Mr. Dusak, who sent a roofer out in April. Mr. Dusak says the leak has been fixed, but in a heavy storm there's still a problem.	6/20/96 Client Interview Memo
		Roach Infestation	6/20/96 Client Interview Memo

CHART 11C CONTINUED

Factual Propositions	Facts	Source
	In late March, Ms. Ransom began having a roach problem. She tried using Raid but to no avail. Finally, she called Mr. Dusak around April 12.	
	On April 19, Mr. Dusak sent an exterminator to the apartment. The exterminator arrived at the apartment unannounced at 8:00 a.m., while Ms. Ransom was leaving for work. She told him to call back to make an appointment. He never came back. The whole apartment is now infested with roaches.	
	Tom Daniels, an inspector from the Health Department, inspected 289 Hudson on May 6 and found moderate swarming of roaches in the kitchen and a few roaches in other areas of the apartment.	5/8/96 Health Department Report
4 The lack of heat, the leak in the bedroom, and the roach infestation at 289 Hudson Street caused Ms. Ransom to pay rent for an apartment she could not fully use and to pay medical bills for illness caused by the conditions.	Ms. Ransom has paid $650.00 rent for each month from January to June 1996 for an apartment she cannot use.	Rent receipts
	Her children came down with bronchitis, and she has doctor bills for $250.00.	6/20/96 Client Interview Memo

CHART 11C CONTINUED

	Factual Propositions	Facts	Source
5	Mr. Dusak knew of the lack of heat, the leak in the bedroom, and roach infestation, yet failed to remedy these problems	*Lack of Heat* Ms. Ransom called Mr. Dusak in January, but it took him until the beginning of February to send out a plumber.	6/20/96 Client Interview Memo
		Leak in Bedroom Ms. Ransom called Mr. Dusak, who sent a roofer out in April. Mr. Dusak says the leak has been fixed, but in a heavy storm, there's still a problem.	6/20/96 Client Interview Memo
		Roach Infestation Ms. Ransom called Mr. Dusak around April 12 to complain about the roach infestation. Mr. Dusak sent out an exterminator. The whole apartment is still infested with roaches.	6/20/96 Client Interview Memo; 4/22/96 letter from Mr. Dusak

At this stage, you have probably already identified issues about the sufficiency of the facts to support certain factual propositions and the credibility of some of the sources of facts—and probably have also anticipated possible defenses for Mr. Dusak. We will deal with those issues at a later time, in §15.1, §15.2, and Chapter 17. The important point here is to understand the nature of the process. The "Facts" column is the proof that can be presented at trial through either a witness or a document to establish the factual proposition. Of course, you will also have to consider whether the evidentiary rules allow the introduction of such evidence. The "Source" column identifies the witness or document that will present the fact at trial. As you can see from the chart, you can have more than one fact supporting a single factual proposition and more than one source establishing a fact. For the third element, for example, you can establish the roach infestation through both the testimony of Ms. Ransom and the Health Department Report. Unless you have at least one source for a fact, however, you will not be able to establish the factual proposition and prove that element.

Like a geometric proof, this model helps lawyers and judges in applying general legal rules to a given case. Obviously, this process is not finished once and for all after the initial client interview. Lawyers engage in marshaling facts throughout the case. Whenever they discover new facts, the charts must be updated.

While this discussion has focused on the use of the legal elements model in the context of possible litigation between parties, lawyers use a similar mode of analysis in non-litigation settings. In drafting a will, for example, you will need to examine the applicable statutes and case law to determine the legal elements required for making particular bequests, for escaping adverse tax consequences, and for avoiding technical problems such as the rule against perpetuities. And through your fact investigation—interviews with the client, review of your client's assets, and examination of the applicable documents—you can draft charts, stating those elements as factual propositions and then relating them to the particular facts of your case.[4] The process is identical to the one we used in this chapter: by marshaling the particular facts in your client's case according to the legal elements, you will draft a will reflecting both the legal requirements in your jurisdiction and the intentions of your client.

---

4. See generally Thomas L. Shaffer & Carol Ann Mooney, *The Planning and Drafting of Wills and Trusts* 185–186 (3d ed. 1991).

CHAPTER

12

THE CHRONOLOGY MODEL OF ORGANIZING FACTS[1]

As you learned in §10.2, one method people use to organize facts is the creation of "scripts"—schemas about sequences in which causally-related events are expected to occur. Scripts are arranged in chronological order. Indeed, psychologists theorize that the tendency to order events in chronological order is embedded in human nature. One study, for example, showed that even when the subjects were told popular stories with their plots out of sequential order, they would reconfigure the stories in their minds and retell them in sequence.[2]

Besides the paradigmatic model, then, chronology is a useful method for organizing facts. By focusing on the chronological relationship of facts to each other, rather than on the connection of facts to general legal propositions, the chronological model provides benefits that are not furnished by the paradigmatic

---

1. The following sources were consulted in writing this chapter and can be referred to for further reading on the subject of the chronological method for organizing facts: W. Lance Bennett & Martha S. Feldman, *Reconstructing Reality in the Courtroom: Justice and Judgment in American Culture* 41, 48 (1981); David A. Binder & Paul Bergman, *Fact Investigation: From Hypothesis to Proof* 11, 44–56 (1984); Richard K. Sherwin, *Law Frames: Historical Truth and Narrative Necessity in a Criminal Case*, 47 Stan. L. Rev. 39, 50–51 (1994); Nancy Pennington & Reid Hastie, *A Cognitive Theory of Juror Decision Making: The Story Model*, 13 Cardozo L. Rev. 519, 525, 541–542 (1991).
2. Sherwin, *supra* note 1, at 51. See also Reid Hastie, *The Role of "Stories" in Civil Jury Judgments*, 32 U. Mich. J.L. Reform 227, 234 (1999) (describing how individual jurors in a mock trial began their decision-making by constructing a model of the events in the case in the form of a chronological, causally-connected narrative).

approach. It locates a particular fact in the context of the surrounding circumstances. Moreover, a fact that may not appear important standing by itself may have much significance when viewed in a chronological sequence. Or a fact that, by itself, may suggest one interpretation in one setting may indicate a very different explanation when examined in another context. In the Ransom case, for example, the fact that Ms. Ransom did not call her landlord to schedule a new appointment for the exterminator after she canceled his first visit, when viewed by itself, could indicate either that the roach problem was not significant or that Ms. Ransom was negligent in attempting to remedy the problem. Nevertheless, when viewed in the context of the fact that her landlord yelled at her when she had called him one week previously, Ms. Ransom has a reasonable, if not totally convincing, explanation for her behavior.

The chronological model also assists us in assessing the internal consistency of the different accounts of "what really happened." One factor we all use in evaluating the credibility of a witness's account of a situation is the extent to which it adheres to our mental scripts about what should happen in a particular situation. In a criminal assault case, for instance, the jury probably will reject the prosecution's case if the complaining witness enjoyed himself at a party immediately after the alleged incident, failed to mention the attack to anyone for two days, and only visited the police a week later. Under most people's schemas, the victim would not behave in this manner after an assault. The chronological model helps us to compare the sequence of events presented by the different witnesses with our scripts for the sequences of such events.

Finally, in a similar manner, the chronological approach also enables lawyers to fill in the gaps of the accounts given to them by their clients. When someone recounts to us what has happened in a particular situation, we naturally ask questions such as "What happened next?" or "What did you do to cause that reaction?" or "Why did he act that way?" We are constantly looking for causes and effects to make sense of the account. By viewing the facts of an incident in a chronological sequence, you can identify the missing links in the account. And then, by considering scripts for that type of incident and asking the question "What should have happened if this account is correct?" you can develop areas for future fact investigation.

Given these benefits of the chronological approach, we suggest that, in addition to the legal elements chart, you prepare Chart 12A. It is the only way to prepare systematically, for presentation in court, negotiations, or elsewhere, a theory about what actually happened. Unless you carefully note the sources of proof (the third column) and the proof issues (the fourth column), you have only the vaguest idea of what is going on with the facts.

CHART 12A CHRONOLOGY TEMPLATE

Date/Time	Episode	Source	Gaps/Internal Consistency

In the Date/Time column, you put the date and, if relevant, the time of the episode. For some cases, all you will need is the day or even month when an event occurred. But in other cases, the precise hour and even minute might be significant.

For example, the time frame for a breach of contract dispute between parties who have transacted business with each other for many years will probably be very different from one for an automobile accident case, in which the movements of the parties both leading up to and after the accident might be pertinent in terms of minutes and seconds.

With regard to the issue of when to begin your time line, most novice lawyers are apt to start their chronology too late in the sequence of events. The starting point for a breach of contract action, for instance, is not necessarily the execution of the contract or even the negotiations leading up to its execution. Prior dealings of the parties might be very significant for understanding the terms of the disputed contract or methods anticipated for performing the contract. Or the beginning date for a medical malpractice case may not be the plaintiff's initial visit to the doctor but could be the first time she experienced symptoms of the condition or that the doctor treated a patient with a similar condition. We certainly are not recommending that all chronologies go back to Adam and Eve. But after you draft your initial chronology, ask yourself whether anything could possibly have happened before that date that could be relevant—even indirectly—to the case. In other words, what brought the parties or a party to that point? Given our scripts of how similar situations transpire, what could (or should) have happened before the initial entry on the chronology? What could have precipitated that first event you have identified?[2]

Similarly, do not prematurely end your chronology on the date of the disputed event or shortly thereafter. In an automobile accident case, for instance, the efforts of the plaintiff after the collision to seek medical care can obviously be very relevant to the issue of damages. When you come to the end of your chronology, ask yourself what could (or should) have happened after that point. What effect could the last episode have on the chain of events?

At times, you may have some difficulty determining the precise date or time of an event. Your client or a witness to the incident may complain that the event happened so long ago that they cannot recall when it occurred, that they were not in any condition at the time to remember what happened, or that they do not have very good memories. Since the purpose of the chronology is to understand the sequence of causes and effect, this lack of information can be quite significant. Obviously, the time when a defendant in a DWI case left the bar prior to his arrest may be crucial to both the prosecution and defense cases. Therefore, identify in the Gaps/Internal Consistency column those dates and times you want to pin down more exactly during your fact investigation. You may want to probe the issue more thoroughly with your client (see §7.6), identify another witness who observed the

---

2. In a death penalty case, for example, defense counsel should attempt "to expand the time frame of the client's story to include those aspects of his life that narrowed his choices and frustrated his hopes and dreams to the point that he lashed out in violence." Sean D. O'Brien, *Death Penalty Stories: Lessons in Life-Saving Narratives*, 71 UMKC L. Rev. 831 (2009). In fact, experts in death penalty litigation assert that defense counsel must investigate the defendant's family extending at least three generations back. *Supplementary Guidelines for the Mitigation Function of Defense Teams in Death Penalty Cases*, 36 Hofstra L. Rev. 677, 690–701 (2008).

event, proffer formal discovery to the opposing party on this issue, or seek documentation (e.g., a log book, telephone record, or medical report) to pinpoint the time.

The second column of the chart requires identification of each episode in the case. In this column, describe each relevant event in the case. In every case, a multitude of events will have occurred, and your chronology will become useless if you try to include every one. Every telephone call, every letter, and every conversation between the parties may not bear on the dispute. As a new lawyer, you should err on the side of overinclusion so as not to ignore significant events. But when trying to select the relevant events, keep focused on the "central action" in the case, the key event upon which the case is based: the breach of contract, the publication of the libelous statement, the seller's misrepresentation, or the assault on the complainant. Then, consider whether or not a particular event is part of the "cause and effect" chain leading to or resulting from that "central action." As your case progresses, you may find that the "central action" is no longer the one you originally identified. Then, revise your chronology to include additional episodes relevant to the newly discovered key event. Throughout, consider the elements of your causes of action. But try not to limit your thinking to paradigmatic notions about the case. Focus on your commonsense idea of how a situation like your case should evolve, not just on how legal doctrine views it.

Also include in this column, where appropriate, the setting of the event, the participants involved, and their physical and mental states. For the chronological approach to be helpful in identifying a sequence of causes and effects, it is important to identify not only the action which took place on a particular date, but also where an event took place, who was present, and how they felt. In an automobile accident case, for example, issues of lighting, road and weather conditions, and the physical and mental states of the different drivers are obviously relevant to the cause and effect of the collision. Exclusion of the facts surrounding each event can defeat the purpose of the chronology. Consider each episode as a scene in a play or situation comedy, and, as with the events themselves, identify those facts relevant to set the scene for the occurrence (see §15.3.2).

In the third column of the chronology chart, list the source of the facts concerning the episode: your client, a witness, an item of correspondence, some other document, an answer obtained at a deposition or in discovery, or an admission of fact in a stipulation or pleading. The credibility of a fact will largely depend on its source. (See §15.2.) As with the legal elements chart, identification of the sources of the facts helps in the later assessment of their credibility and assists you in determining which facts can be relied on in the presentation of the case.

The final column of the chart asks you to identify gap and internal consistency issues. After you draft your chronology, review each episode and ask yourself three questions:

1. What other details do we want to know about each episode to set the scene?
2. Consistent with our mental scripts for this kind of sequence of events, what else could or should have occurred before or after this particular episode? and,
3. Consistent with our mental scripts for this kind of sequence of events, is each episode in the chronology consistent with other episodes?

The answer to the first question helps you develop a credible case. We will discuss this issue in depth in §15.3. For purposes of this discussion, however, consider what additional information you need about the setting, the characters, and the nature of their actions to give a full context to the event.

The answer to the second question helps you fill in the gaps in the chronology. Assume, for example, that you represent a client who seeks damages because of the poor condition of the used car she purchased. In our script of such a transaction, we would expect her to lodge a complaint with the dealer immediately after the car broke down or at least to take some other steps to have it repaired. If you did not obtain this information on these issues in your first interview, you will certainly want to conduct a follow-up interview to assure that you have a complete sequence of the events.

When answering the second question, remember that different people have different scripts depending on their cultures, their social groups, or their own experiences (see §10.2). Accordingly, your scripts about a dispute might be very different from those of the judge, jurors, or agency official who is deciding your case. When you begin to organize your facts, there is no problem in focusing on your own scripts about sequence of events. When you are preparing to present your case, however, consider the schemas of your audience (see §13.3).

Finally, the answer to the third question will aid you in testing the internal consistency of your case. If, for example, in our used-car hypothetical your client waited four months after the breakdown to contact the dealer or took a cross-country trip with the car after it experienced problems, you might have a problem at trial persuading the judge or jury that the car in fact broke down. Your client may have a legitimate explanation for the delay, but the credibility of your case will depend on discovering that explanation. Therefore, you will have to explore this issue with your client in a future interview. Your goal is to develop a coherent and credible chain of events.

Now that we have described the different columns for your chronology chart, let us turn to Chart 12B to explore how it can be applied in the Ransom case.

The questions raised in the fourth column of this chart demonstrate concretely the benefits of the chronological approach in analyzing the facts. First, it places

CHART 12B RANSOM CHRONOLOGY

Date/ Time	Episode	Source	Gaps/Internal Consistency
12/15/95	Lease signed by Samuel Dusak and Keith Ransom for 289 Hudson St. for the term 1/1/96 to 12/31/97.	Lease	How did the Ransoms find the apartment? Did client examine the apartment before moving in? Did she notice any problems with the apartment at that time?

CHART 12B CONTINUED

Date/ Time	Episode	Source	Gaps/Internal Consistency
1/5/96	Client, her husband, and two children (ages two and four) move into the apartment.	Client interview	Did they notice any problems when they moved into the apartment?
1/1/96–6/1/96	Client paid $650.00 in rent each month.	Rent receipts	Did Dusak ever question why the checks were from Mrs. Ransom, not Mr. Ransom?
1/96 (Third or fourth week)	Not enough heat in the apartment because furnace was not functioning properly. She called Mr. Dusak.	Client interview	More exact date? What does client mean by "not enough heat"? When did she call Dusak? What did she say? What did he say?
2/96 (Beginning)	Plumber comes out.	Client interview	More exact date? Did she call Dusak back when no one came out immediately to fix the furnace? Who was plumber? What did he do? Did anyone speak with him? When? What did he say? What was the response?
Throughout winter	Temperature would drop into low fifties at night.	Client interview	What was temperature like during the day? How does client know the exact temperature? What did she do about this problem?
?	Children came down with bronchitis. Doctor's bill of $250.00.	Client interview	When? Name of doctor? Corroboration of diagnosis?
2/96	Client and her husband separated, and husband left the apartment.	Client interview	When? What were the circumstances? Had husband handled any dealings with Dusak? Did Dusak know about the separation?

CHART 12B CONTINUED

Date/ Time	Episode	Source	Gaps/Internal Consistency
Late February	After a large snowstorm, roof began leaking in client's bedroom. Every time it rained, there was a downpour in the bedroom. She could not sleep in bedroom and slept on couch in the living room. She called Dusak.	Client interview	When was the snowstorm? When were the rainstorms? What was the precise extent of the leak? When did she start sleeping in the living room? When did she call Dusak? What did she say? What did he say?
4/96	Roofer came out. After roofer came out, Dusak says roof has been fixed, but in a heavy rainstorm, there's still a problem.	Client interview	Why the delay in fixing the roof? Did she call Dusak anytime between February and April? Content of calls? Exact date? Who was roofer? What did he do? What did he say? When did Dusak say the roof was fixed? What else did he say? What did she say? What does client mean when she says, "There's still a problem."
Late March	Client began having a roach problem. She tried using Raid, but to no avail.	Client interview	Exact date? What was the extent of the roach problem? How often did she use Raid and where did she spray?
4/12/96	Client called Dusak. Dusak yelled at her and said he had never had a roach problem before and that she was the cause of it.	Client interview	Why did she wait until this date to call Dusak? How did she respond to Dusak?
4/19/96; 8:00 a.m.	Exterminator arrived at apartment unannounced. Ms. Ransom was leaving for work and told him to call back to make an appointment.	Client interview; Dusak's 4/22/96 letter	Name of exterminator? Did he leave his address, phone number? Was there any way client could have delayed going to work so extermination could take place?

CHART 12B CONTINUED

Date/ Time	Episode	Source	Gaps/Internal Consistency
4/19/96	In kitchen there were open boxes of food on the drain board.	Dusak's 4/22/96 letter	Is exterminator correct? If he is correct, why were the open boxes of food left out? Were there roaches on the drain board?
4/22/96	Dusak asks client to call him to set up an appointment for exterminator.	Dusak's 4/22/96 letter	
After 4/22/96	Client does not call Dusak to get exterminator because she does not want to be yelled at again. Exterminator does not return.	Client interview	By not calling Dusak, what did client expect?
5/6/96	Client calls Health Department. Tom Daniels inspects apartment and finds moderate swarming of roaches in kitchen and a few roaches in other areas of the apartment.	Client interview; 5/8/96 Health Dept. Report	Was client or any one else present during Daniels' inspection? What did he inspect? How long was he there? What did he say? Why did he say only a few roaches in areas other than the kitchen? What are "moderate swarming" and a "few" roaches?
After 5/6/96	The whole apartment is now infested with roaches.	Client interview	Description of the roach infestation? Did client have any further contact with the Health Dept.? Or Dusak? Why did she wait until June 20 to interview at our office?

each fact in chronological relation to other facts and thereby suggests possible causes and effects of certain events. For instance, on lines 34–36, we list the fact that Ms. Ransom's husband separated from her and left the apartment. From a paradigmatic thinking standpoint, that fact is irrelevant to any legal element in the case. But that event may be crucial for determining "what really happened" in the case. Consider when the separation occurs: February 1996, immediately after the initial problems with the furnace and right before the leak in the bedroom. Given the date of the event, hypothesize some of the possible scripts relating to that event:

- Ms. Ransom's husband had conducted most of the dealings with the landlord until he left, and the landlord only ignored the problems in the apartment after the separation;
- the leak in the bedroom was caused by damage inflicted by Mr. Ransom's violent conduct before the separation;
- Ms. Ransom found it difficult to manage the apartment after her husband left;
- Ms. Ransom overstated the problems because of the stress of being a single parent;
- Mr. Dusak believed all women complain too much and often exaggerate.

While none of these scripts may be accurate, the important point is that the listing of facts in chronological order can help you brainstorm possible causes and effects of different events and lead to fruitful fact investigation.

Second, the chronological model helps you assess the internal consistency of Ms. Ransom's case. By comparing the different episodes with our scripts for similar situations, we can evaluate the credibility of our client's account of the events. In the Gaps/Internal Consistency column, for example, we ask why Ms. Ransom waited until April 12 to complain to Mr. Dusak about the roach problem (lines 63–64) or why she waited until June 20 to come into our office for an interview (lines 102–103). These delays do not comport with a script for "a Mother Faced with an Apartment Infested with Roaches," who would seek immediate help, especially if she had small children. Ms. Ransom may have good explanations for her actions, but the chronology does not show actions consistent with a significant roach problem. Accordingly, we need to explore this issue with our client.

In assessing the internal consistency of the chronology of your case, you need to consider facts from sources other than your client or friendly witnesses. As you can see in the third column, we have in fact included sources that may not be favorable to Ms. Ransom: for example, the exterminator's comments that there were open boxes of food on the drain board when he came to the apartment (lines 73–75) or the health inspector's observations that there were few roaches in other areas of the apartment (lines 102–104). Remember that the purpose of a chronology is to organize the facts in a sequence so you can attempt to discover the cause and effect of particular events. Ignoring unfavorable sources and facts will not assist you in the process. Whether Ms. Ransom denies or admits that she had left any open boxes of food on the drain board, unless we prepare a response to the exterminator's testimony on this issue, the trier-of-fact may conclude that Ms. Ransom's failure to keep food boxes in cupboards caused the increase in roach population at her apartment.

Finally, the chronological approach assists us in identifying factual gaps. In terms of time gaps the model helps us to pin down important dates. In the gaps column, for instance, we have listed those dates that are imprecise (lines 13, 18, 39, and 51) so that we can conduct future investigations to improve the chronology. The significance of pinpointing exact dates can be seen in relation to the heat problem. Lines 15–18 of the chart reflect that in the third or fourth week in January the furnace began to malfunction, and that Ms. Ransom called her landlord to complain; line 21 indicates that the plumber came to the apartment to fix the furnace in early February. Depending on the precise dates of these events, the period between the call to the landlord and the plumber's visit could be anywhere from a few days to three weeks. Pinning down the exact dates will significantly enhance or impede our ability to show that the landlord ignored Ms. Ransom's complaints.

The date column also identifies areas for investigation both before and after the "central action." Our script for "a Tenant Renting an Apartment" includes some events before the signing of the lease (lines 1–4). Usually, tenants visit and inspect the apartment for which they sign a lease and often speak to the landlord or her agent about any problems that have been identified or any repairs that may be required. Such information in Ms. Ransom's case may be helpful in determining whether the problems faced by Ms. Ransom were preexisting and whether Mr. Dusak knew of their existence. Likewise, our script for "Inspector from the Health Department Finds Tenant Living with Her Two Small Children in Roach-Infested Apartment" assumes that most Health Departments will take action to remedy the problem. Our examination of the chronology suggests that we should contact the Health Department to explore what happened between the last date on the time line—May 6—and our June 20 interview of the client.

In terms of the episodes themselves, the chronological approach aids us in discovering gaps as to the setting, characters, and nature of the actions. For example, we seek additional details about the interchange between the exterminator and Ms. Ransom on April 19. In the context of later events—the failure of the landlord to reschedule an appointment and Ms. Ransom's refusal to call her landlord—these details may be essential to determine whether the lack of extermination was caused by the unreasonable refusal of Ms. Ransom to allow the exterminator to enter her apartment or by the arbitrary decision by the exterminator (or landlord) not to reschedule the appointment. We will want to investigate whether Ms. Ransom could have delayed going to work, whether the exterminator offered to return at another time, or whether the exterminator mentioned that he would talk to the landlord about the problem. All of those questions are relevant to the chain of events leading to the failure of the landlord to exterminate the apartment.

CHAPTER 13

THE STORY MODEL OF ORGANIZING FACTS

§13.1 INTRODUCTION

Lisa: *Perhaps there is no moral to this story.*
Homer: *Exactly! It's just a bunch of stuff that happened.*

Epilogue to a *Simpsons* episode[1]

Besides the paradigmatic and chronological models, you can use a story approach to organize facts and present cases. Like the chronological model, the story model often organizes facts as a causal sequence of facts. It is not, however, synonymous with that model. Remember that narrative thinking—structuring the facts in the context of stories—strives to endow a sequence of events with meaning (see §10.3). It serves this function by highlighting certain facts while filtering out others, by focusing on particular details and images while downplaying others, by arranging facts and episodes in a particular order, or by presenting the facts in the context of certain images and symbols. A story does more than set out a

1. *Simpsons: Blood Feud* (Fox television broadcast, December 17, 1991).

chronological series of events. It tries to make *sense* of those events. Consider, for example, the following example:

> a man learned of a plot against England from a woman who was killed in his flat later that night. Eluding the police and the killers, he set out to warn the authorities, but then changed his mind and went abroad to live.[2]

In this account, a chronology is presented, and the cause and effect links between the different facts are clear. But the rationale for the series of events is not. We know nothing, for instance, about the motivations for the man's action, his relationship to the woman, or the woman's connection to the plot. It is not a "story" because we are left bewildered after hearing it, asking, "What is this all about? What does this account mean? What is the moral of the story?"

The essential elements of a story are "Agents who Act to achieve Goals in a recognizable Setting by the use of certain Means and who run into Trouble."[3] A narrative moves from a steady, usual state of affairs through the disruption by Trouble, and then is either resolved through a return to the original steady state or the establishment of a new one.[4] The spin the storyteller gives to the facts surrounding each of these elements—the Agents, Act, Goals, Setting, Means, and Trouble—and the account of how the Trouble is or is not resolved provide the narrative with a particular meaning. In any given case, the description of each of these elements is amenable to construction into many different stories. Indeed, studies have shown that even in uncomplicated cases, lawyers have wide latitude in choosing the stories they tell at trial regarding their cases. By crafting the facts into a meaningful story, a lawyer can greatly enhance her client's chances of success. This chapter describes how you can organize and present facts to endow them with a meaning that supports your client's case.

§13.2 IDENTIFYING UNCONTESTED FACTS

Unlike authors of fictional stories, lawyers are limited in the facts they can use in the presentation of their cases. While we may be able to elude the full impact of some harmful facts through certain storytelling techniques,[5] there are facts in every case that are incontestable and cannot be avoided. While psychological research suggests that some jurors, when faced with a very persuasive narrative, simply disregard facts that are inconsistent with the story, it also shows that other jurors are more skeptical and are more likely to be persuaded by the story that is most

---

2. Thomas M. Leitch, *What Stories Are: Narrative Theory and Interpretation* 11 (1986). See also Janet Malcolm, *The Crime of Sheila McGough* 11 (1999) (describing how a defendant, herself a criminal defense lawyer, lost her case because she "was not interested in telling a plausible and persuasive story [but] was out for the bigger game of imparting a great number of accurate and numbingly boring facts").
3. Anthony G. Amsterdam & Jerome Bruner, *Minding the Law* 46 (2000). See also Brian J. Foley & Ruth Anne Robbins, *Fiction 101: A Primer for Lawyers on How to Use Fiction Writing Techniques to Write Persuasive Facts Sections*, 32 Rutgers L.J. 459, 466 (2001).
4. Amsterdam & Bruner, *supra* note 3, at 46.
5. See §13.4 and §13.5. Those techniques raise ethical questions. See §13.8.

consistent with all the evidence.[6] In crafting stories, then, we need to identify the uncontested facts and recognize that our narratives may have to take them into account.

There are several types of uncontested facts. First, some facts in a case are accepted by all parties as true. For instance, your client acknowledges that he was in the bar at the time of the brawl; she concedes that her signature is on the installment sales contract for the purchase of the car; or your adversary has admitted in her answer that at the time of the accident she had an expired license; or Ms. Ransom admits she leaves open boxes of food on the drain board. Second, the credibility of some sources of facts may be beyond challenge. If a disinterested priest, rabbi, and imam witnessed your client's car going through the red light, you will probably be compelled to admit that fact. Finally, facts reflecting readily verifiable natural phenomena will usually be uncontested. The fact that ice melts at 32 degrees, that the average temperature on a particular date, as recorded by the National Weather Service, was 20 below zero, or that in December the sun sets by 8:00 p.m. in Buffalo will usually be undisputed at trial.

The nature of a fact as contested or uncontested is not fixed. The fact, for example, that a signature on a contract looks just like your client's does not preclude the assertion that the signing was a forgery. Likewise, the fact that the temperature was 20 degrees at a certain time does not prevent the argument that ice was melting because of sunshine beaming on a surface. The important point is that certain facts are more likely to be considered uncontested than others. Although you may be able to develop explanations to contest such facts, your storytelling will more likely than not have to contend with those facts.

To identify uncontested facts in a given case, review the "Facts" column on your Legal Elements Chart (see Chart 11C, the *Ransom Legal Elements Chart* and the "Episodes" column on your Chronology Chart (see Chart 12B, the *Ransom Chronology*) and determine those facts that you will not dispute in the presentation of your case. Also, based on the pleadings and discovery (interrogatory answers, deposition testimony, and responses to requests to admit), you will be able to identify those facts your adversary will consider uncontested. In some jurisdictions, courts will require the submission of a pretrial order setting forth the uncontested facts agreed to by the parties. After making a list of these facts, you will have an idea of the facts that you will not be able to ignore in crafting your story.

---

6. Deanna Kuhn, *How Do People Know?* 12 Psychological Science 1, 1–2 (2001). In fact, a story that ignores key pieces of evidence can likely backfire.

> While there is a strong parallel between lawsuit storytelling and storytelling as entertainment, the parallel is not exact. Like any analogy, it can be taken too far. Therefore, a word of caution is appropriate. If the jury ever comes to believe that a lawyer is trying to tell a good yarn, then the effort is a total failure. The lawyer loses credibility, and the client loses the case. . . . Thus, exaggeration, melodrama, or the use of props, dialogue, or other such overtly theatrical devices can doom the storyteller to failure. As with anything done in the courtroom, sincerity is the watchword.

Gerald R. Powell, *Opening Statements: The Art of Storytelling*, 31 Stetson L. Rev. 89, 91 (2001).

§13.3 IDENTIFYING YOUR AUDIENCE

We saw in §10.3 that, as witnesses tell their stories at a trial, fact-finders reconstruct their own stories about "what really happened," focusing on certain facts and de-emphasizing others.

> [S]tories are not just facts in themselves. They are ways of learning and talking about facts, a way of communicating. In narrative, we take experience and configure it in a conventional and comprehensible form. This is what gives narrative its communicative power. Since human beings think about social interaction in story form, persuasion—a critical task for a lawyer—requires the ability to tell a plausible and compelling story—one that moves the decision-maker to grant the remedy we want.[7]

Different fact-finders are capable of giving different meanings to the telling of the very same story. In one study of a simulated jury trial, for example, jurors in one case constructed radically different stories from the same presentation of evidence in one case. The case concerned the theft of property that the defendant asserted he thought was abandoned. Some jurors concluded that the defendant unlawfully stole the property, while others thought it was the mistake of a well-intentioned, ignorant man who had no sense of what he was stealing. Some saw the situation as the act of a "Good Samaritan" cleaning up the neighborhood while others viewed it as the commission of the perfect, plotted crime, carried out "in broad daylight" to make the act appear innocent. From 48 groups of jurors viewing the very same video-taped trial, 15 different versions of the story were constructed.[8]

The meaning imputed to the "facts" by a fact-finder, then, depends in large part on the process by which that fact-finder constructs his own story of "what really happened" in the case. Accordingly, you must understand the nature of your audience. One of your tasks is to organize and present the facts of your case in a way that they will have meaning to that particular decision-maker. You can craft a story about the facts that might work very effectively with one fact-finder, fail dismally with another, and leave still another totally baffled. Indeed, recent studies in the area of linguistics and communications theory have shown that the most important part of fitting a story to an audience is not "buttering them up" but entering into a dialogue with them, attempting to address the particular concerns in their minds.[9] To be effective as a storyteller, think of yourself as a translator. Impersonate your audience and try to understand the process through which your audience—the fact-finder in your case—ascribes meaning to the story told.[10]

---

7. Jane B. Baron, *The Many Promises of Storytelling in Law*, 23 Rutgers L.J. 79, 95 (1991).
8. James A. Holstein, *Jurors' Interpretations and Jury Decision Making*, 9 Law & Hum. Behav. 83, 86–90 (1985).
9. Amsterdam & Bruner, *supra* note 3, at 136.
10. Christopher P. Gilkerson, *Poverty Law Narratives: The Critical Practice and Theory of Receiving and Translating Client Stories*, 43 Hastings L.J. 861, 915 (1992); Gerald P. Lopez, *Lay Lawyering*, 32 UCLA L. Rev. 1, 15 (1984).

To translate the facts of your client's case to your audience, try to comprehend the "language" used by your listeners. One aspect of that language is the audience's norms, experiences, and assumptions—their schemas[11] (see Chapter 10). Obviously, decision-makers who come from different cultural, social, or religious backgrounds or have had different experiences may construct varying stories about the meaning of certain facts. For example, a juror who is an upper-income Wall Street investment banker may view an alleged misrepresentation by a used car seller as an inadvertent misstatement while an inner-city unemployed mother may perceive it as a premeditated rip-off.

A second, related component of a decision-maker's language is her own repertoire of stock stories, images, and myths. Each regional, ethnic, social, or religious group has its own unique stories which, in just two or three sentences, encapsulate a particular situation. Consider, for example, the significance of the reference to "Curse of the Bambino" to a judge who is a sports fanatic, a mention of "No Soup for you!" or "voted off the island" to a jury of television watchers, the image of traffic gridlock to decision makers in a large city, an allusion to "garbage in, garbage out" to an agency hearing examiner who is a computer geek.

Finally, the translation process must recognize what Thomas Leitch terms the principle of enjoyment.[12] Leitch notes that storytellers not only communicate information to their audience but also provide them with some form of enjoyment. As he observes, many of us enjoy a story in which the teller piles detail upon repetitive detail because we savor the storytelling process of imagining what is going to happen next. (And, it should also be pointed out, many of us have experienced the agony of listening to a storyteller who does not know when to move his story along.) For the legal storyteller, the significance of this insight is that decision-makers might find it difficult to discover meaning in a story if it is unenjoyable. Try to understand what will make the presentation of a story most enjoyable to the fact-finder and craft your story accordingly.

To determine the nature of your audience you must investigate the background of the decision-makers to discover their schemas, stock stories, and interests. In a bench trial, for example, research the professional, political, and social background of the judge. Try to contact other lawyers who have practiced before the judge to determine what kinds of approaches the judge appreciates in the courtroom and the sympathies expressed by that judge in similar cases. A visit to a court session prior to the trial will certainly be helpful. Besides learning the judge's understanding of the applicable legal doctrine, you can discover—through informal courtroom banter, rulings on objections, and interchanges with other

---

11. W. Lance Bennett & Martha S. Feldman, *Reconstructing Reality in the Courtroom: Justice and Judgment in American Culture* 171 (1981); Mark Cammack, *In Search of the Post-Positivist Jury*, 70 Ind. L.J. 405, 474 (1995). See also Malcolm, *supra* note 2, at 131 ("The jury system is posited on the idea that people are capable of suspending their normal state of having a fixed opinion about everything and allowing new ideas to penetrate the defenses of their old ones. But this is like believing people capable of suspending the peristaltic motion of their stomachs. It is like imaging a ballpark filled with placidly neutral spectators. Every juror listens to the testimony through the filter of his preconceptions and as a (conscious or unconscious) rooter for one side or the other.").

12. Leitch, *supra* note 2, at 28. See generally Richard K. Sherwin, *Nomos and Cinema*, 48 UCLA L. Rev. 1519, 1524–1526 (2001) (describing the role of enchantment in the legal system).

lawyers—the judge's interests, attitudes toward clients similar to yours, and reactions to the stories told in other cases.[13]

Similarly, in an administrative proceeding, you will want to conduct some reconnaissance on the hearing examiner or administrative law judge who is hearing the case. Although such officers, like judges, are restricted in their discretion by legal standards, their fact-finding will inevitably be influenced by their own schemas. In an unemployment compensation, immigration, or social security hearing, for example, different hearing examiners have different sympathies, and you should try to craft your story to address those of the officer in your case.

In a jury trial, you will want to reflect on the social milieu of the prospective pool of jurors in the area. When, for example, the skilled trial lawyer Michael Tigar tries a case in a new city, he begins his preparation by switching on radio talk shows, scanning the local newspapers, and watching local television news to determine what is on people's minds.[14] In some cases you may even want to convene a focus group of nonlawyers in your community to explore their attitudes toward the issues in your case. By identifying the schemas, stock stories, and images of those potential jurors, you can begin to craft a story. Then, in the jury selection process ("voir dire") you can explore the nature of your actual audience. Depending upon the jurisdiction, the voir dire process involves the questioning of prospective jurors either by the judge, the lawyers, or both the judge and lawyers. The principal legal justification for this process is to permit counsel to select a fair and impartial jury by the removal of prospective jurors who are biased against their respective clients. But, in regard to legal storytelling, the process also has another benefit for the lawyers in the case. Prospective jurors' answers to questions about education, employment history, family background, hobbies, reading habits, interests, and prior experiences can help lawyers understand the schemas of their audience. With this knowledge, they can challenge prospective jurors who may not have schemas that are responsive to the stories they have crafted. And, if challenges are not available, they can attempt to redesign their stories to address the schemas of the jurors who have been selected.

§13.4 DEVELOPING A UNIFYING THEME

After you have identified the uncontested facts in your case and the nature of your audience, the next step in the process of crafting a story is the development of a unifying theme. A theme is the controlling idea or core insight of a story. It provokes your audience to have a particular feeling about the case and to act on

---

13. Unlike a jury trial, in a bench trial a lawyer can often actually gauge the effectiveness of her storytelling during the proceedings. Judges, due to their experience and training, frequently express their opinions openly on the gaps or weaknesses in the lawyers' narrative. Accordingly, depending on the judge, bench trials can require lawyers to make adjustments to their stories at every stage of the trial to address the concerns of the decision-maker. Paul Holland, *Sharing Stories: Narrative Lawyering in Bench Trials*, 16 Clinical L. Rev. 195, 197 (2009).

14. Richard K. Sherwin, *When Law Goes Pop: The Vanishing Line Between Law and Popular Culture* 26 (2000).

it.[15] A good theme establishes a "thread of common meaning" that runs throughout the entire case.[16] Ideally, you build your case around that theme.

> One of the figures of the Jewish communities of Eastern Europe was the *magid*, an itinerant teller of tales who spoke in the synagogues on the Sabbath. One of these, the *Magid* of Dubno, was famous for his ability to come up with just the right story or parable on any subject for every occasion. An admirer once asked the *magid* how he did it: How could he possibly learn and remember so many stories and parables? The *magid* responded with the following story:
>
>> A traveller walking in the forest came across an extraordinary sight. On virtually every tree, there was a target with an arrow dead center. Marvelling at the marksmanship, the traveller followed the trail of bull's-eyes in search of the archer. Eventually, he came across a small boy with a bow and arrow. The traveller asked the boy where he had learned such skillful archery. "Well," the boy explained, "first I shoot at a tree. Then I draw a target around the arrow."
>>
>> "It's the same with me," said the *magid*. "First I find out the subject, then I make up a story to fit."[17]

Like the *magid*, it is your task as a lawyer to find the bull's-eye that will make your client's story convincing to the decision-maker.

In a single sentence, state the central meaning of your client's case that you want to communicate to the decision-maker. Try not to think in legal terms. Here, you are not developing a logical, legal argument. Rather, attempt to think in a narrative mode, and try to identify succinctly the principal point of your client's story that will compel the decision-maker to decide in your client's favor. In other words, when the jury begins its deliberations, when the judge retires to her chambers, or when the opposing party considers your settlement offer, what is the one message you want to have delivered to them? For example, in a products liability case, the plaintiff's theme may be that the greedy corporate defendant simply disregarded any concerns that may have been raised about the safety of the ordinary people that use its products. In a criminal case, a defense lawyer might adopt a theme that the key prosecution witness jumped to conclusions because it was impossible for him to identify clearly the assailant in a narrow, unlit alley on a moonless night. Or in an employment discrimination case, the defendant might develop a theme that the plaintiff simply could not do her job and is using the civil rights laws to hide her incompetence.

The identification of a unifying theme is a creative process. There are no mechanical rules for finding the *magid*'s bull's-eye because each case is unique, and each decision-maker is different. But here are some suggestions for questions you should ask in brainstorming possible themes:

---

15. Philip N. Meyer, *Storytelling for Lawyers* 16 (2014).
16. Janice Schuetz & Kathryn Holmes Snedaker, *Communication and Litigation: Case Studies of Famous Trials* 80 (1988).
17. Steven L. Winter, *The Cognitive Dimension of the Agon Between Legal Power and Narrative Meaning*, 87 Mich. L. Rev. 2225, 2255 (1989).

1. From the standpoint of your audience, what is the injustice that has been done (or will be done) to your client? Appeals to justice, in contrast to injustice, can be ineffective. While justice is an elusive ideal, "[i]njustice is real. Everybody has suffered injustice. Injustice has the power to stir people's blood."[18] For the plaintiff, try to identify—in one concise statement—the injustice that entitles him to relief. For the defendant, attempt to pinpoint the injustice that will occur if the plaintiff prevails. Think in terms of some of the high-profile stories in the media about perceived injustices (for example, about child abuse, insurance scams, oil spills, police brutality, deadbeat dads, corporate fraud) and try to find a hook into your case onto which the decision-maker will latch. Understanding of the nature of your audience is crucial to your analysis because what is deemed unjust in one community may be judged just in another.
2. How do you define the "Trouble" in your case? As we discussed in §13.1, most stories concern a character who strives to attain a goal but runs into Trouble. A story is only compelling to a particular audience, however, if they believe that the Trouble is a deviation from the orderly or proper state of affairs in such a situation. Otherwise, the troublesome situation seems incomprehensible or nonsensical. In the Ransom case, for example, most judges or juries would reject out of hand a story for Mr. Dusak (the landlord) that identified his Trouble in making the repairs as his need to save money to pay for a vacation in the Bahamas. By defining the Trouble faced by your client in the case, you also identify what your audience might believe should have occurred in that particular situation.[19] That "ought-to-be" scenario can become the theme for your story (for example, the police ought to have conducted a more thorough investigation before jumping to conclusions and bringing charges against your client; Child Protective Services ought to have provided more services to the parents before filing a neglect petition; the accountant ought to have examined all the financial records before approving the disclosure statement). For Mr. Dusak, it could be, "Ms. Ransom ought to have taken better care of her apartment."
3. What are the three "best" facts in your case? Review your legal elements and chronology charts and jot down what strikes you intuitively as the most persuasive facts. Then, try to conflate those facts into a theme. For example, Ms. Ransom's three "best facts" might be (a) that her husband left her with two small children; (b) that there were numerous problems in the apartment—lack of heat, leaking roof, and roaches—which were not remedied; and (c) that the Health Department found roach infestation. From this list you might use the theme, "This is a case about a single mother of two young children whose complaints to the landlord about dangerous conditions in her apartment were ignored even after verification of the problems by the Health Department."

---

18. James W. McElhaney, *Opening Statements: To Be Effective with the Jury, Tell a Good Story*, 81 A.B.A. J. 73, 74 (1995). As Edmond Cahn, the great lawyer, philosopher, and teacher, put it, "Where justice is thought of in the customary manner as an ideal mode or condition, the human response will be merely contemplative, and contemplation bakes no loaves. But the response to a real or imagined instance of injustice is something quite different; it is alive with movement and warmth." Edmond Cahn, *The Sense of Injustice: An Anthropocentric View of Law* 13–14 (1964).
19. Amsterdam & Bruner, *supra* note 3, at 129–131.

4. Are there any refrains that recur in the sequence of events in the case? Again, return to your chronology and try to identify patterns of conduct, conversation, or conflict and consider whether these patterns reflect a theme. Your theme should weave together all the principal facts in your case, and identification of refrains can assist you in that process.[20] Ask yourself: If you were directing a film about your case, what recurring images and setting shots would you include to evoke the audience's sympathy for your client or antipathy for your opponent?[21] In the Ransom case, for example, Mr. Dusak can point to a pattern of prompt response to Ms. Ransom's complaints (at the beginning of February, he sent the plumber to the apartment; in April, the roofer fixed the roof; and on April 19, the exterminator came to the apartment) and the failure of Ms. Ransom to follow up when the problems persisted. His theme might be, "This case is about a landlord who always tried to repair his tenant's apartment even though the tenant did not live up to her responsibilities to keep the landlord fully informed about problems."
5. What stock stories favorable to your client are similar to your case? Identify different popular television shows, books, films, music, commercials, even well-known Biblical references, and consider whether any of those themes might resonate with your audience and reflect positively on your case. Prosecutors, for example, have used themes from *Oliver Twist*, *Doctor Jekyll and Mr. Hyde*, *Pinocchio*, the Cain and Abel story, and *The Godfather* for their stories in summation.[22] In a bench trial, consider the judge's "scripts" for the particular type of proceeding: her expectations for the kinds of witnesses and testimony that are usually presented to tell this type of story.[23] Although evidentiary rules in some jurisdictions may prohibit explicit references to a particular story as prejudicial,[24] identification of these stock stories can help you discover a shared reference that connects with your audience.

   A good example of the successful use of stock stories in litigation is an actual complex corporate case in which the plaintiff sued the defendant for breach of contract, and the defendant impleaded the subcontractor arguing that it in fact had not done its job. The testimony in large part came from accounting experts, and, by the time of closing arguments, the jury was bored and bewildered. Then the plaintiff's attorney rose for his closing: "You know this reminds me of a story, and it's a story you already know from Aesop's fables." The jurors' eyes lit up, and the lawyer continued with the story of the *Butcher and His Two Customers*. Two men were buying chicken at a butcher's stall in the marketplace, and, while the butcher's back was turned for a moment, one of them snatched up the chicken and quickly thrust it under the other's coat, where it could not be seen.

20. Even patterns of ostensibly minor errors or problems can, when viewed in the aggregate, appear quite significant. See Malcolm, *supra* note 2, at 121 ("[W]hen there are so many [minor] incidents, a feeling of suspicion begins to arise and, finally, one of antipathy toward the person who appears to be trying to get away with something.").
21. Meyer, *supra* note 15, at 17.
22. See cases described in Thomas M. Fleming, Annotation, *Negative Characterization or Description of Defendant, by Prosecutor During Summation of Criminal Trial, As Ground for Reversal, New Trial, or Mistrial—Modern Cases*, 88 A.L.R. 4th 8, 195–202 (1991).
23. Holland, *supra* note 13, at 225.
24. *Id.*; see, e.g., *Commonwealth v. Graziano*, 368 Mass. 325, 331 N.E.2d 808 (1975).

When the butcher turned round, he missed the chicken at once and accused both customers with stealing it. But the one who had taken it said he did not have it, and the one who had it said he had not taken it. The butcher looked back and forth at each of them and said, "This is interesting for I can see that though each of you tells half the truth, put together, your two half truths make *one complete lie*." After deliberations, the foreperson of the jury announced a verdict for the plaintiff "because we think the other parties tell one complete lie."[25]

6. Will your theme still have meaning at the end of the trial? In traditional fiction, "[a] primary function of narrative endings is . . . to provide or confirm a teleology or retrospective rationale for the story as a whole, and stories which lack such endings, whatever their fascinations, are often accounted unsatisfactory."[26] Similarly, in legal storytelling, unless your theme holds up through the presentation of your adversary's case until the closure of the trial, the decision-maker may find little meaning in your story. Of course, your adversary's case may challenge the credibility of much of your case. But, in developing a unifying theme, consider all the possible facts that will be presented at trial—especially those that are uncontested—and ask yourself whether your theme can withstand these challenges. If, for example, in the Ransom case, Ms. Ransom's husband left her because she allegedly mistreated her children, a theme focusing on Ms. Ransom's plight as a single mother may not be very effective. The theme must unify your case from start to finish. It cannot just be a slick slogan.

In some situations, especially more complex cases, you might have multiple themes for your case. Like popular entertainment films, your stories will weave these themes together simultaneously. But when you use multiple themes, you need to make sure that they are consistent and that both will hold up at the end of the case. Representing the landlord in the Ransom case, for example, an attorney would have problems persuading a decision-maker if she used both the theme that the apartment had no problems as well as the theme that her client always tried to repair the problems in the tenant's apartment. Pleading in the alternative might be allowed under the rules of civil procedure, but telling a story with alternative themes has the potential for losing narrative impact.

§13.5 CHOOSING PERSUASIVE IMAGES

The crafting of a convincing story also requires the selection of persuasive images and metaphors. Try to visualize "word pictures that call up a vivid mental representation of [the] persons and circumstances" of your case.[27] Remember that narrative thinking is not solely an intellectual process. One or two powerful images can persuade a decision-maker in ways that a logical argument cannot. As trial attorney Gerry Spence observes:

---

25. *Panel Discussion: Developing the 5th MacCrate Skill—the Art of Storytelling*, 26 Pace L. Rev. 501, 506–507 (2006) [hereinafter, *Art of Storytelling*] (story told by Joel ben Izzy, a storytelling consultant for the United States Attorney's Office and major law firms in California).
26. Leitch, *supra* note 2, at 43.
27. Schuetz & Snedaker, *supra* note 16, at 46.

I don't choose the intellectual words like, "My client suffered grave emotional distress as a result of the evil fraud committed against him by the defendant bank." Instead, in my mind's eye I see my client coming home at night, and I tell the story:

> I see Joe . . . trudging home at night to face a heap of unpaid bills sitting on the kitchen table. Nothing but the bills greet him in that cold, empty place, the pipes frozen, the heat turned off by the power company. He couldn't pay the utility bill, remember? I see my client, . . . worn out, exhausted, a man without a penny, without pride, without hope. An empty man. The bank had it all. Even all of Joe.[28]

Although images may grow out of your themes, their purpose is not to capture the meaning of your entire story, but rather to paint a picture of a particular character or event in your story. As to characters, consider, for example, what mental picture you want the decision-maker to have of your client, your adversary, or a key witness in the case. Consistent with the uncontested facts and your theme, what characteristics would you attribute to each of them? What are the two or three adjectives you can apply to them? What images would you use to describe their motives? What television or movie characters are similar to them?

Also, imagine how your adversary will characterize your client and what image can counteract that portrayal. This process is especially important when your client may appear unsympathetic to your audience. The lawyer for subway vigilante Bernhard Goetz, for example, sought to create sympathy for his client by portraying him as a person "just like you and me" with the same fears and emotions.[29] Lawyers for corporate defendants may respond to the negative image of faceless "big business" by painting their clients as employers of decent, hard-working people who serve socially beneficial functions.[30] Or consider the story told by the defense in a mob trial. One of the defendants, Louis Failla, was a reputed mafia soldier who was accused of conspiracy to murder.[31] Relying on taped conversations of Failla, the prosecution sought to portray him as a sinister character who methodically plotted an execution. In response, Failla's lawyer depicted Failla as a comic character, "the exaggerator," who was only engaging in wild speculation in the taped conversation. Failla's attorney painted him as a sympathetic character, "a low-level Mafioso struggling to make a living, trapped by the orders and commands coming down from the . . . capo."[32] To undermine the prosecution's image of a cold-blooded mafia murderer, the defense sought to portray Failla as the "bumbling everyman."

---

28. Gerry Spence, *Let Me Tell You a Story*, Trial, Feb. 1995, at 72, 77.
29. Sherwin, *supra* note 14, at 218.
30. See generally Foley & Robbins, *supra* note 3, at 474–475.
31. This description is based on articles discussing the storytelling techniques used by the defense in this trial, see Meyer, *supra* note 15, at 90–114; Phil Meyer, *Why a Jury Trial Is More Like a Movie Than a Novel*, 28 J.L. & Soc'y 133, 138–146 (2001); Philip N. Meyer, "*Desperate for Love III*": *Rethinking Closing Arguments as Stories*, 50 S.C. L. Rev. 715 (1999) [hereinafter Meyer, *Rethinking Closing Arguments*] and Philip M. Meyer, "*Desperate for Love*": *Cinematic Influences Upon a Defendant's Closing Argument to a Jury*, 18 Vt. L. Rev. 721 (1994) [hereinafter Meyer, *Cinematic Influences*]. The judge, however, departed from the federal sentencing guidelines and gave Failla a lenient sentence. Meyer, *supra* note 15, at 207.
32. Meyer, *Cinematic Influences*, *supra* note 31, at 728.

This process of characterization requires selection of key, appropriate details about your client—her physical and psychological description, her dialogue, and, most importantly, her actions. Overloading the description with identifying details can detract from your attempt to create a clear, compelling image. It is primarily through what your client said and did that the audience can come to an understanding of her character traits.[33]

Also, consider that the character of your client does not have to remain fixed or static. As in a film or television series, individuals can have "character arcs"; their character may be transformed as the story progresses. In fact, the "Trouble" in the case may have a significant impact on the way your client responds to events. In a domestic violence case, for example, a partner, who up to that point had been a passive victim, may finally take control of her situation after a particularly abusive event. On the other hand, consider that in narrative, the image of a character can often foreshadow what will happen next. In your presentation of the story, take into account whether the character of your client previews for the audience the upcoming events or paints a picture that ultimately will appear unrealistic.[34]

In some cases, the image of particular events in a case will also be significant. Here, focus on what images or metaphors capture the feelings of those events. Remember that a story proceeds from a steady state of affairs to Trouble to some kind of outcome (see §13.1). Consider the image you want to paint for the pre-Trouble times and the aftermath. In the Ransom case, for example, try to visualize Ms. Ransom and her family moving into the apartment, eager to establish a new home. Then, imagine the setting when she telephoned Mr. Dusak on April 12 and complained about the roach problem, and he accused her of causing the infestation. One possible portrait of that event would be a mother, clutching her baby, being tormented by the roaches overrunning her apartment as her landlord berates her on the phone. Depending upon the nature of the audience, these images and similar ones can effectively be used throughout the trial to support a unifying theme that Ms. Ransom was the victim of terrible housing conditions and a callous landlord.

You should be wary, however, of the dangers of weak metaphors. As storyteller Joel ben Izzy puts it, "Finding the right [metaphor] is like striking gold. Finding a bad one is like striking fool's gold—you think you've got something until you run to show everyone in the saloon and they laugh in your face."[35] Accordingly, once you have identified a possible metaphor, test it against your chronology and see if it is consistent with the facts in the case. If, for example, Ms. Ransom's lawyer portrays the persistent leaking ceiling as causing her client's family to "drown in a sea of rainwater," the metaphor will only strike a resonance with the decision maker if she can demonstrate substantial damage to her client's property or inconvenience to the family. If the damage merely stained some wallpaper and did not significantly intrude on daily life, the use of the metaphor might actually harm Ms. Ransom's case.

---

33. Meyer, *supra* note 15, at 83–85.
34. Philip N. Meyer, *Vignettes from a Narrative Primer*, 12 Legal Writing J. 229, 263–264 (2006).
35. Joel ben Izzy, *10 Ways to Know if Your Story Is Ready to Tell in Court*, Trial, July 1998, at 91, 93.

§13.6 SELECTING A STORY GENRE

When most of us hear the term genre, we think in terms of "science fiction," "comedy," "tragedy," "western," or, in the cinematic context, "melodrama" or "film noir." Although such categories do not appear very applicable to the lawyer's craft, genre means more than simply different types of literature or films. Narrative genres are "mental models representing possible ways in which events in the world can go."[36] When we read or hear a story in a given genre, we have specific expectations that it will conform to certain norms and conventions, rules of that genre. In a comedy, for example, we expect that the characters will find themselves in a humorous situation that will be resolved in a comical manner and do not anticipate encountering mass murders. The expectations created by a genre assist an audience in finding meaning in a story. Stated in a different way: the conventions of a genre help to give a story internal logic.

For a lawyer, three different aspects of genre are important: sequencing, perspective, and tone. In regard to sequencing, you have several options in telling the story. You can follow the conventional chronological approach and present the story as a linear series of events. You can use a flashback approach, starting at the end of the story and then returning to tell the events that built up to the conclusion. Or you can adopt an episodic structure, moving back and forth between different events in the chronology.

The choice of sequencing genre depends on a number of factors: the complexity of the fact situation, the significance of one or two key facts in either your or your adversary's case, and your unifying theme. If your case is a simple factual situation of cause and effect events, you will probably want to stick to the standard chronological order. Most people find such an approach to be the easiest to understand (see Chapter 12). If, however, your case is very complex and the audience can become distracted waiting for the climax, consider the flashback or episodic approaches. The use of flashback sequencing can be very helpful if you want your listeners to be focusing on one or two key facts throughout the storytelling. In a products liability case with serious medical injury, for example, the plaintiff might want to start off the story with the details of the accident before presenting facts about the purchase of the product. As trial lawyer Gerry Spence recounts:

> If I want the jury to understand the devastation of defective brakes on a vehicle and the responsibility of the car manufacturer for having loosed such killing monsters on the road for profit, I begin with a picture of my client driving along on a pleasant Sunday afternoon.
>
> > It is one of those fresh spring days when we are glad to be alive. The sky is a deep Wyoming blue. The sun is warm and the wildflowers are on stage. Suddenly, a cow jumps up out of the barrow pit, and Sammy slams on the brakes. The rear brakes—something is the matter with them! Sammy's veins are suddenly flooded with adrenaline. His heart is in his throat. His brand-new car begins to swerve and the rear of the car begins

---

36. Amsterdam & Bruner, *supra* note 3, at 133.

> to come around. He is trapped! If he takes his foot off the brake, he will hit the cow and be seriously injured or killed. If he doesn't, his car will careen out of control and wreck. He realizes he is about to die.[37]

Such an approach may hold the listener's attention to the very end of the story.

An episodic approach can be useful, especially in a complex case, for focusing on certain events and downplaying others. In a criminal case, for example, where the defense theme is that the complainant is biased against the defendant, the defendant's story may downplay the events surrounding the incident and concentrate on the different episodes when the complainant displayed his animosity toward the defendant. In an automobile accident case, a plaintiff's lawyer might want to tell the story in different episodes: (1) the actual injury inflicted on the client; (2) the defendant's conduct prior to the accident; (3) the plaintiff's conduct before the accident; (4) the money damages incurred by the plaintiff; and (5) the expert reconstruction of the accident. In a complex case, the cumulative effect of these discrete episodes may be more powerful than the standard chronology. Although in the initial episodes, the audience might be a bit bewildered about "what really happened," by the end of the case, the fact-finder can put all the pieces together.

The second aspect of storytelling genre that is important for lawyers is perspective. Perhaps the simplest and clearest understanding of perspective or point of view may be derived from watching movies. Perspective may be conceptualized and understood simply as (1) where the cameras and microphones are placed to record the action, (2) who the story centers on (typically most films track the movements of the protagonist), and (3) the stance of the moviemaker in relationship to the subject matter and theme of the story and the characters within it.[38]

You can choose the point of view from which to tell your stories. You can adopt the viewpoint of your client, a witness to the event, or a third-party narrator. The selection of a perspective is important because of its impact on the meaning of the story to the audience. In choosing your point of view, it is essential to consider your unifying theme. If it is very personal to your client and you believe the decision-maker can sympathize with your client, the story should probably be told from your client's perspective.

In the Ransom case, for example, if Ms. Ransom's theme is that she was victimized by her landlord, a first-person narrative could be very effective. If, however, your theme relies on the credibility of a certain witness who is not your client, you might want to frame the story from that person's point of view. If the Department of Health inspector had written a dynamite report and visited the apartment on a number of occasions, a story from his perspective might be very helpful. If you want the decision-maker to view the case from a number of viewpoints or to view the facts as "the objective onlooker," you will probably adopt the third-person narrator approach. Prosecutors often strategically use a third-person, omniscient perspective to appear as if they are presenting the

---

37. Spence, *supra* note 28, at 74.
38. Meyer, *supra* note 15, at 138.

undisputable "objective" truth.[39] If you adopt an episodic approach to your story, there is no impediment to telling your story from a number of different perspectives. A very effective example of this narrative technique is the film *Rashomon*, in which a crime is described by several witnesses with very different perspectives.

Finally, consider the tone of your story. Many lawyers simply adopt a somber tone to their storytelling and do not consider any other alternative. Audiences, however, want to enjoy the stories they hear and are not always receptive to the stereotypical lawyerly style. Your tone obviously is affected somewhat by the nature of the case. In most murder cases, for example, a comical tone is not appropriate. But, again, it is important to consider your underlying theme. If your theme focuses on the grave wrong committed against your client, certainly an indignant tone is appropriate. But if your theme is the weakness of your adversary's case, a humorous tone—with dashes of sarcasm and irony—might be very effective. A melodramatic tone might be useful for the defendant in a negligence case when her theme is the senseless tragedy that has befallen both the plaintiff and herself.[40] In a political trial, the defendants may want to adopt a satiric tone, highlighting the absurdity of the government's case.[41] And in a post-conviction brief for a criminal defendant in a death penalty case, the lawyer might want to use the tone of a detective story to wean the decision maker from the impression that the version of "facts" presented in the trial court proceedings is open to question.[42]

Also consider your opponent's genre and the possibility of using a counter-trope to undermine his story. In the Failla case discussed in §13.5, for example, in response to the prosecutor's stern morality tale about a crime family of evil mobsters, the defense attorney attempted to tell a poignant counter-story about his tender-hearted client who simply stumbled into trouble because of his tendency to exaggerate. In this way, the attorney attempted to convert an ostensibly straightforward historical account of a mob crime into a more nuanced psychological narrative.[43]

After choosing your genre—selecting your sequencing approach, perspective, and tone—try to remain consistent with the genre throughout your story. Genre creates expectations in the audience about the conventions that will be used in the storytelling. Deviations from these conventions will negatively impact the effectiveness of the storytelling.[44] Thus, for example, if you abruptly switch from a

---

39. *Id.* at 152.
40. "The genre of melodrama presents the battle between good and evil reduced to its simplest form, where the hero-protagonist battles to the death against the . . . evil, black-caped villain, the antagonistic force against whom the hero's worth is measured." Meyer, *supra* note 15, at 20. See Neil Feigenson, *Legal Blame: How Jurors Think and Talk about Accidents* 119 (2000) (describing why melodrama is a good genre for plaintiffs in accident cases because it focuses on the plaintiff and her suffering and the conception of the accident as the personal agency of the "bad guy").
41. See Schuetz and Snedaker, *supra* note 16, at 223 for a discussion of the use of a burlesque genre by the defense in the "Chicago Eight" case.
42. Plilip N. Meyer, *Adaptation: What Post-Conviction Relief Practitioners in Death Penalty Cases Might Learn from Popular Storytellers About Narrative Persuasion,* in 7 *Law and Popular Culture* 651, 665 (Michael Freedman ed., 2005).
43. See Meyer, *Rethinking Closing Arguments, supra* note 31, at 740–741.
44. Research on mood effects on judgments demonstrates that people evaluate a story more favorably when it puts them in a mood that they expect to hear from that kind of story. Feigenson, *supra* note 40, at 117 n.4.

chronological approach to an episodic approach, or from a first-person to a third-person narrative, or from a tragic to a comic approach, the story will lose its coherence.

§13.7 FINDING THE STORY IN THE FACTS

Once you have identified the uncontested facts, the nature of your audience, your unifying theme, the persuasive images supporting that theme, and your genre, you are ready to put together your story. As with any creative project, there is no mechanical formula for spinning a persuasive yarn. Psychological research on the creative writing process, however, provides some helpful insights into the craft of drafting a persuasive story.[45]

1. Visualizing the story.

As lawyers, we have a tendency to view cases primarily in verbal terms: causes of action, legal rights, case law, statutes, witness statements, and legal documents. Such an approach is in the realm of paradigmatic thinking. Narrative thinking, however, focuses not only on the verbal and logical but also on the emotional and irrational. For that reason, begin finding your story by visualizing the narrative flow.

To visualize their tales, many filmmakers create storyboards with sketches depicting the significant changes of action in the movie and consider alternative sequencing of the scenes. You can adapt this approach to legal storytelling by experimenting with different sequencing of the episodes listed on your chronology. Do not just rely on a linear presentation of your story. Review your chronology and select the key episodes with which you might want to frame your movie or cable series to introduce the audience to your client and the case. Ask yourself, "What episode encapsulates the theme of my narrative?" "What event foreshadows the Trouble in the story?" "What scene starkly shows my client's or the opponent's character?"

Then, from your opening scene, refashion the sequence of episodes in your chronology to show a clear flow of the action in the case. Filter out extraneous episodes with details that will only detract from that flow and highlight those episodes that will capture the audience's interest in knowing what happens next. Consider whether you can arrange the action to reflect a familiar stock story, film, or cable series. In addition, imagine how your sequencing will conclude. Does the

45. The following sources were consulted in writing this section and can be referred to for further reading on the subject of drafting stories: Jerome Bruner, *The Conditions of Creativity*, in H. Gruber et al., *Contemporary Approaches to Creative Thinking* 1 (1962); Mihaly Csikszentmihalyi, *Creativity: Flow and the Psychology of Discovery and Invention* 235–258 (1996); Meyer, *supra* note 15; *Art of Storytelling*, *supra* note 25; Charlotte L. Doyle, *The Writer Tells: The Creative Process in the Writing of Literary Fiction*, 11 Creativity Res. J. 29 (1998).

ending give the audience an understanding of the meaning of the action or does it leave the audience bewildered, or at worst, let the audience down?[46]

Then, reviewing your sequencing, consider how the action shows the images and the character arcs for your client and other key players. Remember, in developing your story, to try to show your characters' motivations and reactions to experiences through speech and concrete action rather than through abstract, third-party summarizations of their feelings—in other words, through *showing* rather than *telling*.[47] Accordingly, review your chronology after you have reorganized it. Picture the images of your client and other characters shown by the flow of scenes.

Ask yourself, for example, whether the image of your client has been clearly shown, whether the trajectory of your client's character arc has been fully developed, and whether your adversary's motivations are reflected in these episodes. What additional scenes will complete the picture you want to paint? What scenes can you eliminate to help the audience visualize those images better? And have your scenes not only shown your client's action but also her emotions? In other words, as Ms. Ransom's lawyer, instead of simply telling the audience that your client felt distressed, you should use her dialogue and interactions with her landlord to show that fact.

Finally, review your reorganized chronology and consider whether the mental picture it presents to the audience reflects your story's theme. Do the key episodes help the audience clearly visualize the Trouble? Are the refrains—patterns of conduct, conversation, or conflict—presented? Have you highlighted your best facts? And, most importantly, does your theme still hold up for the audience after the presentation of all the episodes?

2. *Hearing your client's voice.*

Writers of fiction do not simply present information about their characters. They often construct a new reality by letting their characters take on a life of their own. They hear them, get into their minds, and even feel their emotions. Through this process, they enter into their characters' world. Similarly, in a legal case, your storytelling should not simply repeat the chronology of events. Your client, even if it is a large corporation, has its own point of view, experience, and personality, not just a legal claim or defense.[48] In your client and witness interviews, you should try to enter your client's world, identify her feelings and outlooks, and consider the

---

46. "The concept of purposeful motion is crucial in all storytelling: the narrative must be directed to a culmination—some ending or termination (either restorative or transformative) that the sequence of events anticipates." Meyer, *supra* note 15, at 64.

47. See David Lodge, *Showing and Telling*, in *The Art of Fiction* 121, 122 (1992) (arguing that "[t]he purest from of showing is the quoted speech of characters, in which language exactly mirrors the event. . . . The purest form of telling is the authorial summary in which the conciseness and abstraction of the narrator's language effaces the particularity and individuality of the characters and their actions"); Meyer, *supra* note 34, at 241–43, 251–53; Meyer, *supra* note 42, at 669.

48. This task can be quite daunting for a large institutional client. An analysis of how litigators against the gun industry tell their stories demonstrates that lawsuits brought by private individuals who were victims of gun violence have been more successful than those initiated by governmental bodies because the government cases were much more difficult to translate into melodramatic dramatic form. Allen

motivations for her actions or inactions. Through this process, you can start to construct a perspective and tone for your story.

3. Paying attention to the rhythms and textures of the events in the case.

Writers also report that their craft requires focusing on patterns of events and behavior. In a compelling story, episodes do not occur willy-nilly. Rather, there is usually a rhythm to the plot with emphasis on particular events and silence as to others. A skilled writer pays attention to these rhythms and textures.[49] Moreover, they recognize the importance of *stretch*: the slow-motion telling of a particular part of a story to clue the audience into the relative importance of that scene.[50] In crafting a legal story, then, try to identify patterns in the parties' conduct, character, and relationship and the key events on which you wish to focus. As you imagine the events unfolding from a steady state to Trouble to resolution, pay attention to these rhythms. This process can help you identify a unifying theme, persuasive images for characters, and the best approach for sequencing the narrative.

4. Recognizing the role of detail in storytelling.

Creative storytellers recognize the benefits and weaknesses of the use of detail in narrative. On the one hand, a story that is rich in detail can create vivid images in the audience's mind. It can make the characters and episodes come alive. Also, by creating a mental reality, it facilitates memory.[51] On the other hand, "[t]he person who insists on speaking the whole truth, who painfully spells out every last detail of an action and interrupts his wife to say it was Tuesday, not Wednesday . . . is not honored for his honesty but is shunned for his tiresomeness."[52] In crafting your stories, consider those details that make your images seem real, the voice of your client heard, and the patterns seem clear. At the same time, eliminate those details that might simply lose the audience's attention.

5. Making the story both novel and appropriate.

A creative product is not only novel, but it is also entirely appropriate. It produces the "Aha!" experience—we recognize that it reflects a fitting insight into a particular situation or problem but are surprised by the inventive spin the product gives it. In crafting stories, writers attempt to balance these two contradictory goals: to construct a novel view of reality but in a form suitable to the particular narrative. Likewise, when you attempt to draft a story about your case,

---

Rostron, *Shooting Stories: The Creation of Narrative and Melodrama in Real and Fictional Litigation Against the Gun Industry,* 73 UMKC L. Rev. 1047, 1070 (2005).

49. Ben Izzy, *supra* note 35, at 92 (noting that, "Every good story revolves around a pause. Somewhere in your tale is a point where you can stop, take a breath, and feel your audience's interest mount. It is a moment of silence that you can actually hear, when listeners ask themselves, 'And then what happened?'").

50. Meyer, *supra* note 15, at 127.

51. Hendall Haven, *Story Proof: The Science Behind the Startling Power of Story* 63 (2007).

52. Malcolm, *supra* note 2, at 4.

you need to consider not only how to present an imaginative and inventive version of the facts but also how to make that narrative persuasive to your particular audience given the uncontested facts in the case. You want them to respond, "Aha! That's a different but believable way of viewing these facts!"

Think of this task as a creative writing assignment, not a legal drafting project. Write out a complete draft of your case as a short story and not just jot down your ideas about a possible narrative. You will not actually present your story at the hearing, in a negotiation, or in your brief. Nor, for that matter, will you present verbatim the multitude of legal memos that you drafted to prepare your case. But, just as the writing of memoranda helps you to hone your legal arguments, the process of carefully crafting your story will assist you in developing a persuasive and imaginative narrative. Only by putting your story on paper will you be able to assess adequately, for example, whether or not you have chosen the appropriate genre for presentation of the facts, the most persuasive theme for the audience, or the most compelling images to support that theme.

Finally, after writing your story, read it aloud to colleagues, friends, or relatives and obtain their feedback about whether they were persuaded. Did they identify your theme? What images, metaphors, or word choice caught their fancy and what left them cold? How do they feel about your sequencing? Did they enjoy listening to it? How do they think your fact-finder will respond to the story? In other words, ask them whether or not the story "spoke" to them or whether or not it left them indifferent.

§13.8 ETHICAL STORYTELLING

The law of rhetoric . . . is that one must lie in order to speak the truth.

Sartre

By its very nature, storytelling distorts facts. By placing the facts within the context of a narrative with a unifying theme, a specific genre, and persuasive images, all fashioned for a particular audience, a storyteller seeks to convey a particular meaning to that audience. In so doing, she "hides [any] discontinuities, ellipses, and contradictory experiences that would undermine the intended meaning."[53] Obviously, another storyteller (your adversary) could craft the same facts into an entirely different story with an entirely different meaning.

This does not mean, however, that your use of storytelling to present the facts is unethical. Just as the ethical rules permit you, within certain limits, to fashion interpretations of legal authority to support your client's case,[54] they also allow you to present facts in a light most favorable to your client. The only ethical limitation on this ability is that the story must be supported by facts that the lawyer

53. William Cronon, *A Place for Stories: Nature, History and Narrative*, 78 J. Am. Hist. 1347, 1349–1350 (1992).
54. See Rule 3.3(a)(1) and (2) of the Model Rules of Professional Conduct.

"knows or believes, or has a good faith basis to believe, are true."[55] In particular, a lawyer cannot "make a false statement of fact . . . to a tribunal or fail to correct a false statement of material fact . . . previously made to the tribunal by the lawyer"; cannot "offer evidence that the lawyer knows to be false"; and shall, in an adjudicative proceeding, take reasonable remedial measures, including, if necessary, disclosure to the tribunal, if she has knowledge that a person intends to "engage, is engaging or has engaged in criminal or fraudulent conduct related to the proceeding."[56] You may not coach a client or a witness to change a story merely because it will make a more persuasive one.[57] But where the client's good faith version of the facts differs from that of the adversary, the ethical rules require you to defer to the client.[58]

55. Steven Lubet, *The Trial As a Persuasive Story*, 14 Am. J. of Tr. Advoc. 77, 84 (1990). For a discussion of the ethics of lawyer storytelling, see *id.* at 81–86.
56. Model Rules 3.3(a)(1) and (3) and 3.3(b).
57. Model Rule 3.4(b).
58. Model Rule 1.2(a).

CHAPTER 14

SELECTING A MODEL FOR PRESENTATION OF THE CASE

A judge decides for ten reasons
nine of which nobody knows.

Chinese proverb

The three models described in Chapters 11, 12, and 13—legal elements, chronology, and story—are tools for organizing our thinking about the facts of a case. They help us to recognize that the significance of a particular fact depends, in large part, on the mode of thinking we are using in processing it. In the paradigmatic, legal elements model a fact is important insofar as it supports or undermines a given legal proposition. In the chronological model, a fact's significance lies in its relation to other facts in a cause and effect chain of events. And in stories, facts are of consequence to the extent that they are woven into a tale, with a genre, theme, and images, intended to convey a meaning to the audience. Just as the briefing of cases helps lawyers understand how judges interpret the law, these models help lawyers determine how their audience will construct the facts.

The presentation of facts, however, is not so simple. No lawyer presents to the judge, jury, hearing officer, or adversary—in oral argument, brief, witness examination, or negotiation—a legal elements or chronology chart or the draft of a short story. In most forums, the procedural and evidentiary rules would prohibit such a presentation of the facts. Although in briefs, opening statements, and closing arguments you have some ability to use one of the three models as your template, there are many restrictions even on these forms of advocacy. Legal argument, for example, is usually not permitted in opening statements to juries. And in witness examination—when many facts are presented at a trial—the question and answer format and rules of evidence significantly inhibit the use of these models for the presentation of facts. You obviously cannot start your direct examination by asking, "Referring to the proximate cause element, please give us the facts to show how the defendant proximately caused this accident?"

But more importantly, even if the procedural and evidentiary rules allowed for presentation of these charts and stories at trials, decision-makers usually do not separate their thinking about the facts in a case into such discrete categories. At a bench trial, for example, the judge will almost certainly be relating the facts to the legal elements of the cause of action at the same time she is considering whether there is a consistent sequencing of the events presented in a party's case and determining whether the story told by each party has meaning to her. As Kim Lane Scheppele has observed with respect to judicial decision-making:

> Courts don't first settle on an interpretation of the facts and then figure out what the law means. The practice of judging simultaneously engages both in an on-going project of meaning-making, producing a single opinion in which fact and law are woven together in one coherent whole. Constructing the facts and constructing the law are not two separate enterprises, but are mutually implicated in the same project.[1]

Indeed, in most cases, you will use a combination of all three models at trial, in an appeal, or in negotiation.

Even though the models themselves cannot be used in a brief or at trial, they can be very helpful for selecting the most persuasive approach for presenting the facts. In some cases, a decision-maker will prefer the use of a particular approach for the presentation of facts, and these models will aid you in determining the significant facts upon which to focus. For example, in a high-volume state court (for example, an eviction or consumer collection courtroom), a judge will probably prefer almost a pure legal elements approach. In fact, in such tribunals, plaintiff's lawyers in closing argument will simply marshal the facts to the legal elements. On the other hand, in an informal administrative hearing, such as an unemployment compensation proceeding before a nonlawyer, the hearing officer will probably favor a simple presentation of the facts in a chronological format. And in a high-stakes medical malpractice trial, the jurors will probably expect to hear a

---

1. Kim Lane Scheppele, *Facing Facts in Legal Interpretation*, 30 Representations 42, 60 (1990). Similarly, Jerome Bruner and Tony Amsterdam assert,

> To be sure, results in the law are achieved by the application of specialized legal reasoning—reasoning within and about doctrinal rules, procedural requirements, constitutional and other jurisprudential theories—and are articulated almost wholly in those terms. But final results are *underdetermined* by such rules, requirements, and theories. They are influenced as well by how people think, categorize, tell stories, deploy rhetorics, and make cultural sense as they go about interpreting and applying rules, requirements, and theories.

Anthony G. Amsterdam & Jerome Bruner, *Minding the Law* 287–288 (2000).

good story. In any of these cases, the models will help you to identify which facts are essential to the presentation of the case.

You are not necessarily bound by a decision-maker's preference for a particular kind of presentation based on customs of the tribunal or time pressures. By reviewing the legal elements, chronology, and story models, you can determine which organization of the facts is most convincing for your client. The lawyer for Ms. Ransom, for example, might reject an approach which restricts the presentation to those facts necessary to support the legal elements of the claim because telling the whole story offers a more compelling account of Ms. Ransom's case. In fact, some commentators contend that stories can have a "transformative" power to compel decision-makers to overcome existing legal rules (the paradigmatic approach) and challenge the status quo.[2] Because of the legal requirements of the case, Ms. Ransom's lawyer will also have to take the legal elements model into account, but she will try to infuse the elements into her story.

Finally, the models can help you prepare arguments and witnesses. Because this is not a text on trial or appellate advocacy, we will not discuss at length techniques for applying the three models at different stages of the trial, appellate, or administrative process. Some general examples, however, can demonstrate how these models can be applied in practice:

1. a lawyer concentrating on a chronology of events will probably try, as much as possible, to sequence her witnesses and the testimony in each of their examinations so that a clear presentation of the chain of events is presented;
2. if a lawyer decides to focus on a legal elements approach in her appeal, she will probably want to organize the different points in her brief in terms of the language of the factual propositions which her elements chart shows that the plaintiff must prove;
3. in a jury trial in which the legal elements are complex and potentially confusing to the jury, an attorney cannot ignore the fact the judge will instruct the jurors on the issues, but she can try to create a narrative "hook" to translate the issues into simpler terms;[3]
4. a storytelling lawyer will attempt to inject into her entire case—opening statement, direct examination, cross-examination, closing argument—language and images that reflect her unifying theme;
5. a lawyer who adopts a storytelling approach with a jury will use word choice, voice inflection, and body language throughout the presentation of her case consistent with the tone she has adopted for the story;
6. if a criminal defendant's story is not very strong, his attorney will probably choose to use a legal elements approach raising reasonable doubt as to particular

---

2. See, for example, Richard Delgado, *Storytelling for Oppositionists and Others: A Plea for Narrative*, 87 Mich. L. Rev. 2411 (1989); Richard K. Sherwin, *The Narrative Construction of Legal Reality*, 18 Vt. L. Rev. 681, 709–716 (1994) (describing the successful use of storytelling in the petitioner's brief in *Miranda v. Arizona*, 384 U.S. 436 (1966)).

3. Philip N. Meyer, *Storytelling for Lawyers* 33–35 (2014) (describing how the plaintiff's attorney in a complex strict liability case used the narrative hook of an Old English case ("If the lion gets away, [the owner] pays") to simplify the legal theory for the jury).

elements of the prosecution's case rather than attempting to present the weak counter-narrative.[4]

7. if a case is being tried in a courtroom with the facilities for projecting exhibits and visual aids, the lawyers can help the judge or jury visualize their cases—for example by creating a case timeline in the courtroom as the witnesses testify about particular events; by highlighting on a diagram key aspects of a particular scene or event; or by displaying in dramatic order multiple photographs of the injury or contested condition.

A lawyer might use one approach in one part of a case and another at a different stage. In arguing a motion for a judgment as a matter of law after the presentation of a party's case, for example, the parties will certainly focus their arguments on the legal elements model. The issue on such a motion is whether there is no legally sufficient evidentiary basis for a reasonable jury to have found for that party with respect to that issue. (In some jurisdictions, this motion is called a directed verdict motion.) On the other hand, in a closing argument in a jury trial, you will rarely present the facts solely in their relationship to the legal elements without presenting some chronology, if not a full-blown story. A chronology or story helps jurors to make sense out of all the facts.[5]

In selecting the mode of presentation, the question is not reduced to the old adage that when you are weak on the facts, argue the law and when you are weak on the law, argue the facts. Rather, it is which approach to the facts (legal elements, chronology, or story) will most likely present them in a convincing light to the fact-finder at that stage of the litigation. The different models help you sort out these issues.

---

4. See Reid Hastie, *The Role of "Stories" in Civil Jury Judgments*, 32 U. Mich. J.L. Reform 227, 232 (1999) (describing a study that suggests that in criminal trials a weak defense story results in slightly elevated conviction rates as compared to no defense story at all).

5. In closing arguments in a jury trial, however, it may be very dangerous for a lawyer to ignore totally the legal elements model. In an empirical study on the effect of organizational structure in opening and closings on juror decision making in a breach-of-contract case, the researchers found that strategically it was beneficial for both the plaintiff and defendant to organize their closing arguments using the legal elements model. Shelly C. Spiecker & Debra L. Worthington, *The Influence of Opening Statement/Closing Argument Organizational Strategy on Juror Verdict and Damages Awards*, 27 Law & Hum. Behav. 437, 452 (2003). They note that most jurors use the jury instructions (which reflect the legal elements model) in analyzing the evidence. They conclude, "[T]elling a story is not enough; it is also important to show jurors what to do with the story created." *Id.* at 451.

CHAPTER 15

STRENGTHENING THE PERSUASIVENESS OF YOUR FACTS

The drafting of your fact organization charts and story is an ongoing process. It is not a one-shot event occurring only after the interview of your client. Rather, after you have organized your facts, closely examine these instruments, assess the persuasiveness of your facts, and identify areas for future formal and informal discovery. As you receive responses to this discovery, update the charts and story and reevaluate them accordingly. As you ascertain your adversary's story, consider its effect on your construction of the facts. And as you uncover more information about the schemas of the audience, reconsider the approach you will take in presenting your facts at trial or in negotiation. In short, just as you continue legal research throughout your preparation of a case, frequently revisit your interpretation of the facts.

§15.1 ASSESSING THE LEGAL SUFFICIENCY OF YOUR FACTS

As you learned in Chapter 11, lawyers use the legal elements model to organize the facts according to the propositions underlying a legal right. The plaintiff's lawyer marshals the facts in support of each of the causes of action, and the defendant's lawyer organizes the facts in terms of the legal elements for the affirmative defenses and counterclaims. In this way, lawyers for both the prosecution/plaintiff and defendant can evaluate the adequacy of the facts in relation to the requirements of the relevant case law, statutes, and regulations. Specifically, the legal elements chart assists lawyers for all sides in examining two issues: (1) whether there are sufficient facts to establish each element of the claim or affirmative defense and (2) whether there are additional claims or affirmative defenses that the party might raise.

The first issue—whether there are sufficient facts to establish each element of the claim or affirmative defense—initially requires research of the legal meaning of each of the elements under the relevant case law, statutes, or regulations in the context of the facts of the case. In other words, you need to examine the factual proposition and fact columns of the legal elements chart and consider whether any issues arise concerning the interpretation of any of the legal elements. This is not necessarily an easy process since, as you have learned so far in law school, most cases arise precisely because of disputes over the meaning of particular elements.

Consider, for example, the Ransom case. On Chart 11A, *Sources of Legal Elements*, page 152, we show that the first legal element required by §500(a) of the Property Code is a "written or oral lease." And on Chart 11B, *Legal Elements to Factual Propositions*, page 152, we restate that general proposition as the following factual proposition: "Ms. Ransom has a written lease for 289 Hudson Street." When we marshal the facts, however, we find in Chart 11C, the *Ransom Legal Elements Chart*, page 153, that although Ms. Ransom told us at her interview she has a lease with Mr. Dusak (the landlord), the lease itself shows that it was signed only by Keith Ransom, Ms. Ransom's husband, from whom she is now separated. Ms. Ransom is not a signatory to the lease.

By matching all the facts discovered to the legal elements, we have identified a possible serious deficiency in Ms. Ransom's case. The protections of Property Code §500(a) only apply if Ms. Ransom has a written or oral lease with Mr. Dusak. Unless the meaning of the term "written or oral lease" can be expanded to Ms. Ransom's situation, she will not have a cause of action under that section. Examination of the legal elements chart helps you identify areas for further legal research. For example:

- Can a nonsignator of a written lease be considered a tenant under the lease for purposes of Property Code §500(a) if she was the spouse of the signatory at the time of the signing?
- Can a nonsignator of a written lease be considered a tenant under the lease for purposes of Property Code §500(a) if the landlord knew that she would be living in the dwelling at the time of the signing?
- Can a nonsignator of a written lease be considered a tenant for purposes of §500(a) if the landlord treated her as the tenant and accepted rent from her?
- After the signatory on a lease moves out of a dwelling, is an oral lease established with the remaining occupant when the landlord allows her to remain in the apartment and accepts rent from her?

Each of these legal issues, and perhaps others, must be researched to determine if, given the situation of Ms. Ransom's case, she can present any facts to support a claim that falls within the meaning of "written or oral lease" under the Property Code.

Once you have researched whether the facts of this case fall within the legal meaning of the elements, determine whether there are sufficient facts to establish each element of the claim or affirmative defense. At trial, you must present enough evidence on each element to establish a prima facie case. In other words, you must present facts "such that a reasonable person could draw from it the inference of the existence of the particular fact to be proved."[1] This inquiry may require not only research of the meaning of the elements but also additional fact investigation.

Again, let us consider the Ransom case. In Chart 11A, *Sources of Legal Elements*, the third element is "Premises unfit for human habitation by the occupants." Restated as a factual proposition in Chart 11B, *Legal Elements to Factual Propositions*, this element requires that Ms. Ransom present facts showing that "The premises at 289 Hudson Street are and have been unfit for human habitation because of the lack of sufficient heat, the leak in the bedroom, and the roach infestation." This factual proposition raises an issue for further legal research: are lack of heat, a leaky roof, and roach infestation sufficient conditions to constitute "premises unfit for human habitation." Obviously, Ms. Ransom will want to find cases construing that element very broadly ("any problems that adversely affect the occupants") while Mr. Dusak will seek authority for a very narrow reading ("only problems that make the dwelling totally uninhabitable"). Restating the element as a factual proposition helps to focus the legal research.

In row 3 of column 2 in Chart 11C, the *Ransom Legal Elements Chart,* we marshal the facts we have discovered at Ms. Ransom's interview in support of this factual proposition. Examining this list assists Ms. Ransom's lawyer in assessing the sufficiency of the facts to prove the element and in identifying areas for future investigation. In regard to sufficient heat, for example, the only facts Ms. Ransom has in support of her claim is that she says there was a lack of heat from the second or third week of January to the beginning of February, and interior temperatures in the low fifties at night after that time. Ms. Ransom's lawyer will certainly want to investigate whether adequate heat was provided during the daytime after the beginning of February and pin down the exact time periods in the nighttime when the temperature was in the fifties. If the apartment temperature remained in the seventies during the day and only fell into the fifties in the middle of the night, Ms. Ransom may not have sufficient facts to show that the lack of heat constituted conditions "unfit for human habitation." Likewise, there is a similar question as to the leak in the bedroom. Column 2 of row 3 in Chart 11C shows that Mr. Dusak arranged for a roofer to repair the leak and that subsequently there was still a problem during a heavy storm. The sufficiency of these facts to support a claim that the apartment was unfit for human habitation may depend on the adequacy of the roofer's repairs and the nature of the heavy storm that caused the leak afterwards. These are areas for fact investigation by Ms. Ransom's lawyer.

Finally, even if Ms. Ransom's lawyer discovers that she does not have facts within the meaning of the legal elements or that she does not have sufficient facts to prove a prima facie case, the legal elements chart can assist in developing other possible causes of action. If, for instance, the applicable case law does not support Ms. Ransom's interpretation of the first element ("written or oral lease"), an examination of the facts marshaled for that element raises the possibility of alternative claims: because her husband signed the lease for her family to live in the apartment, she may have a claim for breach of a third-party obligation against

1. Kenneth S. Broun, *McCormick on Evidence* 565 (6th ed. 2006).

Mr. Dusak under her husband's lease, or because Mr. Dusak was notified about the problems in the apartment, he may be liable under a negligence theory.

§15.2 ASSESSING THE SOURCES OF YOUR FACTS

In Chapters 11 and 12, we suggested that you identify the sources of your facts in drafting your legal elements and chronology charts (see Charts 11C and 12B, the *Ransom Legal Elements Chart* and *Chronology*, respectively). This process is important because all sources of facts obviously are not equal. In the Ransom case, for example, statements by Ms. Ransom and Mr. Dusak as to the condition of the apartment are not as credible as those by the apparently neutral observer, Tom Daniels from the Health Department. By identifying the sources of your facts, you can better assess the overall credibility of your case. Moreover, people commonly suffer from what is known as "source amnesia"; they have a vivid memory but are unable to identify the source of the information. As part of the assessment process, you should probe to assist witnesses in pinning down these sources.[2]

§15.2.1 TANGIBLE AND ORAL SOURCES OF FACTS

In the assessment process, it is helpful to distinguish between tangible and oral sources of the facts. Tangible sources of proof are objects involved in the incident (for example, the weapon used to commit the crime or the allegedly defective product) or documents reflecting the occurrence of an event (for instance, papers, photographs, or x-rays). They usually have greater credibility than oral statements describing the object or event because, under most of our schemas, physical proof seems to be more compelling than intangible descriptions. Consider, for example, the issue of the existence of the lease or payment of rent in the Ransom case. Certainly, Ms. Ransom could testify at trial that Mr. Dusak signed a lease with her husband for the apartment and that she, and not her husband, paid the rent for the months she lived there. But most of us would agree that a more credible presentation of those same facts would involve production of the lease itself and the rent receipts acknowledging payment by Mr. Dusak. While the documents almost speak for themselves, the oral description of events requires a more complex assessment process because we must evaluate Ms. Ransom's credibility in observing, recalling, and relating the events about the lease and rental payments.

Just because they are physical, however, not all tangible sources of facts are credible. Parties can forge signatures and can tamper with originals. For tangible sources of proof, then, the focus for credibility assessment should be on the issue of whether the object or document is what it purports to be. If it is a signed document, for example, you need to determine if the signature(s) are valid. If it is an unsigned document, consider whether there are any distinguishing marks or characteristics that would establish its authenticity. If the source of facts is an object, you need to

2. Susan Engel, *Context Is Everything: The Nature of Memory* 15 (1999).

evaluate whether or not anyone could have tampered with it subsequent to the incident.

§15.2.2 CREDIBILITY OF ORAL SOURCES OF FACTS[3]

While evaluating the credibility of tangible sources of facts focuses primarily on whether the object is what it purports to be, credibility assessment of oral sources of facts requires a somewhat different process. Remember that when a witness processes information about an event, she does not merely photograph the event in her mind. Instead, the witness filters and organizes the information to give meaning to that event. This process is ongoing: from the moment the witness first perceives the event, to the time when she later recalls it, to the occasions when she communicates the "facts" about the event to another person. At each of these levels, the witness uses her schemas to construct her version of the "facts" (see §10.2). Even putting aside issues of outright fabrication, by the time a witness testifies at a trial or hearing, the actual occurrence can be very different from the story told by the witness immediately following the event. Credibility assessment of oral sources of facts, therefore, requires an examination of how a particular witness processed the "facts" at all three levels (perception, recall, and communication) and of the schemas used by that witness in the filtering process.

Processing issues. First, perception of the event: Initially, in assessing the credibility of your sources, evaluate the ability of the witness to perceive the facts the witness has related to you. Consider the distance between the witness and the occurrence, the lighting at the location, the period of time of the observation, the length of time of the event, and the existence of any obstructions or distractions. Then, focusing on this particular witness, examine the witness's familiarity with that situation or location, any temporary or permanent physical or mental disability which may have affected her observation, such as diminished eyesight or hearing, and the possible effect of age on perception. If special expertise in observation is relevant, consider the education, training, and employment background of the witness.

Second, recall of the event: A witness's credibility in processing facts is affected not only by perception factors but also by issues relating to the witness's ability to recall the event accurately. Consider whether the period of time between the witness's observation of the event and its later recall might affect the witness's credibility, whether the significance or insignificance of the event could influence reliable recall at a later time, and whether the possible occurrence of intervening events might have affected the version of the facts related by that witness. If, for instance, the witness has met with the opposing party or the opposing lawyer to discuss the case or has suffered a serious illness or incurred a disability since the event, the witness's recall might be significantly altered. Also, evaluate this

---

3. The following sources were consulted in writing this section and can be referred to for further reading on the subject of source credibility: Paul Bergman, *Trial Advocacy* 45–57 (2d ed. 1989); Engel, *supra* note 2, at 58; Robert E. Oliphant, *Basic Concepts in the Law of Evidence* 35–43 (1982); Patrick J. Flynn, *Preparing the Case Before We Initiate Litigation: What We Need Is a Plan*, 18 Am. J. Trial Advoc. 509, 530–532 (1995); Peter Tillers & David Schum, *A Theory of Preliminary Fact Investigation*, 24 U.C. Davis L. Rev. 931, 952–953 (1991).

witness's ability to remember details and whether it is consistent with her recollection of the events in this case. And determine whether the witness's recall of events has remained substantially the same from the time of her initial observations onward. Obviously, a witness who has recollected inconsistent versions of the facts will have credibility problems.

Third, communication about the event: A witness's credibility will be influenced by her ability to communicate her version of the facts to the trier of fact. A witness can have excellent powers of observation with an unobstructed view of the event, and have an extremely accurate and consistent recall of that event, but still fail to communicate a credible version of the facts. Consider, then, the ability of the witness to relate her version of the facts in an articulate, clear, sincere, and engaging manner. Also, evaluate the possible effect of the witness's appearance and demeanor on her credibility. Some fact-finders might not believe witnesses who appear to be disheveled and shifty while others might be influenced by the physical attractiveness or repulsiveness of a witness. Likewise, consider the witness's reputation for truthfulness or untruthfulness and whether or not it will affect the credibility of her story.

Schema issues. In addition to issues relating to the processing of facts, it is helpful to evaluate the influence of the witness's schemas on the credibility of her story. While the witness's abilities to perceive, recall, and communicate her version of the facts impact on a witness's believability, the schemas by which the witness filters and organizes those facts also affect her credibility. Three related sets of schemas are relevant to this aspect of credibility assessment: bias, prejudice, and personal.

First, bias schemas: These schemas relate to a predisposition in favor of a particular party, or persons similar to that party, which might influence the witness's processing of the facts. In the Ransom case, for example, the credibility of Tom Daniels, the Health Department inspector, might be affected by his schemas about the behavior and conduct of landlords and tenants. If Daniels' previous inspection reports reflect a bias towards landlords, his report in favor of Ms. Ransom would appear to be very believable. If, on the other hand, his reports were predominantly pro-tenant, he might be less credible as a witness for Ms. Ransom.

Second, prejudice schemas: In contrast to bias schemas, these schemas concern predispositions against a particular party or persons like that party. Again looking at the Ransom case, it might be helpful for her lawyer to explore possible prejudices of both her client and Mr. Dusak. If Ms. Ransom previously lived in other substandard housing with uncooperative landlords, her version of the facts about Mr. Dusak's failure to repair the apartment might be influenced by her prejudice against those landlords. And if Mr. Dusak was a good friend of Ms. Ransom's husband, and the Ransoms had separated on a hostile basis, Mr. Dusak's story about Ms. Ransom's requests for help might be affected by his negative schema about Ms. Ransom.

Third, personal schemas: Finally, a witness's credibility can be influenced by personal schemas related to the dispute. Although a witness might not be biased in favor of a particular party or prejudiced against another, she still might have certain schemas concerning the events in a case depending upon her social status, prior experiences, or personal interests. These predispositions can easily affect her perception and interpretation of the events. For example, in a sexual harassment employment discrimination case, it is possible that the versions of the facts related by two witnesses to the incident—a male executive in the company and his female secretary—will be quite different. Neither the executive nor the secretary may know the parties involved or have ever experienced a sexual harassment situation, but both will have their own schemas about how employees should interact.

§15.3 ASSESSING YOUR CONTEXTUAL FACTS

> What makes a particular fact or bit of evidence take on meaning in a case is not its physical form, the credibility of the witness who introduced it, or the corroborating testimony of several witnesses. These things all play important roles when we weigh evidence and assess its reliability, but they do not determine its significance. What makes a fact or piece of evidence meaningful in a particular case is its contextual role in the stories that make up the case.[4]

Although this quotation may be a bit overstated, it cannot be disputed that the significance of a fact depends in large part on its context. As you learned in Chapter 12, the importance of a fact may depend on its chronological relationship to other facts. And even within a given episode at a particular time, the relationship of the different facts to each other—the players, the setting, and the actions—can be crucial to our understanding of "what really happened." Simply put, it is a mistake to focus on a particular event in a vacuum without an examination of its full context. Accordingly, to assess the strengths and weaknesses of your client's case, consider not only the credibility of the sources of the facts, but also the context in which events occurred.

To assess contextual facts, focus on the episode column in your chronology chart (see the *Ransom Chronology* in Chart 12B on page 163). As you read each entry, consider five questions:

1. Is the episode stated as a conclusion or simply as facts?
2. Do you have the complete setting of the scene for each episode?
3. What "stage directions" are significant for this episode?
4. What explanatory facts are necessary?
5. What personal facts are important to a full understanding of the episode?

§15.3.1 FOCUS ON FACTS, NOT CONCLUSIONS

When Sergeant Joe Friday on the old television series *Dragnet* used to interview witnesses after the commission of the crime, he would always advise them, "Just the facts." Similarly, when assessing facts in your cases, you need to focus on facts—not conclusions, not characterizations, not opinions. The "facts" are significant because conclusions, characterizations, and opinions can be very ambiguous. They do not provide the necessary details to paint a clear picture of a situation.

---

4. W. Lance Bennett & Martha S. Feldman, *Reconstructing Reality in the Courtroom: Justice and Judgment in American Culture* 117 (1981).

Consider, for example, the entry on the *Ransom Chronology* chart (Chart 12B, lines 108 and 109): "The whole apartment is now infested with roaches." This statement is so conclusory that it is difficult to know for certain the extent of the infestation. Hearing this statement, we do not know how many rooms in the apartment were affected, how many rooms there are in the apartment, approximately how many roaches were in each room, or for what period of time the infestation occurred. A fact-finder or adversary, especially one from a background different from Ms. Ransom's, may not be very persuaded by such bald assertions and may, therefore, dismiss it as the hyperbole of an overly emotional tenant. To make this episode clearer for any audience, it would be helpful for Ms. Ransom's lawyer to avoid the characterizations and, instead, to provide details to portray specifically the conditions in the apartment. Not only do details add credibility to a conclusion. They can also help to convince a fact-finder that the witness has a particularly good memory of the specific event.[5]

Avoidance of characterizations is especially important for conversations. Such characterizations do not have the same impact as accounts of what the witness believes was said. Take, for example, the April 12, 1996 entry on lines 71–72 of the chronology chart: "Client called Dusak. Dusak yelled at her. . . ." This entry is unclear because it lacks a specific description of the tone of his voice or the substance of his statement. Moreover, it fails to describe what Ms. Ransom said to Mr. Dusak before he yelled at her. A number of possible scenarios could have occurred: Mr. Dusak spoke in a loud voice because of some background noise on his end of the line. He could have been merely expressing general dismay that there were roaches in one of his buildings. Or he could have been responding to Ms. Ransom's yelling at him. The entry, "Dusak yelled at her" does not consist of enough facts to describe fully Ms. Ransom's version of "what really happened." This information is crucial to the development of a full picture of Mr. Dusak's treatment of Ms. Ransom.

As our previous discussion of the nature of facts has shown, all versions of the facts, to some extent, are characterizations. They are based on the schemas of the witnesses and their attempts to place the events they have observed into a meaningful narrative. The fact that a witness testifies to what was said does not mean that those exact words were said. Her testimony merely reflects her version based on her schemas and memory. By suggesting that you avoid characterizations in your chronologies, we are not proposing that you accept all the facts related by your client as the correct version of "what really happened." Rather, probe beneath the characterizations so that you can more accurately assess the content of your client's story—as tainted as it may be by her schemas and narrative thinking—and eventually develop a more persuasive presentation of the case to the particular audience.

§15.3.2 SETTING THE SCENE

As you draft your chronology charts, you may be prone to focus solely on the actions and statements of the parties. Perhaps because of our training in legal

---

5. David A. Binder & Paul Bergman, *Fact Investigation: From Hypothesis to Proof* 142 (1984).

doctrine, we concentrate primarily on events as they relate to the elements of the case. For example, in a breach of contract action, we fix our attention on these events: seller made an offer, buyer accepted, buyer paid the consideration, but seller breached by not delivering the goods. But each of those events took place against a backdrop of a particular setting. A description of the setting may be as crucial to understanding "what really happened" as the events themselves. Even in this simple contract dispute, the contexts of the offer and acceptance, the payment of the consideration, and the manner in which the breach occurred may affect our interpretation of the facts. If the offer and acceptance took place in a noisy restaurant, for instance, possible confusion of the parties in regard to the terms of the agreement may be very understandable.

Accordingly, in your assessment of the facts, revisit the episode column on the chronology chart and attempt to describe the setting in which each episode took place. Imagine that each episode is a series of snapshots. The key action (physical movement or verbal statement) is at the center of the photo. Now, consider what background details are relevant to this central action and fill your picture with them. The same details will, of course, not be relevant to each episode. But in the assessment of your facts, it is often helpful to try to determine the significance of four aspects of setting to each event: location of the event, environment of the event, objects in the environment, and the other persons present at the event.

Location of the event. Initially, identify the location of the action. We all have schemas about expected behavior in particular situations, for example, an evaluation meeting between an employee and her boss or an announcement by a lover when he is breaking up with his companion. Accordingly, the venue of a meeting or conversation might be very significant in understanding the mind-set and expectations of the participants and in assessing how a fact-finder will interpret the parties' actions. In a case in which the plaintiff seeks to hold a company liable for the actions of its agent, for example, the location of the negligent conduct might be critical for determining whether or not the agent was acting within the scope of her employment. Consider, then, the exact location where the episode occurred. Determine whether the action occurred inside or outside the place of business, and, if inside, in what room or area. And, if the action was a communication between the parties, determine whether it occurred in a face-to-face conversation, in a phone call, by fax, in written documents, or by email.

Environment of the event. In addition to location, consider the environment at that locale. Environmental considerations should help you (and the trier-of-fact) assess the ability of the parties to act in certain ways, to observe the event when it occurred, and the mood when the event occurred. Think about the effects of weather conditions, terrain, lighting, and sounds on the parties, and try to determine the location of relevant objects, the distance between those objects and the parties, and the possible obstructions between them. In an automobile accident case, for example, consider how the road conditions, possible distractions of the drivers, the direction of the road, the location of the intersections, and the angle of the sunlight could affect the fact-finder's interpretation of the actions of the different parties.

Objects in the environment. A scene is not merely a sterile location and environment but is occupied with objects. Those objects often provide the visual details that bring a story to life. Some commonplace objects, for example, can vividly reflect the theme of your narrative. As an immigration attorney recounts, while his presentation of documents and affidavits failed to persuade an immigration officer of the cohabitation of his client and an American citizen, the client's description of her sudden anger at her husband's failure to put down the toilet seat after use convinced the official that the couple was married.[6] Other objects, while seemingly out of place or irrelevant, may actually strengthen your case by giving it a feeling of reality. The purchase by Ms. Ransom of an expensive piece of furniture, for example, may at first seem inconsistent with your story, but actually it may reflect her attempt to ameliorate her family's dismal living conditions

Other persons present. Finally, determine whether other persons were present during the event. Often, we incorrectly assume that the central action in a case involved only the parties to the litigation. Other persons may be present, however, and these individuals can have a significant effect on the actions or statements of the primary participants. In a breach of contract action, for example, in which the terms of an oral contract are in dispute, the statements made by all the participants in the contract negotiation might be important, not just those of the lead bargainers. An added benefit of determining all those present for a particular event is that you can identify other witnesses who can either corroborate or contradict a party's version of "what really happened."

§15.3.3 IDENTIFYING THE STAGE DIRECTIONS

Continuing with the theater metaphor, not only do you want to identify the setting of each specific episode, but you also want to consider the stage directions. In any particular episode, the parties may move around, physically interact with other persons, handle objects, have facial expressions, and speak with distinctive intonations. These physical movements and intonations can significantly impact our assessment of the action. In a murder case, for example, in which the defendant pleads self-defense, the distance between the victim and the defendant, their tones of voice, and the distance between each of them and the weapon may be very relevant to our understanding of "what really happened." Accordingly, as you assess each episode, consider what parenthetical stage directions are necessary to lay a complete context for the central action or event in dispute.

§15.3.4 EXPLANATORY FACTS

The context of each episode does not include just the physical setting of the event or the physical movements of the participants. To assess fully what is happening in an episode, it is often essential to consider the reasons why each of the participants acted in the ways they did. Certain actions or omissions, which may seem inconsistent with a party's position in a case, may appear to be reasonable

---

6. See James Parry Eyster, *Lawyer as Artist: Using Significant Moments and Obtuse Objects to Enhance Advocacy*, 14 Legal Writing J. 87, 102–114 (2008).

once the explanations for these actions are identified. On the other hand, the parties' explanations may seem quite feeble. Accordingly, as you review your chronology, it is helpful to evaluate the strengths and weaknesses of these explanations.[7]

In the Ransom case, for instance, consider lines 82–85 of Chart 12B (the *Ransom Chronology* on page 163): "Client does not call Dusak to get exterminator because she does not want to be yelled at again." Does that explanation seem very credible to you? Will it persuade the fact-finder? Under some persons' schemas, if a tenant actually had a significant problem with roach infestation and had small children, she would continually pester her landlord, even if he had previously yelled at her. For such a fact-finder, Ms. Ransom's explanation might appear fairly weak. Other details, however, might strengthen the explanation: for example, if Mr. Dusak had warned her never to call again or had threatened her with eviction, Ms. Ransom's failure to call him might appear very reasonable. As Ms. Ransom's lawyer, you do not want to rely simply on the explanations given to you by your client, but rather to appraise whether that explanation will be persuasive at trial or in your negotiations.

§15.3.5 PERSONAL FACTS

Another category of contextual facts are personal facts about the different parties and other actors in the case. These facts are "observable characteristics such as physical attributes and dress; personality; attitude . . . ; and personal background including economic status, job status, educational status, family status, residence, and previous similar involvements."[8] Personal facts include insights into the parties' emotional state—not just their states of mind but also their "psychic apparatuses," how they generally behave and react in similar situations.[9] They give us a richer understanding of the interactions of the different actors. In the Ransom case, for example, the character and attitudes of both Ms. Ransom and Mr. Dusak in their different conversations may significantly affect the fact-finder's determination of whether Ms. Ransom was unreasonable in her demands to Mr. Dusak or whether Mr. Dusak callously ignored those demands.

Similarly, personal facts can provide additional explanations for the actions or omissions of the parties. Take, for example, Ms. Ransom's actions on April 19 (Chart 12B, lines 79–82): she refused to allow the exterminator to treat the apartment because she was leaving for work. Obviously, the nature of Ms. Ransom's economic and job status is relevant to an assessment of the reasonableness of this refusal. If Ms. Ransom held a flex-time job that did not require her arrival at a specific time or if her job was not essential to support of her family, her response to the exterminator might appear to be unreasonable, especially in light of the alleged roach infestation. If, on the other hand, Ms. Ransom was required to punch a time clock for a job that was the sole source of her family's income, her refusal would appear to be quite understandable.

---

7. Binder & Bergman, *supra* note 5, at 140.
8. *Id.* at 107.
9. David Dante Troutt, *Screws, Koon, and Routine Aberrations: The Use of Fictional Narratives in Federal Police Brutality Prosecutions*, 74 N.Y.U. L. Rev. 18, 69 (1999).

Although some personal facts, such as previous, similar experiences, may already appear on your chronological chart, others, such as personality, attitude, or economic and job status, may not. Therefore, include a "Cast of Characters" section at the beginning of your chronology, identifying each player in the case and noting personal information you have obtained about the principal players in your case. Then, as you later examine your chronology, consider the significance of these personal facts to each of the different episodes and, when you identify new information about a player, update your "Cast of Characters" list.

§15.3.6 DEVELOPING ADDITIONAL CONTEXTUAL FACTS

The process we suggest for assessing your contextual facts can at times become unmanageable, especially in a large case. Few lawyers have the time to develop all the contextual facts for each episode in a case, and few clients have the funds to pay fees for such an endeavor. Therefore, when you review your chronology, start off by identifying the four or five episodes that are crucial to an interpretation of the facts of the case. These will include the central action—the car accident, the assault, the breach of contract—and the significant events either leading up to that action or occurring thereafter. In developing additional facts, focus first on these key episodes.

§15.4 ASSESSING YOUR CIRCUMSTANTIAL EVIDENCE

In assessing the facts you have marshaled in your legal elements chart, it is helpful to distinguish between "direct evidence" and "circumstantial evidence" that supports a particular element. Direct evidence is a fact that proves a legal element without the need for an inference. Circumstantial evidence is a fact that permits the fact-finder to infer the existence of another fact (see §7.1).[10] The distinction between the two kinds of evidence can be seen by an examination of column 2 on Chart 11C on page 153, the legal elements chart in the Ransom case. Consider the evidence in regard to the third factual proposition—that the conditions at 289 Hudson Street were unfit for human habitation at least in part because of roach infestation. Ms. Ransom's statements that in late March she began having a roach problem and that she used Raid but to no avail are direct evidence of the factual proposition. No inference is necessary to connect Ms. Ransom's statements with the proposition that there was roach infestation. In contrast, the fact that Mr. Dusak sent an exterminator to the apartment on April 19 is circumstantial evidence that there was roach infestation at the premises. The fact that a landlord sends an exterminator to one of his apartments does not directly establish the existence of roach infestation. To draw that conclusion, one must make the inference that a landlord would send an exterminator only to an apartment where roach infestation existed.

10. *Id.* at 77.

To assess direct evidence, evaluate its sufficiency in supporting the particular legal element and the credibility of its source. In the Ransom case, for example, the sufficiency of Ms. Ransom's statements about roach infestation to support the claim that the conditions rendered the apartment "unfit for human habitation" will depend upon the legal interpretation of that phrase (see §15.1). Moreover, the strength of this evidence will hinge in large part on Ms. Ransom's credibility as a witness and her ability to establish the contextual facts for her observations (see §§15.2 and 15.3).

The assessment of circumstantial evidence, on the other hand, requires an evaluation of the strength of the inference which connects the evidence and the factual proposition. Binder, Bergman, and Moore suggest use of the model in Chart 15A to help make this evaluation.[11]

CHART 15A ASSESSMENT OF CIRCUMSTANTIAL EVIDENCE TEMPLATE

Facts	Generalization	Conclusion

The facts are the circumstantial evidence you have marshaled in support of particular elements, and the conclusion is the factual proposition you want to prove with this evidence. The generalization is the general statement about people or things that connects the facts to the factual proposition, that lets you draw the inference. Applying this model to the above example, we get Chart 15B.

CHART 15B DRAWING THE INFERENCE

Facts	Generalization	Conclusion
On April 19, Mr. Dusak sent an exterminator to Ms. Ransom's apartment.	Landlords send exterminators only to apartments where roach infestation exists.	The premises at 289 Hudson Street have been unfit for human habitation because of roach infestation.

Generalizations "are assertions derived from beliefs about how events normally occur."[12] As you learned in §10.2, those beliefs are based on our schemas about what should happen in particular situations. Because different people can have different schemas, however, the generalizations that support your inferences may not always be accepted by your fact-finders. The experience that you have had about certain situations may be different from theirs. Not everyone, for example, will automatically agree with the generalization that *landlords send exterminators only to apartments where roach infestation exists.* Some might assume that landlords regularly send out exterminators on a preventive basis. Others might

11. See *id.* at 82; Albert J. Moore et al., *Trial Advocacy: Inferences, Arguments and Techniques* 5 (1996).
12. Moore et al., *supra* note 11, at 5.

believe that since exterminators inspect, as well as treat for insect infestation, their presence at a dwelling does not establish the existence of insects at those premises.

Indeed, at times, depending on the generalization, two different inferences can be drawn from the same item of circumstantial evidence. Again, consider the Ransom case. As you may remember, the landlord alleged in his letter that the exterminator saw open boxes of food on the drain board when he visited the apartment. Based on this evidence, the landlord may make the argument presented in Chart 15C. From these same facts, however, the tenant can assert the argument in Chart 15D.

CHART 15C THE LANDLORD'S INFERENCE

Facts	Generalization	Conclusion
Ms. Ransom left open boxes of food on the drain board.	When a tenant leaves open boxes of food on the drain board, it is difficult to eradicate a roach infestation.	Because Ms. Ransom left open boxes of food on the drain board, it was difficult to eradicate the roach infestation in her apartment, and she was the cause of the problem.

Because different generalizations can lead to different conclusions, it is often helpful to articulate the generalization in order to assess its strength or weakness in supporting the inference sought to be drawn.[13] Accordingly, after you have drafted your legal elements chart, review the facts you have marshaled and identify each item of circumstantial evidence. Some of those items will relate to elements that are uncontroverted, and you will not need to evaluate them with the generalization model. Other elements, however, will be hotly contested. For those elements, consider each item of circumstantial evidence using the generalization model. After you have articulated the generalization, consider whether or not your fact-finder will accept it. Ask your friends or family if the generalization is consistent with their schemas. And then determine whether or not you want to rely on this circumstantial evidence.

Articulation of the generalization can also assist you in identifying areas for additional fact investigation. Part of the investigation process consists of brainstorming possible facts that will support the inference you want to draw. To do this, after you have articulated the generalization underlying your inferences, consider the possible circumstances under which the generalization would be more accurate and those under which it would be less accurate. In other words, add the terms *especially when* or *except when* to your generalizations, and consider what facts would either support or weaken it.[14] Then, explore whether or not those facts can be discovered from some source.

---

13. See generally Bergman, *supra* note 3, at 27–30.
14. Binder & Bergman, *supra* note 5, at 94–97.

CHART 15D RANSOM'S INFERENCE

Facts	Generalization	Conclusion
Ms. Ransom left open boxes of food on the drain board.	When a tenant's apartment is roach infested, she may take open boxes of food from the cupboard when she sprays with Raid.	Ms. Ransom left open boxes of food on the drain board because her apartment was infested with roaches, and she had to spray the cupboards with Raid.

In applying the "especially when/except when" analysis to the Ransom case, we can identify possible facts strengthening the generalization for Mr. Dusak by adding "especially when" to the generalization in Chart 15C:

> When a tenant leaves open boxes of food on the drain board, it is difficult to eradicate a roach infestation, *especially when:* (1) the boxes are left on the drain board for a lengthy period of time, (2) the boxes are wide open, or (3) the boxes have crumbs on the outside.

Conversely, by adding "except when" to the generalization, we can identify possible facts weakening the generalization:

> When a tenant leaves open boxes of food on the drain board, it is difficult to eradicate a roach infestation, *except when:* (1) the boxes are in closed plastic containers, (2) there are few cabinets, and the occupant has no other place to store them, and (3) the boxes have been left out only for the preparation of a meal.

As you can see, this analysis helps the parties identify areas for fact investigation. Certainly, Ms. Ransom's lawyer will want to explore with her client the facts surrounding the open boxes in order to buttress the "except when's." Likewise, Mr. Dusak's lawyer will want to probe the memory of the exterminator about his observations of the apartment on the morning of his visit to support his "especially when's." Both lawyers may not want to confine themselves to the obvious witnesses, but instead investigate other sources of proof—for example, visitors to the apartment—to develop those facts that strengthen the inference they want to draw.

§15.5 ASSESSING THE STRUCTURAL INTEGRITY OF YOUR STORY

Until now, we have been focusing solely on the assessment of your facts in the context of the legal elements and chronology models. But another method for considering facts is the story model (see Chapter 13). In assessing your stories, focus on the structural integrity of the story. This process requires evaluation of the story's coverage, consistency, and ambiguity.

Coverage. A story's coverage is complete to the extent that it takes into account all the facts that will be presented at the trial or hearing. In most cases, you cannot craft a very persuasive story by ignoring the negative facts. In fact, audiences appreciate a storyteller who acknowledges the dark side of his characters and deals honestly with them.[15] The trick is to be able to develop a compelling tale that in some way recognizes the existence of these facts. From your assessment of your facts, consider the following questions:

1. Of the facts you have marshaled on the legal elements chart, which are the weakest in supporting your factual propositions and which are the strongest in supporting your adversary's case?
2. What are your least credible sources of proof and what are your adversary's most credible sources?
3. Considering the contextual facts for the central events on your chronology, whose version of the facts seems most persuasive?
4. For the important circumstantial evidence, what conclusions are most likely to be drawn by the fact-finder?

From this assessment, identify the three or four "best" facts for *your adversary*. Then, ask yourself whether you have handled these facts effectively in your story. Depending upon the case, you may try to rebut these facts directly, downplay their importance, or attempt to explain them away (see Chapter 17).

Consistency. Besides assessing whether or not your story covers damaging—as well as supporting—facts, also evaluate whether the story hangs together. First, consider if the story is consistent with the uncontested facts in the case. The fact-finder will not view a story as very persuasive if it ignores facts that are undisputed (see §13.2). Second, determine whether the actors, images, and actions throughout the story are consistent. If, for example, as Ms. Ransom's lawyer, you initially portray your client as the victim of her husband and the landlord, but she is later shown to have abused her husband and aggressively confronted Mr. Dusak, you may find it difficult to paint a persuasive positive picture of your client. "Based on common experience, most of us believe that events proceed in recognizable patterns and that people's emotional state and actions remain relatively consistent from one moment to the next. Therefore, when the different parts of the story are in harmony, we tend to trust the story."[16] Finally, evaluate whether the genre has remained consistent throughout the tale. A serious story of revenge may lose much of its effectiveness if it is abruptly interrupted with a comical interlude.

15. Robert McKee, *Storytelling that Moves People*, Harv. Bus. Rev., June 2003, at 51, 54.
16. Binder & Bergman, *supra* note 5, at 138. See also Janet Malcolm, *The Crime of Sheila McGough* 67 (1999) ("Trials are won by attorneys whose stories fit, and lost by those whose stories are like the shapeless housecoat that truth, in her disdain for appearances, has chosen as her uniform."). On the other hand, if a story seems to fit too perfectly, the audience, especially in the litigation context, might become a bit wary. Anthony G. Amsterdam & Jerome Bruner, *Minding the Law* 174 (2000) ("The more a story told by a visibly good advocate hangs together, . . . the more susceptible it is to being taken as a clever concoction.").

Ambiguity. Studies have shown that the higher the frequency of ambiguities in a story, the more difficult it will be for the fact-finder to interpret it.[17] Ambiguities are cleared up by the presentation of details that connect the different parts of the story. In an appropriate case, attention to detail can provide a story with the coherence necessary to persuade the fact-finder. The impact of a detailed portrayal of the setting, the characters, their motivations, and their step-by-step actions, for example, can be much more compelling than a summary description of the same events.

On the other hand, ambiguity may at times be helpful to lawyers. Literary critics note that stories often gain their dynamism from the omission of facts. "Long-winded storytellers can ruin the most promising material by piling on irrelevant details, broadly foreshadowing later developments, and specifying in advance the emotional reactions they intend to arouse. The problem with such stories is not that they are overlong—many of the great stories are extremely long—but that they are pointless."[18] The same can be true for a lawyer's storytelling. For the fact-finder to become involved in the storytelling process, you may want to hold it in suspense, may want to present a "surprise ending," or leave some matters unclear. The important point is that such ambiguity should be deliberate: to improve the impact of the storytelling. Careless disregard of detail may result in the type of ambiguity that leaves the audience unpersuaded.

---

17. See Bennett & Feldman, *supra* note 4, at 68–90. In fact, these researchers found that, "regardless of a story's truth status, the more ambiguities the story [has], . . . the less plausible it is." *Id.* at 88.
18. Thomas M. Leitch, *What Stories Are: Narrative Theory and Interpretation* 35 (1986).

CHAPTER

16

INVESTIGATING THE FACTS

§16.1 A FACT INVESTIGATION CASE STUDY

After you have assessed the persuasiveness of your facts, you usually need to investigate further to strengthen your case. You are about to read the description of two students' fact investigation in an actual case in a political asylum clinic. As this story demonstrates, while you often run into dead ends in fact investigation, if you are persistent, you can discover the facts you want.

AGATA SZYPSZAK, CLINICAL ESSAY, *WHERE IN THE WORLD IS DR. DETCHAKANDI? A STORY OF FACT INVESTIGATION*
6 CLINICAL L. REV. 517, 518–529 (2000)

Introduction

Dolores Wilson sought asylum in the United States to escape the years of persecution that she had suffered in Liberia at the hands of armed forces loyal to the faction led by Charles Taylor [the President of Liberia]. The Immigration and Naturalization Service (INS) refused to grant that request. My partner, Daniel Williams, and I interviewed Ms. Wilson many times over the course of several months as we prepared for the hearing in which Ms. Wilson could renew her request for asylum by asserting it as a defense to her being deported from the United States. Gradually, she unfolded the horrific details of her story.

Ms. Wilson and her family were targeted by Charles Taylor's forces because of her past service in the government of the late President Samuel Doe. In 1990, several months after Charles Taylor invaded Liberia and began a violent campaign to overthrow President Doe, Ms. Wilson and her children fled Monrovia, the capital of Liberia, in a government car. They were on their way to Guinea, but stopped at the Catholic Education Center (CEC), where Ms. Wilson's daughter attended school.

The CEC was far from the fighting in Monrovia and it housed many refugees. Thinking that she and her children would be safe there, Ms. Wilson decided to stay at the Center and abandoned her plan to attempt the difficult journey to Guinea. She thought that the fighting in Liberia would end before it reached the Center's campus. She expected that the Doe government would prevail and that peace would be restored. She did not realize that within months, President Doe would be assassinated and that the fighting in Monrovia would be only the beginning of seven years of civil war.

About a month and a half after Ms. Wilson and her children had taken refuge in the CEC, Charles Taylor's forces attacked the campus. They searched for anyone who had been associated with the Doe government, demanded that such people be turned in, and threatened death to all of the refugees unless everyone obeyed their orders. During their search of the campus, the rebel soldiers found the government car that Ms. Wilson had used to get to the CEC. A frightened refugee informed the rebels that the car belonged to Ms. Wilson.

When the rebels learned that Ms. Wilson had held office in the Doe government, they took Ms. Wilson and her children as prisoners. The rebels would have killed them, but Dr. Detchakandi, the headmaster of the CEC, intervened. Dr. Detchakandi gave the rebel soldiers the equivalent of two hundred dollars to free Ms. Wilson and her children. The soldiers allowed Ms. Wilson and her children to return to the campus cottage where they had been living. That same evening, however, several rebels went to the cottage. Two of them told Ms. Wilson to go into the bedroom so that they could inspect her personal belongings. They then pushed her down on the floor and raped her at gunpoint. After the rebels left, Ms. Wilson found her seven-year-old daughter bleeding in another room and learned that she too had been raped. . . .

The civil war ended with a cease fire and elections in 1997. Charles Taylor won the elections and was inaugurated, that same year, as president of Liberia. But his brutal vendetta against his enemies continued. Taylor's security forces continued to threaten, harass, and murder political opponents, and many people disappeared without a trace. During this time, Ms. Wilson learned that Taylor's troops were looking for her. Afraid for their lives, Ms. Wilson and her children fled to Guinea. Shortly thereafter, Ms. Wilson came to the United States to visit her relatives, who persuaded her to apply for asylum.

I. Fact Investigation

As a legal matter, Ms. Wilson's circumstances made her a strong candidate for asylum. The United States government can grant asylum to a person who has fled to the United States and has been persecuted or has a well-founded fear of persecution on account of race, religion, nationality, political opinion, or membership in a particular social group. Ms. Wilson, however, had not succeeded in persuading an INS asylum officer to grant her asylum. Thus, instead of allowing

Ms. Wilson to remain safely in the United States, the INS instituted deportation proceedings against her. Our main task, as we prepared for the hearing, would be to find documentary or testimonial evidence to corroborate Ms. Wilson's claim. But finding corroborating evidence would not be easy. Because of the war, Ms. Wilson had not been able to seek medical attention after being raped. Most of her documents had been destroyed. Nearly all of the people who had known about Ms. Wilson's political activities in Liberia and her treatment at the hands of the rebels had been scattered throughout Liberia and other parts of Africa. Furthermore, Ms. Wilson asked us not to contact anyone in Liberia because communications were not secure and she did not want to put her friends and family in any more danger.

Our advisor, Phil, suggested that we make a chart to organize our fact investigation. At his urging, we listed each fact in Ms. Wilson's story that we would have to corroborate. For each of these facts, we specified its relative importance on a scale of 1 through 3, the relevant evidence we already had, the evidence we still needed, and our ideas about how we might obtain the missing documents, find the crucial witnesses, and generate supporting affidavits. During many hours of brainstorming, Dan and I produced a nineteen page, fine print reminder of all the work we still had to do. . . .

We started our fact investigation with online research. LEXIS and the World Wide Web turned up many country condition reports and reports on human rights abuses which had occurred during the war, but we did not find any corroboration for Ms. Wilson's particular claim of persecution. We did not expect Ms. Wilson's story to have been plastered on the front page of an African newspaper, but we hoped that by chance the attack on the CEC had been reported by a newspaper or a human rights organization. Unfortunately, the only media accounts that we found involving fighting in Liberia during the 1990s at a Catholic institution concerned a military clash in Monrovia, far from the CEC.

In planning our fact investigation, we knew . . . [t]here were no witnesses to . . . the rapes. But we hoped to find someone who was at the CEC in 1990 and who could confirm that Ms. Wilson and her children had been threatened with execution before being saved by Dr. Detchakandi's bribe. Unfortunately, most of the people who had worked at the CEC in 1990 or had taken refuge there had later fled from Liberia. Ms. Wilson could not provide us with any of their names or whereabouts and it was clear that they could be in Guinea, the Ivory Coast, or anywhere else in the world. Thus, our only choice was to find Dr. Detchakandi.

II. The Search for Dr. Detchakandi

Initially, trying to find Dr. Detchakandi was a low priority in our fact investigation. Our nineteen page chart gave us plenty of leads to follow up that were more promising than locating the former headmaster of a school that had been attacked nine years earlier. We did not know Dr. Detchakandi's first name, and we did not know whether he was still alive, much less where he might be. But when Phil saw the low priority that our chart assigned to this task, he said, "If Dr. Detchakandi is still alive, he has to be somewhere. Wouldn't it be worth spending some of your time trying to locate this key witness who could save your client's life?" . . .

I started the search for Dr. Detchakandi on the Internet. I hoped that he would be mentioned somewhere. I looked at education and medical websites; I ran queries for Dr. Detchakandi in databases concerned with Liberia and then with all of Africa, but I had no luck. Meanwhile, my partner Dan tried to find leads by calling people. His calls led to our first big break. Dan called an office of the Catholic Church in the United States to ask whether someone there had any information on the Catholic Education Center or Dr. Detchakandi. Jennifer Campbell, a church official, informed Dan that the CEC and all of its records had been destroyed in a fire, but she also told him that the Bishop of Liberia was currently on sabbatical in Pennsylvania. Dan obtained permission from Ms. Wilson to talk to the Bishop about her and then called him immediately. He learned that Bishop Brown actually knew Ms. Wilson. Moreover, the Bishop had heard about the Taylor rebels' attack on the CEC and about Ms. Wilson's rape. Bishop Brown also told Dan that Dr. Detchakandi had fled to Ghana shortly after the CEC attack and was probably still there.

Around the same time, Ms. Wilson gave us the name of a Catholic priest, Father Anthony Gooden, who might be able to corroborate the attack because he was "near" the CEC in 1990. Ms. Wilson informed us that she thought that Father Gooden was now in Minnesota, but the only contact information she had was a beeper number to which I never received a response, and no Father Gooden was listed in any Minnesota telephone directory. Finding Father Gooden was crucial both because he could himself confirm that the CEC had been attacked, and because he might give us more clues on how to find Dr. Detchakandi. I left a message for Jennifer Campbell to see whether she could help us locate him.

I went to our weekly meeting with Phil frustrated and impatient with our lack of progress. After a month and a half, it was clear that we might never find Dr. Detchakandi. Dan and I told Phil what we had done and asked whether he had any suggestions. Phil asked whether, in view of Bishop Brown's report of Dr. Detchakandi's flight to Ghana, we had called the Ghanaian embassy to ask whether Ghana had records of Liberian refugees who had entered during the past decade. If Ghana lacked such records, he suggested, the embassy might at least have a current set of phone books for the country. I knew that Phil's first suggestion was a long-shot; as for his second idea, I was not sure whether looking up phone numbers was a service that an embassy would provide. In fact, I was pretty sure that the embassy would refuse to serve as a telephone information service, but who was I to argue with a professor who seemed so convinced that calling the embassy was a sensible idea?

As I expected, the Ghanaian Embassy had no records of the Liberian refugees who had escaped into Ghana. But Tom, the man who answered the phone, found the most current phone book and agreed to look for a number for Dr. Detchakandi. The "most current" phone book happened to be from the year 1994, but one cannot ask for everything. There were three entries for Detchakandi: one for a business, one for a residence (but with an incomplete phone number), and one for a "Dr. Nk Detchakandi" in Accra!

I could not contain my excitement. I tried to be rational and tell myself that the phone number could be a false lead, but I just knew that I had found Dr. Detchakandi! I quickly estimated that Accra was five hours ahead of Washington, D.C. time. Since it was 1:00 p.m. in D.C., the time difference would not be a problem. I picked up the phone and called. I could not stop shaking when a woman answered and I asked for Dr. Detchakandi. I tried to sound coherent when I quickly explained that I was calling from the United States regarding a political asylum case, but I was far from calm. I wanted to scream for joy when she said that I had reached Dr. Detchakandi's residence. Unfortunately, Dr. Detchakandi was not home. I had to call back at 9:00 p.m. (4:00 p.m. our time). I hung up the phone and called my partner Dan to tell him the good news. . . . I called Dr. Nk Detchakandi at exactly 4:00 p.m. I was a little bit more prepared and collected this time. I told Dr. Detchakandi that I was a student representing a woman from Liberia in her political asylum case and I asked a few questions to make sure that he was the right Dr. Detchakandi. Very quickly, it became apparent that he was not! He had never lived in Liberia. . . .

III. Finding Dr. Detchakandi

[During the next week] Dan and I had to focus our energy and attention on preparing Ms. Wilson's documentary evidence, writing a trial brief, developing opening and closing statements, and rehearsing Ms. Wilson's testimony. We were awaiting emails, phone calls, and affidavits from many expert witnesses. We were also working on affidavits from Bishop Brown and Father Gooden, whom we finally located with Jennifer Campbell's help. Bishop Brown and Father Gooden both said that they had heard about Ms. Wilson's having been raped at the Catholic Education Center, but neither of them had been present at the Center at the time of the attack. In fact, neither of them had been in Liberia in the early 1990s. . . . In addition, due to prior commitments, the Bishop was unable to come to court in Maryland and testify on Ms. Wilson's behalf. His failure to make the trip from Pennsylvania and subject himself to cross-examination could have made the court suspicious of the truthfulness of his affidavit. That is why, although Dan and I were very grateful for the affidavits that we had, we still wanted an eyewitness who could directly confirm the testimony Ms. Wilson would give. The issue was not the admissibility of the hearsay because proceedings in Immigration Court are not governed by the Federal Rules of Evidence. Dan and I simply wanted to find as much evidence as possible to bolster the credibility of Ms. Wilson's claim. . . .

Since I thought that I had already done everything humanly possible to find [Dr. Detchakandi], I knew the only solution was to retrace my steps, and that is exactly what I did. I called Dan and asked him to repeat exactly what Bishop Brown told him about Dr. Detchakandi to see if we missed any clues. In my crazed state, I started showering Dan with questions, and he suggested that I call Bishop Brown myself. At that point in my clinic work, I had already learned that sometimes asking the same question a different way, or at a different time, can lead to a major breakthrough so I called the Bishop.

Bishop Brown was not in, and I had to leave a message. Instead of just leaving my name and number and asking him to return my call, I started rambling to the poor receptionist about my predicament of not being able to find Dr. Detchakandi and how I needed the Bishop's help. The receptionist, sympathetic to my desperation, took down a detailed message and even asked me for the correct spelling of Dr. Detchakandi's name. Minutes later, Bishop Brown called back and told me that Dr. "Mike" Detchakandi was currently living in the Ho Area in Ghana, but he was no longer teaching. I still lacked a mailing address and phone number, but at least now I knew Dr. Detchakandi's first name and the city that he was living in. Then, as I sat there contemplating how I could use the new information, Bishop Brown called me again.

That is when, less than a month before our affidavits and other documents had to be filed in court, I learned that Dr. Detchakandi's son, who had been a physician in Liberia, was currently living somewhere in the United States, married to a Liberian woman who was also a doctor. I could not believe my ears. I knew that this was the key to finding Dr. Detchakandi. I was so close. I quickly logged on the Internet to do a search and then I received a third phone call from the Bishop.

"By the way," he said, "you're spelling the name wrong." "What!" I exclaimed. "The name is not D-e-t-c-h-a-k-a-n-d-i. The correct spelling is D-e-k-y-a-k-a-n-d-i," said the Bishop. And there it was, two months of searching and not turning up anything—all because we had the wrong spelling of the last name. I did not know whether to laugh or cry.

I quickly did an online people search and came up with twenty-five entries for "Dekyakandi," none of them, of course, with the prefix "Dr." or followed by "MD." With the prior incident of mistaken identity still fresh in my mind, I did not want to call and explain myself to each of these people. There had to be another way. "I wonder if there is an association for doctors comparable to the American Bar Association?" I mused out loud to my fellow students in our clinic room. "There is," said my colleague Jill Sheldon. Before she could say, "it's called the American Medical Association," I was already searching for it. I quickly accessed the AMA website and began my search. Finding Dr. Dekyakandi's son in the AMA's physician listing was a long shot. I did not know whether he was practicing medicine in the United States. Even if he was, he might not be included in the online listing, but it was certainly worth a try. As usual, however, searching was not going to be easy. The AMA website does not have an alphabetical listing of all its members (or at least none that I could find). Thus, I had to search for Dr. Dekyakandi's son by typing his last name and using the scroll down menu to try each possible state of residence—a very time consuming process. But I diligently checked each state, one-by-one in alphabetical order, and, in Michigan, I got a hit: Dr. Tom Dekyakandi.

As I dialed the phone number, I was painfully aware that this attempt was my last. If Tom Dekyakandi was not Dr. Dekyakandi's son, there would almost be no point for me to keep looking. Our court submission was due in about three weeks and getting an affidavit from Dekyakandi in Ghana could take twice as long. I was nervous and excited, but I did not want to get my hopes up because the phone call could be another dead end. It was not. Almost two months after I began the hunt for Dr. Dekyakandi, I finally found Dr. Dekyakandi's son, who eventually led me to his father. I also learned that Tom Dekyakandi's wife had visited the Catholic Education Center in Liberia shortly after it was attacked by the Taylor rebels. While she was there, she had met Ms. Wilson, who had told her about her harrowing experience. Words cannot describe the exhilaration that I felt at that moment. Everything I had done to reach that point was suddenly all worth it. Surprisingly, I still felt that way even after Aimen Mir, another clinic colleague, told me that LEXIS has a professional licenses database that can be used to retrieve information about a physician simply by typing in the physician's last name—a much easier search process than the one that I used. This reminder of the multiple paths in fact investigation was an appropriate ending for a search that started with a misspelled last name. . . .

Four months after the hearing, the judge granted Ms. Wilson political asylum, and, in his written opinion, he specifically cited to Dr. Dekyakandi's affidavit as one of the many documents that corroborated her claim.

As this essay demonstrates, fact investigation is a grueling, and at times rewarding, task. As with most of the lawyering process, no easy formulas exist for uncovering facts in a case. As the law students in this case discovered, thorough fact investigation requires asking the same question in different ways, conducting often tedious examination of directories, running into numerous brick walls (including the misspelling of names), and a bit of luck. In this chapter we describe some suggested methods for investigating facts in a case, but we caution that in each case you will face different obstacles to unearthing the facts you need, and you must adopt your approach to respond to each of them.

§16.2 DEVELOPING ADDITIONAL SOURCES OF PROOF

As discussed in §15.2, your assessment of the persuasiveness of your existing facts requires an evaluation of the strength of the sources of the facts supporting the legal elements and the episodes listed in your chronology. After you have assessed the credibility of your sources of proof, you need to try to develop additional, more credible sources. Follow the approach used by the students in Ms. Wilson's case. Reviewing your legal elements chart and chronology, you should identify each contested fact that needs further support and specify its relative importance on a scale of 1 to 3. Although in each case a number of contested facts will exist, you will usually need to search for corroborating evidence for only a few elements or episodes. (In the Wilson case, the students identified the attack at the CEC as the key episode that needed corroboration because it would strongly show that Ms. Wilson had a "well-founded fear of persecution.") Then, brainstorm possible additional sources of corroborating evidence for the high priority elements or episodes.

In undertaking this process, think in terms of a "spectrum" of possible sources of proof.[1] Remember that the credibility of a source of proof will depend on the nature of the source (tangible or oral), processing factors of the witnesses, and schema factors of the witnesses (see §15.2). It is helpful, then, to think about possible additional sources of proof in terms of their range of credibility. Initially, consider whether any document or other tangible evidence exists that reflects what

---

1. Patrick J. Flynn, *Preparing the Case Before We Initiate Litigation: What We Need Is a Plan*, 18 Am. J. Trial Advoc. 509, 538–539 (1995).

happened in a particular episode. A medical record may exist, for example, recording the nature of an injury. A police report might contain information about an accident or altercation. Or a personal diary might record a witness's observations about the event. Then try to identify all the possible witnesses of the event and rank them according to their ability to perceive the event, recall it, and communicate their information to the fact-finder. In the Wilson case, for example, the students considered relying solely on affidavits from Bishop Brown and Father Gooden generally describing the conditions in Liberia at the time of the attacks on their client, but they were concerned about the credibility of these affidavits given that neither man had been in Liberia in the early 1990s, and Father Brown was unavailable for cross-examination.

Finally, consider additional sources of proof in terms of their bias, prejudice, and personal schemas. Start with perhaps the most credible witnesses of an event, possible neutral observers of an event. Then consider persons associated with your adversary—friends, relatives, friendly co-workers. Finally, identify persons connected with your client. If the facts concerning an episode are not easily understandable by a layperson, you might want to consider obtaining an expert whose unique schemas about a particular subject, based on her education and training, can help you, and possibly the fact-finder, interpret what happened. In a products liability case, for example, it will probably be essential for both parties to obtain experts to try to explain what occurred when the product in dispute malfunctioned.

§16.3 TRACKING DOWN ADDITIONAL SOURCES

Once you have brainstormed possible sources of corroborating facts, you need to track them down. While you will have to adapt this process in each case depending on the particular sources you are searching, we suggest that you consider five general approaches: following the people trail; following the paper and electronic trails; probing the institutional context; exploring organizational relationships; and understanding the organization's operations.[2]

§16.3.1 FOLLOWING THE PEOPLE TRAIL

If you are trying to track down a particular individual or learn about his reputation or character, you might seek out his neighbors, co-workers, business associates, or social acquaintances. For a corporation, you might contact its customers, suppliers, stockholders, or employees. If the person or corporation has been the subject of prior litigation, you might want to talk to the other party to that suit or its attorneys. And, even if you are trying to uncover damaging information about the person (for example, a complaining witness in a criminal case), you

2. These suggested approaches are based on methods described in Dennis King, *Get the Facts on Anyone* 3–6 (1999). See also Brant Houston et al., *The Investigative Reporter's Handbook: A Guide to Documents, Databases and Techniques* (5th ed. 2009).

might want to contact his best friends to uncover positive facts to which you may later have to respond.[3]

In following the people trail, you need to probe each person thoroughly for additional information (see §7.6). Often, your contact will initially deny having information about the individual or assert a lack of memory. As the student in the Wilson case learned in her second call to Bishop Brown, you need to ask the same question in different ways or at different times. The person may be busy, may not be free to talk openly, or may misunderstand the purpose of your inquiry. In addition, even if the contact has no helpful information about your subject, you should ask him for the names of any other persons who might have such information.

§16.3.2 FOLLOWING THE PAPER AND ELECTRONIC TRAILS

We live in a record-keeping society and whether you are investigating information on a particular person, weather conditions at a particular time, background on a particular company, or government filings and inspections, tangible records of these parties and events are likely to exist. Many of these records are accessible either on the Internet or on specialized databases, such as LEXIS and Westlaw. Unfortunately, as the description of the fact investigation in the Wilson case demonstrates, searching on the Web for this information is not as easy as it may seem. The students had no luck with specific queries on search engines for the name "Dr. Detchakandi" or general research for news articles on the attack on the CEC. Even when they found that the doctor had a son who was a physician in the United States, they could not simply type the name into a directory on the AMA website but had to scroll down menus for each state.

For these reasons, we suggest that you develop an investigation strategy before searching for a paper trail on the Internet. If a basic query on a search engine (such as *www.google.com* or *www.bing.com*) does not succeed, try to use one of the advanced search functions. Depending on the particular search engine, you can limit your query, for instance, to documents with particular words or phrases; specific keywords in the title or URL; date ranges; file format (e.g., pdf, Excel, or PowerPoint); or pages from a particular country or location. For a more targeted search, on Google you can use the proximity connector, "AROUND(n)," to narrow your search to retrieve results within a certain number (*n*) of words from each other. For example, if in the Ransom case, you want to search for complaints against the landlord Dusak, a search for "Dusak complaints" will retrieve results with both words anywhere in the documents; the search "Dusak AROUND(5) complaints" will limit the results only to documents in which the two terms are within five words of each other.

If these searches do not succeed, spend some time learning what types of information are in fact available on different websites and databases before you launch your search. Some websites can be particularly helpful to lawyers. To give

---

3. King *supra* note 2, at 4.

you a sense of what you might look for, here are a few websites that were in good operating condition at the time this book was published:

http://fedstats.sites.usa.gov (statistics collected by the federal government)
www.iTools.com/search (a library's reference desk on the Web)
http://tvnews.vanderbilt.edu (an archive of news reported on television)
www.anywho.com (a people finder)
www.pipl.com (comprehensive people search)
www.searchsystems.net (index of all online public records)
statelocalgov.net (directory for public records of state agencies and local governments)
http://ssdi-search.com (social security death index)
Blackbookonline.info (directory for free public record searches).

There are *thousands* of other sites through which you can access data. (Web addresses and the quality of websites change often. By the time you read this book, one or more of the websites listed above might have disappeared or changed addresses.)

But the wide range of data on the Web does not guarantee that the information you seek is available. Tax and property records for some jurisdictions, for instance, are not current, and other records might not be available for a particular state or county.

LEXIS and Westlaw include some directories on corporations, real estate transactions, court filings, and professional listings. The student in the Wilson case, for example, conducted a tedious search on the AMA website because she did not know that LEXIS had a professional licenses database that could be used to retrieve information about a physician simply by typing in his or her name.

LEXIS and Westlaw both include news libraries that archive newspaper stories. Sometimes a newspaper or magazine article will contain something useful to you about the person, subject, or organization you are trying to learn about. Check both LEXIS and Westlaw. Each includes publications not archived by the other.

Social networking sites, such as Facebook and Linkedin, can also be used as effective investigative tools. If the person you are investigating, a member of her family, or a friend has a public profile on one of these sites, you can obtain information about her lifestyle, interests, activities, and employment. In a drunken driving case in Santa Barbara, California, for example, in which a passenger was killed, the defendant pleaded guilty, expressed deep remorse, and sought a long probation. But the prosecutor used a photo and comments from her social networking site to show her partying lifestyle, and the judge sentenced her to two years in prison.[4] Additionally, these sites can be used affirmatively to request information about a particular problem or event. A lawyer, for instance, seeking support for his client's claim that a landlord rejected members of particular groups

4. Justin Rebello, *Using Social Networks to Investigate Your Case*, *Minnesota Lawyer*, Aug. 18, 2008, *available at* 2008 WLNR 25703417. The use of social networking sites in fact investigation raises some serious ethical issues (see §16.4).

as tenants can create an account soliciting information from other persons who believe they were victims of the landlord's discriminatory conduct.

Like social media platforms, Google Groups (*http://groups.google.com*) contains discussions by individuals with a community of interest (e.g., hobbies, politics, social issues). Using Google Groups, you can anonymously search through postings to find messages from particular people and to identify their email addresses. You can also attempt to email the author of a message.

With Internet sources, you need to be suspicious of the credibility of the information you retrieve. As with any sources of proof, issues of bias and prejudice come into play (see §§15.2.1 and 15.2.2). Some sources on the Internet are obviously more credible than others. A real estate agency's assessment of the strength of the market in a particular area is less believable, for example, than a county government report on the subject, and the county report is less credible than an official listing of all property transactions in the area within the last year. (Reliable data is objective. Even unbiased opinions, such as the ones you might find in the county government's report, are subjective.)

The fact that a computer is providing information does not certify that that information is complete or accurate. Anybody can create a website, and any time you use a search engine some of the sites you find will reflect narrow and perhaps bizarre points of view. How can you improve the quality of what you find on the Web?[5]

First, rely on sites sponsored by the best organizations in the field. If you want medical information, go to the websites of the federal Centers for Disease Control, the Mayo Clinic, and other organizations with national reputations. Also discover who else relies on the site by typing the search operator "link:" before the website's address in a Google search (e.g., the search "link:mayoclinic.org" will retrieve the sites that cite that address).

Second, look for data collected comprehensively and in depth. A danger sign is an isolated fact that you like but does not cite to any authority that would give it credibility and is not presented in a context that would help you understand how that fact was learned and what it means. Moreover, consider whether the site is current and determine whether or not it is missing any content. Oftentimes a website will only include an abbreviated version of an original printed publication. You are not interested in the kind of informational tidbits that people mention in casual conversation. You want hard facts from reliable sources.

Third, identify the site owner and her credentials. Be suspicious if you cannot easily find the name. If you cannot find the name, you can run the domain name through a registry database such as *www.betterwhois.com* to attempt to find the owner's identity. Once you have a name, you can track down the owner's credentials by doing an independent search, for example, on the Library of Congress online catalog, *http://catalog.loc.gov*.

---

5. These suggestions are based on those recommended in Carole A. Levitt & Mark E. Rosch, *The Lawyer's Guide to Fact Finding on the Internet* (3d ed. 2006). See also Carole A. Levitt & Mark E. Rosch, *The Cybersleuth's Guide to the Internet* (12th ed. 2013).

Fourth, if you need to prove something in court, ask yourself how you can get the evidence. Most websites are not admissible evidence, but they can lead you to evidence that is admissible in a courtroom.

Unfortunately, in this day of computer research, students often give up on tracking down records if they cannot be found on the Internet. The students in the Wilson case, for example, after searching LEXIS and the Web for articles on the CEC attack apparently did not attempt to search for newspaper or magazine articles that may have been written on the attack but not posted on the Web. Numerous newspaper and periodical articles, especially those in local weeklies and specialty newsletters, are not available online. Other sources of records, especially those relating to the work of local governments (for instance, city and county legislative reports), concerning vital statistics (for example, birth and death records), or produced before the 1990s, may not be available through computer research. And records relating to particular incidents or transactions (for instance, hospital and police records or records of payments of government fees) may only be available in hard copy.

In many of your cases, the paper and electronic trails will lead you to issues concerning government regulation of the transaction involved or similar incidents involving different parties (for example, zoning decisions, housing inspections, community development grants, corporate filings, or fraud investigations). Many of these records will not be available on the Web. Depending on the jurisdiction that maintains the records, you will need to file a request for the documents under a state Open Records Act or Freedom of Information Law or the federal Freedom of Information Act ("FOIA").[6] In making these requests, you need to determine the specific official to whom the request must be addressed, the applicability of the statute and any exemptions to your specific request, the deadlines for responses, and the procedures for processing requests.

Successful investigation requires the skillful interweaving of the paper and electronic trails with the people trail.[7] In your search of friends and associates of your subject, you should be asking questions about any documentation that might assist you in your investigation. And, as you review any records you unearth, you should be alert to the names of other persons you might want to interview.

§16.3.3 PROBING THE INSTITUTIONAL CONTEXT

If the subject of your search is connected with or concerns a particular business or organization, you should also consider exploring the institutional context of your subject: investigating the people, paper, and electronic trails within that organization.[8] In the Wilson case, for example, when the initial investigation failed to disclose information about the CEC attack, the students called an office of the Catholic Church for information on Dr. Detchakandi. And through those contacts with the church, they found the doctor. Similarly, in cases involving players acting

---

6. See, e.g., 5 U.S.C. §552 (Freedom of Information Act); N.Y. Pub. Off. Law §§84–90 (McKinney 2008 & Supp. 2014) (Freedom of Information Law); and Tex. Gov't Code Ann. §§552.001–552.353 (Vernon 2012 & Supp. 2014) (Open Records Act).
7. King, *supra* note 2, at 4.
8. *Id.* at 4–5.

within any organization—police officers in criminal cases, managers in employment discrimination cases, superintendents in landlord/tenant cases—crucial records and information from associates likely will exist in the files and offices of those organizations.

The same approach works in reverse: if the subject of your inquiry is the business itself, you should focus on the identities and backgrounds of the principals, officers, and directors of that company. If, for example, your client is attempting to enforce a judgment against a corporation that recently transferred all its assets to a third party, you probably will want to investigate the relationship between the principals of the corporation and the transferee to determine if the conveyance was fraudulent. Or, if you are representing a developer who is having difficulty purchasing property owned by a particular business, you will want to identify the owners of the business to find out if your client might have some possible allies to approach. To determine the names of the principals of corporations, partnerships, and limited liability companies, you will need to follow the trail of filings with the appropriate state office, often the Secretary of State. For businesses operating under an assumed name, you must track down the state, county, or city registry for such names to discover the principals for the business.

§16.3.4 EXPLORING ORGANIZATIONAL RELATIONSHIPS

In some cases, you will not only want to investigate the institutional context of your subject, but also the associations of that institution with other organizations. "You may find that your subject is linked in complex ways to various economic or political interests. The only way to understand the significance of the relationships involved . . . is to analyze this larger environment."[9] Such an approach is very helpful when you are investigating the actions of a business that is affiliated with a number of other companies. Focusing on the activities of a single company might disclose very little information, but inquiry into the actions of other companies associated with the subject might help to put all the pieces together. To determine, for instance, if a corporation is hiding assets with an affiliate or is using a subsidiary to avoid disclosing certain expenses, investigation might include an examination of the people, paper, and electronic trails for all companies associated with that corporation.

§16.3.5 UNDERSTANDING AN ORGANIZATION'S OPERATIONS

This approach is the process of figuring out how things work in a particular business, institution, profession, association, or government.[10] In your fact investigation using people, paper, and electronic trails, you will usually uncover a significant amount of information, but it will only be helpful if you have a framework for understanding it. In a medical malpractice suit, for example, your examination of the relevant hospital record and interviews with the nurses and

9. *Id.* at 5–6.
10. *Id.* at 6.

physicians will disclose a number of facts about the underlying incident. But unless you understand the hierarchy of responsibility in the hospital, the professional relationships between the different players in the treatment of the patient, and the procedures for generating records about that treatment, you might not fully understand the different stories about "what really happened" and the documents you are examining. These same issues arise if you are investigating the operations of a local government, a local gang, an accounting firm, or a not-for-profit group.

As a new attorney in a particular field, you will have very limited knowledge about the operations of the institutions and businesses involved in your cases. An initial part of the fact investigation process, then, requires getting a grasp of how these groups work. Depending on your case, you can obtain this information through different sources: employees at the organization or similar groups; websites for professional or business groups; government guides; or operational documents from the company.[11] In some instances, you may need to consult with an expert to obtain a full understanding of the operations of the subject institution.

§16.3.6 VEHICLES FOR TRACKING DOWN ADDITIONAL FACTS

Much fact investigation occurs either before litigation or in a context that will never lead to litigation. You will have to follow the people, paper, and electronic trails and conduct any exploration of the background of your subject without the assistance of formal discovery rules. Except in the context of government records (see §16.3.2), parties usually will have no obligation to disclose information to you. You will simply have to rely on your own prowess to uncover relevant documents or corroborating witnesses.

Once litigation has been commenced, you often will have the opportunity to engage in some kind of pre-trial discovery, for example, interrogatories, requests to produce documents, and depositions. At trial or hearing, you usually can subpoena documents. Since this book is not a civil procedure text, we will not describe the use of these and other discovery mechanisms. You should understand, however, that even in the litigation context, much fact investigation occurs outside the context of formal discovery. Often your client will be unable to afford large-scale formal discovery; information, especially from third parties, will be more easily accessible through informal means; and sometimes it is a better strategy to unearth crucial information without informing your opponent of your find.

§16.4 ETHICS IN FACT INVESTIGATION

Unlike a reporter or private investigator, a lawyer has unique professional obligations in the fact investigation process. In the course of representing a client, a lawyer shall not knowingly "make a false statement of material fact to a third

11. To investigate a not-for-profit organization, for example, you probably will want to review the organization's IRS Form 990, which contains a wealth of financial information. Most of these forms can be obtained from *www.guidestar.org*.

person."[12] Accordingly, in contacting individuals for information about your client's case, you cannot falsely represent your role, for example, by stating that you are a reporter.[13] Moreover, in representing a client, a lawyer "shall not communicate about the subject of the representation with a person the lawyer knows to be represented by another lawyer in the matter, unless the lawyer has the consent of the other lawyer or is authorized to do so by law or a court order."[14] This obligation can raise difficult issues when the other side is a corporation, and you are seeking information from one of its employees.[15] In addition, "[I]n dealing on behalf of a client with a person who is not represented by counsel, a lawyer shall not state or imply that the lawyer is disinterested."[16] Finally, a lawyer shall not "use methods of obtaining evidence that violate the legal rights of such a person."[17]

---

12. Model Rule 4.1(a).
13. This issue has recently arisen in the context of the use of social networking sites for fact investigation. Two bar association ethics committees have categorically proscribed lawyers and investigators under their supervision from "friending" an unrepresented person in a case to obtain information without revealing the true purpose of the request. Ass'n of the Bar of the City of N.Y. Comm. on Prof'l Ethics, Formal Op. 2010-2; Philadelphia Bar Ass'n Prof'l Guidance Comm., Op. 2009-02. They found that such a communication would be deceptive because it would omit the highly material fact that the lawyer planned to use the information obtained from the person in a lawsuit. One ethics committee, however, has suggested that dissemblance for the purpose of gathering evidence may be permissible in the limited circumstances where the investigation concerns a violation of civil rights or intellectual property rights, and the lawyer believes in good faith that such violation is taking place or will take place imminently; the dissemblance is authorized by law; the evidence sought is not reasonably available through other lawful means; and the dissemblance does not unlawfully or unethically violate the rights of the third party. Ass'n of the Bar of the City of N.Y. Comm. on Prof'l Ethics, Formal Op. 737 (2007). See also New York State Bar Ass'n Comm. on Prof'l Ethics, Op. 843 (2010) (concluding that a lawyer who represents a client in pending litigation, and who has access to the public social network pages of another party, may access and review those pages as long as the lawyer does not friend the other party or direct a third party to do so). Given the divergent opinions on this issue, it is essential that lawyers consult the ethics opinions in their jurisdiction before using social networking for this type of fact investigation.
14. Model Rule 4.2.
15. Charles W. Wolfram, *Modern Legal Ethics* §11.6.2 at 613 (1986).
16. Model Rule 4.3.
17. Model Rule 4.4(a).

CHAPTER

17

RESPONDING TO YOUR ADVERSARY'S FACTS

§17.1 IMAGINING YOUR ADVERSARY'S FACTS

Thus far, we have discussed the organization of facts in your own case and the assessment of their credibility. In most cases, however, your adversary is also presenting facts, and part of your case preparation will involve developing a response to these facts. Obviously, you will not know all the facts that will be used by your adversaries until the trial or hearing, but, in your case preparation, you should be able to get some idea of what facts they will be introducing. To identify those facts, examine your adversary's pleadings, her responses to written discovery, any documents written by the adversary or persons associated with her, and, if depositions are conducted in the case, the answers of your adversary and her witnesses in their examinations. Also, consider whether information you have obtained from third parties in the fact investigation process suggests the views of your adversary about the events in the case. In addition, explore with your own client and witnesses what positions they believe your adversary will be taking in the case. Finally, for those areas about which you cannot discover the facts, brainstorm what facts you envision your adversary will present in light of her schemas about such situations.

After discovering your adversary's facts, identify the principal conflicts between your client's version of key events and your opponent's account. In terms of the legal elements model of organizing facts (Chapter 11), identify those elements for which there is a factual dispute. In regard to the chronology model for organizing facts (Chapter 12), note any conflicts between your client's version of particular episodes and your adversary's account. Then, consider the significance of each of the contested facts and select those on which you will need to focus to establish your case. In many cases, you will find that the key factual disputes only concern two or three significant events.

After you have identified the contested facts in terms of the legal elements and chronology models, try to imagine the adversary's story. Consider the injustices your adversary will be asserting, the "best" facts upon which she will be relying, and the refrains that occur throughout her (and her witnesses') telling of their versions. Then, try to imagine what possible unifying themes your adversary will be weaving throughout the presentation of her case. Also, attempt to identify the persuasive images that your adversary may be using: for example, her characterization of herself and the key events in the case. Finally, in many cases, it might be helpful to identify what genre the opposing party will be using for the presentation of the facts. Then, consider how you might want to adjust the sequencing, perspective, and tone of your own story to counter your adversary. In short, ask yourself how you believe the adversary will be packaging her presentation to the fact-finder.

§17.2 ATTACKING YOUR ADVERSARY'S SOURCES OF FACT

Once you have identified the key facts in dispute, we suggest that you identify the sources of your version and those of your adversary. You should then evaluate the credibility of the sources for both versions.

Consider, for example, a possible discrepancy in the Ransom case. Remember the following episode described in the Ransom chronology for April 19, 1996:

> Exterminator arrived at apartment unannounced. Ms. Ransom was leaving for work and told him to call back to make an appointment.

(Chart 12B, lines 77–82). The source of these facts is Ms. Ransom's interview on June 20, 1996. Now, suppose that at his deposition on May 6, 1997, the exterminator testified,

> I arrived at Ms. Ransom's apartment about 8:00 a.m. on April 19. She met me at the door in a house dress. She looked as if she had just got out of bed and said nothing about going to work. The kids were running around, and the TV was blaring with cartoons. She yelled at me for coming unannounced and slammed the door in my face.

The lawyers for both parties will need to consider how the fact-finder will assess the credibility of the sources for these two versions of this event. Using the methods described in Chapter 15, we first consider processing issues (§15.2.2). For this episode, there are probably few questions about the perception of the event, although the blaring of the television may have interfered with both Ms. Ransom's and the exterminator's hearing of the conversation or could have accounted for the volume of each of their voices.

On the other hand, there are some significant recall issues about this episode. While Ms. Ransom told you about the events only two months after the event, the exterminator is telling his account more than one year later. Under most of our schemas, if this exterminator has visited many apartments during that year, it is possible that his memory of the visit to Ms. Ransom's apartment one year later is not very clear. But the exterminator may have a vivid memory of these events because tenants rarely slam doors in his face. This would be an issue that the landlord's lawyer would want to explore with the exterminator during trial preparation and that Ms. Ransom's lawyer would have wanted to address at the deposition.

Moreover, the only tangible fact reflecting the events of that morning—the April 22 letter from Mr. Dusak to Ms. Ransom—contains no information in regard to the hostile reception described by the exterminator. Because, under most of our schemas, a landlord would include such negative references in a letter to his tenant, the accuracy of the exterminator's recall one year after the events can be called into question. For this reason, Ms. Ransom appears more credible in regard to processing issues.

As to schema issues, however, it is unclear which source is more credible. Ms. Ransom certainly has a bias in favor of her case and may have a prejudice against any worker for the landlord. The schemas of the exterminator will need to be investigated by both parties. If he is an independent contractor who works for many landlords, homeowners, and tenants and has no preconceived notions against tenants, he may appear to be unbiased and a very credible witness. If, on the other hand, he works primarily for Mr. Dusak, has spoken to others negatively about tenants, or expresses such feelings in a personal interview or at a deposition, the fact-finder may consider that Ms. Ransom and the exterminator are equally credible in regard to this episode.

§17.3 ATTACKING YOUR ADVERSARY'S INFERENCES

In examining the key conflicts in versions, identify your adversary's circumstantial evidence and assess the strength of her inferences. Return to the Circumstantial Evidence–Generalization–Conclusion model, and assess the strength of your adversary's generalizations (see §15.4). Then, attempt to develop "except when's" to undermine these generalizations.

Again, let us return to the Ransom case, and assume that the landlord has denied that the leak in the bedroom has not been adequately repaired. In support of that denial, assume that Mr. Dusak testified at his deposition,

> I received a call from Ms. Ransom in early March about the problem with the leaking roof. Immediately, I called ABC Roofing. They sent out workers a week later and finished the work by April 2. Ms. Ransom never called me after April 2 to complain about the leaking roof so I assumed it was repaired.

CHART 17A ATTACKING DUSAK'S INFERENCE

Facts	Generalization	Conclusion
Ms. Ransom never called Mr. Dusak after April 2 to complain about problem of leaking roof.	If a tenant does not complain to her landlord about a repair job, the repair has been made.	Since Ms. Ransom did not complain after April 2 about the leak in the roof, it was adequately repaired, and the premises was fit for human habitation.

To attack Mr. Dusak's inference that the leak was adequately repaired, Ms. Ransom's lawyer should try to brainstorm possible "except when's" to this generalization: *If a tenant does not complain about a repair job, the repair has been made*, except when: (1) the tenant tells the superintendent in the building about the problem; (2) the tenant is scared that the landlord will verbally abuse her if she complains; (3) the tenant has consistently complained about different problems prior to this one, and nothing has been done; or (4) she has other, more serious problems in her life, not necessarily related to the apartment, to which she must attend. After she conducts further fact investigation (in this case, a follow-up interview with the client), Ms. Ransom's lawyer will have to consider how she can incorporate the "except when" into her presentation of the case. If, for example, Ms. Ransom tells her that she did not call Mr. Dusak because she was afraid of him, her lawyer may be able to argue to the fact-finder that this "except when" is consistent with the theme of her case: victimization by the landlord. In this way, Ms. Ransom's attorney can use the very same circumstantial evidence used by Mr. Dusak to support her own case.

§17.4 ATTACKING YOUR ADVERSARY'S CONTEXTUAL FACTS

The credibility of your adversary's story can also be assessed by examining your adversary's descriptions of episodes in the chronology. Even if there is no conflict in regard to the specific actions in an episode, there may be a dispute as to the context for those actions. An evaluation of the facts setting the scene, the facts reflecting stage directions, explanatory facts, and personal facts will assist you in developing responses to your adversary's version of the events.

Consider, for example, the exterminator's account of his visit to the apartment that he gave at his deposition. Even assuming this account has some accuracy, the context for that meeting is very significant in determining "what really happened." For example, we do not know how the exterminator announced his arrival. Think of possible scenarios that could affect a fact-finder's reaction to the events. On the one hand, the exterminator could have politely knocked on the door and requested entrance into the apartment, while Ms. Ransom could have immediately yelled at him and pushed him out the door. In such a context, Ms. Ransom's conduct appears very unreasonable. On the other hand, the exterminator could have knocked vigorously and repeatedly at the door, demanding entry. When Ms. Ransom opened the door, he could have pushed Ms. Ransom aside to get into the apartment, shoved the children out of the way, and started to prepare for spraying. In that context, Ms. Ransom seems to have acted quite reasonably in response to the exterminator.

To challenge the exterminator's account, then, Ms. Ransom's lawyer will not only focus on the credibility of the exterminator as a witness—his ability to perceive and recall the events and his possible biases and prejudices—but also the facts surrounding that account. The exterminator's version at his deposition was very conclusory. In fact, it did not even include a description of his portion of the conversation. To challenge this account, Ms. Ransom's lawyer will want to explore the context of the conversation with her client, with the exterminator in an interview or at his deposition, or with Ms. Ransom's four-year-old child, who may have witnessed the encounter.

§17.5 ATTACKING YOUR ADVERSARY'S STORY

Finally, the process of responding to your adversary's case usually requires an assessment of your adversary's story. First, compare your unifying theme with your adversary's and consider which will make more sense to the fact-finder. Ask yourself whether there is any way to fine tune your theme to respond more effectively to your adversary. If your adversary's theme is based on a powerful slogan or stock story, attempt to develop a counter-slogan or counter-story to undermine this theme.[1] Second, consider whether your adversary's story takes into account all the facts that will be presented at the hearing or trial. Can you attack her story on the grounds that it is incomplete? Third, determine whether the adversary's story is consistent with the uncontested facts in the case and portrays the actors and actions consistently. In the Ransom case, for example, her lawyer will want to consider whether all of Mr. Dusak's actions accord with the image his lawyer wants to paint of a concerned and dependable landlord. Finally, examine the amount of ambiguity in your adversary's story. What details are missing and how crucial are they to the adversary's case? Again, in the Ransom case, if Mr. Dusak is unable to remember key conversations with Ms. Ransom, her lawyer can possibly attack any story based on the theme that Mr. Dusak was responsive to his tenants' complaints.

---

1. See Anthony G. Amsterdam & Jerome Bruner, *Minding the Law* 188–189 (2000) (examining the types of rhetoric that can be used in arguing a death penalty case in the United States Supreme Court: "This case puts the criminal justice system at risk" versus "This case goes to the heart of the Nation's constitutional commitment to equality and justice").

PART IV

COUNSELING

CHAPTER

18

WHAT HAPPENS WHEN A LAWYER COUNSELS A CLIENT

§18.1 COUNSELING AND ADVICE IN LEGAL WORK

It's no accident that when judges talk to lawyers or when lawyers talk to each other, they traditionally use the word "counselor" as a form of address.[1] Some clients hire a lawyer to get advocacy, but *all* clients need and expect advice. For that reason, "[c]ounseling lies at the heart of the professional relationship between lawyer and client."[2] For many lawyers, it also dominates their workday. "Surveys suggest that lawyers spend most of their time in activities that the lawyers themselves describe as 'counseling.'"[3]

What exactly is counseling? Simply put, it is "the process in which lawyers help clients reach decisions."[4] How do lawyers do that? There are two parts to counseling. The first, preparation, includes identifying the client's goals and developing two or more alternative potential solutions that, to varying degrees, might accomplish those goals. (Chapter 20 explains how to do that.) The second is a meeting with the

---

1. For example: "Good morning, counselor, when will you be ready to proceed?"
2. Paul Brest, *The Responsibility of Law Schools: Educating Lawyers as Counselors and Problem Solvers* (Issues 3 & 4), 58 Law & Contemp. Probs. 5, 8 (Summer/Autumn 1995).
3. Thomas L. Shaffer & James R. Elkins, *Legal Interviewing and Counseling in a Nutshell* 7 (4th ed. 2004). "Lawyers spend less time in court or in the library than one would think. . . ." *Id.* at 8.
4. David A. Binder & Susan C. Price, *Legal Interviewing and Counseling: A Client-Centered Approach* 5 (1977).

client in which the lawyer explains the potential solutions so the client can choose between or among them. Chapter 21 explains how to conduct that meeting. A simple example occurs when a defendant makes a pretrial offer to settle. For the plaintiff, one potential solution is to accept the offer. Another is to go to trial in hopes of getting more there. A much more complex example is given in Chapter 19.

"Advice" is a broader concept. Counseling is a form of advice, but not all advice is counseling. For example, suppose a judge has just preliminarily enjoined a client; the client asks you whether such an order can be appealed; and you say yes. You have provided advice because you have decoded some of the mystery of the law for a layperson. But you have not counseled because you have not helped the client make a decision—here whether to appeal this particular preliminary injunction. The decision would require weighing the advantages, costs, risks, and chances of success of one option (in this instance, appealing the injunction) against the advantages, costs, risks, and chances of success of another option (not appealing). Counseling is working out those variables and explaining them to the client in a way that will help the client decide.

Clients want counseling and other advice in two kinds of situations. The first is transactions, such as business contracts, when the client wants to know how to accomplish a given goal at minimum cost and risk (see §18.2). The second is dispute resolution, which is dominated by conflict and where litigation is at least an option and might already be happening (§18.3).

These two categories can overlap. In part, that is because a transaction-focused client wants to avoid conflict. For example, a client buying land on which to build a shopping center would want to know how to structure the transaction so as to cause the least amount of disagreement with the tax, land use, and environmental authorities. Another reason for overlap is that one method of resolving conflict is to find a way for both parties to improve their situations by collaborating (which often involves a transaction). For example, two home owners feuding over who pays for the care of trees that overhang both plots of land might be able to get a volume discount if they ask tree care companies to bid on working on all the trees on both plots. This solves conflict and requires two transactions: one between the property owners themselves and the other between them and the tree care company submitting the best bid.

Counseling and interviewing can overlap, too. Where a deadline or an emergency threatens, you might need to counsel a client on some questions during the initial interview. And if interviewing is for the most part learning facts orally, you will need to do that many times during the representation of a given client, sometimes in preparation for or in the midst of counseling.

Bear in mind three other things if the client is an organization which usually means a business but might mean a nonprofit organization. First, as you learned in §2.2, the more you know the client's business and industry, the better you can perform all of this work. Second, organizations might look monolithic from the outside, but they are not really "cold, impersonal, and rational decision-makers."[5] Instead, organizations "are composed of people, and a merger or acquisition is as likely to occur because someone is empire-building as for any completely rational

5. Robert F. Seibel, LAWCLINIC listserv posting dated Nov. 16, 1994.

business reason."[6] Third, organizations speak to their lawyers through managers, executives, and other employees, who may have their own personal worries. But the lawyer represents the organization and not any of the people who work for it. When the interests of employees diverge from those of the organization, the lawyer owes an entire duty of loyalty to it and little, other than some warnings, to the people involved. See §22.4 for an explanation of what the law expects you to do in this situation.

Finally, to be a good counselor no matter who your client is, you have to be able to combine empathy and detachment, two things that do not naturally exist side by side. Empathy helps you understand the client's goals and needs. Detachment helps you see the problem as it really is, without delusion. "The wise counselor is one who is able to see his client's situation from within and yet, at the same time, from a distance, and thus to give advice that is at once compassionate and objective."[7]

§18.2 TRANSACTIONAL COUNSELING

When organizational clients want transactional counseling and advice, it is most typically about how to structure deals with other organizations and how to conduct their affairs so as to minimize their taxes and their legal liability (say, in tort). When an individual or a family wants counseling and advice, it might, for example, be about how to plan an estate or buy a home.

Chapters 19 through 22 explain how to do full counseling of individuals and organizations. But much of what lawyers add to transactions is in the form of advice that might fall short of full counseling. In an organizational setting, the advice might be given in varying degrees of formality:

Answering a point-blank question from the client, often over the telephone. You sit in your office writing or reading. The phone rings, and you pick it up. A client describes a proposed transaction and asks pointedly about several concerns, among them perhaps "whether the transaction is lawful, whether it is consistent with loan or other commitments that the corporation has previously undertaken, whether it will lead to a desired tax treatment,"[8] and so on. Or the client asks a single general question: "Do you see any problems with this?" When you answer, you are not doing full-blown counseling because your role is not to structure the decision as described in Chapter 21. But your answer is advice, and there is a technique to giving it. Take careful written notes of what the other person is telling you. Before answering, make certain that you understand the facts. Summarize them as you think you have heard them and ask the person at the other end of the line whether you have got them right ("Let me make sure I've got the facts right . . ."). Do not answer the other person's questions until you are confident that you know exactly what the law is, and if that involves delay, estimate how

---

6. *Id.*
7. Anthony Kronman, *Living in the Law*, 54 U. Chi. L. Rev. 835, 866 (1987).
8. Robert W. Hamilton, *Fundamentals of Modern Business* 517 (1989).

long the delay will be ("I want to check a few things, and I'll get back to you later this morning"). Make a written note of the advice you gave over the phone, and keep all of your notes in the client's file in case a misunderstanding later occurs about what you said or why you said it.

Participation in business planning. This might happen in a meeting in which the lawyer is only one of several people in the room. Depending on the situation, the lawyer might figuratively sit on the sidelines, interjecting advice about legal concerns as they become relevant, or the lawyer might counsel by framing alternatives and estimating their effectiveness, as described in Chapter 20.

Counseling about a transaction that is in the formation stage. The client and another business have talked about how each could earn some money buying or selling something to the other. They have already agreed to some of the terms—perhaps price, quantity, delivery dates, and so forth. You have not been part of these discussions because you would not be able to add value to them. At a point when the deal seems to be jelling, the client consults you to "run it past our lawyers" (find out whether the deal would create legal problems) and "reduce it to writing" (ask you to produce a contract, which will govern the transaction). After you and the client talk things over, you write a draft of an agreement. This is not the final version. After you and the client review the draft, you rewrite it and send it to the other business's lawyer. Or if the other business's lawyer has already written a draft, you rewrite that instead. Negotiations ensue. Afterward, you rewrite the agreement again to reflect the results of the negotiations. At some or a number of points in this story, you and the client have conversations in which you frame alternative ways of solving problems and estimate each alternative's effectiveness, as described in Chapters 20 and 21.

Section 8.3.1 lists a number of things about which you should be curious when a client brings you a business transaction. In addition, ask yourself what *practical* problems you see as a disinterested observer. This does not necessarily have anything to do with law, but it is among the most valuable things a lawyer can provide for a client. A lawyer who confines her-or himself to legal questions is a technician. A lawyer who also goes beyond the legal questions is a problem-solver.

In sum, "The mark of a successful corporation lawyer in giving advice can be simply stated: He or she must consistently give advice that the client believes it can rely on, and that, when followed, usually leads to the desired result (which may simply be that nothing bad happens when the advice is followed)."[9]

§18.3 DISPUTE RESOLUTION COUNSELING

If you were asked to imagine dispute resolution counseling, you would probably visualize either or both of two scenes. One would be a prelitigation conversation in which the lawyer helps the client decide whether a lawsuit would

9. *Id.* at 517.

be worth the effort, stress, and expense. The other would be a conversation during litigation: the other side has offered to settle, and the question is whether to accept or go to trial. But litigation is not the only way to settle disputes, and, although these scenes are very common, they are not the only ways in which dispute resolution counseling occurs.

When litigation has not yet begun, it is too simple and too narrow to think of the counseling question as "Should we sue?" The real question is "What method of dispute resolution is best suited to this problem?" These are among the things you might think about:

- Should we negotiate *without* suing? The other side will usually negotiate if you have leverage, and in some circumstances, you might have economic or other leverage even if you do not have a provable cause of action.
- Should we negotiate *before* suing? This might be worthwhile if the other side is confident that you will sue if negotiation fails, and if you are confident that to negotiate you will not need to depose witnesses or pose interrogatories to the other side (which you can do only after suing).
- Should we *arbitrate*? Arbitration is essentially private litigation. The parties can create their own rules of procedure, making them as simple or as complicated as they like. They can choose their own judge (the arbitrator). Or, if they want a panel of three arbitrators, each party names one arbitrator, and those two choose the third. The parties can stipulate that the arbitrator or arbitrators have experience in the subject matter of the dispute. If the dispute involves a collision of ships at sea, for example, the parties can make sure that the arbitrators all have admiralty law experience. Not all arbitrators, however, are lawyers. With very narrow exceptions, the decision of the arbitrators cannot be appealed. Some clients find that frightening; others find it reassuring. Arbitration can be private in another sense as well: the parties can agree that neither they nor the arbitrators will tell anybody else that the arbitration ever happened. Arbitration includes no juries, which makes it unattractive to a client whose case has jury appeal (many tort plaintiffs, for example) but especially attractive to a client (such as a large corporation) distrusted by ordinary people. Arbitrators tend to award less in damages than juries.
- *Can* we arbitrate? By law, some issues cannot be arbitrated. For example, in many states an arbitrator cannot dissolve a marriage or award child custody, but an arbitrator can determine the money and property issues in a divorce.
- *Must* we arbitrate? In some industries, arbitration is difficult to avoid. For example, most stockbrokers and many health maintenance organizations will not do business with you unless you agree in advance to arbitrate any dispute that might subsequently arise. Has the client signed anything that contains an agreement to arbitrate disputes like the one before you? And in some court systems, certain cases are diverted to arbitration rather than to the courtroom.
- Should we *mediate*? Rather than adjudicating a dispute, a mediator tries to help the parties work it out themselves by suggesting possible solutions or helping the parties brainstorm them and by helping the parties to understand each other's point of view. Mediation can be useful where the parties have had and want to continue a relationship important to both of them. It is sometimes attractive where the parties do not anticipate a continuing relationship but for some

reason want to resolve their dispute in a way that does not create an obvious "winner" and "loser." Mediation can, however, create hidden winners and losers. If one party is psychologically powerful and the other is psychological vulnerable, the former might intimidate the latter despite the best efforts of the mediator. An example might be where one party has a conciliatory and accommodating temperament and the other is by nature stubborn and unyielding. Another might be a divorce where the money and property issues are being mediated and one spouse is bullying and manipulative and the other lacks self-confidence. In both situations, one of these parties needs the advice of somebody who owes a total duty of loyalty to that party—a lawyer who will participate in the mediation on the party's behalf.

Arbitration and mediation are categorized as alternative dispute resolution, or ADR. Businesses are finding them increasingly useful as ways to settle disputes without incurring the expense and delay of litigation. That does not mean that a business client will be eager to mediate or arbitrate. The proportion of business disputes that are arbitrated or mediated is probably still relatively small, although it will likely grow in the future. And although arbitration and mediation are overall cheaper than litigation because they are simpler and faster, they include two expenses that litigation does not. The parties pay arbitrators and mediators for their services, and the parties provide the site at which the arbitration or mediation occurs. (In litigation, the taxpayers provide the judge and courtroom.)

If the client does not have a provable cause of action and has no leverage or other means of getting the adversary into dispute resolution, tell the client that as soon as you know it (see §22.1 for how). Delaying unpleasant news makes it harder on the client to hear it and harder for the lawyer to say it. But do not reject a case just because the means for winning it are not immediately apparent to you when you hear the client's story in the initial interview. Effective theories and strategies take time to develop.

Advice without full counseling can happen inside a dispute resolution situation. Suppose that a corporation has been sued. The complaint alleges that the corporation has dumped lead and mercury in a river, destroying the fishing industry there. The answer denies everything. You represent the corporation, and you receive a phone call from the factory manager, who says, "Environmentalists are in a boat in the river next to our drain pipe. They're sampling the water. Can we have them arrested for doing that?" You read the corporation's deed to the factory land and note that the corporation's property stops at the water's edge. "The answer is no," you say. In this conversation, you are only answering a question about how the law treats certain facts.

§18.4 "DECISION MAKING IS AN ART"[10]

A well-made decision of any kind is a product of professional problem solving operating through the six steps laid out in §4.2. In client counseling the steps can be stated as follows:

---

10. Warren Lehman, *The Pursuit of a Client's Interest*, 77 Mich. L. Rev. 1078, 1094 (1979).

1. Identify the problem, focusing on the client's goals as described in (§20.1).
2. Gather and evaluate information and raw materials that can be used to resolve the problem.
3. Generate options (§20.2).
4. Evaluate each option to measure its advantages, costs, risks, and odds of success (Chapter 20) and explain those predictions to the client (Chapter 21).
5. Choose the best option (§21.5).
6. Act on the solution chosen.

You will become better at this as you develop an effective problem-solving style and learn the thinking described in §4.2: identify the few things that really matter; identify the decisive event; and organize strategy around the decisive event. In dispute resolution, plan to prevent the adversary from achieving her or his own decisive event. Treat the entire problem or conflict as an integrated whole. Protect against weaknesses. And resist the temptation to act on motivations that are not strategic, such as your own emotional needs.

§18.5 THE PROCESS OF HELPING ANOTHER PERSON MAKE A DECISION

Counseling falls into two parts.

The first is preparation before meeting with the client. You identify the client's goals; gather and evaluate relevant information about both the law and the facts; generate alternative potential solutions that, to varying degrees, might accomplish those goals; and analyze the advantages, costs, risks, and chances of success of each potential solution. In other words, you go through the first four steps of decision-making listed in §18.4. Chapter 20 explains how to do this preparation.

In generating and evaluating potential solutions, consider both the legal and the nonlegal aspects and ramifications of the decision. In some settings, business or financial considerations matter. In others, political considerations might matter. And in most settings, interpersonal or emotional factors are important, even if not immediately apparent.

We sometimes uses interchangeably the terms "potential solutions," "choices," and "options." But not all options are potential solutions. Where the client has suffered a loss, doing nothing is one of the options, and sometimes the only realistic one. But it usually does not solve the client's problem.

If this were your own decision to make, you would continue through the fifth and sixth steps listed in §18.4 and then be done. But it is not your decision to make. You are designing a decision, but you will not make it. Because someone else will, counseling has a second part, the meeting with the client, in which you give the client your preparation in a way that helps the client make the decision.

During the meeting that is the second part of counseling, go back through the first four steps. Ask questions to make sure that you have understood the client's goals and that they have not recently changed. If any facts or aspects of the law will dominate the decision, describe them to the client (or remind the client of them if she already knows). List the options available to the client and explain what each one is together with its advantages, costs, risks, and chances of success. Then ask the client to choose an option (the fifth step from §18.4). After the client decides—which might not happen until after the meeting—the counseling job is complete, and you and the client act on that decision (the sixth step from §18.4). Chapter 21 explains how to conduct the meeting with the client.

§18.6 THE FOUR CHALLENGES IN COUNSELING

The four biggest challenges in counseling are:

1. *Creating options:* It is not enough just to identify options that are immediately obvious from comparison of the law to the facts. *Create* options that would not be there except for your problem-solving skills. And the options should go beyond the law. They should be practical solutions that will work in the real world where the client lives, not just in law books.
2. *Working out each option precisely:* Do not stop short of precisely defining the value of an option—especially where the value can be stated in numbers and with certainty. The following does not help the client:

   > If you choose the fourth option, you will be paid $219,000, and you'll have to pay tax on it.

   Here is what the client really needs to know:

   > If you choose the fourth option, you will be paid $219,000 within 30 days, on which you will owe tax of 35% or $76,650, so that you will get to keep $142,350. Therefore, this option is worth $142,350 to you.

   Sometimes defining an option precisely requires predictions that you might not feel confident making. Suppose that another option in the example above is not a certainty but instead a probability or possibility, requiring a prediction concerning odds. Using the concept of expected valuation (§20.3.2), you can carry precision to this level:

   > If you choose the second option, I estimate that you stand two chances in three of being paid $400,000, on which you will owe tax of 35%. Because this is a probability and not a certainty, the value of this option—so you can compare it with the other options—is really two-thirds of $400,000, minus tax. [*lawyer then explains why and works out the numbers*]

   It might be hard to work this out, but clients need to know it.
3. *Clarity with the client:* Counseling a client involves teaching the client what the decision is, what the options are, and how to choose among them. You already know a lot about the difference between good teaching and bad teaching. For many beginning lawyers, that is the key to realizing how to explain the decision and the options clearly and in a well-organized way so that the client truly

understands them. But counseling is different in one important way from the teaching you have experienced in school. Not only might the client be senior to the lawyer-teacher in age, but the client is in charge because the client has hired the lawyer and, if dissatisfied with the lawyer's work, can fire her.

4. *A helpful professional affect:* Clients need empathy combined with intellectual detachment. When you learn how to do this, you are also learning in general how to relate to somebody else in a professional way.

CHAPTER

19

AN EXAMPLE OF COUNSELING: THE PLANT CLOSING

You have been hired by a labor union that represents the 432 employees of a local manufacturing plant. They were told last week that the plant will close 21 days later (two weeks from today) because the huge corporation that owns it is no longer satisfied with the modest profit earned by the product the employees make and because the corporation has been unable to persuade anybody else to buy and operate the plant. The corporation wants to concentrate its efforts only in product lines where the profits are spectacular. The employees want to continue working in this plant. They have families to support and are unlikely to find equivalent work in the local economy. The corporation says that such things are not relevant to bottom lines on corporate balance sheets, and that the employees' paychecks will end on the day the plant closes.

§19.1 PREPARING TO COUNSEL THE EMPLOYEES

Identifying the union's goals. The union members want to keep their jobs. You have spoken with many of them individually and it seems that, aside from the obvious and paramount need to preserve income, the workers want these jobs for three reasons: (1) most of them have worked in this plant for years, know each other, and feel a sense of community which they do not want to lose; (2) most of them are in middle or late-middle age and fear that they will not be able to find equivalent work elsewhere or adapt to it if it is available; and (3) many of them say that the work, although hard, is satisfying. (It would have been easy for you to just take the union's goal as "save jobs," but you learned so much more when you looked beyond that.) The workers are not interested in revenge. And although they think it would be nice if the world were to operate so that this kind of thing did not happen, they are not out to change the world.

Gathering and evaluating relevant information about both the law and the facts. You check the law and find the following:

Your state is one of the few with a plant-closing statute, and it might be the strongest statute in the country. It requires employers to give 120 days notice to employees before permanently closing an employment site at which the work force has exceeded 250 people at any time during the preceding 24 months. An employer who does not do so is liable to affected employees for triple the wages not paid between the time the plant does close and a date that occurs 120 days after notice is given. Nothing in the statute requires an employer to pay employees after the 120-day notice expires, and nothing requires the employer actually to operate the plant during the 120 days. The statute is relatively new. Business groups claim that it violates the interstate commerce clause of the federal constitution as well as the due process and equal protection clauses of the Fourteenth Amendment. No court in your state has ruled on the question, but in other states courts have upheld weaker plant closing statutes against similar challenges.

The federal Worker Adjustment and Retraining Notification Act (WARN) requires notification 60 days before a plant closing. There are big exceptions, but these facts are not within them. The penalty for violations is much softer than under your state's statute. An employer who violates both statutes pays only the larger penalty (not both).

Nothing else in state or federal law requires an employer to give employees any severance payments of any kind.

The federal Consolidated Omnibus Budget Reconciliation Act of 1985 (COBRA) provides that—under the circumstances that exist here—an employer must arrange for discharged employees to continue temporarily their health insurance coverage, but at the employees' own expense. Insurance through COBRA has two advantages. First, it can be, but is not always, cheaper than insurance bought on the open market. Second, because it is a continuation of, rather than new, insurance, employees with chronic illnesses, which the insurance industry calls "preexisting conditions," will not be discriminated against.

Your state's unemployment compensation plan will pay the equivalent of one-third of each employee's wages for 26 weeks after they cease to be employed.

Some lawyers would stop here on the idea that lawyers apply law to facts and do not do not much else. But you know that lawyers are problem-solvers and not mere technicians, so you go further and find out the following:

The land on which the plant sits is zoned only for industrial use and is surrounded for some distance in every direction by similar land. Some other neighboring plants have also closed within the past few years, and several of them are now dilapidated shells. There are few buyers for this kind of real estate locally. Most of the dilapidated factories are still owned by the companies that once operated them, and these companies continue to pay property taxes on them. A few are now owned by the local government because bids at tax foreclosure sales were insufficient.

Most of the equipment in the plant will be serviceable for at least a decade. It is not new, but it is not obsolete either. The manufacturing process is labor-intensive. That means that although the equipment is essential, there is not much of it in the factory. There is a market for used equipment of this kind, but it is erratic. That means that if the corporation tried to sell the equipment, it might find a buyer right away or never.

The product manufactured in the plant is bought by other businesses for use in their own work. It is the kind of product that one buys continually rather than only once in a while. Because the brand made in this factory is known for its high quality, many customers habitually buy it rather than competing brands. But profits in manufacturing this product will never be more than modest because customers will not pay more than a certain price for it, no matter how good it is.

None of the workers has any significant savings. All are blue or pink collar, and many are literally the working poor. None has any managerial experience or knows anything about finance or marketing.

The corporation is exclusively profit-minded. (It does whatever earns or saves money.) It operates no other plant in this state.

Visiting the plant and using a telephone, a law library, and the Internet, a lawyer would probably need between 12 and 20 hours of work to collect all this information.

Generating potential solutions. You come up with the following list. (These are not alternatives. The union could decide to do more than one of them.)

1. Take action to get the corporation to obey the state's plant closing statute;
2. Advise the workers of their COBRA rights and give them the information they would need to file unemployment compensation claims;
3. Organize protests, lobbying efforts, and media exposure to persuade Congress, the state legislature, or both to adopt remedial legislation; and,
4. Find a way for the workers to buy the plant and keep on manufacturing the product.

Evaluating potential solutions. When you tally up the advantages, costs, risks, and chances of success for each of these options, this is what you get:

1. *Action under the plant closing statutes.* Under the state statute, this would get the workers an additional 99 days of income but would accomplish nothing else. The corporation's obligation is clear under the statute. Although there is a possibility that the corporation might be able to get the statute held unconstitutional, that seems unlikely, given the case law. And the corporation is unlikely to try. It has little motivation because it owns no other plant in the state, might be accruing triple penalties while challenging the statute, and, even if the state statute were struck down, the federal statute would still impose some penalties, although they would be weaker. The chances of success here are high. (A prudent lawyer does not promise that a particular result is 100% certain: facts that you do not yet know about might defeat a client's claim.) The cost to the union would be anywhere from your hourly rate for a few hours of work (if the corporation voluntarily agrees to obey the statute) to a very high sum (if the

corporation challenges the statute in court). You predict that the cost will be toward the low end of that scale, although the corporation will not agree easily.

2. *Advising the workers of their COBRA and unemployment compensation rights.* There's no reason to believe that the workers do not qualify for COBRA and unemployment compensation, both of which are better than nothing. But that, too, does not accomplish the union's goals. Unemployment compensation is not a job; it is not the job each worker now has; it is temporary; and it will provide less money than a paycheck would. The unemployment benefits for these workers might be so low that they might not be able to afford COBRA insurance. Although the value of this option is low, the cost of obtaining it is also low. It would take you no more than a few hours to make sure that all the workers are fully informed of what they are entitled to and how to get it.

3. *Lobbying, etc.* The state already has the strongest plant closing statute in the country. You might be able to imagine other legislation, but it would not be applied retroactively to these workers. Although legislation applied prospectively might improve society, this option does nothing to advance the goals of the workers, who are worried about their families.

4. *Buying the plant.* If it were possible, this option would satisfy nearly all the union's goals and also give the workers more control over their lives than they have had as employees. It would require capital to buy the plant; managerial, financial, and marketing expertise to keep it going and sell the product; and a transition plan that would maintain the existing market for the product, keep raw materials coming in, and keep the new worker-owners from being overwhelmed immediately by snafus and operating expenses.

   Taken together, that seems impossible. But you break it down into its parts:

   The plant and its equipment will not easily find any other ready buyer, and if the corporation does not sell the real estate soon, it will have to continue to pay property taxes on it. You have already established that the corporation owes each worker 99 days more wages than the corporation thought it did. This is not a huge expense for a giant corporation, but you have increased the cost to the corporation of closing the factory. And you might be able to show the company that it would be cheaper to help the workers buy the place.

   An operating plant pumps money into a local economy that a closed plant does not. From the local government's point of view, it might be a good investment to give the new worker-owners, all local voters, a temporary or long-term rebate on the plant's property taxes to help get the plant established in their hands.

   If, on the other hand, the corporation continues to own the plant, it will still owe property taxes even though the plant would produce no revenue. To avoid this expense, which will recur every year indefinitely, the corporation might save money by selling the plant to the employees now at a discounted price or by lending the employees the money they would need to buy the plant. And even though the corporation might do that to save money, it could portray the sale for public relations purposes as an act of generosity by a responsible corporate citizen. You have seen many advertisements in which companies bragged about things they have done for communities or the environment so that the public will feel better buying the companies' products. You wonder whether the opportunity to do this is an asset to which corporations and their accountants can assign a dollar value. And you wonder whether this corporation cares enough about public relations to consider selling to the employees to be a good investment.

Some corporations would not see it that way. And some corporations would eliminate their property taxes on hard-to-sell land simply by no longer paying them and waiting for the local government to seize the property to pay off the tax deficiency. But that would take the property off the tax rolls because the local government would not be able to sell it, in addition to the local unemployment that would be generated when the plant closes. If the corporation takes this approach, we are taken back to the local government as a potential source of assistance for the employees. These two results—a reduction in property tax revenue and an increase in unemployment—can damage the government's budget and the local economy, which gives the local government an incentive to help.

You see the germ of something here, although you also see problems. Things can get harsher when workers own the business. For example, it is always true that some employees are less efficient than others. Will the more efficient employees resent the less efficient ones when profitability affects everybody's income? Right now, this is at best an incomplete option. You have not been able to create a plan that would make it work. For that reason, you are not yet in a position to estimate costs for this option.

§19.2 MEETING WITH THE STEERING COMMITTEE

This is an unusual counseling session because you are meeting not with one or two people, but with the nine that the union members have elected as their steering committee to address this problem. You begin by stating your understanding of the union's goals so that if your understanding is wrong, it will be corrected. (It is not.) You then describe some of the facts that you consider especially important: the difficulty the corporation will have selling the plant and equipment, the loyalty of the plant's customers, the reputation of its product, and so on.

You say that you have thought of four options, but before you list them you would like to ask for patience. You will list them all first and then afterward describe how each would work and its advantages, costs, risks, and chances of success. You add that three of the options will sound inadequate and the fourth will sound impossible, but you ask for patience because you think that you and the steering committee might be able to brainstorm the fourth option into something the union could find acceptable.

You then list the options, and body language tells you that the group is not pleased. "You mean there's nothing in the law," someone asks, "that says they have to keep this plant open as long as we are making a profit for them?" You say, "No," but this question makes you realize that if the workers buy the plant, they do not have to make any profit at all. If they borrow money to buy the plant, all profit, or what used to be profit, can go to debt repayment.

You then go through the options one by one, describing their advantages, costs, risks, and chances of success. You present the last option (buying the plant) as an incomplete idea and point to the problems: The workers would need to hire managers and financial and marketing people. It would be awkward because hired managers would be supervising the owners of the business. And where would the money come from to buy the plant?

"I've worked for this company for 37 years," says one of the steering committee members, "and in the last 5 or 6 years they did nothing to make this plant work. They didn't like the product and treated it like a stepchild. They sent us dumb managers who belong in a Dilbert cartoon, probably rejects from other factories. We made this place work, and now they throw us out in the street!"

"I know of a manager who does not belong in a Dilbert cartoon," says someone else. "Isaiah Joyner's daughter got a college degree in business, works in some high stress job in a big city, and hates it. Think she'd like to come back here?"

This meeting goes on for a long time. At the end, the steering committee votes to make a conditional recommendation to the union membership that they negotiate with the corporation to buy the plant, using the severance that the corporation would otherwise have to pay as part of the purchase price and borrowing the rest from the corporation itself or elsewhere.

There are two conditions. The first is that a business plan be developed first demonstrating that the workers could buy and operate the plant while retaining its customers. The second condition is that the county and municipal governments commit themselves to rebate most of the property taxes for several years if the workers buy the plant.

The steering committee also votes that if these conditions are not met, the recommendation to the union membership will be to get what they are entitled to under the state plant closing statute, COBRA, and unemployment compensation and start looking for other jobs.

The business plan would have to be developed very quickly because not much time is left before the corporation otherwise will close the plant. The next morning you pick up the phone to call Isaiah Joyner's daughter. As you dial, you hope that she is very capable, has time to spare right now, can help you estimate the costs of the buy-out option and its chances of success, and would like to come back to live in your community.

CHAPTER

20

PREPARING FOR COUNSELING: STRUCTURING THE OPTIONS

The process of preparation is outlined in §18.4: You identify the client's goals and preferences; gather and evaluate relevant information about both the law and the facts; generate alternative potential solutions that, to varying degrees, might accomplish those goals; and analyze the advantages, costs, risks, and chances of success of each potential solution.

§20.1 FOCUSING ON CLIENT GOALS AND PREFERENCES

Transactional goals. Make sure that you have clear answers to the following questions: "What do you [the client] want to gain out of this transaction? What should we try to make sure that you get? How does this transaction fit into your overall plans for the future?"

Do not assume you know the client's goals. Even two clients who want the same kind of transaction might want it for very different reasons and therefore have very different goals. A client whom you are helping to buy land last week might have wanted it to preserve wilderness (you might have represented the Nature Conservancy). Another client whom you are helping to buy a different plot of land this week want it for reasons that would have the opposite effect (you might be representing a developer of shopping centers).

Clients who do not use lawyers very often are sometimes unsure of their goals and instead seem to have a vague feeling that the transaction at hand is just called for by the circumstances. This is especially frequent in estate planning. It sometimes helps to ask the client to imagine the scene after the transaction and its effects and consequences have run their course: "This may seem indelicate, but could I ask you to imagine how the people in your life would be managing if you were to pass away? What would be their needs? Is there anything you would like to do about what you imagine?" It can also help to mention the sorts of things that clients generally seem to want in such situations: "People with young children usually want to designate a guardian in case both parents pass away. Is that something you would want to do?"

Virtually all transaction clients will want to minimize any taxes or legal liability that might grow out of the transaction.

Dispute resolution goals. If the client has suffered a loss, what might she want? The possibilities include money or other measures to make up for that loss (damages, etc.); something that would prevent the defendant and others from causing similar losses in the future (punitive damages, an injunction, legislation); an official and public finding that the defendant acted wrongfully (a favorable judgment); and punishment for the defendant (punitive damages, publicity from the judgment). One client might want one or two of these things, while another client might want them all.

If the client is being sued or prosecuted, the primary goal usually is a successful defense. But the client might want more than a technical victory. The client might want victory in a form that clears the client's name. Often, a name-clearing victory can be gotten only with more risk—such as at trial—than a technical victory, which might come out of negotiations or pretrial motions that are hard for the public to understand.

Ranking client goals. You need to know how important each goal is to the client. Sometimes it is necessary to sacrifice what the client wants to get what the client needs. You are not in a position to counsel until you know where the client would draw the line between those two things.

Client preferences. A goal is what the client hired you to get. A preference is something the client would like you to do or not do while pursuing goals. "If you can avoid it, don't call my Aunt Sally as a witness" is a preference. The client did not hire you to prevent Aunt Sally from testifying. The client hired you to obtain something else and would prefer that the cost not include Aunt Sally's testimony. Some common client preferences include avoiding trials and other confrontations, avoiding taking time off from a job or other occupation, and avoiding publicity (although some clients want publicity). You can assume that all clients would prefer to get relief sooner rather than later and to pay as little as possible in attorney's fees and other expenses.

Client preferences are important because they will affect each option's value to the client. You need to know not only the preferences, but also how intense they are. There's a big difference between "If you can avoid it . . ." and "Under no circumstances . . ." And you need to know why the preference exists. One client might prefer to get money soon because, once invested, early money earns more in interest, dividends, and capital gains than late money does. Another client might prefer to get money soon to pay mounting medical bills—a much more compelling reason.

For many clients, the most important preference is represented by their tolerance or intolerance for risk (see §20.4).

§20.2 DEVELOPING POTENTIAL SOLUTIONS

Notice that the solution developed in §19.1 (buying the factory) did not leap out of a law book. The lawyer created it by combining a number of raw ingredients. Some of the raw ingredients came from law books, and some came from common sense and an understanding of the business practicalities of the situation.

The lesson is this: Do not simply itemize the solutions that are obvious ("the law will let you do X, but it will not let you do Y"). Find ways to *create* solutions that—without your imagination and problem solving—would not otherwise exist. More than anything else, that is what clients believe they are paying you to do. Chapter 4 explains how. Inclusive solutions (§4.5) are often the most long-lasting and satisfying.

What clients want from you are practical solutions that produce good results. Do not limit yourself to how the law will treat the client. Think in bigger terms. Consider the people involved and their human needs. If money is involved, think about the wisest way to deal with it, taking into account all the costs and the way the relevant markets and financial institutions operate. Think in practical terms. Use good judgment (§2.2.1) and good common sense.

§20.3 PREDICTING WHAT EACH POTENTIAL SOLUTION WOULD CAUSE

Ben Franklin said that complicated decisions are hard to make because:

> all the reasons pro and con are not present in the mind at the same time; but sometimes one set present themselves, and at other times another, the first being out of sight . . . [and] uncertainty . . . perplexes us.
>
> To get over this, my way is to divide half a sheet of paper by a line into two columns; writing over the one Pro, and over the other Con. Then, . . . I [write] down under the different head[ing]s short hints of the different motives, that at different times occur to me, for or against the measure. When I have thus got them all together in one view, I endeavor to estimate their respective weights . . . and thus proceeding I find at length where the balance lies. . . .
>
> And, though the weight of reasons cannot be taken with the precision of algebraic quantities, . . . when each is thus considered, separately and comparatively, and the whole lies before me, I think I can judge better, and am less liable to make a rash step. . . .[1]

1. Letter from Franklin to Joseph Priestley, from *The Benjamin Franklin Sampler* (1956).

This is option evaluation as explained in §4.2 You estimate—in detail—the advantages, costs, risks, and chances of success of each option. That requires you to make predictions. You can express a prediction either in descriptive phrases (such as "a good chance of success" or "highly likely") or in numbers ("odds of about two out of three" or "a 50/50 chance of success"). Both methods have problems.

Descriptive phrases might be too vague to be meaningful to the client, or even to you. An optimistic client might hear "the chances are good" to mean "we are definitely going to win." And how much probability do we have when there is "an excellent chance of success"? A client making one of the most important decisions of her life should want a more meaningful measurement of probability.

On the other hand, numbers can imply a precision that is not really there. Predictive estimates are by nature inexact, and a prediction that something is 65% likely to happen is not significantly different from a prediction that it is 60% or 70% likely to happen—although a client could easily think otherwise because you are using exact numbers. Unless you have done a detailed predictive analysis using something like the decision tree explained in §20.3.4, it would be better to avoid predicting in percentage terms and instead limit yourself to more general statements expressed in fractions, such as "odds of three in four." Without a detailed predictive analysis using a decision tree or similar device, you cannot really be more accurate than odds expressed in fifths ("two chances in five"), and you should resist the temptation to use smaller fractions. The only exception is where you believe the odds are even: it's hard to say that without using a phrase like "a 50/50 chance."

Predicting is frightening business. How can you possibly assure a client that you know what the future will bring? You cannot, but you have to predict anyway. It might help to remember that every day trillions of dollars are invested, lent, or otherwise committed based on predictions of whether customers will like a product or hate it, whether stock prices or interest rates will rise or fall, whether Congress will do this or that, or even whether there will be lots of rain or only a little over the next few months in the wheat belt or the corn belt or the cotton belt or some other place where crops are grown. Many of those predictions turn out to be wrong. The earth will not swallow you up if a prediction you make turns out to be inaccurate. But people whose predictions tend mostly to be right gain the loyalty and respect of their clients, both in investing and in law.

Out of fear of being wrong, you may want to hedge, which might be either bad or good. One form of hedging—waffling—makes your advice less useful to a client, who must make a decision and needs the best prediction you are capable of. From the client's point of view if you waffle, you are not really predicting. Another form of hedging—adding qualifications or conditions—makes your prediction *more* precise because qualifications and conditions identify variables that might change and alter your prediction ("we stand less than a 50/50 chance at trial unless we can get the Britz letter into evidence").

Often, you will have to predict without complete knowledge of the facts or the law. Some facts might not become available to you until later, or only at some expense, or only after fighting with an adversary, or never. And as you know, some parts of the law are unsettled. When you predict, you need to identify not only what you know, but also what you do not know. And where you see a gap in knowledge, you need to define exactly how the gap would influence the prediction and estimate how and when that gap can be filled and how much it would cost to do so. (Sometimes the cost of filling the gap will exceed the value to be gained in making the prediction more accurate.)

Predictions cannot be set in stone. They evolve as you learn more about the facts and as other things change. Your prediction about the results at trial might change when you find out who the judge will be, and it might change again after you have chosen a jury. Even the law itself can change in the midst of your representation of a client. But when a client has to make a decision, the client has to work with the predictions you are able to make at the time the decision must be made.

To make a good decision, the client will need to know what variables might change enough to alter your prediction as well as any gaps in the facts or the law that qualify your prediction. If you fail to make these qualifications clear to a client, you risk the kind of misunderstanding that leads to ethics complaints and malpractice actions.

And your predictions should be frank and disinterested. If there is bad news, the client needs to know it. Hiding it from the client does neither her nor you a favor (and again, risks the kind of misunderstanding that can turn into an ethics complaint or a malpractice action).

You should be able to articulate a reason for each prediction. When you meet with the client, you will have to explain that reason. And if you force yourself to articulate it now, while preparing, your predictions will be more accurate because the act of articulating will force you to bring your unconscious thinking out in the open where you will notice its gaps and inconsistencies.

For two reasons, it may be a good idea to reduce to writing your predictions and the reasoning behind them. The first is preservation for the future, in case there is any later misunderstanding about the advice you gave the client. The second reason is that the act of writing improves the quality of the prediction. The writing process and the thinking process are inseparable. When an idea is spoken about, it might be half-formed, but if it is written about with care, it will have to become fully developed. The number of variables to be considered can make predictive judgments so complex that a lawyer can easily become lost unless thoughts can be worked out on paper. It is not unusual for a lawyer to start writing on the basis of a tentative prediction already made, only to find, after much writing—and rewriting—that the prediction "won't write" and must be changed. Depending on the complexity and importance of the issues, the writing could range from handwritten (but careful and complete) notes for the file to a formal office memorandum of law.

§20.3.1 THE POTENTIAL SOLUTION'S CHANCES OF ACHIEVING THE CLIENT'S GOALS

Construct three scenarios for each option: the best case, the worst case, and the most likely case. Imagine the best result that could *reasonably* happen and the worst result that could reasonably happen. Neither of these should be far-fetched. They should define the range of what is genuinely possible—the range of things that really could happen to the client. Now imagine the result you think most likely to happen.

In especially important situations, you might want to construct five scenarios:

best possible	most likely	worst possible

←——————————————————→

the three above, plus two more that define a range of *probability*. What is the best result that would not surprise you? What is the worst result that would not surprise you?

best possible	best unsurprising	most likely	worst unsurprising	worst possible

←——————————————————————————→

The range of outcomes that would not surprise you helps the client put your "most likely" scenario into a sharper context. What happens if your estimate of what is most likely turns out to be wrong? Into what range of probability will you and the client be falling back? In less important situations, you can dispense with the "best unsurprising" and "worst unsurprising" scenarios if you explain to the client that any prediction contains a plus-or-minus factor: your "most likely" prediction implies at least some margin of error on both sides.

Because legal reasoning is so difficult to learn, law school inadvertently encourages students to think formalistically—to think that courts will rule in a certain way once the legal tests have been satisfied. But in prediction, there is a step that comes after formal legal reasoning. After analogizing, distinguishing, focusing on policy, synthesizing fragmented authority, and reconciling conflicting or adverse authority, step back from what you are doing and test the result of your reasoning for realism. That requires taking into account how judges, juries, and administrative agencies think.

For issues to be decided by a judge, ask yourself whether the result you predict will seem right to the judge who will rule (if you know who that judge will be) or to the typical judge. The experience of adjudicating creates what Roscoe Pound called "the trained intuition of the judge,"[2] an instinct for how the law ought to treat each set of facts. If the result of your reasoning would strike the judicial mind as unrealistic and unreasonable, that mind will reject what you have done no matter how nice your reasoning is. Karl Llewellyn wrote that "rules *guide*, but they do not *control* decision. There is no precedent that the judge may not at his need either file down to razor thinness or expand into a bludgeon."[3] Or, put less delicately: judges first decide what they think is right and then dress it up with legal argument so that it looks presentable (although what they think is right can also be influenced by legal argument).

Llewellyn also wrote two other things that are particularly important here. The first is that law *as practicing lawyers know it* is "[w]hat officials [including judges] do about disputes"[4]—and not what statutes and cases say they should do

2. Roscoe Pound, *The Theory of Judicial Decision*, 36 Harv. L. Rev. 940, 951 (1923).
3. Karl N. Llewellyn, *The Bramble Bush* 180 (1930).
4. *Id.* at 3.

about disputes. The second is that "'rights' which cannot be realized are worse than useless; they are traps of delay, expense, and heartache."[5] Your client might seem to have rights under a literal reading of a statute, but if judges will find ways to rule otherwise, you will not help your client by counseling with false optimism.

Thus, you need to evaluate not only the strength and weakness of the case in terms of legal abstractions, but also predict what the actual court involved would decide. For example, in a high-volume eviction or consumer credit court, although case law may support the dismissal of a complaint for failure to plead a specific element, a particular trial judge might expedite cases by ignoring precedent and denying motions to dismiss where the complaint's defect is technical and the plaintiff would probably amend the complaint anyway. Or, in a criminal case, while appellate precedent may strongly require the suppression of certain evidence, many trial court judges will find ways of ignoring this authority if a ruling to suppress would lead to dismissal of the case. These kinds of predictions are fairly simple if you have had experience with a particular judge or with typical local juries.

If you know who the judge will be but have never litigated before that judge, ask the advice of lawyers who have. Use Lexis or Westlaw to find and read the judge's opinions on similar issues. And visit the judge's courtroom to get a sense of her personality.

If you do not know who the judge will be, try to think realistically about judges and how they view the world. You might feel that all law school has taught you is legal argument and that you do not know any judges, or at least enough judges for you to be able to generalize about what they would do in the infinite variety of cases that clients will bring you. Certainly, it will take a long time for you to understand fully how "the trained intuition of the judge" operates. But you can, in a rudimentary way, test your predictions for realism by thinking of one or more persons you do know very well who seem typical of respected and responsible people in their 40's, 50's, and 60's (which is the age of most judges). It would help if these people were lawyers, but that is not essential. It is much more important that these people are instinctively responsible and that their good common sense naturally gains the respect of others. After you have worked out the legal reasoning, ask yourself how these people would react to the result you predict. Would they scoff at it? Or would they say that it is nice to see the law coming to the result it ought to? This is not going to give you the same feel for judicial realism that a good lawyer has after ten years of experience. But it can help you break out of the abstract view of law that legal education sometimes inadvertently encourages.

For issues to be decided by a jury, you have a different problem. Juries are randomly selected groups of people and often behave in unpredictable ways. But over time, juries from a community tend to render verdicts in a range that roughly reflects some of the community's values. And you can make approximate predictions by (1) "determining the distribution of verdicts in similar claims" tried in the same community, (2) "adjusting the distributions of verdicts in similar claims to reflect the unique facts of" the client's claim, and (3) "adjusting the revised

---

5. *Id.* at 9.

distribution to reflect transaction costs."[6] In addition, if the client is deciding whether to settle or go to trial, the two options have to be compared in terms of expected value, the time value of money, and the effect of taxes. All of this is explained below.

How do you find out what *verdicts juries have returned in similar cases*? Lawyers who practice in large urban areas can subscribe to verdict reporting services. There are also some national services,[7] but the verdicts they report might be more or less generous to plaintiffs than juries typical of your community might return. If you are on the defense side of a tort action and are being paid by an insurance company, the company itself might have a database on past jury verdicts. If none of these sources produces the information you need, you might ask the advice of a lawyer who has long experience litigating your kind of case in your community.[8] In predicting personal injury verdicts, some attorneys use "rule of thumb" formulas such as "three times specials" or other multiples of the plaintiff's out-of-pocket expenses. In many instances, these rough estimates ignore the unique facts in the case and over-simplify.[9]

Once you have gotten data on other jury verdicts, how do you *adjust to get something comparable to your case*? Ask yourself the following questions: Are the facts of your case more or less favorable than the facts of prior verdicts? Are the injuries being remedied more or less egregious than the injuries in your case? How do the jurisdictions and communities involved compare with yours? (Other jurisdictions might have different law, and other communities might produce different kinds of jurors.) How recent are the verdicts you are comparing to your case? In some communities, juries have over time grown more generous to plaintiffs, while in others the opposite has happened. And how many verdicts are you comparing? The smaller the number, the less reliable the sample is as a basis for prediction. The most reliable sample would be a large one in which most of the juries appear to be behaving consistently with one another.

§20.3.2 TRANSACTION COSTS, EXPECTED VALUE, THE TIME VALUE OF MONEY, AND TAX

Suppose you predict that the jury will award your client $100,000 and that the defendant will lose any appeal. Should your client start looking for ways to spend $100,000? Suppose the defendant makes an offer to settle now for $65,000. Which is more valuable—a $100,000 judgment in the future or $65,000 now?

To understand the value today of a predicted gain of money in the future, or to compare a predicted future gain of money with a competing possible gain of money now, or to know how much of a gain can be kept after taxes, your calculations need to take into account four facts of financial life:

---

6. Peter Toll Hoffman, *Valuation of Cases for Settlement: Theory and Practice*, 1991 J. Disp. Resol. 1, 7. The next few paragraphs in the text rely heavily on pages 10–31 of Professor Hoffman's thorough article.
7. See, for example, Association of Trial Lawyers of America, Jury Verdicts & Settlements (available in the Lexis Verdict library) and National Jury Review & Analysis (available in the Lexis Verdict library).
8. If you have to go outside your law firm to get this kind of advice, you might have to pay for it. You are taking up another lawyer's time, although some lawyers will talk to you informally for free as a professional courtesy.
9. Donald G. Gifford, *Legal Negotiation: Theory and Applications* 53 (1989).

1. It costs money to get money (*transaction costs*), and those expenses reduce the value of a financial gain.
2. Unless you are 100% confident that a future gain will occur, its real value today (its *expected value*) is reduced because of doubt.
3. The value of money differs over time (the *time value of money*) because future money will suffer from inflation and because money you have now could be invested and grow in the future.
4. Whenever money changes hands, a government might—or might not—take some of it to pay for things like streets, schools, and national defense (*tax*).

Let's consider each of these concepts as well as how to use them.

Transaction costs. How do you adjust to reflect transaction costs? The most obvious transaction cost is what the client would have to pay to go to trial and get the verdict you predict. How much would the client have to pay you, and how much would your client have to pay for things like expert witnesses and deposition transcripts? These estimates merit precision, at least within a range. When a lawyer gives an off-the-cuff guess and costs steadily mount until they greatly exceed that guess, the client can justifiably become distrustful and angry. If there is an appeal, how much would the client have to pay to defend the verdict? If the client is a plaintiff and if the judgment would not be chargeable to an insurance company or some other party that promptly satisfies judgments, how much would the client have to pay to enforce the judgment you predict? Some defendants go to elaborate lengths to hide their assets. For that matter—and this is critically important—do you have good reason to believe that the defendant actually has the assets or insurance to satisfy the judgment you predict? And how much of the client's own time and effort would all this litigation consume? Some transaction costs are not financial. An example is the emotional drain of being a litigant.

Expected value. If you just bought a lottery ticket that might pay $5 million, its value as you walk away from the lottery counter is much less than $5 million because your odds of winning are low. If a total of ten million tickets have been sold, your ticket is worth fifty cents, computed by the future payout multiplied by your chances of getting it ($5 million multiplied by 1/10,000,000 or 0.0000001). If you paid a dollar for the ticket, a financial analyst would tell you that you paid more than it was worth. But if only two tickets have been sold, which means that your odds of winning are 50%, your one dollar ticket is worth $2.5 million ($5 million multiplied by 0.50).

But if you win, you'll get $5 million, and if you lose, you'll get nothing. Why is the expected value more than nothing and less than $5 million—the only two things that could happen in the future? Either you will get $5 million or you will get nothing. The reason is that we need some way of assigning value to a speculative gain, and the math outlined above is used in a wide variety of situations. For example, when one company is being sold to another, the first company's assets and liabilities are appraised in determining the purchase price. Current lawsuits are appraised as assets where the company is a plaintiff and liabilities where it is a defendant, and the appraisals can be done through expected value calculations—the odds of various future outcomes in those lawsuits.

When you are negotiating on behalf of your client, you can compare a proposed settlement with a predicted verdict by computing the expected value of the verdict. If you predict that there are two chances in three that a jury would return a verdict in a plaintiff's favor, and that such a verdict would be for $100,000, the verdict's expected value is $67,000. This is more meaningful to frequent litigants such as insurance companies, because over time their bets even out. But it can still be meaningful to an individual client who otherwise would have no real way of comparing the worth and risk of a predicted verdict with the certainty of a settlement offer.

The time value of money. Money's value differs over time. Money delivered now is worth more than the same amount delivered later because the money you get now can be invested and will grow in the meantime. If the client is choosing between going to trial and accepting a settlement offer, you have to estimate how long it would take to get payment on a judgment and what investment income the amount offered in settlement would earn in the meantime. A safe assumable investment income is the current annualized rate paid by Treasury bills or money market funds, which can be found in the business sections of daily newspapers.

Suppose you believe the most likely result at trial would be a $100,000 judgment in favor of the client, the plaintiff, who would not receive that money until three years from now. What is the present value of that $100,000? We will ignore temporarily the other three variables: transaction costs, expected value, and tax. In other words, we are assuming that attorney's fees and other expenses are not being paid by the client, that the odds of winning the $100,000 are 100%, and that no part of it will be taxed. Realistically, there will be transaction costs, the odds will be less than 100%, and there might be tax. But to illustrate present value we will ignore the other variables temporarily. Let's also assume that a relatively risk-free investment would earn 6% interest annually over the next three years.

The present value of $100,000 under these circumstances is $83,962. Put another way, if today you invested $83,962 at 6% interest, compounded annually, you would have $100,000 in three years. (More frequent compounding would change that, but we are trying to keep the illustration simple.) Here's the formula for computing the present value of a future amount:

$$\text{FV divided by } (1 + i)^n = \text{PV}$$

If you are mathphobic, don't panic. We'll walk you through this. Here's what the abbreviations mean: FV = future value; i = the interest rate; n = the number of years between now and the future payment; and PV = present value. Now here's the formula applied to the $100,000 judgment that we are convinced our client will get in three years

$$\$100{,}000 \text{ divided by } (1 + 0.06 = 1.06)^3 = \$83{,}962$$

Here's the same calculation in words: Add 0.06 (6%) to 1 to get 1.06. Multiply 1.06 by 1.06 by 1.06 (because of the three years) to get 1.191016. Do *not* multiply 1.06 by 3. That's because the interest will *compound* annually. Divide $100,000 by 1.191016 to get $83,962.

Business calculators (which cost a little more than ordinary pocket calculators) and spreadsheets will do this calculation for you, but if you are mathphobic you might have a hard time understanding their instructions. If you don't have a business calculator and don't know how to use a spreadsheet, just follow the formula above.

Tax. Because some kinds of awards are taxed and others are not, the effect of taxes might be different depending on how a case is settled. In a verdict, the client is taxed according to the kind of award the jury provides. For example, compensatory damages for personal physical injury or property loss are not taxable. But the client will pay taxes on damages for breach of contract, compensation for lost income, or punitive damages. In a negotiated settlement, on the other hand, the parties can sometimes limit the taxes one or both of them will pay.

For example, suppose a plaintiff has sued for $120,000 in compensatory damages for personal physical injury and $80,000 in punitive damages. The defendant is willing to settle for half of the total $200,000 sought by the plaintiff. If the parties agree to allocate that settlement proportionately between the two categories of damages—producing $60,000 in compensatory damages for personal physical injury and $40,000 in punitive damages—the plaintiff will pay federal income taxes (and possibly state income taxes as well) on $40,000 because punitive damages are taxable. But if all of the settlement is allocated to compensatory damages, and if the evidence supports compensatory damages in the range of $100,000, the plaintiff will pay no federal income tax on any of the settlement because compensatory damages for personal physical injury are not taxable.

Although you may be able to reduce taxes by the way you develop options, the converse can be frightening. If you *ignore* the tax consequences of the options you offer a client in counseling, you commit malpractice. And a client who later must pay a surprising tax bill will be highly motivated to sue you.

If the options are valued in monetary terms, even only partially, you *must* do the math to determine what each option is really worth. For example, if in a damages lawsuit the client will decide whether to accept a settlement offer or go to trial, the client has no way of choosing between the two unless you place a value—in *numbers of dollars*—on each option.

To do the math, you need to answer two questions. *Is it taxed*? And if so, *at what rate*? Some income is taxed by the federal government at 15%; other income is taxed at well over 30%. For federal tax, the ultimate answers to these questions are in the tax code, IRS regulations, and cases interpreting them, although reading a tax service, like CCH's, will usually give you the answers faster. For state tax, the answers are in state tax statutes, regulations, and cases.

Let's go back to the question posed at the beginning of this section: which is financially more valuable—the $100,000 judgment we predict or the $65,000 offer to settle? The client has suffered a physical injury, which means that compensation for it will not be taxed. The contingency fee agreement provides that attorney's fees will be 25% of a negotiated settlement and 33% of a judgment achieved through trial. There are a few other transaction costs, but they are small enough that we can ignore them in this illustration.

The predicted judgment minus transaction costs is $67,000 ($100,000 times 0.67, which is what's left after deducting your 0.33). Using the formula illustrated above, the present value of $67,000 is $56,254. Suppose that you believe the likelihood of that verdict is three chances in four, or 75%. The expected value of the judgment is $42,191 (0.75 times $56,254).

The $65,000 settlement offer is immediate (it already is a present value), certain (it has 100% expected value), and as tax-free as the judgment. The only thing to deduct is transaction costs of 25% (your free), which reduce its real value to the client to $48,750 ($65,000 times 0.75). That is more—but not dramatically more—that the $42,191 value we assigned to the predicted judgment.

All of this ignores other, nonfinancial considerations, such as the client's feelings about risk, the emotional toll and client effort required by further litigation, the client's need for or fear of public adjudication, and other factors listed below in §20.3.3. They may be more important to the client than the exact amounts of money involved. But doing these calculations is the only way we can assign numerical values to separate financial options that differ in likelihood, time of delivery, and transaction costs. Sometimes, they will also differ in tax consequences.

§20.3.3 SIDE-EFFECTS—DESIRABLE AND UNDESIRABLE

In dispute resolution counseling, consider the following:

- Would a lawsuit or other confrontational option disrupt relationships the client considers important? Would it give the adversary an opportunity to impugn the client's character? If the client's honesty or another character trait could be made an issue, you can be sure that the adversary will do so.
- Would continued conflict build stress up to a level that the client would want to be relieved of? Most individual clients experience litigation as "emotional turmoil,"[10] but some do not care.
- Could litigation compound harm the client has already suffered? For example, if the client has been defamed, but the damage to reputation has been limited to a small circle of people, litigation—and especially a trial—could give the defamatory claims much wider circulation.
- Could a verdict provide a public vindication important to the client?
- Is vengeance ("making them pay") important to the client? One of law's functions is give people an avenue of vengeance more socially acceptable than murder or mayhem. But there are limits. You learned in first-year Civil Procedure that in federal court you may not use a paper filed in court "for any improper purpose, such as to harass, cause unnecessary delay, or needlessly increase the cost of litigation."[11] Nearly all state courts have similar provisions. And ethical rules everywhere impose other constraints and provide mechanisms for you to decline to pursue client goals under some circumstances.
- If the client is a frequent litigant (such as an insurance company) or an attractive target for litigation (such as a newspaper that aspires to print the truth no matter

10. *Id.* at 33.
11. Fed. R. Civ. P. 11(b)(1).

whom it offends), is it important to force plaintiffs to trial in order to discourage the impression that the client is a "soft touch"?

- In a criminal case in which the client is being offered a plea bargain, what problems, aside from the sentence itself, would the resulting conviction or other disposition cause the client? Does the client risk deportation or loss of a license or a job?

Finally, consider the moral dimension. We are too used to assuming that when people act in their own self-interest, they will act selfishly. In a world where material success and conspicuous consumption are so important, people are led to believe that in many situations, especially where lawyers are involved, maximizing their own gain is what they are *supposed* to do. But for more clients than you might suppose, doing the morally right thing can be in their own self-interest. Being fair or even generous can be a pleasure for its own sake, and for some clients it can introduce a degree of inner peace into an experience that might otherwise be more distressful. Years after the decision the client is about to make, will the client feel guilt, shame, or a loss of self-respect remembering how others suffered because the client chose to maximize her own gain? Or, if the client tries to do the morally right thing now, will the client look back on it later with satisfaction?

Some clients are open to this kind of counseling, while others are not. The best way to find out how a client will react is to raise the subject gradually. For example, you might point out the ways in which another person in the dispute or transaction will suffer if the client chooses a certain option and then ask whether that is something the client wants to consider. The answer, and the tone and body language that accompany it, will tell you whether it is worth continuing down that path.

§20.3.4 DECISION TREES

If you have one decision to make with only two options ("do we go for ice cream or do we go for beer?"), it's easy to keep track of the consequences of each option ("advantages of ice cream vs. advantages of beer"). But if you have several decisions to make and they are all interconnected, a decision tree can help you keep track of how one decision affects another.

A decision tree also has a much more complicated use. Suppose your client has one decision with two options ("do we accept the other side's settlement offer or do we go to trial?"), and suppose that assessing the value of trial is difficult because there are so many variables ("will the jury believe our expert witness? will the judge admit document X into evidence? will we discredit the other side's star witness through cross examination?") How do you keep track of all the variables? And how do you figure out their effect on each other? A decision tree helps you predict the result at trial and compute an expected value for the option of going to trial.

Suppose your client has suffered $1 million in easily provable losses, and the defendant has offered to settle before trial by paying your client $200,000 now. You have negotiated hard to get a settlement offer, and you believe that the one the defendant has made is the best you can get. Your client has two options: accept the offer or go to trial. The value of the offer is easy to compute. It is immediate money, so you don't need to compute the present value of future payments. And if your client accepts, payment is a certainty, so you don't need to compute the expected value of a speculative event. The value of the settlement offer is \$200,000 minus transaction costs and any tax that might apply.

But how do you estimate the value of trial? Identify the future events on which the result at trial depends, predict their likelihood, figure out their effect on each other, and figure out their effect on the eventual verdict. The following reading by Richard Birke explains how.

RICHARD BIRKE, *DECISION TREES—MADE EASY* (2004)

In some cases, the client is unsure of how to compare an offer to settle to the continuation of litigation, and in these cases, the client would do well to understand how to use a simple decision tree. The tree would help them determine the ballpark for an appropriate settlement.

There are seven simple steps that any person can take that will enable them to set up and use a decision tree to help them evaluate their claim. These are:

Use numbers when speaking about probability.

Pare the case down to no more than four major areas of uncertainty (fewer is better).

Learn to set up a simple tree in a logical order.

Assign probabilities based on the strengths and weaknesses in the case, working from left to right.

Add in the financial awards associated with the various ways the case might end.

Solve the tree.

Add in costs as appropriate.

Using Numbers

When lawyers talk about the value of trial with their clients, they tend to shy away from using numbers to express probabilities. This reluctance is understandable— law is not an exact science, and lawyers fear overpromising. So instead of saying "we have a 90% chance of winning," lawyers use phrases like "we have a good shot at winning" or "our case is strong." In workshops I have run in which I ask lawyers to assign a number to these phrases, they exhibit spreads of more than 50% between the intended probability and the understood probability. That is, the lawyer could say "we have a good shot," intending to express that the case is a winner 40% of the time, and the client could understand that the lawyer expressed an 80% likelihood. Words simply do not adequately express probabilistic estimates. . . .

Determining the Significant Uncertainties

Lawsuits may be complicated, but disputes about the value of these lawsuits typically boil down to a small handful of disagreements between the parties. Ask what are the areas about which the parties are really far apart, and the answers are usually things like one side believes that a motion in limine will be granted and the other believes it will be denied. One side believes that their client will be believed by the jury and the other side believes that the client will be easily impeached. Each side is optimistic that the judge will use their jury instruction. The potential number of such disagreements is vast, but in any particular lawsuit, the number of really significant areas of disagreement is small. These disagreements represent the significant uncertainties in the case.

Setting up Trees

Decision trees [are like] roadmaps with a few intersections, and each intersection has some discrete number of forks in the road. The intersections represent the areas of uncertainty and the number of forks represents the number of ways the issue could come out. For example, in a simple tort case in which the uncertainties are "will plaintiff prove duty," "will plaintiff prove breach," and "will plaintiff prove causation," there are three intersections, each with two forks—one for yes and one for no. Some intersections in some cases could have more than two forks. In a case in which one of the major areas of uncertainty is the credibility of a witness, there could be a fork representing "jury believes every bit of testimony," another for "jury believes nothing," and a third for "jury believes some but not all." Similarly, an intersection representing the various monetary awards that a jury might assign could have many forks.

An easy way to make sure that the tree is set up in a logical manner is to start at the left and move chronologically through the dispute. Our tort case might have duty as the first intersection, breach as the second, and causation as the third. A tree might be set up in a different manner (perhaps in order of most contested issue to least), but a chronological effort usually yields a competent result.

Each fork in the tree will end at a terminal point, and the package of terminal points represents all the different ways that a case could come out. In our tort liability case, there are four terminal points. One is where plaintiff fails to prove duty, in which case the lawsuit is over. The second is where plaintiff proves duty, but fails to prove breach, in which case the lawsuit is over. The third is where plaintiff proves duty and breach but not causation, and the fourth is where plaintiff proves all three elements.

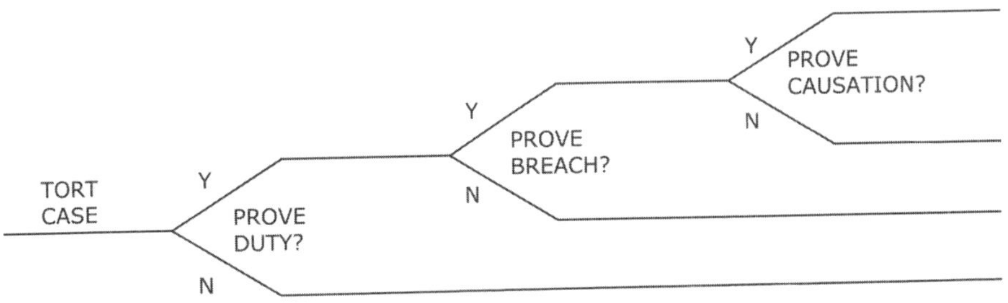

Figure 1 —The Basic Tree

Probabilities

First, look at each intersection and write down all the reasons why a case may travel each fork. In the tort case, the fork labeled "plaintiff proves duty" will have a yes fork and a no fork. The reasons why the case might go to the yes fork may be that plaintiff has good witnesses, a friendly judge, a good legal ruling or case, etc. The reasons why the case might go to the no fork might be related to uncertainty about witnesses, opposing legal case law, etc. . . .

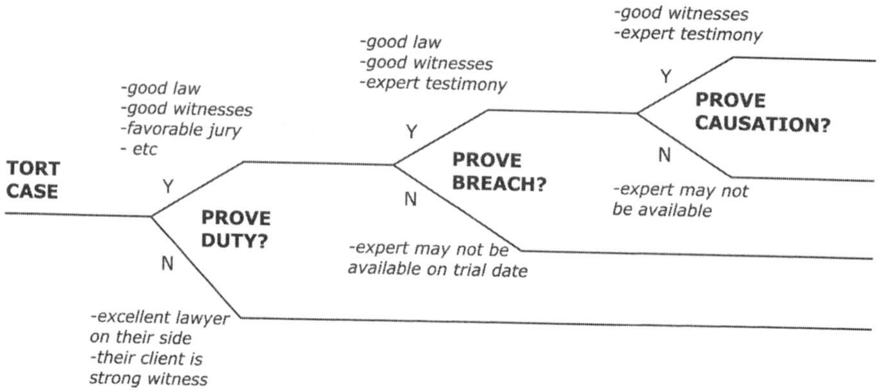

Figure 2 — The Tree with Strengths & Weaknesses

Add in the Awards

[Assume for this example that if the plaintiff were to win at trial,] the award would be $1,000,000. In other cases, the awards might be highly variable, and that uncertainty would be another intersection in the tree with an appropriate number of forks.

Solving the Tree

Now comes simple math. . . . Assume for the moment that each element of our tort case has a 50/50 probability. [Specifically, the plaintiff has 50% odds of proving a duty, 50% odds of proving breach, and 50% odds of proving causation. The plaintiff therefore has a 25% probability of proving both duty and breach. That is because the plaintiff's case has half a chance (50%) of surviving the duty issue and half a chance (another 50%) of surviving the breach issue—and half of half is a quarter (25%). If the plaintiff gets that far, the probability is cut in half again because of the 50% odds on proving causation. Thus the plaintiff has a 12.5% probability of proving all three contested elements. And] a 12.5% chance of a million dollars is worth $125,000. The sum is $125,000, and that is the solution of the tree.

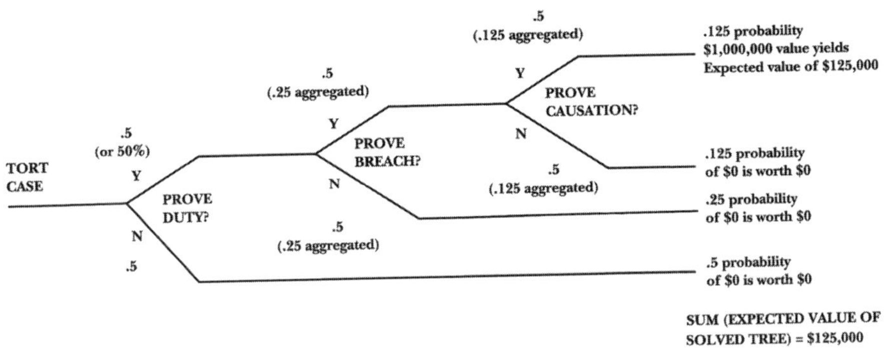

Figure 3 — The Tree Solved

Deduct Costs

If the trial would cost plaintiff $100,000—win or lose—we can deduct $100,000 from the solution of the tree, so that the net value of this lawsuit would be $25,000.

However, sometimes the costs vary depending on the nature of the uncertainties. For example, if the case has been tried already and is pending appeal, the uncertainties may be "will appellant win at the court of appeal" and "if they do, will they win at trial?" In this instance, if appellant loses at the court of appeal, they bear the costs of pursuing the appeal win or lose. If they win at the court of appeal and go to trial, they bear the cost of pursuing the appeal and the cost of the new trial. Thus the deductions of costs come not from the total expected value of the case, but at the end of each terminal point.

Still Not Simple Enough?

Here's a simple analogy that [shows] how these trees work. Imagine that there are 100 runners at the start of a race. The race course has a number of unmarked intersections. At each intersection, some number of runners will run in a way that brings them closer to the podium, and some will turn in ways that will run them into a ditch, out of the race. Only runners who run the whole race will get a financial prize, and the rest will get nothing, and they may pay a fee for running.

Our 100 runners start, and 50 of them turn one way at the intersection of "prove duty" street and "don't prove duty" street. The 50 who run one way are still in the race with many intersections ahead, and the other 50 have run into a ditch and are out of the race. The remaining 50 split equally at the intersection of "prove breach" street and "don't prove breach" street, send 25 more into a ditch and 25 still in the race. At our third intersection, half run into a ditch and half run to the finish line where they each get a $1,000 prize. The average prize for each runner entering the race is $125, and if it cost each runner $100 to enter the race, the average take home reward is $25. If someone were to offer an individual runner $50 to buy her spot in the race, the runner would be well advised to take the money.

Of course, this assumes that the runner was in the race just for the money, and not to prove something to the defendant, or to herself, or to create a precedent. If the motivation for litigating has little to do with money, the decision tree is not a useful tool.

The example in this reading assumes that each of the events on which trial depends has a 50% probability: the plaintiff has a 50% chance of proving duty, a 50% chance of proving breach, and a 50% chance of proving causation. Solving the tree was mostly multiplying by half several times. On those odds, the expected value of trial is $125,000 minus $100,000 in transaction costs and any taxes that might apply. If the defendant has offered $200,000 to settle the case, settlement is financially the better option. (Money might, however, be only part of what matters to the client, who might add other values to the option of trial, such as the cathartic value of telling the story of loss in court.)

The math—and the value of trial as an option—would have been quite different if the plaintiff had a 100% chance of proving duty, an 80% chance of proving breach, and a 60% chance of proving causation. That produces a 48% chance of a favorable verdict. Because the $1 million in losses are beyond question—the jury can return a verdict of $1 million or nothing—the expected value of trial on those predictions is $480,000, minus $100,000 in transaction costs and taxes, if there are any. On these probabilities, trial is financially the better option. (Again, money might be only part of what matters to the client, who might feel it important to avoid the trauma of reliving in public a terrible event—or who might be risk-averse and prefer taking a certain but lesser amount of money to hoping for a speculative larger amount at trial.)

Whatever the probabilities, any money gained at trial—or on appeal after trial, or at a second trial after a reversal on appeal—is far into the future. Unlike the settlement offer, it is not immediate money. So in computing the value of trial, you would have to do a present value analysis. It might be only the roughest estimate because you can't predict when litigation will end. You can't predict whether an appeal would follow trial, for example, and whether a retrial would follow an appeal.

§20.4 ADAPTING TO THE CLIENT'S TOLERANCE FOR RISK

Some people will bet small amounts of money—$5 on a lottery ticket or $25 on the office World Series or Superbowl pool. Some people will not bet at all; they have no taste for it, or it violates their convictions. Some people feel comfortable staking relatively large bets, such as $1,000 in a poker game. Some people bet with money they cannot afford to lose.

If you think of gambling as limited to lotteries, office pools, poker, and the like, you will probably say that you do not gamble often or that you never gamble. But the fact is that every time you make a decision based on a prediction of the future, you are gambling. You gamble every day in small ways. If it takes you 20 minutes to drive to school and if your first class of the day is with a teacher who will not tolerate tardiness, you're gambling that you will have no trouble finding a parking space when you leave home 25 minutes before class.

We win a lot of the small gambles of everyday life, but we also lose a lot of them. In the end, it doesn't matter much because both the benefits of winning and the costs of losing are not terribly great. You're embarrassed if you walk into class five minutes late, and the embarrassment might cause you to stop making that particular gamble. But you still have your family and friends, your net worth is unchanged, and you have not significantly added to the amount of injustice in the world. Even if you win, what have you won? Maybe an extra five minutes at home.

The big gambles are much more frightening. Tolerance for risk decreases as the stakes get bigger. A person who will casually bet $20 on a horse race might be a lot more hesitant if three zeros were added to that amount. And the size of the stake is always relative. To some people with very large financial resources, even a $20,000 bet is not significant enough to cause anxiety. And to others in precarious circumstances, $20 can be a lot of money.

Whatever the client's tolerance for risk, it is entitled to your respect. The client, after all, must live with the consequences of the decision long after you have disappeared from the client's life. You do, however, have an obligation to point out the disadvantages of betting to clients with high tolerances for risk and the disadvantages of not betting to clients with low tolerances.

How can you structure the options to take the client's level of tolerance into account? First, you can make sure that the menu of choices you offer addresses the client's level of tolerance. If you offer four risky options and one safe one to a client who has a low tolerance, your creativity may have been focused on the wrong end of the scale. Might there have been more than one safe option?

Second, if money or something else quantifiable is at the heart of the matter, you can calculate the expected value of each option. (See §20.3.2.)

Third, you can help a client understand whether her tolerance for risk is realistic *in this situation*. A client with a high tolerance who wants to make an unrealistic gamble might gain insight if you explain that you think most clients would not bet that steeply against the odds, and *why* most clients would not do that. On the other hand, it might be overbearing, if not oppressive, to tell a person with a low tolerance for risk that most clients would make a bet the client does not want to make. (In your first few years practicing law, you won't enough of a data base to know how "most clients" decide. Sometimes you will prepare by asking a senior lawyer how most clients would make the bet your client will make.)

§20.5 WHY SOME CLIENTS EXCLUDE THEIR LAWYERS FROM IMPORTANT DECISIONS

Lani Guinier tells the following story about a construction company, Bovis General Contractors, and an office building:

> Before beginning construction, but after the contracts were formally negotiated by the lawyers, a team from Bovis arranged a meeting attended by the [future] owners of the building, the architects, the engineers, and those who would be using the building. The Bovis team encouraged those present to identify important issues at the outset. Everyone agreed they wanted the project to come in on time and under budget; to meet the needs of the building's users; and to lead to long-term relationships with each of the other parties.
>
> Most poignant is that these business people *did not invite lawyers* to their meeting. The lawyers negotiated the contract under which everyone was operating, but the [meeting] participants negotiated duties without ever referring to or consulting [that] contract. . . . The lawyers' approach, which is understandably based on avoiding client [liability] in the event things go awry, often forecloses the *human interaction*—the pleasant exchanges and gestures—*which assure that things go right.* Indeed, *Bovis boasts that it has never had a lawsuit filed when it leaves lawyers out of the room and negotiates interpersonal agreements among the participants themselves.*[12]

Some clients believe that lawyers listen too little, dominate conversations, poison relationships by generating conflict, and raise objections when they should be developing solutions. Business people call this kind of lawyer a "deal killer"—a lawyer who can sabotage a deal the client really wants.

Deborah Tannen tells this story:[13]

> For my book *Talking from 9 to 5*, I spent time in companies observing people, interviewing them, and having individuals tape-record their conversations when I wasn't there. The companies . . . were all happy to proceed on the basis of our [oral] agreement on certain ground rules: The individuals would control the taping, any identifying names would be changed, and I would show them what I wrote about conversations that had taken place in their company and change or take out anything they did not approve. In some cases, I also signed a confidentiality agreement, promising not to reveal anything I learned about the company's business.

Some companies ran this past their lawyers, and in every one of those instances agreement became impossible.

> Negotiations with one company stand out. They had approached me to help them figure out why women were not advancing to the highest levels of management. I explained that to answer this question I would need to examine closely what was going on in the day-to-day business and that I would like to use my findings in my book. . . . But six months later, after thousands of dollars in legal fees and untold hours of everyone's time, the company's lawyers called the negotiations a bust, advising the company that the risk was too great.
>
> . . . The company's lawyer was demanding approval and veto power over my entire book. I could not agree to that; it meant I might write a three-hundred-page book in which a half-dozen examples came from this company and then have the company . . . tell me I could not publish the book. My lawyer was demanding for

---

12. Lani Guinier, *Lessons and Challenges of Becoming Gentlemen*, 24 Rev. of L. & Soc. Change 1, 13–14 (1998) (emphasis added).
13. Deborah Tannen, *The Argument Culture* 135–136 (1998).

> me total rights to the videotapes of conversations to use any way I wanted. The company could not agree to that; it meant I could put videotapes of their employees on national television. . . . Yet the people I was working with at the company had no desire to pass judgment on any part of my book that did not involve them, and I had no intention of using the videotapes except for analysis. The lawyers apparently figured they ought to ask for everything. . . . Rather than focusing on what the company and I had [already] agreed to do to help each other, the lawyers tried to foresee and forfend everything we could do to hurt each other. . . .

This company *had asked Tannen for help*. She and the company's managers had agreed on all the practicalities. Then the company made the mistake of running the deal past its lawyers. Because a lawyer was now on the company's side of the table, Tannen had to hire a lawyer. The lawyers then charged lots of money to kill the deal. Without lawyers, the same kind of deal worked out well elsewhere.

What went wrong? These lawyers overreacted and made big issues out of little ones. The company's lawyer's demand for veto power over the whole book was absurd. The company would have been fully protected with veto power limited to the very few passages where the company's name was mentioned. Tannen's lawyer's demand for total rights over the videotapes was equally absurd. Tannen had no interest in the opportunity the lawyer was trying to get for her.

The lawyers could have helped their clients by focusing on how the deal would have benefitted both parties. For example, suppose the company's lawyer asked only for veto power over book passages mentioning the company. And suppose Tannen refused on the quite reasonable ground that authors lose credibility if they aren't allowed to say what they think is accurate. Suppose the company's lawyer then asked that the company be identified in the book by a pseudonym and not by its real name. And suppose Tannen explained that for some reason a pseudonym would not work. If all those solutions fail, the company's lawyer should explain the risks to the managers who had negotiated with Tannen and ask whether they feel the benefits to the company outweigh the risks. If they say yes and also say that they trust her to be fair, at that point the lawyer has done his job and need do little more or nothing.

When lawyers focus only on the worst in human nature, they can bring out the worst in everyone involved, including themselves and their own clients. Before the lawyers in this story came into the picture, Tannen and the company had a good relationship. The lawyers killed that relationship and probably got their clients upset with each other. To accomplish good results—ones that make a client better off—a lawyer can often be more effective by finding ways to bring out the best in everyone's personalities and by building relationships based on pluses rather than sowing suspicion and conflict based on minuses.

Sometimes the pluses are too few to help, and the best way of protecting a client is to handle a situation forcefully with negatives. But that is true less often than many lawyers assume. Some clients lock their lawyers out of decisions—or fire them—because of too much negativity and conflict and not enough problem solving.

Another example: the Ebola virus usually leads to death after horrible suffering. In the earliest known outbreaks, 89% of the people infected in Congo died, as did 53% of those infected in the Sudan. Like many diseases, Ebola can spread from other primates to humans. For that reason, monkeys imported into the United States must be kept in temporary quarantine to make sure that they are not bringing infectious diseases into the country. In the late 1980s, monkeys in one quarantine facility had become infected with Ebola. This building was in a small industrial park adjacent to an elementary school and near a residential neighborhood in Reston, Virginia, a suburb of Washington, D.C.

The U.S. Army Medical Research Institute of Infectious Diseases (USAMRIID) was responsible for developing defenses against biological weapons that might be used by terrorists or by an enemy in war. If the United States were attacked with biological weapons, USAMRIID would have been expected to send biohazard SWAT teams immediately to limit infection and treat victims. Although the monkey infections were a naturally occurring outbreak and not an attack, the owner of the quarantine facility invited USAMRIID to take over the building, set up bio-containment barriers to keep Ebola from spreading outside the facility, kill the infected monkeys, and decontaminate the building. No statute gives the Army the authority to do this when the country is not being attacked, and if the Army did anything wrong and spread Ebola to the surrounding area, the potential legal liabilities could be enormous. To prevent public panic, USAMRIID decided to send its team in secretly without telling anyone nearby—including officials at the elementary school.

Before beginning this operation, USAMRIID consulted an Army general in the Pentagon. No lawyer was present during this conversation.

> Was this legal? Could the Army simply put together a biohazard SWAT team and move in on the monkey house? General Russell was afraid that the Army's lawyers would tell him that it could not, and should not, be done, so he answered the legal doubts with these words: "A policy of moving out and doing it, and asking forgiveness afterward, is better than a policy of asking permission and having it denied. *You never ask a lawyer for permission to do something. We are going to do the needful, and [afterward] the lawyers are going to tell us why it's legal.*"[14]

Fortunately, no human became ill. Scientists later discovered that this strain of Ebola—now called Ebola-Reston—does not make humans ill as other strains do.

What could General Russell have been afraid of? He might have had bad experiences with lawyers who raise objections in a single-minded effort to reduce legal risks even if the client is willing to take those risks to achieve an important goal. Why do some lawyers behave this way? Here are some possibilities:

First, some lawyers think bureaucratically, dividing everything into what is legal and what is illegal, even though a large gray area, where the law is unclear, exists between the plainly legal and the plainly illegal. An early twentieth-century lawyer named Elihu Root is often cited for the statement that most of the practice of law is telling clients that they are acting like fools and should stop. There is some truth in that, and a wise lawyer knows how to deliver that kind of advice in a way the client can accept. But perhaps a more important quote is this: "I don't want a

---

14. Richard Preston, *The Hot Zone* 159 (1994) (emphasis added).

lawyer to tell me what I cannot do; I hire him to tell me *how* to do what I want to do." That quote has an unattractive reputation because of the person who said it—J. P. Morgan, a robber-baron financier who was a contemporary of Root. But stripped of that association, it actually states what all clients want from their lawyers—not just the rich and powerful but also clients who are oppressed by society.

Second, some lawyers—especially inexperienced ones—do not know when or how to take risks, even necessary ones. Business people cannot make money without taking risks, and the most effective business people are good at separating profitable risks from pointless ones. People at the top of large organizations (such as generals) can sometimes feel the same way, even where profit is not an issue (as in the Army), because they can see the bigger picture and more easily balance need against risk.

Third, law school teaches students how to read cases and statutes, but not necessarily how to solve problems. Our job is to *create solutions*. We should say no only when there truly are no viable solutions. Lawyers who say no too easily might lack solution-generation skills (see §4.1.2). Clients view them as obstructionists. A few students go to the opposite extreme: they confidently propose off-the-wall solutions that have almost no chance of success. These students might be good at option generation but not at option evaluation (again, see §4.1.2).

Fourth, law school so emphasizes shooting down ideas that some students may think that that is the heart of what lawyers are paid to do. But shooting down potentially valuable ideas makes a lawyer a destructive presence rather than a constructive one. Some business people say that when confronted with an idea that has some faults, the bureaucratic mind will reject it to avoid risk while the entrepreneurial mind will find a way to improve it to create an opportunity. By that measure, the lawyer who reflexively shoots down every idea with a fault in it subtracts value from a situation rather than adding it.

If General Russell had called in the Army's lawyers, what would have been good counseling?

The lawyer should make sure that the clients—the general and the people from USAMRIID—understand the potential for liability, and the lawyer should brainstorm with them ways to minimize the legal risks. The lawyer should also brainstorm ways to minimize public hostility if the operation is less than fully successful. For example, from both a liability and a public relations standpoint, conducting this operation in secret, using disguised vehicles, while an elementary school is in session nearby, seems like an unnecessary risk. A monkey that escapes during the operation could get onto the school grounds and infect children.

But that should not cause a lawyer to say no automatically. Instead, the lawyer should help work out a way of achieving client goals while reducing legal risks. A good problem-solving lawyer might explore the possibility of enlisting the highest official in the school district as a collaborator, if that person will be both decisive and discreet, and closing the school for some reason other than Ebola, even if it is a ruse to avoid public panic.

CHAPTER

21

THE COUNSELING MEETING WITH THE CLIENT

§21.1 MOOD, SETTING, AND THE LAWYER'S AFFECT

A client who is making a momentous decision will be presented with a large amount of information while under stress. Remember that *how* you say something has an enormous effect on how people respond (see Chapter 5). What should you be careful about in this situation?

Involve the client so that you have a genuine conversation. This is collaborative decision-making. Do not be a talking head.

Suppose you are at home, looking at the television, surfing channels with the remote control in your hand. On the screen you see two or three people sitting in easy chairs in a television studio, talking about the great issues of the day. How long will you watch this before moving on to the next channel? They might be marveling at the recent discovery of an unlimited number of superb jobs for recent law school graduates in a place with a wonderful climate and local laws that make student loans uncollectible. Why, as soon as you see the talking heads, will you change the channel so fast that you will never learn of this remarkable place? Because, like most people, you dislike being put in a passive position while somebody talks at you.

In client counseling, a lawyer who is a talking head might explain the choices nonstop for perhaps a half hour and then ask the client whether she has any questions. The client then says her first word: "No." The lawyer concludes by saying, "Well, go home, think about it, and call me when you've decided."

Be an active listener, using all the techniques you learned in Chapter 8.

Give the client helpful respect. You may know some things the client does not, but the client hired you, can fire you, and therefore is your boss. Moreover, the client has to live with the consequences of this decision long after you have forgotten about it.

Why do some lawyers forget this and patronize clients? "[I]n almost every advisory relationship, the client is usually untrained in the professional's specialty, while the professional may have seen the client's problem (or variants of it) many times before. There is thus an almost natural tendency to come across to the client as patronizing, pompous, and arrogant. . . . Although advising clients sometimes feels like explaining things to a child, the secret to becoming a good adviser is to do exactly the opposite: Act as if you were trying to advise your mother or father . . . with immense amounts of respect. . . ."[1]

Consider in advance how you will explain legal concepts and terminology. If you try to find the right words off the cuff, they will either be incomprehensible or sound condescending. You want plain words that accurately describe the concept without implying that you are talking down to the client. Compare three examples, the second of which flunks these criteria:

1. A doctor, speaking to a patient with a neurological disorder.

> Although you feel a tingling in your knee sometimes, but nothing is really happening in the knee. When that tingling happens, it is because of something going on in your brain. Every part of your body is controlled by nerves that report to some specific part of your brain. The nerves use low levels of electricity to report, and your brain also uses low levels of electricity. The part of your brain that controls your knee sometimes has a kind of short-circuit in which the brain thinks it has received a signal from the knee, but it hasn't. That part of your brain, which is very small, probably has been slightly damaged in some way. But even if that weren't true, the brain can still fool itself. People who have had a leg amputated sometimes report that shortly afterward they can still feel their toes wiggling.

2. A lawyer, speaking to a client who owns a gas station and who has just been served with a temporary restraining order.

> A TRO can be granted while a motion for a preliminary injunction is pending for the purpose of preserving the status quo until the motion can be decided. You have been restrained from selling gasoline from the pumps alleged by the Department of Environmental Protection to be an environmental hazard, and violation of the order is punishable as a contempt. The order is effective until it is vacated, which probably will not be before the court decides the pending motion for a preliminary injunction, which has a return date of next Friday.

3. Another lawyer, conveying the same information to the same client.

> A judge can command you not to do something for a short period, which is what has happened here through this order, which lawyers call a temporary restraining order or TRO. This TRO orders you not to sell gas from the pumps that the DEP complained

1. David H. Maister, *How to Give Advice*, The American Lawyer, Mar. 1997 57, 57–58.

to you about last week. If you do that anyway, the judge can make you pay a fine or even lock you up in jail. The DEP has also asked for another kind of order called a preliminary injunction, which would do the same thing but for a much longer period of time. The judge has not given DEP a preliminary injunction, although she might do so later. The TRO—the order that was delivered to you yesterday—will last until the judge decides whether to issue the other order, the preliminary injunction. We go to court on that next Friday, but the judge will not decide on that day.

Do doctors usually talk to you the way the doctor in the first example does? Do you wish they would? In the third example, has the client been given all the information contained in the second example? Is the third example more clear to a client?

Don't talk to a client using words you would say to another lawyer. Clients want you to respect their intelligence but to use words that nonlawyers can understand. This requires careful forethought. Before you sit down with a client, ask yourself what words will most clearly communicate to the client the legal situation.

Ignore your own emotional needs. Don't show off. Be patient even if you have a lot of other things to do. If the meeting is taking longer than you thought it would and if you are due in court or elsewhere, break off the meeting and reschedule as soon as possible. Don't try to do a one-hour job in a half hour.

Explain the options neutrally. Remember everything you've already learned about client-centered lawyering in Chapter 3. Don't let your wording or body language convey that you like some options better than others. That would put pressure on the client to make a choice she might not make otherwise. If the client wants your recommendation, the client will ask for it (see §21.4 for how to answer that question). If the client has not asked for your recommendation, keep it to yourself and don't even hint at it.

Give the client empathy. If you were in the client's position, you would want the person advising you to be supportive and understanding, but you would not want that person to be unctuous and insincere about it. See §5.2.2.

Face the harsh facts. If the client gets an unrealistically optimistic picture, the decision will probably be the wrong one. And clients poorly advised in this way are tempted later to consider ethics complaints and malpractice actions.

Use an appropriate seating arrangement. You should not be behind a desk, where you look authoritative, distant, and uninterested. (If you were interested, why would you put a big piece of furniture between you and the client?) Sit together at a conference table or in chairs together so you can talk close at hand. The best seating arrangement lets you and the client look together at pieces of paper. The seating arrangement should allow you to use a large note pad or a whiteboard on the wall or an easel, or some other way of outlining the options visually.

§21.2 BEGINNING THE MEETING

When scheduling the meeting, you undoubtedly told the client what decision you would be asking the client to make, and you probably also explained the reason for the decision and its importance unless the client already knew anyway. If not, now is the time to do so. Even if you have said these things before, it helps focus the client's attention if you at least summarize them as you begin the meeting.

Depending on how experienced the client is in dealing with lawyers, you should explain that this is the client's decision; why it should be the client's decision; how you can help the client make the decision by framing choices and working out their advantages, costs, risks, and chances for success; and how you and the client can work together at doing this. You can dispense with some of these explanations with repeat clients, who might find them pedantic. But if a client has dealt with lawyers only infrequently, or has dealt in the past with lawyers who have not been very good counselors, the client might really need an orientation.

Before explaining the choices, make sure that you have understood the client's goals and that they have not recently changed. If they have, you will need to adapt. If they have changed greatly, you may be able to do only some of the counseling job in this meeting because you may need a break to prepare some new options or evaluations.

If any facts or aspects of the law will dominate the decision, you can describe them to the client or remind the client of them if she already knows. Do not give a detailed recitation unless the client asks for it. You are trying to avoid being a talking head. But if something will be a theme from option to option, it helps to explain it early.

Warn the client against premature judgment (see §4.2). Brainstorming will happen only if the client keeps an open mind.

Then, simply outline the options, letting the client see the outline on paper or on a whiteboard. Describe each one only enough so that the client knows what it is. Then go on to the next option. Do not evaluate the options yet. You are just trying to give the client an overview before you go into the details. In what sequence should you mention the options? Put yourself in the client's position and ask yourself which sequence would help this client understand the nature of the decision. For example, you might start with the options the client already knows about and work toward the ones that would be news to the client. Or you might start with the most serious options and then mention the more marginal ones.

In preparing for this meeting, you worked out in detail each option's advantages, costs, risks, and chance of success. The client can better see how these all fit together if you show the client something visual. It can be as simple as a handwritten list on a notepad. If the choices and their ramifications are complicated, you might want it typed to get everything on a single page. If the client has to turn from one page to the next, the big picture can disappear.

Afterward, ask the client whether she sees any additional options. Clients can be creative about this. Sometimes they can change some of your ideas into new and additional potential solutions as the steering committee did in §19.2. Sometimes they can remember ideas that you have mentioned in the past but have unaccountably forgotten about now. Your memory is not perfect. And sometimes they can think of potential solutions that have escaped you. Clients are closer to the problem than you are, and many of them spend more time than you can thinking about the it.

You are now ready to explain each choice's advantages, costs, risks, and chances of success.

§21.3 DISCUSSING THE CHOICES AND WHAT THEY WOULD DO

The best transition is to ask the client which options she would like to talk about first. If the client has no preference, you might discuss them in the same sequence in which you introduced them earlier.

Brainstorming with a client is different from brainstorming with another lawyer. Many clients will assume that their problem-solving skills are inferior to yours, and they will need your encouragement to believe otherwise. The best encouragement is not flattery, but instead a sincere interest in how the client thinks and feels about the problem and how it might be resolved. Treat the client as an equal whose views you respect.

Seek additional insights from the client frequently. Every time you find yourself finishing some aspect of a particular option (its risks, for example), ask the client whether she sees something else. If the client offers something, ask again until the answer, finally, is no. As you learned in §8.3.2, a person with several related pieces of information will usually offer them only one at a time when being asked questions. If you ask once, get one piece of information, and then go onto something else, the client might not tell you the others. After going through all the options, you might ask the client whether any new ones have occurred to her during the conversation. Do not be surprised if the answer is yes.

Be clear about what will happen upon success or loss. Suppose your client has read in the newspaper of multimillion dollar jury verdicts. You have drafted a complaint seeking two million dollars in damages. You fail to tell the client that a complaint customarily asks for the most the lawyer thinks the client could possibly get from a jury. You also do not tell the client that a typical jury verdict in this kind of case would be less than half a million; that local judges might reduce a verdict like that by one-third or even one-half; that nothing will be paid during the pendency of an appeal; and that a reasonable settlement offer by the other side—before or after a verdict—would probably be less than you predict that a jury would award. By failing to tell your client all this, you are not treating your client fairly, and you are asking for trouble.

Also be clear about what your efforts will cost the client. For the client, cost is not limited to your fee. In litigation, the client will also have to pay some itemizeable costs within your office (photocopying and messenger expenses, for example, and perhaps fees for court reporters at depositions). The client also might have to pay court costs. And even in regard to your fee, when does it end? Many clients are astonished to learn that even if they win at trial, they will have to keep paying your hourly rate while the other side appeals.

There are also less tangible costs to the client—in time, missed vacations, annoyed employers, and pure stress. Intangible costs are too often overlooked in counseling. Clients who have never been litigants sometimes find it hard to imagine the frustrations and anxiety litigants suffer, or the ways in which the opposing side in litigation might try to impugn their motives or character.

§21.4 IF THE CLIENT ASKS FOR A RECOMMENDATION, SHOULD YOU GIVE ONE?

In the client-centered lawyering explained in §§3.1–3.3, the lawyer helps, but the client decides. In counseling, that means laying out the choices neutrally—without telling the client which ones you like.

This book assumes that most clients want client-centered counseling, and that client-centered counseling produces better decisions. Some clients, however, really do want to be counseled in a different and more traditional way, and a client is entitled to have advice given in a style with which the client is comfortable. If the client is uninterested in an array of options and wants to focus immediately on the one you would recommend, you should try to persuade the client to choose without your recommendation.

But if the client persists and wants your recommendation at the beginning, then the client is making a decision about how she wants to be counseled, and that decision is one you should respect. But be very careful not to let your own needs—your ego or your tight schedule—delude you about what a client really wants. *If it is absolutely clear, despite your attempts to persuade otherwise, that this really is what the client feels most comfortable with,* you should counsel the client in the manner the client prefers. In client-centered lawyering, the client is, after all, the boss. Recommend a solution while explaining its benefits and drawbacks, but mention the alternatives and explain why they are worth considering.

Clients who want to hear *only* your recommendation tend, paradoxically, to be either sophisticated or unsophisticated.

Some unsophisticated clients might not function well in a participatory relationship with a professional and might want guidance from an authority figure in the old tradition where "[t]he client is expected to stand by passively while the lawyer lays out what he considers to be all the relevant legal considerations and selects for the client's rubber-stamping the course of action" that the lawyer thinks best.[2] But, in our experience, that is not true of most unsophisticated clients. Some unsophisticated clients have very good problem-solving skills which you will, with pleasure, learn to respect. For some, brainstorming with you is an opportunity to awaken skills and thus gain some mastery and empowerment. And for some, when you presume to recommend, your "opinions may tend to silence and dominate"[3]—rather than enlighten.

At the opposite extreme, a repeat business client who has dealt with lawyers often and who knows you and trusts your judgment might not want to hear about other options because she is confident that the one you would recommend is the best one. Successful business people know how to use time efficiently, and to them

---

2. Martin J. Solomon, *Client Relations: Ethics and Economics*, 23 Ariz. St. L.J. 155, 181 (1991).
3. Robert D. Dinerstein, *Clinical Texts and Contexts*, 39 UCLA L. Rev. 697, 710 (1992).

a 30-minute conversation seems to be a mistake if a 5-minute conversation would yield the same result. This client has already decided how to use her time. Respect that—unless you believe the problem at issue is much more complicated and important than the client assumes. If that's so, say that your recommendation is that she set aside time for extended discussion with you about the options.

Only with caution should you accede to a client's preference for "recommendation only" counseling. Three things disappear when you give your recommendation and mention the alternatives only as an afterthought.

The first is an opportunity to brainstorm the options with the client. Not only are two minds better than one, but the client usually knows more than you do about some of the factual situation as well as the kinds of solutions the client feels more comfortable with. If you suspect that brainstorming might improve the options in a significant way, say something like: "If we can work together for a few minutes to think about the options, it might be a good investment of time. Before I make a recommendation, I want to be sure about the situation."

The second is a process that can give both you and the client assurance that the right decision is being made. People sometimes think of a process as an inconvenient thing one has to go through in order to get a certain result. But a good process often has its own value even if the same result might be obtained without it. Among other things, a good process creates or deepens confidence that the result is the best one available.

For example, you meet with a client on a Monday. At the client's request, you state your recommendation, and the meeting lasts only ten minutes because the client makes a fast decision on the spot. On Tuesday, you and the client act on that decision, and the action is irrevocable. No matter how hard you try, you will never be able to undo it. On Wednesday and Thursday, lots of unexplored issues keep popping into the client's mind. Finally, on Friday, the client cannot stand it any longer and calls you, listing all these issues for you. You explain how, although they are reasonable concerns, none of them would change your recommendation. You have very good reasons, and the client is completely persuaded. After that conversation, the client thinks of a few more unexplored issues. The client might call you again. Or the client might be too embarrassed to do so and might for a very long time wonder whether what you recommended was really the right thing to do.

Some lawyers would dismiss this client as antsy, but the real problem is that you did not insist on a process that was thorough enough to give this client confidence from the very beginning that your recommendation was the right thing to do. Some things are too important to be settled on your recommendation, even if at the time that is how the client wants to handle decision-making.

The third thing that disappears when you give "recommendation only" counseling is full disclosure sufficient to protect you from the law of malpractice if your recommended solution fails. Suppose you recommend option A and do not mention option B. Based on what you and the client know at the time, option A is so much better than option B that no reasonable person would seriously consider option B. In other words, you have given exactly the right advice. But later the situation changes. New facts cause option A to fail and to make option B much more attractive. The client hires another lawyer, who sues you in malpractice because you never mentioned option B. You say that it would not have made any difference because the client would still have chosen option A, which was the better choice at the time the client had to make a decision. The client says otherwise. You might win at trial, or you might lose, or your liability insurer might settle before trial. Even if you "win" this dispute, you will lose an enormous amount of time, probably in hours that would otherwise be billable, as well as peace of mind. You may suffer some bad publicity. Your insurance rates will probably go up. *And*, you might not win.

In addition, "recommendation only" counseling creates a potential for confrontation, which might be either open or hidden. You describe option C and recommend it, telling the client that it is the only thing that will work. The client dislikes option C and says, "But what about option D? There are things about it I like, and I really hope it will work." You have researched this thoroughly and know that the last time option D worked for anybody was in 1919, and even then on distinguishable facts. You try to explain why option D will not work. You might persuade the client, and the conversation might end with sincere friendliness on both sides. But two other things are just as likely, or even more likely. One is that you and the client argue about it. The other, which is worse, is that the client does not argue, but you see some stiffening body language, after which the client goes away and follows your advice reluctantly, or does nothing, or hires another lawyer. The problem is that you have taken a position, and once you do that, conflict rather than brainstorming is the usual result. An assertive client might argue with you, and it is difficult to convert arguing into brainstorming. An unassertive client would rather go away than argue, but the problem remains.

Everything said in this section is different from the scene in which the client asks you *what you would do if you were in the client's situation*. In our experience, that is a very good question from a smart client. You should ask the same question of a mechanic who tells you that your eight-year-old car needs a valve job ("if this were your car, what would you do?") or a home contractor who is giving you a quote on an expensive but not urgent repair ("if this were your home, what would you do?").

This client is asking for information—not for your recommendation. The client wants to know how other informed and responsible people—for example, you—deal with problems like the client's. You can answer while at the same time explaining exactly how your values, goals, tolerance for risk, taste, and situation in life are different from the client's. If you have enough experience to be able to describe how most people in your community decide similar questions, the client might also find that helpful.

§21.5 ASKING THE CLIENT TO DECIDE

Ask the client to decide among the options. Understandably, the client might want time to think about it. In fact, you ought to encourage that unless there is some reason for an immediate decision. And don't be surprised if the client telephones with one or two follow-up questions before deciding.

If the decision will be delayed, try to work out a "soft" (flexible) deadline before the client leaves the meeting. Legal work seems to go on interminably because few of the people involved impose deadlines on themselves. A client faced with a tough decision may delay making it but then regret the delay. You can help by asking the client if she wants to set a date by which she will get back to you.

After the client decides, the counseling job is complete, and you and the client then act on that decision.

§21.6 SOMETIMES A CLIENT'S STATED GOAL MIGHT NOT BE THE CLIENT'S TRUE PREFERENCE

What clients tell us about their goals is entitled to respect. Many clients have thought about this deeply and know themselves and their situations far better than a lawyer ever will.

But sometimes what a client most needs is for a detached observer, such as a lawyer, to sense an inner truth about the client's situation and then help the client face it. That is particularly so when a client assumes or has been forced into thinking that a particular legal solution is what the client should be seeking. How can you help here? Start by listening with your heart rather than with the rational part of your brain. Then ask questions that probe the client's feelings. As you read the following, notice how the lawyer listened and the questions he asked.

STEVEN KEEVA, WHAT CLIENTS WANT
ABA Journal, June 2002, at 49

[Attorney Arnie Herz believes that any] legal situation holds the seeds of transformation. . . .

A case in point: Macie Scherick. When she hired Herz . . . , all she needed was for him to draft documents so she could sell her 50 percent share of a SoHo art gallery. At least, that's . . . all she thought she needed.

But Herz sensed there might be more to think about. He asked Scherick about the business and about her partner of 15 years, and he listened carefully to her answers.

The result? Well, here's how Scherick puts it: "He profoundly transformed my life." . . .

. . . Whether clients come to discuss a business dispute, a will or a contract, they almost invariably bring confusion, fear and anger, Herz says. "The problem," he adds, "is that when they come in such a condition, they are apt to accept legal solutions that don't serve them as well as they might."

That's exactly what Scherick was ready to do. But as she talked about selling her stake in the gallery, Herz didn't hear a woman who wanted out. He heard a woman who loved her work but had been intimidated by her business partner. At the time, Scherick had a 2-year-old child, plus another one on the way. Her partner was insisting that the demands of motherhood were inhibiting the gallery's success and, therefore her own. Scherick said she was willing to step aside.

But Herz heard between the lines. "For Macie, what first appeared to be a simple legal transaction powered by a solid business rationale turned out to be a complex situation involving two disempowered people," says Herz. "She . . . was fearful of confrontation, intimidated by her partner's emotions and aggressiveness, and not aware of her legal rights. So she was brought to the brink of selling a business she loved, was good at, and that was rightfully hers."

When Herz explained to Scherick that she was legally entitled to stay in the business, and that her partner could not force dissolution or push her out, she didn't believe it. "But then she began to see that she was not powerless," says Herz. "In fact, it became clear to her that, with all the legal leverage she had, she held the power and not her partner."

This gets at another premise that underlies Herz's work. "You have to identify and acknowledge any fear and/or anger or confusion that clients may be experiencing. When you do that, the relationship is totally transformed. They then know what it means to be heard, because you're seeing their true interests—which they rarely know they have. . . ."

When he did that, says Scherick, "I never felt so understood in my life." . . . Because Herz had helped her reclaim her own sense of self-worth, she realized she wanted more of a fair shake than she had sought.

Then Herz asked her to do what he asks all his clients to do. "I ask them to step outside the legal situation, to forget about all the drama of the moment and instead think about what they'd like their lives to look like three or four months down the line. Suddenly they see possibilities that never would have occurred to them before."

Scherick allowed [Herz] to negotiate a fair deal for her. The result was that the partner left the business to start her own.

Scherick, along with a new partner, continues to run the business, which has grown substantially in both revenues and square footage. Their Sears Peyton Gallery is about to double its space in a move to Chelsea, the very epicenter of the New York art world.

§21.7 WHAT TO DO IF THE CLIENT IS PERSUADED BY COGNITIVE BIASES AND ILLUSIONS

If you ask clients how they are making decisions, you will frequently, but not always, hear availability bias, anchoring bias, confirmation bias, and confidence illusions (see §4.4).

You will already be struggling to keep cognitive biases and illusions from misleading your own thinking (see §4.4 again). When you hear them from your client, what can you do?

Sometimes cognitive biases and illusions are just background noise. A client might voice them. But if your reasoning seems sound, the client might understand you and make a good choice among your options—while still voicing cognitive biases and illusions. This is typical human behavior. Nothing is wrong, and no harm is done.

Things are different when a bias or illusion prevents a client from understanding the situation or appreciating the options. Trying to argue a client out of a cognitive error usually does not work and can make the client resentful. The most effective thing is to ask questions, like the ones Frank was asked in the vignette that begins §4.4. Ask them with respect and genuine curiosity, not like a classroom

Socratic dialogue. It is easier for a client to abandon a cognitive error if the client is *helped* respectfully to see it.

What if the client will not give up the bias or illusion? That is the client's right. You have fulfilled your obligation if you do a good job of trying to help through questions. Cognitive biases and illusions permeate everyday life, and it might not be possible to persuade a client to think differently.

CHAPTER 22

OVERCOMING SPECIAL PROBLEMS IN COUNSELING

§22.1 ETHICAL ISSUES IN COUNSELING

Candid and complete advice. Rule 2.1 of the Model Rules of Professional Conduct requires lawyers to "render candid advice," and in doing so, the "lawyer may refer not only to law but to other considerations such as moral, economic, social and political factors, that may be relevant to the client's situation." The Comment to Rule 2.1 elaborates:

> A client is entitled to straightforward advice expressing the lawyer's honest assessment. . . .
>
> Advice couched in narrow legal terms may be of little value to a client, especially where practical considerations, such as cost or effects on other people, are predominant. . . . It is proper for a lawyer to refer to relevant moral and ethical considerations in giving advice. Although a lawyer is not a moral advisor as such, moral and ethical considerations impinge upon most legal questions and may decisively influence how the law will be applied.

Rule 1.4 requires you to "explain a matter to the extent reasonably necessary to permit the client to make informed decisions." The Comment to Rule 1.4 notes that, in many instances, the client can make an informed decision only if you explain the damage that some of the options under consideration might cause to others:

> In litigation a lawyer should explain the general strategy and prospects of success and ordinarily should consult the client on tactics that are likely to result in significant expense or to injure or coerce others. On the other hand, a lawyer ordinarily will not be expected to describe trial or negotiation strategy in detail. The guiding principle is that the lawyer should fulfill reasonable client expectations for information consistent with the duty to act in the client's best interests, and the client's overall requirements as to the character of representation.

If you receive an offer of compromise from an opposing party, you must inform the client of the offer and counsel on whether to accept or reject it unless in earlier counseling the client has already decided which offers will be accepted and which rejected.[1]

When the client decides to do something illegal. Illegality can happen on more than one level. One client might decide to commit a crime. Another client might decide to do something that involves an increased risk of negligence liability. Ethics law treats these possibilities differently.

Under Rule 1.2(d) of the Model Rules:

> A lawyer shall not counsel a client to engage, or assist a client, in conduct that the lawyer knows is criminal or fraudulent, but a lawyer may discuss the legal consequences of any proposed course of conduct with a client and may counsel or assist a client to make a good faith effort to determine the validity, scope, meaning or application of the law.

This means that in counseling you may not suggest an option that involves committing a crime or civil fraud. But if a client asks you whether a particular act would be illegal, you may answer the question, regardless of what the answer might be.

If you say that the act would be illegal and if the client then asks what would happen if the client were to do it anyway, you may answer that question as well. You might say that the client could be made to pay damages in tort or contract, or you might explain the judge's sentencing discretion if the act is a crime. If the client further asks you to predict whether the client would be held liable or prosecuted or convicted, you may answer that, too. For example, if the client has a store and wants to open it for business on Sundays, and if your state or county has a Sunday-closing law that has not been enforced for generations, you may tell the client that opening on Sundays is technically illegal, but that there is virtually no chance of the client's being prosecuted. Why may you do that? If law—as practicing lawyers know it—is "[w]hat officials do about disputes,"[2] you are explaining the law to your client.[3]

Rule 1.4(a)(5) requires that a lawyer "consult with the client about any relevant limitation on the lawyer's conduct when the lawyer knows that the client expects assistance not permitted by the Rules of Professional Conduct or other law." That means that if the client asks you to help plan an act that would be

---

1. Comment to Rule 1.4 of the Model Rules of Professional Conduct.
2. Karl N. Llewellyn, *The Bramble Bush* 3 (1930).
3. Monroe H. Freedman, *Lawyers' Ethics in an Adversary System* 59–60 (1975).

criminal, you must say that you cannot and explain why. What's the difference between this and answering the client's question about opening a store on Sunday? It is the difference between describing what the law will do and helping to plan an act. You did not help the client plan to commit the crime of opening on Sunday; you simply predicted the consequences.

When the client makes a decision that you consider immoral. Ethics law gives you a choice between two alternatives. You may act on the client's wishes. Or you may withdraw from the case.[4]

Your withdrawal will probably not cause the client to change the decision. Another lawyer can probably be found who will not object as you did. And if you represent the client in litigation, the court might order you to continue to represent the client "notwithstanding good cause for terminating the representation."[5] If you try to withdraw on the eve of trial, for example, the harm withdrawal would cause to the opposing party, the court, witnesses, and others might outweigh the harm caused by your continuing to represent the client.

Usually, it's more effective to appeal to the client's self-interest. If the client might be able to see a connection between self-interest and moral values, you might try linking them in an approach something like this:

Lawyer: I can understand why you would want to treat your neighbor this badly. If I had a neighbor who behaved that way, I think I would be as upset as you are. But I'm worried about the future. Sometimes, in the heat of hurt feelings, we do things that we later regret. We behave harshly while angry. And later when anger has cooled down, we think that that is not how we want to be remembered by anybody else or even by ourselves. I'm worried that a few years from now you might wish that you had treated your neighbor less harshly on this occasion. I'm not talking about forgiving him. I'm only talking about being less vengeful.

If the client is not likely to see a connection between moral values and self-interest, you might develop a creative plan that does something special for the client's own self-interest in a way that eliminates or reduces the moral problem without describing it as a moral problem.

For example, suppose the client is a real estate developer who has quietly bought up two city blocks of apartment houses. The tenants are all low-income, and the client wants to tear down the buildings and construct a large corporate office complex with upscale stores on the street level. The client has already emptied most of the apartments by refusing to renew leases as they expire and by offering a few thousand dollars each to tenants who would move out while their leases are still in effect. The client predicts that, if this continues, nearly all the apartments will be empty within a few months. But about a dozen tenants have declared that they refuse to move, and each of them has a lease that extends long past the scheduled date of demolition. The client calls these people "the resisters."

---

4. Model Rule 1.16(b)(4).
5. Model Rule 1.16(c).

The client intends to demolish, on a 24-hour-a-day schedule, the buildings in which the resisters do not live, which is legal in that part of town even though the resisters would not be able to get much sleep. The client will make no effort to make access to the resisters' apartments easy during demolition, and the client will cut off the resisters' utilities from time to time, using "demolition safety" as an excuse. You told the client that it would be illegal to cut off utilities unless it was really required for safety reasons, and the client asked whether the resisters could easily prove that the cutoffs were unnecessary. When you answered that proof would be hard, although not impossible, the client chuckled.

What can you do to persuade this client that it would be in the client's own self-interest to treat these people better? Sometimes a client might be influenced if you predict that terrible things would happen to the client if the client were to persist. But the facts here will not support that. This client can probably get away with it if the client is cunning enough. You are not willing to withdraw, and even if you were, it would make no difference because the client can replace you with another lawyer who is not bothered by such things.

The key is to find an incentive that makes sense within the client's way of thinking. Can you show the client that more civilized methods of persuading the resisters to leave would cost less? Can you think up an act of generosity on the client's part that would solve the resisters' housing problems while producing a benefit for the client that the client considers worthwhile? Some clients instinctively think narrowly while ignoring the effects of good and bad publicity. And the tax code can at times be helpful. Money spent in some ways is not taxed or is taxed less than money spent in other ways. You cannot know the true cost of any transaction until its tax consequences are factored in. If Plan X will cost the client $1,000 and is fully taxed, it is more expensive than Plan Y, which will cost $1,150 and is not taxed at all.

In general, there is a limit to the number of times you can tell a client that the client is behaving immorally. With some clients, you will lose your credibility if you do it even once. Even with a particularly fair-minded client, you begin to lose credibility if you do it with any regularity.

When the client is disabled from making a decision. A minor or a person suffering from a mental disability might not be considered by the law to have the capacity to make legally binding decisions. The definition of incapacity differs slightly from state to state. But most people who are incapacitated from making legally binding decisions are still entitled to some autonomy and no less respect than anyone else.

Under Rule 1.14(a), "[w]hen a client's capacity to make adequately considered decisions . . . is diminished, whether because of minority, mental impairment or for some other reason, the lawyer shall, as far as reasonably possible, maintain a normal client-lawyer relationship with the client." The Comment to Rule 1.14 explains that "a client with diminished capacity often has the ability to understand, deliberate upon, and reach conclusions about matters affecting the client's own well-being. . . . [For example,] some persons of advanced age can be quite capable of handling routine financial matters while needing special legal protection concerning major transactions."

Rule 1.14(b) provides that

> When the lawyer reasonably believes that the client has diminished capacity, is at risk of substantial physical, financial or other harm unless action is taken[,] and cannot adequately act in the client's own interest, the lawyer may take reasonably necessary protective action, including consulting with individuals or entities that have the ability to take action to protect the client and, in appropriate cases, seeking the appointment of a guardian ad litem, conservator or guardian.

§22.2 WHEN THE CLIENT'S GOALS CANNOT BE ACCOMPLISHED

Suppose the client wants something that the legal system will not deliver, and you are unable to find or create any other solution to the problem. This is much worse than the situation in which some of the client's goals cannot be accomplished but others can.

How do you break this bad news to the client? After examining the research on how doctors do a bad job of delivering bad news and how they can do it better, Linda F. Smith made some suggestions for lawyers in similar circumstances.[6] Among them are the following:

Do not deliver bad news without thinking long and hard about what you will say and how you will say it. If in the initial interview, you think that the client cannot get what the client wants, do not say so then unless the client's goal is plainly impossible. First, if you give yourself a few days, you might be able to think of a way of accomplishing at least some of the client's goals. Even if you can deliver only 10% of what the client is after, that is better than nothing. Second, clients can accept bad news better if they are told all the reasons why it's bad, and in an initial interview you are usually not prepared to do that. It can take more time to prepare a solid explanation that a layperson will understand. Third, for the client it can be traumatic to be told immediately in an initial interview that what she wants is impossible. It can feel as though the lawyer is not willing to take some time to try to solve even a part of the problem. If in the initial interview you feel that the client will not get what she wants, it would be more appropriate to say that it will be difficult to do so while empathizing with the client's needs.

When you give bad news, allow plenty of time to explain it. A thorough explanation helps the client accept the situation. And the client will need time to talk about frustration and disappointment.

"Be clear, direct, and candid in giving information."[7] Sometimes lawyers communicate bad news ambiguously because they are afraid of a client's negative

---

6. Linda F. Smith, *Medical Paradigms for Counseling: Giving Clients Bad News*, 4 Clinical L. Rev. 391 (1998). The next eight paragraphs in the text rely on pages 418–424 of Professor Smith's thorough article.
7. *Id.* at 419.

reaction. But clients are entitled to truth rather than misleading ambiguities. And it is part of a lawyer's job to help clients deal with negative reactions.

Begin by saying that what you have to report is disappointing. Then give a quick summary ("Your great-aunt's will cannot be successfully challenged even though she left you nothing") and explain in detail why it is so. To avoid ambiguity, keep the discussion focused on the news you are delivering and what it means for the client.

Listen to the client's reaction and empathize with it. It can be brutal to hear bad news from a person who does not seem to care about its effect. Legal rules are designed to do the fair thing in most situations. No rule can cause justice 100% of the time. And many situations are themselves unfair because they cannot be resolved without hurting someone. Your client deserves the same human response that you would give a friend in similar circumstances.

But if you overdramatize your empathy, a resilient client might become depressed because you are treating as tragic something that for the client is only frustrating and disappointing. Listen carefully to what the client says and match it with empathy. If, on the other hand, the client reacts harshly, do not change your prediction for that reason alone. If the news really is bad, you would not be doing the client a favor if you imply false reassurance in order to avoid the client's fury or anguish.

Before ending, develop a plan for handling the situation. What is needed to keep matters from getting worse? Even if the client's goals cannot be accomplished, could anything be done that might benefit the client?

§22.3 WHEN THE CLIENT MAKES A DECISION THE LAWYER CONSIDERS EXTREMELY UNWISE

A decision is *extremely* unwise if it would cause *a great deal more* difficulty for the client than it would solve, or if it would do a *much* less effective job of solving the client's problems than other options that the client rejects.

This is not the same as a decision that you would not make if you were in the client's position. The client, not you, has to live with the consequences of the decision. If the decision reflects the client's tastes and values rather than yours, there is nothing troubling about that.

Why might a client choose an option that would cause many more problems than it would solve or that would do a much less effective job of solving the client's problems than other options would? Here are the three most common possibilities: The client might be ineffectual at making decisions in general. Or the client might be either much less willing or much more willing to take risks than you expected. Or the client might disagree with your predictions of what the various options will cause.

Among the things clients hire us for is to warn them of trouble, and the client who makes an extremely unwise decision is entitled to warning. That client is also entitled to ignore your warning after hearing it. It is not just that the client has to live with the consequences of the decision. The client also decides whether to make risky bets or safer ones. And sometimes clients are right when they disagree with their lawyers' predictions.

How can you deliver this warning? First, do not give a lecture. Instead, raise the matter through questions and through statements of concern about the client's needs. The questions should probe so you can find out why the client is making this decision. You are looking for the places where the client's thinking diverges radically from your own. The client's thinking might diverge radically from your own in only a very few ways, but you do not understand the client's reasoning unless you find those points of disagreement. Second, do not argue with the client. Arguing accomplishes nothing in this situation, and most clients will experience arguing as abuse. A good way to express your concern is to say that you are worried about the client or about some aspect of the situation (see the sample dialog below). Third, check your own thinking to make sure that you really do accept the client's goals and values and are not substituting your own. And fourth, make it clear that you will act faithfully on whatever decision the client makes, but because of the matter's importance, you want to make sure that the client understands the risks and consequences.

Here is an example. The client is a plaintiff, and the defendant has offered to settle on the eve of trial. The lawyer believes that the client has only two chances in five of winning.

Client: I want to reject their offer to settle. They're not offering enough money.

Lawyer: I'm fully ready for trial. Our witnesses are ready, and we can start picking a jury in the morning. But this might be the most important decision you'll make in this case. Let me ask some questions so that I understand not only what you want me to do, but also why you want me to do it.

Client: OK.

Lawyer: Are you more optimistic than I am about what will happen at trial?

Client: I'm a little more optimistic. I don't feel like I'm losing. I feel as though it's a toss up now, a fifty-fifty shot.

Lawyer: That is just a little more optimistic than I am. What worries me is that you expressed real concern last week about getting money for you and for your family. How comfortable do you feel risking all or nothing like this? Because if we lose at trial, there will be nothing. . . .

This conversation would probably go on for some time.

PART

V

NEGOTIATION

CHAPTER 23

HOW NEGOTIATION WORKS

§23.1 AIMS OF NEGOTIATION

Some scholars estimate that as much as 90% of the legal matters handled by lawyers eventually involve negotiation.[1] One study of tort, contract, and real property cases in urban state trial courts found that 61.5% of cases were disposed by a settlement or voluntary dismissal.[2] Approximately 60% of criminal cases are disposed with guilty pleas.[3] In federal courts, 89% of criminal cases end in guilty pleas, presumably negotiated.[4]

Like all other work done by lawyers, negotiations can be separated into two general categories: transactions and dispute resolution. In transactional negotiations, the parties try to enter into relationships in which they voluntarily agree to terms that will govern their future conduct. Examples include transferring or renting real estate, buying and selling goods and services, creating business partnerships and joint ventures, and merging and acquiring companies. In dispute

1. Robert M. Bastress & Joseph D. Harbaugh, *Interviewing, Counseling, and Negotiating: Skills for Effective Representation* 341 (1990).
2. Brian J. Ostrom & Neal B. Kramer, National Center for State Courts, *Examining the Work of State Courts, 1996: A National Perspective from the Court Statistics Project* 24 (1997).
3. See Shauna M. Strickland, *Beyond the Vanishing Trial: A Look at the Composition of State Court Dispositions, http://ncsc.contentdm.oclc.org/cdm/ref/collection/adr/id/41* at 2 (visited Sept. 1, 2014) (examining trends in 19 states).
4. *Judicial Business of the United States Courts, Administrative Office of the United States Court* (2013) (Table D-4), *www.uscourts.gov/uscourts/Statistics/StatisticalTablesForTheFederalJudiciary/2013/december/D04Dec13.pdf* (visited Aug. 25, 2014).

negotiations, the parties are in conflict, and they try to resolve the conflict themselves. The alternative is to have a third party, such as a court, decide. Examples include settlement discussions in a lawsuit, plea bargaining, and negotiations between the Federal Trade Commission and a company before the filing of an antitrust case.

Some negotiations have both dispute and transaction aspects. Labor negotiations, for example, might concern both disputes about safety or other working conditions regulated by legal rules and transactional aspects relating to the long-term relationship between labor and management. Similarly, international trade negotiations may involve disputes about the meaning of provisions in existing contracts and bargaining about future contract terms. Even in an ostensibly "pure" dispute negotiation, transactional issues may arise. In a commercial landlord/tenant case, for instance, in which the tenant alleges breach of contract because of the purported failure of the landlord to provide services required under the lease, the parties may attempt to resolve the dispute by rewriting the terms of the lease to make the requirements more explicit.

Whether transactional or dispute resolution, the goal of any negotiator is to communicate persuasively with the other side. Communication can take many forms: threats that your client will take certain actions or assert power against the other party if a deal is not reached; arguments that a certain case, statute, or rule supports your position; promises that will bind your client in return for concessions from your opponent; appeals to your adversary to display some sympathy to your client; recognition of the views of the other party in an attempt to solve problems collaboratively; or intentional silences to promote discussion with the other side. The forms of communication you choose will depend on the strategy you develop. (See §§27.1 and 27.2.) But, in essence, negotiation—like interviewing, counseling, or legal storytelling—is a communication skill.

Your aim is to get the other party to make an agreement on terms as favorable as possible to your client. It is not to vent your or your client's anger, to show your prowess in researching obscure legal issues, or to demonstrate your ability to display rhetorical flourishes. Negotiation is not a monologue with the other party's lawyer as a passive audience. Rather, it is a dialogue in which you intend to persuade the other party to reach a mutually agreeable decision on issues.

§23.2 CONTEXT OF NEGOTIATION: INTERESTS, RIGHTS, AND POWER

To understand how negotiation works, consider each party's interests, rights, and power.[5] Every dispute or transaction occurs against a backdrop of these three factors. The differing interests of the parties, of course, bring them to the bargaining table. But the rights and power of the parties influence the result because the parties know that if an agreement is not reached, "a more coercive process will

---

5. William L. Ury et al., *Getting Disputes Resolved: Designing Systems to Cut the Costs of Conflict* 4–8 (1988).

ensue."[6] In that more coercive process—litigation or economic conflict, for example—each party will ask for vindication of its rights and use its power. These concepts are introduced here and explained more fully in Chapter 24.

§23.2.1 INTERESTS OF THE PARTIES

"Interests are needs, desires, concerns, fears—the things one cares about or wants. They underlie people's positions—the tangible items they say they want."[7] Common interests are resolving the matter promptly, maximizing financial position, developing or maintaining long-term relationships, or addressing psychological needs.

Consider, for example, the *Ransom v. Dusak* case discussed in Chapter 11. There, Ransom sought damages for breach of the warranty of habitability. Underlying that legal position could be a number of interests: compensation for the partial loss of use of her apartment, for her suffering, and for her medical bills; the desire to have the problems in her home repaired; development of a good relationship with the landlord; peace of mind; revenge. And behind Dusak's defense of the case could be several other interests: protection of his reputation in the community, the desire to get a new tenant, compensation for the money he expended to defend the case, and peace of mind.

Likewise, in the transactional context, the parties will usually have multiple interests. In an employment negotiation for a management position in a company, for instance, an applicant may be concerned not only with the amount of the salary, but also the nature of the fringe and vacation benefits, the title and responsibilities of the position, payment of moving expenses, possibilities for promotion, or geographic location of the office. The company's interests may include not only the applicant's training and experience but also her ability to work with supervisors and subordinates, consistency of salary and benefits with comparable managers, the applicant's willingness to make a long-term commitment, or her professional growth potential.

Each party might have many interests, and some of them might conflict. Although in a commercial transaction, a buyer may want quality goods, timely delivery, and a low price, she may not need to obtain all three. In a plea bargaining negotiation in a case with multiple defendants, an individual defendant might have an interest in reducing the risk of a long sentence but also might have some loyalty to codefendants and want to avoid reprisals. And in an international negotiation, a country might have concerns about secure borders but also want to develop long-term trade relations with neighboring countries.

§23.2.2 RIGHTS OF THE PARTIES

"Rights" are independent standards that demonstrate the legitimacy or fairness of a party's position. They can be based on formal legal rules (case law, statutes, and regulations) or contracts between the parties. Or they can be

---

6. Sally E. Merry, *Disputing Without Culture*, 100 Harv. L. Rev. 2057, 2066 (1987) (reviewing Stephen B. Goldberg et al., *Dispute Resolution* (1985)).
7. Ury et al., *supra* note 5, at 5.

grounded on socially accepted standards of behavior, such as reciprocity, precedent, equality, and seniority.[8] In the *Ransom v. Dusak* case, for example, Ransom might rely on the statutory warranty of habitability, a common law claim for negligent maintenance of the premises, or the argument that, as a matter of fairness, if she pays her rent, she should be entitled to a habitable apartment. Dusak might base his defense on Ransom's failure to prove all the elements on her claim for breach of warranty of habitability or might argue that Ransom's refusal to allow the admittance of the exterminator absolves him of any obligation to pay damages for the vermin infestation.

In dispute-resolution negotiations, bargaining occurs in the "shadow of the law"[9]—in the context of the legal claims and defenses raised by the parties before the particular tribunal. And aside from the substantive legal positions taken by the parties, they may also have different procedural rights that frame the negotiation. Examples are rights to discovery, to joinder of additional parties, to pretrial motions, or to interlocutory appeals. Even a motion for an adjournment or continuance of the proceedings might be a significant right for a party in a particular case.

Unlike dispute negotiations, transactional negotiations do not technically take place in the "shadow of the law." But the rights of the parties do provide some context for transactional bargaining. Sometimes, the parties are limited in their options by specific statutory or regulatory requirements. Usury statutes, for example, limit the amount of interest that a lender can charge a borrower, even if the two want to agree otherwise.[10] Beyond the law, transactional negotiators frequently rely on "common business practice" or "form provisions" in their bargaining.[11] And the parties often refer to socially accepted standards of behavior as a basis for their position. In a negotiation for a sale of residential property, for instance, if the buyer wants a ten-day period to withdraw from the contract after an inspection report, the seller may request that, in return, the buyer give her ten days to withdraw from the contract if she does not want to make the repairs listed in the report.

§23.2.3 POWER OF THE PARTIES

Power is "the ability to coerce someone to do something he would not otherwise do."[12] Although rights can coerce the party against whom they are enforced (see §23.2.2), power—in the sense used in this book—is coercion *without resorting to enforcement of legal rights*. A party asserts power in two common ways. One way is "aggression, such as sabotage or physical attack" (or more commonly, the pressure of bad publicity); the other way is "withholding the

8. *Id.* at 7.
9. This term was coined in Robert H. Mnookin & Lewis Kornhauser, *Bargaining in the Shadow of the Law: the Case of Divorce*, 88 Yale L.J. 950 (1979).
10. See, e.g., N.Y. Gen. Oblig. §5-501(1) (McKinney Supp. 2012).
11. Carrie Menkel-Meadow, *Toward Another View of Legal Negotiation: The Structure of Problem Solving*, 31 UCLA L. Rev. 754, 766 (1984). She terms this kind of negotiation bargaining in the "shadow of the form contract."
12. Ury et al., *supra* note 5, at 7.

benefits that derive from a relationship, as when employees withhold their labor in a strike."[13]

For some people and in some negotiations, relative power is the determinative factor. For example, when you want to buy a computer, the basic terms of the contract—the price, available accessories and software, and warranty—are not negotiable. When you find the computer you want to buy, you must accept the terms on which the manufacturer will let it be sold. But when General Motors wants to buy a computer, it can either dictate terms to a much smaller company or negotiate on an equal footing with a company large enough to have market power that matches GM's.

Even in a setting where one party starts out with a substantial power disadvantage, relative power does not necessarily determine the result. For example, car dealers have bargaining resources vastly superior to those of most car buyers. But dealers must make sales in a competitive market. Indeed, during certain times of the year, dealers need to sell cars to get them out of inventory. At those times, buyers may have significant power, at least in regard to the valuing of the trade-in, the financing package, or the availability of some options. Thus, relative power can be variable and does not always determine the negotiation's outcome.

§23.3 APPROACHES TO NEGOTIATION

The two primary approaches to negotiation are adversarial and problem-solving.[14] The adversarial approach focuses on the rights and power of the parties. The problem-solving approach focuses on the interests of the parties. Nearly all negotiations involve some degree of both approaches, but a description of the distinction between these two types of negotiation will help you make appropriate choices in selecting negotiation strategy and tactics.

§23.3.1 ADVERSARIAL APPROACH TO NEGOTIATION

A negotiator taking an adversarial approach views bargaining as an issue of distribution of limited resources. This type of bargaining is also called "zero-sum" negotiation because each dollar that one side receives (or does not need to pay out) is one dollar that the other side loses. If there are three claimants to a $3,000 pot of money, and if one claimant takes $1,500, the other two must split the remaining $1,500. Haggling over the price of a new car is a classic example of distributive bargaining. For every dollar that the price comes down, the buyer gains a dollar, and the seller loses a dollar.

In an adversarial negotiation, each party takes a position that she or he is entitled to something. In a personal injury case, for example, in which the plaintiff seeks $500,000 damages for injuries incurred in an automobile accident, the parties view the negotiation in terms of a continuum between zero dollars (the amount the defendant initially says it will pay) and the $500,000 demanded in

---

13. *Id.* at 8.
14. Other approaches exist, such as game theory, economic models, and bargaining theory, but they are less helpful when first learning basic negotiation skills.

the plaintiff's complaint. Depending on their assessment of the strength of their respective cases, the plaintiff and the defendant will each select an "opening position" on this continuum and determine a "bottom line"—the position at which the particular party will walk away from the negotiation. Negotiation then becomes a contest in which each party makes concessions, adopts fallback positions, and either eventually agrees to a compromise or leaves the bargaining table (see §25.4).

In the legal context, the adversarial approach to negotiation focuses on the rights and power of the parties. In dispute resolution cases conducted in the "shadow of the law," the negotiators typically—and sometimes wrongly—assume that the bargaining is limited to the judgment that could be entered by a court or other tribunal in deciding the case: "who will get the most money and who can be compelled to do or not to do something [by the court]. Indeed, it may be because litigation negotiations are so often conducted in the shadow of [a potential] court [decision] that they are assumed to be zero-sum games."[15] In a personal injury automobile accident case, for example, parties using an adversarial approach limit their discussions to the strength and weaknesses of the legal claims and defenses and each party's predictions of a jury verdict. Similarly, in transactional negotiations, negotiators adopting the adversarial approach assume that bargaining is limited to the options available under common business practices or form contracts and agreements. Even though a court will probably not render a judgment in the transactional negotiation, prevailing practices in the trade or business can become the "rights" about which the parties negotiate. Moreover, the relative power imbalance between the parties can affect the ultimate distribution of the pot.

When is it wrong to assume that the range of possible settlements is limited to what a court could decide or what one would find in common business practices or form agreements? It is wrong whenever a problem-solving approach would get more for your client. Subsections 23.3.2 and 23.3.3 explain how and when that might occur.

§23.3.2 PROBLEM-SOLVING APPROACH TO NEGOTIATION

While the adversarial approach to negotiation focuses on the distribution of limited resources, the problem-solving approach emphasizes the *integration* of the resources each side brings to the table so that each side ends up better off. Earlier in this book, we used the expression *problem solving* to describe general methods of identifying a client's problem, predicting what will happen in the future, and creating and implementing strategies to control what will happen in the future (see Chapter 4). In the negotiating chapters, we use that term to refer to a lawyer's use of some of these same methods—especially solution generation and solution evaluation—to negotiate a settlement or deal that will meet the interests of all parties.

---

15. Menkel-Meadow, *supra* note 11, at 766.

In the problem-solving model, each side is assumed to bring something of value to the deal that can create benefits to both parties, and the negotiators try to integrate these interests in a settlement or deal. A good illustration is a negotiation to create a joint business venture in which one party puts up the capital and the other provides the research and labor. Such negotiations are not viewed as zero-sum games but win-win situations. Many negotiations present integrative opportunities—even those which initially may appear to be purely distributional. In a personal injury setting, for example, the plaintiff's interest in a quick resolution of the dispute and the defendant's interest in delayed payment of full damages might be conducive to a structured settlement with a lengthy payout schedule. (A structured settlement is one in which the defendant makes payments stretched out over a period of years rather than in one lump sum immediately.)

Rather than concentrating on the rights and power of the parties, problem-solving negotiators focus on accommodating the interests of all the parties (see §4.3). As you saw in §23.3.1, the adversarial approach to negotiation results in positional bargaining: each party takes positions based on its evaluation of the strength or weakness of the parties' "rights" in the case. In their well-known book on problem-solving negotiation, *Getting to Yes*, Roger Fisher and William Ury reject this approach:

> When negotiators bargain over positions, they tend to lock themselves into those positions. The more you clarify your position and defend it against attack, the more committed you become to it. The more you try to convince the other side of the impossibility of changing your opening position, the more difficult it becomes to do so. Your ego becomes identified with your position. You now have a new interest in "saving face"—in reconciling future action with past positions—making it less and less likely that any agreement will wisely reconcile the parties' original interests.[16]

Fisher and Ury argue that by focusing on interests and not positions, parties can generate a variety of options that will provide for mutual gain for both of them.[17] By identifying their own interests and recognizing the interests of the other party, both parties can collaborate to develop an agreement amenable to both.

To illustrate such an approach, they point to the Camp David treaty between Egypt and Israel negotiated in 1978. After the Six Day War of 1967, Israel occupied the Sinai Peninsula. In the 1978 negotiations, Israel took the position that it retain some part of the Sinai, and Egypt insisted that Israel return the entire Sinai. Positional bargaining about alternative boundary lines took the parties nowhere. But then the negotiators began to consider their different interests: Israel was concerned about its security interests and did not want the pre-1967 situation with a military presence on its border. Egypt, after centuries of colonial occupation, did not want any infringement on its sovereignty. The interest-based approach to negotiation led to a solution: Israel returned the Sinai to complete Egyptian

---

16. Roger Fisher et al., *Getting to Yes: Negotiating Agreement Without Giving In* 4–5 (2d ed. 1991).
17. *Id.* at 10–11.

sovereignty, but Egypt agreed to demilitarization of large parts of the peninsula to assure Israeli security.[18]

Nonetheless, problem-solving negotiators do recognize that there are instances where interests cannot be integrated satisfactorily, and negotiation will fail. While adversarial negotiators select "bottom lines" at which they will walk away from the bargaining table, problem-solving negotiators identify a BATNA—a Best Alternative To a Negotiated Agreement—as a standard against which any proposed agreement should be measured. A BATNA is more flexible than a bottom line position.

To develop a BATNA, a negotiator predicts the best thing the negotiator would be able to do if the negotiation fails and an agreement is not reached. In a transactional negotiation where a drug store chain wants to lease space in a building, for example, the building owner will wonder: "What other potential tenants might I lease the space to? Are there any alternative uses for the building? Are there any tax advantages to keeping the store vacant?" Each of these represents a potential alternative to signing an agreement with the drug store chain: finding a different tenant or using the building in a way that does not involve leasing space or leaving the space empty for a time and taking a tax loss. The most profitable of them is the building owner's BATNA—the owner's best alternative to a negotiated agreement with the drug store chain. If during the negotiation, the BATNA looks better than any possible deal with the drug store chain, the building owner can walk away. If not, the building owner will come to an agreement.

Or in a dispute resolution negotiation for settlement of a lawsuit, the plaintiff will wonder, "If this case goes to trial, will I win, how long would I have to wait to win, and how much will it cost to win?" Trial is the only BATNA. The issue is whether it is better than negotiating a settlement, and that depends on the chances of winning at trial, the delay before victory, and the cost of winning.

Good planning involves imagining the other party's BATNA as well. Unless you have a good idea of the other side's alternatives to settling with you, you really do not know how strong or weak you are in the negotiation.

§23.3.3 USE OF THE DIFFERENT APPROACHES

Many commentators express a strong preference for problem solving as a substitute for adversarial negotiation.[19] Others tout the effectiveness of adversarial methods, arguing that the problems often identified as inherent in such an approach are the result of incompetent bargaining, not the method itself.[20] The approach described in this book is more flexible. Most negotiations are not purely adversarial or problem solving. Even a usually adversarial negotiator in a personal injury case, for example, might engage in problem solving on an issue such as the payout schedule, taking into account the plaintiff's immediate financial needs and

18. *Id.* at 41–42.
19. Menkel-Meadow, *supra* note 11, at 771–772.
20. See, e.g., Robert J. Condlin, *"Every Day and in Every Way We Are All Becoming Meta and Meta" or How Communitarian Bargaining Theory Conquered the World (of Bargaining Theory)*, 23 Ohio St. J. on Disp. Resol. 231, 241 (2008); Robert J. Condlin, *Bargaining with a Hugger: The Weaknesses and Limitations of a Communitarian Conception of Legal Dispute Bargaining, or Why Can't All Just Get Along*, 9 Cardozo J. Conflict Resol. 1, 79, 88 (2007).

the defendant's preference to pay at least some of the money later rather than now. And in many problem-solving negotiations, the parties may engage in bazaar-style haggling when it comes down to "nickel and dime" issues at the conclusion of the bargaining.[21]

These mixed approaches reflect the reality of how lawyers really do negotiate effectively. It is a complex process involving both distributive and integrative issues, all against a backdrop of the parties' interests, rights, and power. As you will see in Chapter 25, understanding the differences between the two approaches can be helpful in developing effective strategies on behalf of your client and crafting arguments or appeals to the opposing party.

If you assume that one approach is always preferable to the other, you will be less effective at negotiation than another person who can function well using either approach.

§23.4 ROLES OF THE LAWYER IN NEGOTIATION

In negotiations, a lawyer often acts in four capacities: evaluator, advisor, negotiator, and drafter.

1. ***Evaluator.*** At a minimum, you can help a client by providing a third party's evaluation of the situation. Sometimes clients become fixated on a relatively small part of a dispute or transaction, and the lawyer, who has no personal stake in the matter, can provide some perspective on the problem. Some clients in personal injury cases, for example, encouraged by press reports of huge verdicts in high-profile cases, expect the same results in their cases. One of the functions of a lawyer is to give clients a reality check as to the actual experience in your particular jurisdiction.
2. ***Advisor.*** Lawyers counsel their clients as to their options during the negotiation process, particularly in regard to what offers to make and whether to accept an offer made by the other side. The client, however, decides whether to make an agreement (see §§3.3 and 24.5).
3. ***Negotiator.*** In many dispute situations, the lawyer is the exclusive communicator with the other party or its lawyer, and the client does no more than authorize the lawyer to act (see §24.5). But sometimes the client is an active participant in the negotiations, and the lawyer plays the role of a co-negotiator or backseat advisor. The decision as to who should be the negotiator is a strategic one, depending in part on the communication skills of the client, the expertise of the lawyer or client on the issues raised by the transaction or dispute, the advantages or disadvantages of having a person with authority present, and the concern of the client to be intimately involved in the discussions. In most transactional situations, on the other hand, the clients themselves negotiate the key elements of the deal, such as price, what is being purchased,

---

21. See generally Gerald B. Wetlaufer, *The Limits of Integrative Bargaining*, 85 Geo. L.J. 369, 390 (1996).

and when it will be delivered. Lawyers are brought into the picture to draft the contract, and the lawyers conduct a second negotiation over how the contract will allocate various risks between the parties and other aspects of contract drafting. Occasionally, a transactional client will turn the negotiation of the entire deal over to a lawyer, but that is unusual.

4. ***Drafter.*** Once an agreement is reached, it usually must be reduced to writing (see §28.4.2). Even in those situations where the agreement is made orally, such as stipulations on the record in a courtroom, the lawyers need to work out the precise language of the agreement. When reducing the agreement to writing, other issues often arise, and, as the saying goes, "the devil is in the details." More negotiation is often needed when pinning down the exact language of the agreement.

§23.5 DISCHARGING YOUR ETHICAL AND LEGAL RESPONSIBILITIES

When representing your client in a negotiation, you not only have to examine the different approaches to the process and your role on behalf of your client, but you must also consider your ethical and legal obligations both to your client and the other party. The Model Rules of Professional Responsibility create ethical obligations for attorneys in the negotiation process. Also, the ABA's Section of Litigation has adopted *Ethical Guidelines for Settlement Negotiations*,[22] and the National Legal Aid and Defender Association (NLADA) has adopted *Performance Guidelines for Criminal Defense Representation*, which include guidelines specifically for representing criminal defendants in plea bargaining.[23] Although these guidelines are not binding authority, they provide more detailed guidance than the Rules in regard to a lawyer's responsibility to clients and opposing parties during settlement talks. Finally, a lawyer should be aware of the potential tort and contract liability issues that can arise in the negotiation process.

Under the ABA Model Rules of Professional Conduct, "[a] lawyer shall abide by a client's decision whether to settle a matter. In a criminal case, the lawyer shall abide by the client's decision, after consultation with the lawyer, as to a plea to be entered."[24] Fleshing out this requirement, the *ABA Guidelines for Settlement Negotiations* require attorneys to provide clients with a professional assessment of the advantages and disadvantages of proposed settlements so that they can make fully informed decisions. Moreover, these guidelines caution lawyers to "be particularly sensitive to the risk that the client's practical dependency on the lawyer may give the lawyer immense power to influence or overcome the client's will respecting a proposed settlement," and warn attorneys not to make threats "to

---

22. *www.abanet.org/litigation/ethics/settlementnegotiations.pdf* (visited Aug. 25, 2014).
23. Nat'l Legal Aid & Defenders Ass'n, *Performance Guidelines for Criminal Defense Representation* (1995).
24. Model Rules of Professional Conduct R. 1.2(a).

take actions that may harm the client's interests to induce the client's assent to the lawyer's position respecting a proposed settlement."[25]

In the plea bargaining context, the NLADA guidelines require defense attorneys to explore with their clients the possibility and desirability of reaching a negotiated disposition rather than proceeding to trial. And they advise attorneys to shield their clients from improper "overt or veiled" pressure to plead."[26] Additionally, these guidelines provide that in developing negotiation plans for their clients, attorneys must be fully aware and make their clients fully aware of not only the maximum term of imprisonment and fines but also any possible sentence enhancements or parole consequences; the likely place and manner of confinement; the effect of good-time credits on the sentence; and other possible collateral consequences of the conviction.[27] These consequences include potential effects on voting rights, professional licensing, immigration status, rights to public housing and other public benefits, driving privileges, and parental rights.[28] Finally, these guidelines require that in developing a negotiation strategy, defense counsel must be completely familiar with the types of concessions the client might be able to offer the prosecution as part of a negotiated settlement, and the kinds of benefits that the prosecution might be willing to offer the client in exchange for a plea.[29]

In regard to your responsibilities to opposing counsel, in any negotiation, you will make representations: in regard to particular facts in the case; as to assessments of the strengths and weaknesses of the different parties' cases; or of your opinions about proposed solutions to problems. Indeed, most arguments and threats contain representations of fact, which can raise ethical issues if you misrepresent the facts or omit certain facts.

As to misrepresentations, under Model Rule of Professional Conduct 4.1(a), a lawyer "[i]n the course of representing a client, a lawyer shall not knowingly . . . (a) make a false statement of material fact or law to a third person. . . ."[30] The comment to the rule provides, however, that "[u]nder generally accepted conventions in negotiation, certain types of statements *ordinarily* are not taken as statements of material fact. Estimates of price or value placed on the subject of a transaction and a party's intentions as to an acceptable settlement of a claim are in this category. . . ."[31]

The line between actual misrepresentation and "puffing" is not always clear. And the interpretation of the rule and comment varies from state to state and is influenced by prevailing local practices.[32] The weasel word "ordinarily" in the comment does not necessarily give you broad leeway in your representations in

25. ABA, *supra* note 22.
26. NLADA, *supra* note 23, at 72–73.
27. *Id.* at 77. These requirements are consistent with the Supreme Court's recent plea bargaining jurisprudence, which makes clear "'negotiation of a plea bargain is a critical phase of litigation for purposes of the Sixth Amendment right to effective assistance of counsel.'" *Missouri v. Frye*, 132 S. Ct. 1399, 1406 (2012) (citing *Padilla v. Kentucky*, 559 U.S. 356, 373 (2010)).
28. An excellent website to consult for determining possible collateral consequences of criminal convictions in a particular jurisdictions is *www.lac.org/roadblocks-to-reentry* (visited Aug. 22, 2014).
29. NLADA, *supra* note 23, at 77–78.
30. Model Rules of Professional Conduct 4.1(a).
31. Comment 2 to Model Rule 4.1 (emphasis added).
32. Charles W. Wolfram, *Modern Legal Ethics* §13.5.8 at 727 (1986).

negotiation. In the Ransom case, for instance, consider these three statements by Dusak's lawyer, all of which he knows to be misrepresentations:

1. My client will not agree to exterminations every month.
2. My client has signed an agreement with an exterminator for service every month.
3. My client tells me he thinks it will cost over $150 a month to have an exterminator.

In most jurisdictions, Statement 1 is probably permissible because it merely reflects his client's intentions as to an acceptable settlement and Statement 2 is probably impermissible because it states an untrue fact that materially relates to the negotiation. Statement 3, however, is on the borderline: it could just be Dusak's opinion about a negotiating position, but, by referring to an estimate of cost, it could be considered a statement of fact made to induce a concession by Ransom.

Certainly, then, before you engage in bargaining, research the applicable ethics opinions for that particular jurisdiction.[33] Even as to your assessments of the strengths and weaknesses of your client's case, "a careful lawyer, intent on negotiating a legally protectable bargain, would be very circumspect in making or implying false and misleading statements about intention."[34] A material misrepresentation not only poses an ethics problem but also permits a challenge to the entire agreement. If the other party can establish the elements for a fraud in the inducement claim, the agreement may be rescinded.

In regard to omissions of fact, Rule 4.1(b) provides that a "lawyer shall not knowingly . . . fail to disclose a material fact to a third party when disclosure is necessary to avoid assisting a criminal or fraudulent act by a client, unless disclosure is prohibited by Rule 1.6."[35] With narrow exceptions, Rule 1.6 prohibits a lawyer from revealing "information relating to representation of a client unless the client gives informed consent [or] the disclosure is impliedly authorized in order to carry out the representation. . . ."[36] Generally, under these rules, a lawyer is not obligated to disclose information that will harm her client's negotiating position. Indeed, a lawyer who discloses confidential information without the client's consent commits an ethical violation.

Besides the rules of professional responsibility, you should consider the possible tort and contract liability which can arise from misrepresentations in a negotiation. Because every negotiated agreement, including one entered in court, is a contract, tort liability for fraud in the inducement can result from a misrepresentation.[37] As agents of their clients, lawyers can share in liability for such

---

33. A lawyer admitted to practice in a jurisdiction where the Model Rules apply is subject to the disciplinary authority of that jurisdiction although engaged in practice elsewhere. Model Rule 8.5.
34. Wolfram, *supra* note 32.
35. Model Rule 4.1(b).
36. Model Rule 1.6(a).
37. See Restatement (Second) of Torts §525 (1977) ("One who fraudulently makes a misrepresentation of fact, opinion, intention or law for the purpose of inducing another to act or refrain from action in reliance upon it, is subject to liability to the other in deceit for pecuniary loss caused to him by his justifiable reliance upon the misrepresentation.").

damages.[38] In addition to tort liability for damages, a fraudulent or material misrepresentation can lead to the voiding of the contract.[39] Your client, then, could face not only the possibility of losing the benefits of the deal but also a judgment against her for damages.

Some threats are unethical. In some states, a lawyer may not threaten presentation of criminal charges solely to obtain an advantage in a civil matter.[40] In those states, any threat to bring criminal charges may be risky, as may be a threat to file disciplinary charges with a grievance committee. The best policy is never to threaten criminal or disciplinary consequences in those jurisdictions.

Finally, you should be aware that in most states clients are permitted to sue their attorneys for malpractice for negligently negotiating an agreement even if they consented to settlement.[41] While most courts acknowledge the policy of encouraging negotiated settlements to disputes, they also recognize that lawyers owe their clients the duty to know the law and obtain accurate information upon which the client can make an informed decision. "The test for purposes of malpractice is commonly stated as whether the attorney exercised that degree of skill, prudence, and diligence in investigating the facts, in legal research, and in giving legal advice that lawyers of ordinary skill and capacity would do in similar situations."[42]

---

38. See Restatement (Second) of Agency §348 (1958) ("An agent who fraudulently makes representations . . . is subject to liability in tort to the injured person, although the fraud . . . occurs in a transaction on behalf of the principal.").
39. See Restatement (Second) of Contracts (1981) ("If a party's manifestation of assent is induced either by a fraudulent or material misrepresentation by the other party upon which the recipient is justified in relying, the contract is voidable by the recipient."). Under this Restatement, non-disclosure of a fact can be equivalent to an assertion. See *id.* §161.
40. See generally 2 Geoffrey C. Hazard & W. William Hodes, *The Law of Lawyering* §40.4 at 40-8 to 40-11 (2010).
41. See Lynn A. Epstein, *Post-Settlement Malpractice: Undoing the Done Deal*, 46 Cath. U. L. Rev. 453 (1997).
42. Jay Folberg & Dwight Golann, *Lawyer Negotiation: Theory, Practice, and Law* 272 (2d ed. 2011).

CHAPTER 24

NEGOTIATION PREPARATION: ASSESSING THE PARTIES

§24.1 INTERESTS, RIGHTS, AND POWER

You saw in §23.2 that all negotiations are greatly affected by the parties' interests, rights, and power. Prenegotiation preparation necessarily includes an assessment of the interests, rights, and power of both your client and the other side.

§24.2 ASSESSING THE PARTIES' INTERESTS

This process requires identifying the interests of each party, prioritizing your client's interests, and predicting the other party's priorities.

§24.2.1 TYPES OF INTERESTS

Interests are the needs, desires, concerns, fears, and expectations of a particular party. Although this definition seems quite simple, the process of identifying the interests of your client and those of the other party is not so easy. Your client may be unsure or ambivalent about what she really wants. Or she may be absolutely certain about her needs at the initial interview, only to change her mind completely on the eve of the deal closing or trial.

In regard to identifying the interests of the other parties, your access to them is limited, and their communications to you might not be totally forthright. Your task, therefore, is a reconnaissance mission to learn as much as possible about the other side's interests.[1]

To engage in this process, think of various types of interests to explore. Although the following categories may not be applicable to all cases and some of them overlap, they provide a framework to assure a thorough investigation of interests:

1. ***Financial interests.*** These include not only the short-term money effects of the transaction or dispute but also any long-term financial ramifications or tax consequences for the party.

2. ***Performance interests.*** Especially in transactional settings, performance concerns may be just as important as price. In an installment sales transaction, for example, the seller might be as interested in the security and nonperformance remedy provisions of the agreement as in the payment schedule. Or in the sale of a house, the seller who is relocating to another area in a short time may be willing to accept a much lower price if the buyer pays cash (so that the seller does not have to worry about whether the deal might collapse if the buyer cannot get a mortgage).

3. ***Psychological needs.*** In many transactions and disputes, one or more of the parties has an emotional stake: a seller has lived in her house for 25 years and is ambivalent about having to move; each spouse in a child custody dispute feels that the other is an unfit parent; a commercial buyer feels that it was overcharged in a previous transaction; a plaintiff in an action against an insurance company may have mixed feelings, wanting both vengeance and the certainty that compensation will be forthcoming; an environmental group may be up in arms because it feels that a factory deliberately and greedily ignored clean air standards. Although these feelings might not be rational, they are real and certainly affect the dynamics of bargaining. Indeed, in some dispute resolution negotiations, the primary interest of a party is not the relief requested in the complaint but an apology or public recognition of wrongdoing.

4. ***Reputational interests.*** Some parties might be concerned about the effect of the transaction or dispute on their reputations. They may fear, for example, that this case might set a harmful precedent in the future or that adverse publicity will embarrass them. In the plea bargaining context, some prosecutors may want to buttress their reputations by racking up good win-loss records in which a guilty plea to a reduced charge counts as a win but trials risk being losses. They may also offer less favorable pleas in strong, high-profile cases than in similar low-profile cases hoping to win well-publicized convictions.[2]

---

1. For an extended discussion of this process, see Carrie Menkel-Meadow, *Toward Another View of Legal Negotiation: The Structure of Problem Solving*, 31 UCLA L. Rev. 754, 801–803 (1984).
2. Stephanos Bibas, *Plea Bargaining Outside the Shadow of Trial*, 117 Harv. L. Rev. 2463, 2471, 2474 (2004).

5. ***Relationship interests.*** Many transactional and some dispute-resolution negotiations involve repeat players: buyers frequently purchase from particular sellers; unions regularly bargain with management for collective bargaining agreements; parents in a custody dispute may continue to be in close contact with each other; or public interest groups may consistently litigate against the same governmental regulatory bodies. In those situations, although the relationship between the parties on some level will be adversarial, on another level it will require cooperation. After a collective bargaining agreement is reached, for example, the employees will be working for management, and, even after the public interest group has settled or litigated its case, it will probably be dealing on a regular basis with matters before the regulatory body. In many cases, therefore, parties may have a stake in maintaining a working relationship.

6. ***Liberty interests.*** These may include not only freedom from incarceration in a criminal case but also freedom to travel, to engage in a particular occupation, or to spend time with one's family. Criminal defendants nearly always want to avoid imprisonment. But other dispositions can also have a significant impact on the defendant's liberty: community service obligations may interfere with the defendant's job obligations; a record of a conviction might preclude employment in a particular occupation; or participation in a drug program might interfere with family life.

7. ***Basic human needs.*** This catch-all category is a useful tool in double-checking your investigation of the parties' interests. It includes security, economic well-being, a sense of belonging and of being appreciated, and control over one's life. These needs are not exclusive to individuals. Groups, corporations, government agencies, and nations, to some extent, all have these interests, and they should not be overlooked.

§24.2.2 IDENTIFICATION OF PARTIES' INTERESTS

When interviewing and counseling your client to learn the client's interests, begin with open-ended, rather than closed or leading questions (see §8.3.2). Ask your client what end results she desires, and then why this outcome is so important. Do not rush into accepting the initial response, but try to obtain a complete listing of all the client's concerns. If the client defines her needs and interests only vaguely, you will want to narrow your questions, perhaps by exploring whether the client has any interests in the categories described in §24.2.1. If you do not succeed with this approach, ask about the kinds of concerns that other clients have had in these situations. It is often helpful to write down your client's responses on a pad or whiteboard which the client can read while you write; seeing the answers charted out, the client may be encouraged to articulate other concerns.

During this process, your client may be reluctant to express some concerns, especially those of a psychological nature. In a child custody dispute, for example, a parent may not want to litigate aggressively an issue because she feels that she lacks the stamina to do it. Sensitive, active listening helps in such situations (see §8.1.2). To obtain a thorough account of all your client's interests, be nonjudgmental so that your client feels that she can openly confide in you.

A client's interests will shift often during your representation. Some clients may not be ready to commit and reach a deal; others might be ambivalent about what they want; and still others may view the case differently at the end of a negotiation when faced with concrete options than at the beginning. While you may be tempted to take control and tell the client what to do, we suggest that you work with the client to determine what she genuinely wants. Find out the reasons that the client changed her mind. If the client is not ready to reach an agreement, explain the consequences of her shifting positions, the possibilities of delaying negotiations, and the risks inherent in changing positions.[3]

You also need to identify the interests of the opposing party or parties to understand fully the context for the negotiation. Sometimes the other party articulates its needs and interests clearly and forthrightly. Other times, however, your opponent will leave you bewildered either because of its own negotiation strategy or because it has not thought out its concerns thoroughly. In those situations, you may want to adopt an approach similar to the one you use with your client and ask the other party's lawyer why the other party has adopted a particular position and why the other party rejects your client's position (see §28.1.1).[4] If this does not work, you might want to explore possible interests with your opponent by asking questions such as "it seems to me that you are interested in . . ." to evoke an affirmative or corrective response. A similar technique is to make a proposal, tell the other side that you think the proposal helps to satisfy an interest that you assume it has, and then listen carefully to its reaction. Sometimes phrasing a proposal as a hypothetical results in helpful discussion because the other side may not feel as threatened by it as by an actual offer ("If we were to offer X, what effect would that have on your client's situation?").

The other party and its lawyer, however, are not the only sources for identifying its interests. Your client may know the other side's interests and concerns from personal experience. This is certainly true in domestic relations or labor management disputes. And many commercial and corporate transactions involve repeat players who have intimate knowledge of each other's interests. Try to get your clients to put themselves in the role of the other side and argue its view of the case. Ask them how they think the other side feels about them and what it hopes to attain in the case.[5]

Additional information can be obtained from other lawyers or third parties who have previously dealt with your opponent. And in a dispute or transaction with an organization, news articles or Web postings might reveal its financial, reputational, and policy priorities. Consider the other parties' behavior in similar settings both in style and substance; their training, political, and professional affiliation; the organizational position of the person who has authority for negotiation decisions; and the persons to whom the other side defers or tends to admire.[6] Use your fact investigation not only to explore the substantive issues in

---

3. See generally Robert H. Mnookin et al., *Beyond Winning: Negotiating to Create Value in Deals and Disputes* 201–203 (2000).
4. Roger Fisher et al., *Getting to Yes: Negotiating Agreement Without Giving In* 44–45 (2d ed. 1991).
5. Mnookin et al., *supra* note 3, at 180–182.
6. David A. Lax & James K. Sebenius, *Interests: The Measure of Negotiation*, 2 Negot. J. 73, 89 (1986).

CHART 24A ASSESSMENT OF PARTIES' INTERESTS

Types of Interest	Client's Interests	Other Party's Interests
1. Financial		
2. Performance		
3. Liberty		
4. Psychological		
5. Reputational		
6. Relationship		
7. Basic Human Needs		
HIGHEST PRIORITIES		

the case but also the underlying interests and needs of the other side. (See §§16.3.1–16.3.5.)

§24.2.3 PRIORITIZING INTERESTS

The final step in assessing the interests of the parties is to prioritize the interests of your client and the other party. Obviously, the lists you compile in regard to your client's interests and your guesses as to the other party's interests will in many cases be lengthy. (See Chart 24A for the list's basic structure.) And some interests on a list might be inconsistent with others on the same list. In negotiating a business partnership, for example, your client may articulate interests both in retaining control over the direction of the business and in limiting the time he wants to spend on it.

To get an adequate assessment of the interests of both parties, work with your client to determine her two or three most important interests in this transaction or dispute and try to speculate on the priorities of concerns for the other party. Remember that each of the parties' interests may change as the bargaining progresses. As that happens, you may want to revisit your assessment of interests and priorities. By identifying these priorities you lay the groundwork for determining whether or not a problem-solving approach will settle the issues (see §25.3).

§24.3 ASSESSING THE PARTIES' RIGHTS

Novice lawyers tend to think of negotiations as driven primarily by legal concerns. You saw in §24.2, however, that nonlegal interests—financial, psychological, relationship, reputational needs—can be the driving force behind the parties' behavior. Still, legal negotiations do take place in the "shadow of the law," and it would be a mistake to ignore totally the legal rights of the parties in preparing for negotiation. Although many negotiations do not include lengthy legal arguments, the parties' evaluation of their respective rights can have a significant impact on the outcome. Robert Condlin writes that although explicit legal argumentation is

> common among novice negotiators, [it] is less prominent in negotiations between experienced lawyers who bargain with one another regularly (e.g., personal injury plaintiffs' lawyers and insurance company counsel, prosecutors and criminal defense lawyers). Perhaps this is because personal familiarity and common experiences give lawyers shared views about what law is settled and what evidence counts as persuasive, and enable them to play out arguments privately in their heads so that they need discuss only novel or controversial points openly.[7]

In dispute resolution negotiations, assessment of the parties' rights requires predicting the possible outcome if the case were to be tried in court. This includes evaluating the strengths and weaknesses of the parties' legal and factual theories (see Chart 24B). The lawyer for the party going forward (the plaintiff, the prosecutor, or the movant) should identify all possible claims for relief (or, in a

CHART 24B ASSESSMENT OF PARTIES' RIGHTS—DISPUTE

Analysis of Claims	**Plaintiff/Prosecutor**	**Defendant**
Legal Theory(ies)/ Defense(s) Strengths Weaknesses Factual Theory(ies) Strengths Weaknesses		
WHAT ADDITIONAL INFORMATION IS NEEDED TO REACH A DEAL? **WHO IS LIKELY TO PREVAIL?** **HOW CAN THE RIGHTS RELATIONSHIP BE CHANGED?**		

7. Robert J. Condlin, *"Cases on Both Sides": Patterns of Argument in Legal Dispute-Negotiation*, 44 Md. L. Rev. 65, 69 n.14 (1985).

criminal case, the range of charges) and the legal elements for each. The lawyer should then determine whether the evidence will establish a prima facie case (see Chapter 11). Finally, the lawyer should identify the possible legal remedies that would be available if the case is proved. (Sometimes, a plaintiff in a civil case will have a strong case establishing liability, but only be entitled to limited relief.)

The resisting lawyer (representing the defendant, for example) should consider whether any of the claims is based on an accurate understanding of the law. Then, the resisting lawyer should marshal the available evidence to determine whether the party asserting the claim can establish a prima facie case. Finally, the resisting lawyer should consider whether any affirmative defenses can defeat any of the claims and whether the evidence will establish the minimum facts to prove those defenses.

When considering legal theories in preparation for negotiation, be especially careful about burdens of production and persuasion. In litigation, the winner is the party who either carries all of her burdens or prevents an adversary from carrying all of his. The question is not whether a defendant is liable or guilty, but whether the evidence proves the claim or charge according to the applicable standard. And negotiation "in the shadow of the law" inevitably takes burdens into account. In a criminal case, for example, the prosecution's need to prove its case beyond a reasonable doubt has a substantial effect on the plea bargaining process. (Remember to evaluate not only the strength and weakness of each party's legal theory in the abstract, but also try to predict the probable rulings on these legal issues by the tribunal that will actually decide the case. See §20.3.1.)

In regard to factual theory, consider the persuasiveness of the parties' facts. Using the approach discussed in §§15.2–15.4, evaluate the credibility of each parties' sources of facts, contextual facts, and circumstantial evidence and assess the structural integrity of their stories. Then try to forecast, given the nature of your audience (the particular judge, hearing examiner, arbitrator, or jury), the ultimate judgment. (See §20.3.1 on how to predict damages.)

Rights assessment is also necessary in preparation for a transactional negotiation (see Chart 24C). Here, the inquiry is not about the possible outcome of the case at trial, but about legal requirements governing the transaction or the common business practices that create context for the deal. Many legal form books provide not only sample forms for similar deals but also relevant case law and statutory authority on these transactions. Although you should avoid using form books as the sole basis for your proposal, they can help to identify key legal issues. If you have not handled such a deal before, get copies of similar agreements from experienced lawyers. With the help of your client, investigate also the common business practices for such transactions, such as pricing, performance, and quality control standards. Certainly, you should not feel bound by the sample agreement in the form book or common business practices, but you need to understand that the other parties may be entering the negotiation presuming that these customs constitute their informal "rights."

Often, novice lawyers—out of fear that the negotiations will fail—will prematurely reach a deal with an opponent without learning crucial facts. Identify the information that is indispensable to your appraisal of the situation so that you can adequately prepare a negotiation strategy. In a transactional setting, obtain facts about industry customs, information about past dealings between the parties, and

CHART 24C ASSESSMENT OF PARTIES' RIGHTS—TRANSACTION

Rights	Client's Rights	Other Party's Rights
Statutory/Regulatory Requirements Common Business Practices for Transaction		
WHAT ADDITIONAL INFORMATION IS NEEDED TO REACH A DEAL? **WHAT EFFECT DO THESE RIGHTS HAVE ON THE TRANSACTION?** **HOW CAN THE LEGAL RELATIONSHIP BE CHANGED?**		

technical information about the products or services involved. In a dispute negotiation, examine your Chronology (see Chart 12B on page 163), and identify the missing witnesses, documents, and facts that are essential to a basic understanding of the events. (See Charts 24B and 24C.)

The rights context of most negotiations is not stagnant but can change drastically depending upon the legal maneuvering of the parties. You often have the ability to change the legal relationship of the parties before or during negotiation. In the dispute resolution context, for instance, you can add leverage by suing, making strategically sound motions, conducting extensive discovery, filing a counterclaim, or seeking sanctions for unreasonable conduct. Similar moves can be made in transactional negotiations. For example, in a commercial real estate sale where the price is deflated because of zoning restrictions on the property, the situation will be changed radically if the owner succeeds in getting a zoning variance. In preparing for your negotiation, you should identify those possible changes. (See Charts 24B and 24C.)

§24.4 ASSESSING THE PARTIES' POWER

Power is the ability to coerce someone to do something that person would not otherwise do (see §23.2.3). Assessing the parties' rights means examining how legal or other objective standards affect the parties' strengths and weaknesses. But assessing the power context explores how *nonlegal*, coercive factors do the same thing. Although, as we shall see, power differentials do not necessarily determine negotiation outcomes, they can have a significant impact on the bargaining process. In fact, several studies have shown that power symmetry rather than power imbalance is the most favorable condition for reaching agreement because the more powerful party's coercive tactics can often lead to resistance from the weaker party, suspicion of even its reasonable offers, and extreme threats by the less-powerful party to counter the stronger party's power plays.[8] In your preparation for a negotiation, therefore, you need to assess the potential effects of power imbalances.

§24.4.1 TYPES OF POWER

The primary sources of power in legal negotiations are economic, social, psychological, and political power, and expertise. (See Chart 24D.)

1. *Economic power.* Obviously, the ability of a party to bring its resources to bear on a transaction or dispute can impact the negotiation. When a large corporation negotiates to acquire a smaller, family-run business, for example, the acquiring company will probably have at its disposal a much greater staff of lawyers, accountants, and tax experts. Similarly, in a criminal case, the state can

CHART 24D ASSESSMENT OF PARTIES' POWER

<table>
<tr><th>Types of Power</th><th>Client's Power</th><th>Other Party's Power</th></tr>
<tr><td>1. Economic
2. Social
3. Psychological
4. Political
5. Expertise</td><td></td><td></td></tr>
<tr><td colspan="2">WHAT EFFECT DO THESE POWER RELATIONSHIPS HAVE ON THE TRANSACTION/ DISPUTE?

HOW CAN THE POWER RELATIONSHIP BE CHANGED?</td><td></td></tr>
</table>

8. Robert S. Adler & Elliot M. Silverstein, *When David Meets Goliath: Dealing with Power Differentials in Negotiations*, 5 Harv. Negot. L. Rev. 1, 16–18 (2000).

overwhelm many defendants with its cadre of assistant district attorneys, investigators, and expert witnesses. And in the labor-management context, the company, as owner of its facilities, has the right, within legal limits, to set the conditions of work for its employees. In many cases, the dynamic of the negotiation is driven by these types of power imbalance.

Nevertheless, parties with large resources may suffer from limitations on their power, and parties with ostensibly fewer resources may have access to other means of economic power. The large corporation seeking to acquire the smaller company may be involved in numerous other transactions and litigation and may be able to devote only limited staff to this deal. And the privately-owned company may have retained a small, boutique law firm that specializes in representing "underdogs" in such negotiations. Likewise, while the heavy caseload of many urban prosecutors may severely inhibit their ability to press all cases to the fullest extent possible, some white collar defendants may have the ability to retain legal "dream teams." And in labor-management negotiations, the employees may have an advantage if they are few in number, have highly specialized skills, and operate expensive and complicated machinery. The company may have invested heavily in equipment, and it may be cheaper to raise pay than to let that equipment lie idle while hard-to-replace workers are on strike.

2. *Social power.* Some transactions and disputes occur within a context where the parties can wield significant power within a given geographic, fraternal, religious, or similar community. For instance, suppose a young retailer has recently opened a business in a small town and negotiates a contract with a well-established and prominent wholesaler. Both parties certainly know the pressures that the wholesaler can exert on the retailer's business relationships in the town, on his position in the community, and on his family and personal life. Or, within some traditional religious communities, parties can apply pressure from religious authorities to attempt to influence negotiations on child custody and property distribution issues.[9] Even within the more cosmopolitan world of regulatory transactions and litigation, social power can play a role. Studies have shown, for instance, that because of the ongoing, day-to-day personal relationship between public utilities and their regulators' staffs, close and informal ties develop between them, often resulting in the companies having an undue influence over the process of regulatory negotiations.[10]

And differences in social status between the parties can create power imbalances in the bargaining process. A visit to a high-volume urban eviction or misdemeanor court will starkly reflect this problem. Court personnel and judges often treat the assistant district attorney assigned to a particular courtroom or a "regular" landlords' lawyer who consistently appears in a court with a deference

---

9. See, for example, *Fred Kaplan, Orthodox Jews Struggle with Divorce*, Boston Globe, May 3, 1998, at A-1, available in LEXIS, News Library, Globe File (describing problems created in civil divorce proceedings when Orthodox Jewish men refuse to give their wives religiously required divorces and the religious authorities side with the husbands).

10. David M. Welborn & Anthony E. Brown, *Regulatory Policy and Processes: The Public Service Commissions in Tennessee, Kentucky and Georgia* 66 (1980). See Stefan H. Krieger, *Problems for Captive Ratepayers in Nonunanimous Settlements of Public Utility Rate Cases*, 12 Yale J. on Reg. 257, 306–308 (1995).

that is not shown to low-income litigants or defendants of color. Indeed, in some of these courtrooms, African-American and Latino lawyers are often frequently mistaken by the regular lawyers or court personnel for one of the defendants. A defendant who does not speak English is at an even greater disadvantage in attempting to maneuver through the court process. In such an environment, social factors obviously influence negotiations.

3. *Psychological power.* All parties to a negotiation have certain psychological needs: desires, fears, anger, and other emotions (§24.2). And sometimes one or more of the parties try to exploit those needs in negotiations by wielding psychological power. In a child custody dispute, for example, one parent might threaten to poison the children's minds against the other unless the latter agrees to more liberal visitation terms. Likewise, in some landlord-tenant negotiations, the landlord might threaten to lock the tenant out of his apartment or disconnect the utility service, even though the landlord has no legal right to take such action. Threats like these can have profound effects on low-income tenants who do not know their rights—or on anybody who wants to live in his home in peace. Even in corporate bargaining, negotiators often attempt to play psychological games with their adversaries to obtain an advantage.

4. *Political power* is the ability to influence public officials, decision-makers, or opinion-makers. In high-profile civil rights, antitrust, or products liability cases, parties often attempt to enlist the support of government agencies or key media figures to influence the negotiations.

But even in less dramatic cases, parties can try to exert political power. Consider the *Ransom v. Dusak* case for example. On the one hand, the landlord might attempt to influence the political context by contacting friendly officials in the Department of Health to discourage the filing of any formal charges against him for the conditions at Ransom's apartment. On the other hand, Ransom might work with a community organization to organize the tenants to pressure Dusak to repair the property and to demand prompt action by the Health Department. She might also try to interest a local newspaper in her story. In either case, these political actions or threats of political action by the parties would certainly affect any negotiation of the dispute.

5. *Expertise.* In some negotiations one party has greater expertise on certain issues involved in the transaction or dispute, and that knowledge can result in a power imbalance. Moreover, the more information that a party has about a particular situation, the more likely that she will understand its context and will be able to make a quick decision even with limited resources.[11] Imagine, for instance, a company official with no computer background who is negotiating for the purchase of a software program for all his firm's accounts and records. Even if he educates himself on the basics of computer software, the salesperson will probably be at an advantage because of her superior knowledge about the product.

---

11. Adler & Silverstein, *supra* note 8, at 26.

This situation frequently arises with novice lawyers. Suppose you are negotiating with an experienced lawyer in a routine matter, such as a real estate closing or settlement of a divorce case, and your adversary says, "This is the way attorneys in this area always handle escrow accounts for real estate taxes that will become due," or "They may have taught you this in law school, but let me tell you, Judge Lavagetto won't even countenance a request for joint custody."

You may have carefully researched the law on the subject and spoken to other experienced practitioners about the issue and come to the conclusion that your adversary is dead wrong—but you might still have the nagging feeling that he knows what he is talking about. Your adversary may have nothing more than psychological power over you because your inexperience makes you insecure. But unless you are willing to stand up to your adversary, that psychological power can be intimidating.

6. *Moral power.* Even parties with limited economic or political resources may be able to exert power through appeals to fairness or morality. Day laborers negotiating with a town for the establishment of a hiring site, for example, may have very little political clout but might be successful by appealing to notions of basic human dignity and the right of every person to a job. Although moral power depends in large part on the ability of the more powerful party to empathize with the other side, it can carry a degree of sincerity that is lacking with other assertions of power.[12]

§24.4.2 SHIFTING THE POWER RELATIONSHIP

The power relationship between the parties is not static. You or the other party can take steps either before or during the negotiation to change the power balance. And those changes can significantly impact the course of the negotiations. In preparing for your negotiation, you should also identify those possible changes. (See Chart 24D.)

1. *Using the party's own power to affect the power balance.* Obviously, if one party in a negotiation has substantially more power in a particular area, the other party can either try to increase its power in the same area or develop power in some other area. For instance, a small company with limited resources locked in an antitrust dispute with a large manufacturer that has huge resources can increase its economic power by forging alliances with other small firms that are experiencing similar problems. Or a community organization challenging a powerful corporation's siting of a hazardous waste dump in a low-income neighborhood might attempt to reduce the power imbalance by using media pressure to influence government officials.

2. *Asserting rights to affect the power balance.* Often when a power imbalance exists between the parties to a dispute, the less powerful party can attempt to equalize the playing field by seeking rights-based relief. Litigation, for example,

---

12. *Id.* at 28.

can be used by less powerful parties to protect their interests against more powerful opponents.

The prime example of the use of adjudication for this purpose is a federal civil rights action against a school system alleging racial discrimination, in which the plaintiffs rely on the protections of the civil rights laws and the procedural protections of the federal courts to rectify the power imbalance between themselves and local government officials.

3. Reducing the perception of powerlessness. Some power imbalances are more perceived than real. Although the threats of a spouse in a child custody dispute or of a landlord against a low-income tenant may be empty, they may still cause your client to feel inordinate fear. Likewise, even though your experienced opponent may be completely wrong in his interpretation of the law or his understanding of how a particular judge handles a matter, you, as an inexperienced lawyer, may feel intimidated by his pressure.

A partial remedy is to change the perception of powerlessness. To address your client's fear, counsel her about the actual risks involved in the situation. Certainly, you do not want to downplay actual dangers. But, in many instances, your client will not have been involved previously with a similar transaction or dispute, and the client's fears will be unfounded. In a calm setting, describe to the client your experiences or those of your colleagues in comparable cases, lay out the advantages and disadvantages of different options, and then let the client decide (see §§21.2–21.3).

Psychological power plays—aimed at you, your client, or both of you—often occur in hallway negotiations just before trial or at the last minute before a deal closes. To alleviate the impact of this conduct, prepare your client for the contingency that it will happen, and, if it does occur, counsel your client in a private setting where you and the client can coolly reflect on the odds that the opponent will in fact exercise his power. And be prepared in advance for situations where more experienced lawyers might try to manipulate you because you are still a novice lawyer. If you come prepared with cases and statutes in support of your position or have consulted with other lawyers about the habits of a particular judge, you will be in a better position to resist. Moreover, you should consider the kind of impression you want to give the other attorney. Research suggests that the entire tone of a negotiation may be established through the parties' tones and gestures at the beginning of the discussions.[13] If you initially appear hesitant or tentative, a more experienced lawyer will likely try to take advantage of you. While false bravado will seem phoney, you will most likely set the right tone for the negotiation if you appear comfortable in the situation and are prepared to respond directly and confidently to the other attorney's arguments.

4. Using information to increase power. In some situations the other side initially has more power because it has access to more information. In an employment discrimination case, for example, much of the evidence about the company's personnel policies, its treatment of similar workers, and the personnel

13. *Id.* at 81–82.

records of the offending supervisor will be in the company's files. The plaintiff can level the playing field through the fact investigation process, by both formal discovery of the company's documents and informal interviews with knowledgeable third parties. (See §§16.3.1–16.3.5.) Even in cases in which both sides have equal access to information, you may be able to challenge a more powerful opponent effectively with exhaustive fact investigation. In a high-volume criminal courtroom, for example, the prosecutor may get deference from the judge and court personnel but probably will not have the resources to investigate thoroughly every case. A defense attorney whose investigation uncovers major holes in the prosecution's case may use that information to obtain strong leverage in plea bargaining. Finally, when confronted with an experienced attorney, a novice attorney often can equalize any power imbalance in a negotiation with an effective demonstration of her command of the facts in the case.

§24.5 OBTAINING YOUR CLIENT'S AUTHORITY

Now that you have assessed the interests, rights, and power of the different parties, you can start to develop a strategy for the negotiation. When engaging in this process, remember that your client has the ultimate authority to accept or reject a settlement or plea bargaining offer. As discussed in §23.5, under the ABA Model Rules of Professional Conduct, "[a] lawyer shall abide by a client's decision whether to settle a matter. In a criminal case, the lawyer shall abide by the client's decision, after consultation with the lawyer, as to a plea to be entered."[14] Thus, you are always obligated to inform your client of a settlement offer, even if you suspect that the client will reject it.[15]

Because the client has the ultimate authority in the negotiation process, you should consult with the client from the beginning of your preparation for the negotiation. Have the client identify the core of what she wants in this transaction or dispute and what would be "icing on the cake." As we see in Chapter 25, this process requires a determination of the client's Best Alternative To a Negotiated Agreement. Before the negotiation, ask the client to decide how much authority to settle she will give you. This process consists of counseling the client about her BATNA and exploring with her hypothetical settlement packages, the acceptability of these packages, and the possibility of other packages that are more or less favorable to her.[16] This, of course, is not a one-time process. As the negotiation proceeds, as you learn new information, as you receive offers from the other party, and as your client reevaluates her feelings about the transaction or dispute, your counseling will continue, and your client will determine whether to modify the authority she has given you.

Although your client has the ultimate authority to decide on any agreement, the type of authority your client gives you before and during the negotiation can

---

14. Model Rules of Professional Conduct Rule 1.2(a).
15. ABA Comm. on Prof'l Ethics, Formal Op. 326 (1970).
16. Paul R. Tremblay, *"Pre-Negotiation" Counseling: An Alternative Model*, 13 Clinical L. Rev. 541, 547–556 (2006).

vary greatly. Sometimes lawyers negotiate "without authority." You can say to the other party's lawyer, "I don't have authority to negotiate those particular type of terms," or "At this time, I don't have authority on anything," and then try to work out the most favorable deal to present to the client for approval. Often your clients will want you to take such an approach, telling you to see what you can get and asking you to report back to them. On the other hand, a desperate client might give you unlimited authority, saying to you, in effect, "Get me the best deal you can" and pre-authorizing you to accept it. In most instances, however, clients will give you limited authority, and you will continually consult with them for increased authority as the negotiation progresses.[17]

Two problems can arise from unlimited authority. One is that the client loses a lot of control over her own lawyer's conduct during the negotiation because the lawyer has not been asked to report back for approval at various stages during the negotiation. The other problem is that a lawyer negotiating with unlimited authority can more easily be swept up in the heat of negotiation. Reporting back to the client before the deal is closed provides an opportunity for reflection before making a commitment.

On the other hand, if you have no authority to settle, you might be able to brainstorm more openly and flexibly with the other side, unconfined by limits set in advance by your client. But when you have no authority to settle, your client may delay making a realistic assessment of her case and expect more from the negotiations than is possible. You might solve that problem before negotiating by explaining to the client the possible deals that might result, given the practicalities of the situation.

We suspect that most lawyers generally feel comfortable negotiating with limited authority, which encourages the client to assess the case seriously before negotiation and allows the client to keep control over the process. But there are disadvantages to limited authority, too. For example, social science studies show that lawyers with only limited authority are more likely to be more vigorous and tough in their use of competitive tactics than lawyers who have unlimited authority.[18]

The decision of how much authority you will be given is a strategic one and should fit the situation. What works well in one negotiation for one client might work badly in the next negotiation for another client.

§24.6 IS A STRUCTURED SETTLEMENT IN YOUR CLIENT'S INTEREST?

A structured settlement is an agreement in a damages case through which a defendant pays a plaintiff money over a period of time, usually years, rather than all at once.

Structured settlements can look like an easy way to find agreement. A defendant does not need to pay immediately all the money agreed to. And to a

---

17. Donald G. Gifford, *Legal Negotiation: Theory and Applications* 70 (1989).
18. *Id.*

plaintiff's lawyer who ignores the time value of money (see §20.3.2), agreeing to accept the money later seems like a small concession to facilitate agreement. But because of the time value of money, payments later are worth less than payments now. For example, when a plaintiff agrees to accept $600,000 over five years—the first $100,000 immediately and the rest in five future annual payments of $100,000 each—the plaintiff has actually agreed to accept a present value of $521,237 (if we assume an annual investment rate of return of six percent on the future money). Using the formula in §20.3.2, the present value of the five future $100,000 payments at 6% interest is $421,237. That plus the $100,000 to be paid immediately equals $521,237. In this calculation, there's a separate present value for each future payment:

payment	*future value*	*present value*
immediate	$100,000	$100,000
1 year	100,000	94,340
2 years	100,000	89,000
3 years	100,000	83,962
4 years	100,000	79,209
5 years	100,000	74,726
		total = 521,237

Looking at the deal from the defendant's point of view, if the defendant were to fund this obligation right now by paying $100,000 up front and investing enough to produce the $500,000 for future payments, that would cost the defendant $521,237 in today's money if the rate of return on the investment were 6%.

Some settlements, such as those for personal injury, are not taxable income to the plaintiff (see §2.2.11). But if the settlement would be taxed, the tax consequences could change the math above. A lump sum payment of the entire settlement at once could push the plaintiff into a higher tax bracket in the year it's paid. But if the settlement is structured into smaller payments over several years, those payments—because they're smaller—might be less likely to move the plaintiff into a higher tax bracket in those years. The plaintiff might thus owe less total tax under a structured settlement than with a lump sum payment. This could be more meaningful to a plaintiff with a small income, who starts off in a low tax bracket, than it would to a well-off plaintiff, who might already be in the top tax bracket before receiving any settlement money. You would need to compute the tax consequences for the structured settlement you're considering and compare them to the tax consequences of a lump sum payment.

As a threshold matter, if there is a structured settlement, the plaintiff's lawyer should insist that the defendant's ability to make future payments be guaranteed through the defendant's purchase of a funding vehicle like an annuity. Without such protection, a defendant could go bankrupt or disappear, leaving the plaintiff without the future payments she was promised.

A structured settlement can make sense on the plaintiff's side where the money is not needed immediately or where the plaintiff might lack the financial skills to keep it intact for future needs. And where the lawsuit is over injuries suffered by a child, a structured settlement may be necessary to guarantee that the money is not squandered by the adults responsible for the child. But a plaintiff's lawyer should compute the present value of any proposed structured settlement before agreeing to it. What the plaintiff would really be getting is the present value, not the total of all future payments (which are reduced by the time value of money). If the defendant were to offer the present value as an immediate and total payment, would that be enough to satisfy the plaintiff? If the money is not needed right away, there's no real difference between the defendant buying an annuity for the plaintiff (a structured settlement) and the defendant paying the present value immediately so the plaintiff can invest it on her own. The cost to the defendant is the same in both instances, and it's identical to the present value of the structured settlement. If the present value is not enough to satisfy the plaintiff, it's inadequate no matter how it's paid.

A structured settlement is an extremely complicated arrangement. If you are about to participate in a negotiation where a structured settlement might be proposed, you should spend some time in the library with books or other materials designed to show practitioners how to handle structured settlements. Do that regardless of whether your client is the plaintiff or defendant.

CHAPTER

25

DEVELOPING A NEGOTIATION STRATEGY

§25.1 DETERMINING YOUR CLIENT'S BATNA

The first step in developing a negotiation strategy is to identify your client's BATNA or Best Alternative To a Negotiated Agreement (see §23.3.2).

> Your BATNA is your walkaway alternative. It's your best course of action for satisfying your interests without the other's agreement. If you're negotiating with your boss over a raise, your BATNA might be to find a job with another firm. If you're negotiating with a salesperson, your BATNA might be to talk to the store manager or, if that fails, you might go to another store. If one nation is negotiating with another over unfair trade practices, its BATNA might be to appeal to the appropriate international tribunal [or impose a tariff].[1]

Determining the client's BATNA is valuable whichever approach you eventually use in the negotiation—adversarial, problem solving, or a combination of both.

Only after your client has identified her BATNA should she translate it into a bottom line, the minimum amount she would accept rather than pursue her BATNA. Identification of a bottom line prior to the exploration of different

1. William Ury, *Getting Past No: Negotiating Your Way from Confrontation to Cooperation* 21–22 (1993).

BATNA's has several disadvantages.[2] First, premature identification of bottom lines reduces the potential for problem-solving negotiation. By focusing too early on a fixed preconception of what outcome is acceptable, it ignores the possibility of unforeseen solutions that might develop during the negotiation.[3] If, for example, a client in a contract negotiation initially focuses solely on a monetary bottom line, she may overlook the possibility of other nonmonetary options for addressing her interests. By holding off on the identification of a bottom line at least until the client has considered her BATNA and perhaps until negotiations have begun, you leave open the possibility of productive problem-solving brainstorming.

Second, bottom lines are sometimes set too high. At the beginning of the negotiation process, your client's expectations may be unrealistic. But once they are crystallized into a bottom line, those expectations become a position that is hard to abandon even when it turns out later to be unrealistic. The converse can also be true. In some circumstances the bottom line may be too low, but because it is a position, the client might abandon it only reluctantly.

To determine your client's BATNA, you and your client should review your assessments of the parties' interests, rights, and power (Charts 24A, 24B, 24C, and 24D). From these assessments, generate options by identifying the possible alternatives to a negotiated settlement. From your interests assessment, consider the alternatives that your client can undertake herself to pursue her interests outside of any relationship with the other party. Then, from the rights assessments, identify what rights the client can assert before a court, agency, or arbitrator to address her interests. Finally, from the powers assessment, consider alternative ways that your client can wield power to coerce the other side into meeting her interests.

Assume, for example, that you represent an electric utility that is negotiating for an easement to install a high-voltage transmission line over some farmland. In reviewing its interests, your client might develop a number of possible alternatives to negotiation that it can pursue without any relationship with the property owner: obtaining an easement on other, nearby property; purchasing other property in the area for the installation of the line; enlarging an existing line; or abandoning plans altogether for the new installation. In reviewing its rights, your client might identify still another option: an eminent domain proceeding to obtain a condemnation order allowing an easement on the property. And in reviewing its power, your client might consider the possibility of raising its electric rates to the property owner (because of the extra cost of service) to force the granting of the easement.

Or consider a negotiation in the *Ransom v. Dusak* case. Assume you are counseling Ransom. After reviewing her interests, you might identify several alternatives to negotiation: repairing the conditions herself, moving out of the apartment, or just giving up. Turning to her rights, you might determine that Ransom has other options: withholding her rent and raising the inadequate conditions as a defense in an eviction action, filing an affirmative case against Dusak for breach of the warranty of habitability, or bringing a class action against

2. See Robert H. Mnookin et al., *Beyond Winning: Negotiating to Create Value in Deals and Disputes* 20 (2000).

3. Roger Fisher et al., *Getting to Yes: Negotiating Agreement Without Giving In* 98–99 (2d ed. 1991).

him on behalf of all the tenants in the building. And, finally, considering her power, you might develop even more options, such as persuading the Health Department to prosecute Dusak for his failure to maintain the premises or organizing the tenants to pressure him to sell the building.

After identifying possible alternatives to negotiation, you and your client should evaluate each of them to determine one or two BATNA's. You and the client should try to imagine the potential consequences of each option and consider its advantages and disadvantages. Although there is no simple formula for this evaluation, the client should consider: (1) whether a particular option meets those interests the client considers to be top priorities, (2) the strengths and weaknesses of the different parties' legal and factual theories, and (3) any power imbalance in the relationship with the other side.

In the utility easement hypothetical, for instance, where your client's primary interest is minimizing costs, the utility will need to consider the potential expense of obtaining an easement from other property owners in the area, the costs of enlarging existing lines, the financial necessity for an easement on this particular property, the costs (and risks) of eminent domain litigation, and the dangers of trying to impose increased rates on the property owner. And, in *Ransom v. Dusak*, if Ransom's principal interest is peace of mind and the safety of her children, she will need to weigh seriously the psychological pressures and time delays inherent in rights-based or power-based alternatives to negotiation.

Identification of a BATNA serves several functions. First, it helps your client decide whether to negotiate. If, for example, your rights-based BATNA is very strong and the client has little interest in any compromise, trial may be better than negotiating.

Second, a BATNA sets a standard by which to measure settlement proposals. If the client's BATNA is a very strong legal case which she is willing and financially able to pursue, she will probably reject an offer that does not address most of her interests adequately. If, on the other hand, the BATNA is a difficult defense of a lawsuit, the adjudication of which will strain the client's limited finances, she will be more likely to accept that very same offer.

Finally, as you will see in §25.3, the process of identifying a BATNA helps you select the most effective overall approach to the negotiation.

§25.2 DETERMINING THE OTHER PARTY'S BATNA

After identifying your client's BATNA, go further and try to predict the other side's BATNA. Reviewing the assessment of the other party's interests, rights, and power, you and your client should imagine the other side's alternatives to negotiation. Then, weighing these options in light of their imagined priority interests, try to identify the one or two that would best accomplish the other side's goals. By comparing your client's BATNA with the other side's BATNA, you get a good sense of the settlement range and the probability of achieving a negotiated agreement.

§25.3 SELECTING AN APPROACH TO THE NEGOTIATION

As you know by now, a lawyer using an adversarial approach to negotiation views what is happening as a conflict over distribution of limited resources and tries to persuade the other side to concede that the adversarial lawyer's client is entitled to the maximum gain. A lawyer using a problem-solving approach tries to integrate the resources of each side to reach a settlement or deal and works with the other party to develop mutual agreements. Often a lawyer will use both types of approaches in the same negotiation (see §23.3.3). In preparation for a negotiation, determine the most effective approach or approaches for the situation in which you find yourself. Most of what you do and say while negotiating will depend on the approach you have selected.

The approach you take will depend, in large part, on the kind of authority the client has given you and the BATNA she has identified. Many proponents of problem-solving negotiation assert that almost all transactions and disputes are not zero-sum games, and they argue for the use of such an approach in most negotiations. "While there may be some paradigmatic zero-sum games in legal negotiations," one scholar asserts, "most are not zero-sum. For example, in a random search of 240 cases taken from 15 federal and state reporters most cases, in terms presented to the court, were not zero-sum disputes. . . . Child custody can become joint custody, zoning cases permit variances, and bankruptcy can become financial reorganization."[4]

Although this might be admirable theory, it ignores the fact that the client has the ultimate authority to accept or reject a proposal. Thus, even if the most efficient and reasonable solution to a child custody dispute might be a joint custody agreement, if your client insists on sole custody, a problem-solving approach to negotiation will probably not be useful in addressing her interests. You, of course, can counsel your client as to the benefits of a joint custody arrangement and warn her of the disadvantages of relying on a court proceeding as her BATNA, but the client does have the final say—and, in the end, a court case might be right for her needs, even if we would rather she chose otherwise.

In determining the approach to take, consider the following factors:

1. ***Integrative versus distributive aspects of the transaction or dispute.*** While a problem-solving approach works better when there is good potential for joint gain, an adversarial approach works better when distributive issues predominate. To choose between them, consider the "Highest Priorities" section of your interests assessments chart (Chart 24A) and determine whether any viable solutions are suggested by these priorities that would be mutually acceptable to both parties. In a negotiation for the commercial sale of goods, for example, if the parties care about price more than anything else, an adversarial approach probably will protect each party's interests better because distributive issues predominate. But in a negotiation to create a joint venture, many common interests may exist

---

4. Carrie Menkel-Meadow, *Toward Another View of Legal Negotiation: The Structure of Problem Solving*, 31 UCLA L. Rev. 754, 785 (1984).

that allow for a problem-solving approach; the joint venture will fail if the parties do not develop a sound relationship.

2. ***Relationship interests versus one-shot deal.*** If your interests assessment reflects important relationship interests between the parties, a problem-solving approach may be strongly warranted because positional bargaining can be highly disruptive to relationships. In situations where an ongoing relationship exists between the parties—for example, labor and management, tenant and landlord, spouses, merchants who engage in frequent transactions—an adversarial approach has the potential for adversely affecting that relationship. "Even if you win the battle, you may lose the war. In the process you may destroy your relationship with the other side. And they will often find a way to renege or retaliate the next time they are in a position of power."[5] In contrast, if the dispute or transaction is a "one-shot" deal with a party with whom your client has little or no relationship—and anticipates none in the future—the interest of maintaining the relationship does not predominate and the problem-solving approach is not so strongly indicated. You might, of course, still want to use a problem-solving approach for other reasons—for example, if your client wants to minimize the costs of litigating a dispute.

3. ***Impact of psychological and reputational interests.*** In some negotiations, if your client's psychological or reputational interests matter most, they will dictate the approach you take in bargaining. If, for example, you represent a criminal defendant who is afraid of the effect of a lengthy trial on his family, you may opt for a problem-solving approach even if you believe you can achieve the maximum gain for your client using adversarial methods. Or, if in an action alleging a Clean Air Act violation, in which you represent a defendant company that believes the plaintiffs are unfairly attacking its environmental record and that wants to vindicate its reputation, you may choose an adversarial approach even if your evaluation of the different interests suggests possible integrative solutions.

4. ***Strength or weaknesses of the rights-based or power-based BATNA's.*** Your approach to negotiation may be significantly affected by the strength or weakness of your rights-based or power-based BATNA's. On the one hand, if your client has a strong legal claim or power resources that could coerce the other side into submission, an adversarial approach may be warranted. Unless your client can realize maximum gain from the negotiation, she probably should resort to her BATNA. On the other hand, if her legal claims are more tenuous and you are litigating before a hostile judge or agency or the power balance tips in your opponent's favor, a problem-solving approach may be advisable.

5. ***Importance of a definitive ruling.*** In some disputes one or both of the parties might need a definitive ruling on a particular legal issue. In certain

---

5. Ury, *supra* note 1, at 132 ("[as] the great Chinese strategist Sun Tzu wrote, "To win one hundred victories in one hundred battles is not the acme of skill. To subdue the enemy without fighting is the acme of skill").

constitutional, civil rights, environmental, or other "public interest" litigation, the plaintiff may have a strong interest in attaining a clear vindication of its rights either through a ruling from the court or agency or through a consent decree or other agreement under which the defendant acknowledges some liability. Likewise, in an intellectual property dispute, the plaintiff may want to demonstrate clearly its right to a patent or copyright. In such cases, even though a problem-solving approach might efficiently resolve the dispute, the plaintiff's lawyer may want to adopt an adversarial approach to achieve the maximum gain in the negotiation: an admission of wrongdoing by the defendant.

Consider three cautions about these factors. First, they are merely guidelines to suggest ways of selecting your approach to negotiation; they are not mechanical rules. In some cases, for example, where your client wants a definitive ruling, you may select a problem-solving approach because other overriding client interests, such as maintaining a good relationship with the other side, suggest that an adversarial approach is not warranted. Second, in some if not most cases, different issues in the negotiation will be more amenable to one approach than to another. Third, you may find that your initial approach simply does not work with the other side. Be prepared to adapt your strategy to the negotiation behavior of the other party.

§25.4 CRAFTING A PLAN: ADVERSARIAL APPROACH

In a negotiation in which you have chosen to take an adversarial approach, or for those issues in a particular negotiation for which you have selected that approach, your goal is to maximize your client's gain and minimize your client's loss. To accomplish this goal, you engage in an exchange of offers and counter-offers with the other side until you either reach an impasse or agreement. Along the way, you attempt to persuade the other party to make concessions based on different arguments, threats, warnings, or appeals. On a very basic level, this is not very different from the everyday dickering on a New York street corner between a vendor and a tourist:

Vendor: It sure looks like it's going to rain. These umbrellas are a great buy for $15.00!

Tourist: I saw them on sale at my local Walmart in Tulsa for $5.00 a piece. Fifteen dollars is a rip-off. I'll only pay $7.50.

Vendor: Come on, you know as well as I that a Walmart umbrella would fall to pieces in one wind gust. These umbrellas are high-quality. They have a special patented lining to protect against wind gusts. But, I like you; I once had a good friend from Tulsa. For you today, I'll give you one for $12.50.

Tourist: You have to be kidding! There's no difference between one umbrella and another. I bet you think I'm some sort of hick. In fact, I can go into Macy's basement right now, and I'm sure I can get one for much less than $12.50. [*walking away*] Bottom line, I'll give you $9.00.

Vendor: Wait a second! Do you want to stand in line at Macy's for an hour and then end up paying $20.00. Listen. I need to make a living too; I have a family to support. Did you hear that thunder? OK, for you today, I'll give it to you for $11.00.

Tourist: [*with raindrops falling on his head*] $10.00 and that's it.

Vendor: [*grumbling*] I'm making nothing on this sale, but I'll give it to you for $10.00.

The street vendor and tourist probably did very little, if any, planning for their bargaining. You, on the other hand, will be negotiating for much more than an umbrella. Adversarial exchanges in important matters require serious preparation, including the creation by you and your client of a game plan for the exchange. This plan should identify several key positions in the exchange: (1) the opening offer; (2) the bottom line; (3) the target point (the position on the continuum of offers and counteroffers where you imagine the parties will agree); and (4) concession points (the moves you might make between the opening offer and your bottom line.[6] Section 25.1 warned against premature identification of a bottom line and advised that you initially look for a BATNA instead. Once you decide to take an adversarial approach, however, the identification of a bottom line is essential to effective planning. But counsel your client that circumstances might change, and that she should not become entrenched with that position.

To understand such a plan, consider a simple automobile accident personal injury case in which the plaintiff seeks a judgment of $150,000, and the insurer denies any liability. After meeting with its lawyer and considering the circumstances of the case, the insurer prepares the game plan graphed in Chart 25A.[7] Although we graphed this game plan in terms of dollar amounts, the same format can be used when the controversy is not about money. In a plea bargaining situation, for example, the parties might graph a continuum of different sentences, or, if the defendant has been charged with many crimes, the parties might chart the range of offenses from the major one to all the lesser included ones. Or, in the *Ransom v. Dusak* case, they might graph both monetary and nonmonetary positions, including not only compensation for Ransom, but also different repairs and the time when they will be completed.

After drawing up your own range of positions, graph your prediction of positions the other side will take. The insurer's lawyer, for example, might develop the diagram in Chart 25B. From this diagram, the insurer's lawyer can estimate a settlement range of $50,000 (the plaintiff's bottom line) to $85,000 (his client's bottom line). His goal in the negotiation will be to convince the plaintiff to concede

---

6. Robert M. Bastress & Joseph D. Harbaugh, *Interviewing, Counseling, and Negotiating: Skills for Effective Representation* 475 (1990).
7. Similar graphs appear in *id*. at 476–477 and Thomas F. Guernsey, *A Practical Guide to Negotiation* 2 (1996).

CHART 25A YOUR OWN BARGAINING RANGE

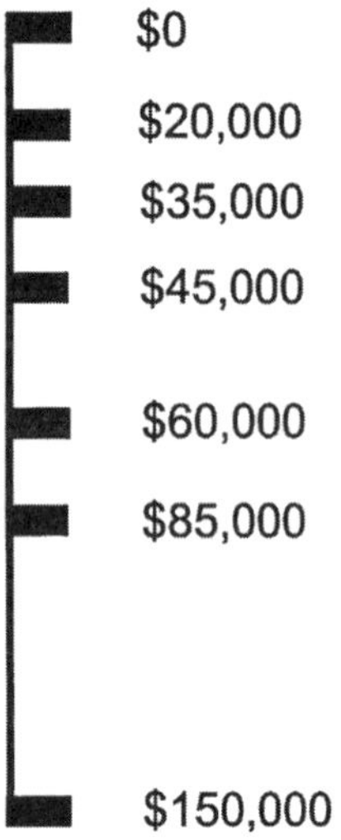

CHART 25B BOTH PARTIES' BARGAINING RANGE

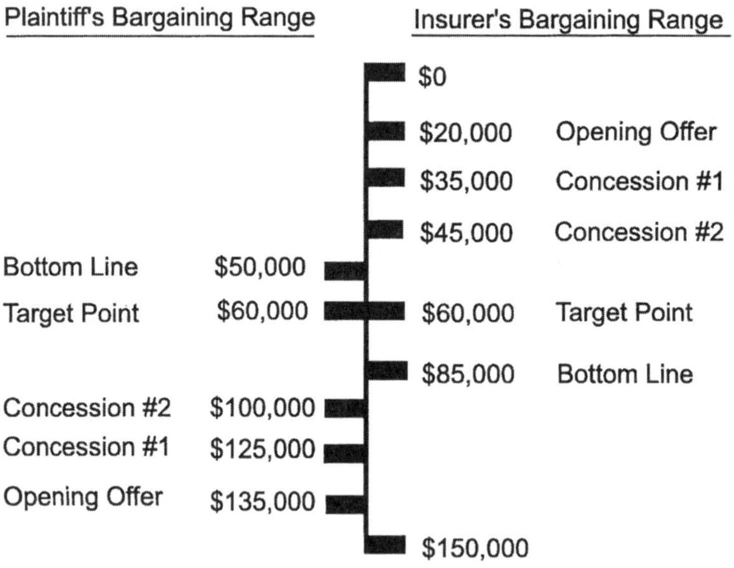

all the way to her bottom line and to fend off the attempts of the plaintiff's lawyer to force the insurance company to its bottom line. Most of the time, your predictions of the other party's positions will not be completely accurate. This process helps, however, to give you and your client a rough estimate of the relationship between the other side's bargaining range and yours.

Although these ranges, by their very nature, are merely estimates, do not pull them out of a hat. You and your client should return to your assessment charts (Charts 24A, 24B, 24C, and 24D) and evaluate your client's and the other party's positions in light of each parties' interests, rights, and power. In the personal injury hypothetical, the insurer's lawyer will certainly consider the strengths and weaknesses of each party's case in terms of both legal and factual theory. But he will also want to examine the interests and power of the plaintiff and its effect on her bargaining range. If the plaintiff is strapped for funds, for example, or at the deposition appeared very reluctant to proceed with the case, these facts will certainly affect the estimate the insurer's lawyer makes of the plaintiff's bottom line. Additionally, he might want to consider his own client's economic and financial interests in developing its bottom line and concession points.

Evaluating interests, rights, and power in terms of the parties' respective bargaining ranges will also help you develop arguments, threats, warnings, and appeals to convince the other side to make concessions. In order to elicit concessions from the other side, you must demonstrate that your offer is better than its BATNA. The process of estimating these ranges helps you to develop ways of causing the other side to make concessions and to know when you should make concessions (see §27.1.4).

Finally, in making these estimates, your client needs to consider the time value of money (see §20.3.2) and the transaction costs of a trial. Even if the recovery at trial is the same as the settlement amount, a dollar now is worth more than a dollar after trial and possible appeal. Attorneys' fees and litigation expenses decrease even further the future value of an eventual award at trial.

§25.5 CRAFTING A PLAN: PROBLEM-SOLVING APPROACH

§25.5.1 THE BRAINSTORMING PROCESS

When you decide to take a problem-solving approach, your goal is to find solutions that will integrate the resources of both sides or to increase the resources available so that a mutually agreeable solution is more likely. You and your client should consider the priorities of each party's interests (Chart 24B) and explore any possible solutions suggested by these priorities. Unlike the adversarial approach, where you concentrate on maximizing the interests of your client and consider the most obvious distributive options, here you try to broaden the number of options for settlement beyond obvious issues of dividing a fixed pie. You attempt to "create value" by considering ways of reaching a deal that makes both parties better off without making the other party worse off.[8]

Problem-solving negotiation then requires brainstorming the sources of value to each party beyond the most obvious. While there are numerous methods for engaging in this process, here are a few suggestions.

1. ***Consider differences between the parties.*** Focusing on different interests of the parties may actually be a better basis for problem-solving negotiation than concentrating solely on similarity of interests.

> The notion that differences can create value is counter-intuitive to many negotiators, who believe that they can reach agreement only by finding common ground. But the truth is that differences are often more useful than similarities in helping parties reach a deal. Differences set the stage for possible gains from trade, and it is through trades that value is most commonly created.[9]

The different resources of the parties, for example, may become the basis for a negotiated solution. In a commercial leasing transaction where the property needs a major renovation, the landlord is strapped for cash, and the potential tenant, an excellent handyman, is worried about whether a profit can be made within the first year, a potential solution might be a reduced rent for the first year, in exchange for which the tenant will repair the property. The different time preferences of the parties may also provide the foundation for a settlement. In a personal injury case, for instance, the plaintiff may need money for medical and rehabilitation expenses in the future, and the uninsured defendant may need to limit his short-term expenditures. With an adversarial approach, the parties simply try to reach an agreement as to the amount of a lump-sum recovery. Under a problem-solving approach, the parties might agree on a structured settlement, paid over time, that might meet the needs of both parties. Likewise, the parties' different risk preferences or valuation of the goods in question might create opportunities for a solution.

2. ***Concentrate on noncompetitive similarities between the parties.*** In some cases, parties share similar, noncompeting interests so that one party's gain does not mean the other party's loss. In an acrimonious divorce case, for example, the parties may disagree about almost every issue but both are very concerned about the well-being of their children. That shared and high priority interest might form the basis for an overall settlement. In fact, the parties may be willing to compromise on many other very contentious issues for the sake of their children.

3. ***Focus on ways to expand existing resources.*** In developing different solutions, look beyond the resources of the parties and ask yourself whether there are ways of creating resources elsewhere. One commentator tells the story, for example, of a large antitrust case against drug manufacturers in which a subgroup

---

8. The following discussion of methods for creating value is based in part on Mnookin et al., *supra* note 2, at 12–17.

9. *Id.* at 14 (footnote omitted).

of plaintiff drug wholesalers and retailers rejected as inadequate the $3 million allocated to them of the $100 million total settlement. Because of time and other logistic constraints, the settlement terms could not be modified, and it appeared that the deal was a failure. The parties developed a solution, however, under which the drug manufacturers placed a large portion of the total settlement in a bank account for one year in trust for the plaintiffs. After that year, the trust account accrued interest, and the protesting drug wholesalers and retailers were able to take a larger award. The bank provided the mechanism for augmenting the resources available to the parties.[10] By considering expansion of resources, the negotiation becomes less of a zero-sum game.

To plan for a problem-solving negotiation, encourage your client to break out of the tendency to view the issues as a simple distributive problem. Ask the client to help you brainstorm other solutions. For example, in representing the buyer in a negotiation for the sale of a house, ask her, "If the seller won't decrease the price, is there anything else he can do that would make you willing to pay that amount?" Another way of increasing the range of options is to enlist the assistance of an expert. Accountants and other financial consultants, for example, can be helpful in devising methods for organizing a settlement or transaction to meet the interests of both parties.

§25.5.2 A CASE STUDY OF THE BRAINSTORMING PROCESS

Consider a concrete example of how to plan an actual case:

Ms. Cassini, a registered nurse, established a group home for people with AIDS in a predominantly African-American neighborhood in the City of Wincliffe. She became interested in this patient population through her nursing practice at a large metropolitan hospital. She rented the house from a local landlord and received funding from the state Department of Social Services for each of the residents at the facility. Cassini chose this neighborhood because of the low rent and because several of the residents originally grew up in the area. Six to eight people lived in the home at any one time, and a nurse or other health attendant was always on duty. The residents shared housekeeping responsibilities, ate their meals together, and spent their spare time in common social activities.

Neighbors around the home became very distressed by its existence. They felt that the city had dumped group homes in their neighborhood. (Just around the block from Cassini's facility was a group home for people with muscular dystrophy.) In fact, they felt that the city discriminated against them because they were African-American, and that it had neglected their area in a number of ways: the schools were some of the worst in the city, services were substandard, and complaints about these conditions were largely ignored. The neighbors feared that their children would come into contact with residents at Cassini's facility, that visitors to the home would congest the streets, and that, because of the number of people living in and visiting the home, the noise level at night would be intolerable.

---

10. Menkel-Meadow, *supra* note 4, at 810.

The neighbors complained to local politicians, who talked to city officials. The city investigated the matter and discovered that its own sanitation workers were also concerned about possible contamination from handling refuse from the home. In response to these complaints and under pressure from the local politicians, the city brought two misdemeanor charges against Cassini for violation of the city's zoning ordinance, which allowed only single-family homes in the area where she operated her facility. If convicted, Cassini was subject to six-months imprisonment and a $1,000 fine for each of the charges.

Ms. Cassini came to a law school clinic, which agreed to represent her. Clinic students investigated the facts and law and decided to file a complaint with the United States Department of Housing and Urban Development (HUD) against the city, arguing that the city's actions constituted discrimination against the handicapped residents of the home in violation of the federal Fair Housing Act.[11]

At this point, the students began to prepare for negotiations with the City Attorney. They met with Cassini and asked her about her interests in the case. She said that she wanted to keep running the home for people with AIDS; that she wanted an apology from the city and the neighbors for the way they treated her; that she was worried about a possible jail sentence and criminal record; and that she wanted the confidentiality for the residents of the facility protected. Although she initially expressed a strong conviction about pressing the case to trial, she eventually broke down crying and said that she just wanted the case to go away.

After the arraignment, the City Attorney told the Clinic students that the city felt obligated to enforce the zoning ordinance and wanted to protect its citizens and sanitation workers from contamination. The City Attorney confided "off the record" that he was under pressure from local politicians to push this case to trial as soon as possible. While he acknowledged that the city was concerned about the HUD investigation and that case precedents were against the city, the students got the sense that the city was equally concerned about complaints from the neighbors that the city was discriminating against African-Americans.

After identifying the interests of the parties, the students, jointly with Cassini, prioritized these interests. For Cassini, they decided that her primary concerns were (1) avoiding a conviction, (2) continuing to maintain a group home for people with AIDS, and (3) restoring her peace of mind. For the city, they guessed that its principal interests were (1) safety of its citizens and workers and (2) risk avoidance (avoiding negative responses from both the neighbors and HUD). Finally, the students decided to identify the interests of the neighbors, even though they were not parties to the case, both because of the pressure they had brought against the city and because of the ongoing relationship they had with Cassini. The students speculated that the neighbors' interests included safety and noise conditions in their area and better treatment of their neighborhood by city officials.

Based on their assessment of these priorities, the students decided to take a problem-solving approach in the plea bargaining. Cassini wanted peace of mind, and to build a good relationship with the neighbors, and the city was risk averse. Perhaps there were ways of integrating the interests of the parties into a solution.

11. See 42 U.S.C. §3604.

The students found that the listing of interests suggested a number of possible options besides the obvious ones, which were conviction of Cassini or dismissal of the charges and a positive ruling from HUD. One possible option was the city's cooperation in helping Cassini find a new location for her facility in an area with fewer group homes. That would allow Cassini to continue her work, and would give her some peace of mind by ending the criminal case and her contact with the neighbors. The city would be relieved of the political pressures, although new problems might be created with the people who lived near the new home, and the fears of the sanitation workers would not be alleviated.

A second possibility was a program to educate the neighbors and sanitation workers about the negligible dangers of contamination with AIDS and to develop a cooperative relationship between the home and the neighbors to avoid safety and noise problems. This option would permit Cassini to keep the home at its present location. It addressed, to some extent, the concerns of the neighbors, and, if it were to satisfy the neighbors, it would also satisfy one of the city's primary interests.

A final option was an expansion of city services (garbage collection, road repair, police surveillance) in the neighborhood. If the neighbors felt that there actually could be benefits from the existence of the group home, they might be less concerned about the existence of such facilities in the area.

Obviously, there were drawbacks with each of these options. The city, for example, might reject any relocation option or the cost of any additional neighborhood services. The neighbors, even with an educational program, might have irrational fears about people with AIDS. The purpose of this planning process, however, is not to develop absolutely acceptable solutions. It is to open the door to the other side so that the two sides can continue brainstorming to find mutually agreeable solutions (see §27.2.2). Just as the adversarial planning method attempts to guess at the responses of the other party and to lay a foundation for a future exchange of offers, this process tries to speculate about the interests of the other parties to establish a basis for future brainstorming.

§25.6 INFORMATION GATHERING, DISCLOSING, AND CONCEALING

Whether you are planning an adversarial approach, a problem-solving approach, or a combination of the two, you need to prepare for "information bargaining." A negotiation involves not only an exchange of offers and counteroffers or brainstorming of possible solutions, but also attempts by each party to learn more information from the other. Bargaining is as much a learning experience as a contest.[12] With this information, each party can readjust its concession strategy in adversarial bargaining or its brainstorming approach in problem-solving negotiation. To prepare, identify: (1) information you want to obtain from

---

12. Robert J. Condlin, *"Every Day and in Every Way We Are All Becoming Meta and Meta" or How Communitarian Bargaining Theory Conquered the World (of Bargaining Theory)*, 23 Ohio St. J. on Disp. Resol. 231, 244 (2008) (observing that "[n]ot all bargainers start with a complete understanding of the issues in a controversy, or access to all of the relevant data. . . . As a consequence, even highly skilled bargainers change their minds about what cases are worth.").

the other party so you can understand its bargaining stance; (2) information you want to disclose voluntarily to the other party to facilitate your overall plan; and (3) information you want to conceal that might weaken your negotiation posture. The next few pages explain how to identify information in each of these categories. We later describe techniques to use during the negotiation to elicit or conceal this information (see §28.1).

1. Gathering information. Remember that the negotiation process itself is by no means the only vehicle for gathering information about the other side's position or interests in the dispute or transaction. Significant information can be obtained through your client, third parties, the Internet, library research, public records, and, in the dispute context, formal discovery. (See §§16.3.1–16.3.5.) In a negotiation for a sale of a business, for example, if the seller had previously engaged in failed negotiations with another potential buyer, that party might be an important source of information for the new buyer about the seller's "bottom line." Likewise, in a medical malpractice suit, the defendant's lawyer may be able to discover much more about the plaintiff's interests in the case at a deposition than might be learned during settlement talks. In other words, before relying on the bargaining process as a means to gather information, try to develop other sources of proof.

In adversarial negotiations, the most important information you need is the other party's bottom line. For that very reason, most opponents will not disclose that information. Your goal, then, is to gather as much circumstantial evidence as possible about the other party's assessment of the transaction or dispute so that you can better estimate its bottom line. Start with your interests assessment of the case and identify what particular interests of the other party might affect its determination of a bargaining range. You might want to explore, for example, the other side's psychological or reputational interests in a lawsuit or its concerns about the transaction costs of the case.

Then, examining your rights assessment of the case, identify both the issues about which your position is strong and the ones in which your position is weak. By obtaining information about the other side's views on these issues, you will learn whether or not its assessment coincides with yours and how it evaluates the merits of its position.

Finally, in regard to your power assessment of the case, consider the types of potential power the other side might wield and how the likelihood of the exercise of that power would affect that party's bottom line. In most cases, you obviously do not want to ask the other side directly if it will exercise a particular form of power if bargaining fails. But if the other side threatens the exercise of that power, you probably will want to gather information to determine whether it is bluffing or is serious.

In problem-solving bargaining, the types of information you want to obtain flow from your interests assessment of the case. Consider the priority interests you have predicted for the other side that lead to the integrative solutions you have brainstormed. In the negotiations, you will want to gather information to confirm whether or not those forecasts are correct. In the group home case, for instance, the students predicted that one of the city's interests would be to avert the risks of a Fair Housing Act enforcement proceeding and brainstormed a possible solution to meet that interest (that the city help Cassini find a new location for her facilities). In the negotiation process, the students would want to explore whether the city in fact was so worried that it would help Cassini relocate.

2. Disclosing information. The process of identifying information that you should disclose during the negotiation requires an analysis converse to the one you used in regard to the information you want to gather from the other side. Thus, in an adversarial negotiation, you want to disclose information that will apprise the other side of facts showing a strong bottom line for your client: that your client's interests support few concessions in bargaining, that your legal and factual theories are convincing, and that you will use power alternatives if negotiations fail. And, in problem-solving negotiations, you will want to reveal information about your client's interests that will facilitate a solution that will integrate both parties' concerns. Indeed, in some cases, your open disclosure of information can reduce the transaction costs for fact investigation and help to neutralize your opponent's adversarial bargaining stance.[13] In any case, however, your disclosure must be limited by tactical considerations (it must be credible or it will not persuade) and ethical constraints (it must be permitted by the rules of professional responsibility; see §23.5).

3. Concealing information. Although many lawyers consider the concealment of damaging information an absolute rule of negotiation, it is better to think of the issue as a tactical one. Initially, consider whether the other side has—or will have—access to the information. If the other side will learn it from other sources anyway, it might be useless to hide it. Second, examine whether candid acknowledgment of damaging facts may have the potential to increase the strength of your negotiating positions. In a negotiation for the sale of a house, for example, consider the impact on the buyer if the seller's lawyer admits, "I know that the ceiling in the upstairs bedroom had some water damage a few years ago, but it was fixed, and there hasn't been a problem since then." Finally, analyze whether the disclosure will facilitate the negotiation. Especially in problem-solving bargaining, your openness as to the interests of your client—even if you disclose some weakness of your client—might encourage a similar response from the other side. If, however, the damaging information is not easily accessible and its disclosure serves no tactical purpose, consider ethically acceptable means of concealing it (see §23.5).

§25.7 PLANNING THE AGENDA

You need to decide the best sequence in which to address issues as well as where and when to negotiate.

13. Mnookin et al., *supra* note 2, at 25–26.

§25.7.1 ISSUES

After you have decided on an approach to the negotiations and considered information issues, plan your issues agenda. Most negotiations concern multiple issues. In the settlement of a police brutality case, for example, the parties might negotiate over the proportionate liability of the different officers, the amount of actual damages, any entitlement to punitive damages, admissions of liability, and the plaintiff's right to attorney's fees. A number of issues can arise even in a routine negotiation for a home sale in those states where lawyers represent the parties to such a transaction. Examples might include responsibility for performing and paying for certain repairs, deadlines for required inspections and obtaining financing, date for closing, and liability for real estate taxes. As part of your strategy development, consider the sequence in which you want to address these issues.

Although there are no hard and fast rules for designing your issues agenda, the primary consideration is whether your sequencing facilitates the overall plan you have developed for the negotiation. Initial consideration of minor issues can be effective if you want to establish a cooperative relationship with the other party that facilitates the negotiation of more difficult issues.[14] This approach can help if you are using problem-solving methods in the negotiation and are concerned about the other party's willingness to engage in such bargaining. But it might delay the inevitable negotiation over the major issues. For that reason, you may want to begin with bargaining over one or two major issues to evaluate the possibility of any settlement or deal. In an adversarial context in which your client has a very strong rights-or power-based BATNA, consideration of a major issue first can give you control over the negotiation. Finally, you might want to negotiate multiple issues simultaneously. In adversarial bargaining, this approach can lead to "log-rolling" or trading off of concessions. In problem-solving negotiation, it can assist in mutual brainstorming of solutions.

Development of your own agenda, of course, does not assure that the other party's lawyer will agree with your sequencing of issues. Therefore, be prepared to explain the advantages of your approach and how it will lead to a quick resolution of the issues. In a negotiation where you want to take a problem-solving approach, this explanation might help you persuade the other side to take such an approach. You might also want to present an initial draft agreement to the other party and propose that you both work off of it. This approach helps you to take control of the negotiation. If, however, you want to develop a cooperative relationship with the other side, the surprise presentation of the document at a negotiation session can be viewed as too controlling and can alienate the other attorney.

§25.7.2 VENUE: TELEPHONE, EMAIL, TEXTING, LOCATION

Where will you negotiate: on the phone, by email, by texting, at one of the lawyers' offices, at one of the parties' homes or businesses, or at a "neutral" location such as the hallway outside the courtroom? In some disputes, you may have the option of holding negotiation sessions at a pretrial conference in court.

---

14. Donald G. Gifford, *Legal Negotiation: Theory and Applications* 76 (1989).

And in many cases, the bargaining will entail multiple negotiation sessions with the possibility of using different modes of communication.

In previous editions of this book we expressed some preference for face-to-face negotiations in contrast to other modes of communication. Recent research comparing different modes of communication in negotiation has shown, however, that for both adversarial and problem-solving negotiations, the particular medium does not necessarily affect the ultimate outcome.[15] It seems more likely that what matters is how a medium is used. Email, for example, can be effective in one situation and counterproductive in another.

Moreover, over the years, younger lawyers, accustomed to electronic communication in their daily lives, have become more comfortable with email or even texting, in contrast to face-to-face, negotiation. Additionally, the economics and time pressures of practice may make the costs of face-to-face bargaining prohibitive. For these reasons, rather than adopting a blanket preference for a particular mode of communication in negotiation, you should consider the advantages and disadvantages of using a particular mode in the context of your case.

Face to Face: The primary advantage of face-to-face bargaining is that the channels of communication are synchronous with parties exchanging ideas at the same time. This exchange is facilitated by the visual and vocal cues of personal contact. As a result, psychological distance can be reduced, and the parties have the opportunity to build trust and rapport.[16] In some situations, however, these visual and vocal cues can actually be a disadvantage. If, for example, a negotiator's body language suggests nervousness or tentativeness, her adversary might assume that she is unprepared and attempt to take advantage of the situation. Similarly, while the give and take of in-person discussion may promote rapport in some contexts, it can instead be exploited by a domineering adversary who tries to "take over the room" and control the discussion.[17]

Telephone: Like in-person bargaining, negotiation by telephone allows for an immediate give-and-take of ideas and small talk and other rapport-building communication techniques. And, unlike face-to-face contact, it has the advantage of reducing the adverse effects of negative visual cues.[18] When your client has limited resources, it is often less expensive than in-person negotiation. Communication by phone also gives each party the ability to control the agenda simply by hanging up.[19] But precisely because phone conversations give parties such control and lack the visual cues of in-person exchange, in contentious situations it is often difficult to develop trust and rapport on the telephone.[20] For that reason, if you want to use a problem-solving approach, and the other side is reluctant to engage in mutual brainstorming, the phone can be very limiting. Moreover, the parties to a phone conversation may become distracted by other calls and office interruptions. For those reasons, unless the parties have committed to a particular time

---

15. Shira Mor & Alexandra Suppes, "The Role of Communication Media in Negotiations," in *Negotiation Excellence: Successful Deal Making* 403-405 (Michael Benoliel ed., 2d ed. 2014).
16. *Id.* at 395.
17. See Noam Ebner, "Negotiation via (the new) Email" in *Negotiation Excellence: Successful Deal Making* 407, 421 (Michael Benoliel ed., 2d ed. 2014).
18. Mor & Suppes, *supra* note 15, at 395.
19. Jay Folberg & Dwight Golann, *Lawyer Negotiation: Theory, Practice, and Law* 164 (2d ed. 2011).
20. Mor & Suppes, *supra* note 15, at 395.

period for telephone bargaining, the use of the phone can often be most effective for "short and sweet" exchanges in adversarial bargaining.

Email: Like the telephone, email provides lawyers with a cost-effective means to negotiate at greater distances. It also gives attorneys the flexibility to communicate at times convenient to each of them. With the widespread use of smartphones, email bargaining has become "semi-synchronous." Although attorneys can respond quickly and engage in real-time give and take, they can also consult with supervisors and colleagues and carefully plan each response.[21] Moreover, because email provides more time for crafting responses than in-person or telephone negotiation, lawyers have the opportunity to set forth "on one page" their ideas on the full range of issues. In a problem-solving setting, such an ability can be helpful in allowing attorneys to bundle multiple issues to stimulate brainstorming alternatives. Moreover, in multiparty negotiations, in which one attorney may attempt to control in-person or telephone bargaining, email provides a better opportunity for fuller participation.[22]

Email negotiations, however, can have some significant disadvantages. Even more so than phone communication, electronic messages are highly "flammable": they are not readily put in context by facial expression or voice inflection. They, therefore, run the risk of being misunderstood by the other attorney. Moreover, given the psychological distance and loss of visual and vocal cues, people have a tendency in electronic communication to attribute negative intentions to the other side. E-negotiation can accentuate competitiveness.[23] Finally, due to the physical distance, reduced social pressure, and sense of anonymity, people sometimes do not have the same inhibitions in email as they do in face-to-face meetings. They may respond too quickly to an email message in a manner that will negatively impact the course of negotiations.[24]

To address these problems, we suggest that you "unmask" yourself in your messages by trying to build (or maintain) rapport and show empathy. In problem-solving negotiations, use interest-based language and frame suggested options as methods of integrating the needs of both parties. Consider the device you are using. If you need to send a lengthy response, instead of immediately dashing off a quick, poorly edited message on your smartphone, wait until you can draft a more thoughtful response on your laptop. Moreover, when you receive a message that you consider hostile, read it twice, reflect on the nature of the sender's intent, and delay sending an angry response. In drafting messages, avoid unnecessary length (the other party may simply ignore or only scan a tome) and be careful with humor, which may be misunderstood. Finally, to overcome the danger of your adversary's inaccurate understanding of your ideas, consider using graphs or tables as attachments to present positions clearly and persuasively.[25]

---

21. *Id.* at 395; Ebner, *supra* note 17, at 419, 423.
22. Ebner, *supra* note 17, at 421.
23. *Id*, at 420-421.
24. For a complete discussion of these disadvantages, see *id.* at 418, 420-421, 428-429.
25. *Id.* at 419-420, 422, 424, 427-428. Also, small talk in telephone conversations can help parties develop the kind of rapport that will lessen misunderstandings about the tone of electronic messages. Janice Nadler, *Rapport in Legal Negotiation: How Small Talk Can Facilitate E-Mail Dealmaking*, 9 Harv. Negot. L. Rev. 223 (2004).

Texting: Even more so than emailing with smartphones, texting is synchronous, with the parties expecting immediate responses to their messages. That aspect of texting is very helpful when an attorney needs a quick response to a specific question and her adversary may be in the midst of another meeting. But precisely because texting can be so fast-paced and interactive, people often have the tendency to send off quick responses without sufficient consideration of different options. In fact, some negotiators try to use this fast-paced tempo to dominate their adversaries.[26] Accordingly, when receiving a text message in negotiation, stop and consider whether you want to continue the exchange—or switch to another mode of communication.

While throughout most negotiations, you will use a combination of modes of communication, at each stage, you should consider whether a particular medium is consistent with your overall strategy.[27] If, for example, you have decided to use a problem-solving approach, you will probably want to start, if possible, with a face-to-face meeting to attempt to develop the kind of rapport that will encourage identification of different interests and brainstorming of options. In your follow-up email communications, you might want to frame your message in terms of the interests that were identified. And, if, in the course of your bargaining, your adversary sends a hostile email or text message, instead of automatically dashing off a harsh response, you may want to call her to try to resolve the problem. If, on the other hand, you are using a more adversarial approach, you might want to begin the negotiations with a phone call or email message laying out your positions and to use well-crafted electronic messages to respond to the other side's positions. If the parties reach an impasse, a face-to-face meeting might resolve the outstanding issues.

Location: In regard to the location of face-to-face negotiations, an advantage to hosting the negotiation is that you can have the resources you need under your command—your files, research materials, and support staff. You feel more in control of the situation. But there are also advantages to negotiating on the other party's turf. You can demonstrate your intent to cooperate by consenting to meet at the other lawyer's office. And when you are away from your own office, you can honestly excuse yourself if you do not have the necessary materials on hand.

Consider also the person you are and where you will perform best. One of the authors of this book believes that the sales operations of new car dealerships are designed to confuse buyers into making mistakes. He never conducts a serious negotiation at a car dealership. Instead, he uses two or three online car brokerage services to establish a low price and then by email asks several local dealers to beat that price. After some of the dealers respond offering prices lower than the online brokerage price, he telephones each of them and tries to get them to beat each others' prices. After everything is agreed to by email and telephone, he signs a sales contract. The other author of this book believes that he is at his best in face-to-face

26. Mor & Suppes, *supra* note 15, at 395. Research has also shown that when texting, the negotiator who makes the first concession is often not met by an equal concession from their counterpart. When texting, "a concession can be perceived . . . as a sign of weakness whereas during face-to-face negotiation a concession is usually interpreted as a gesture of good faith and evidence of the shared goal to reach a mutually beneficial agreement." *Id.* at 405.

27. *Id.* at 404.

negotiations and does all his negotiating at the dealership. Neither author gets better deals than the other. But each gets better deals than he would if he were to negotiate in a way that did not fit his personality.

§25.7.3 TIMING

Most bargaining does not occur in a vacuum where the parties have infinite time to resolve the transaction or dispute. Negotiators regularly face deadlines imposed either by the circumstances of the case (the date when the seller wants to leave her home, the time when the manufacturer needs the goods for production, or the expiration of the collective bargaining agreement); by third-party requirements (a scheduled trial date); or by limitations set by one or both of the parties themselves (an offer that expires next Tuesday). As part of your strategic planning, you should consider how to handle these deadlines.

As to external deadlines—those imposed by circumstances outside of the negotiation—examine the pros and cons of different timing agendas. The most propitious time to negotiate may not be the earliest. You may, for example, need additional information to assess adequately the strengths and weaknesses of your legal case; you may feel that the case is not "ripe" for serious bargaining because the other side has not seriously considered the merits of the case; or you may want to wait until the trial court has decided a pivotal motion. Indeed, especially if you are using the adversarial approach, you may want to wait until the eve of trial or other deadline to pressure a less powerful opponent into a deal.

On the other hand, delay has its disadvantages. The more resources the other party has devoted to preparing for trial, the greater may be the possibility that it will take its risks going to trial. If your client wants to conserve resources or panics at the thought of going to trial, or if you fear that the opposing lawyer will try to take advantage of your client in the court hallway on the eve of trial, you also may want to forgo waiting until the last minute. Moreover, if you are using a problem-solving approach, you need to allow enough time to work out a mutually agreeable solution. The time pressures of deadlines are not always conducive to such a process.

When the other side sets a deadline on an offer, you can try to persuade the other lawyer that deadlines like that are counterproductive. But if that fails, your client will need to decide, based on her BATNA, whether to accept or reject the offer as made.

If you want to make an offer with a deadline, remember that while that might be effective in adversarial bargaining, it can harm a problem-solving negotiation. It not only hinders the development of a cooperative atmosphere but can also harm any long-term relationship your client might want to maintain with the other side. And unless you are serious about such self-imposed deadlines, your credibility will be significantly damaged if the other side calls your bluff and you have to renege on your threat (see §28.2.2).

Quite often, especially in more complex cases, negotiators will reach an impasse, and bargaining will end. Such breakdowns, however, are not necessarily the end of the negotiation process. Parties may actually benefit from some time off. They may calm down, regain concentration, and reassess their interests in the matter. Moreover, in a problem-solving negotiation, such respites can provide necessary time for incubation of new options.[28] Additionally, other events (like a looming trial date, a deposition that significantly impacts one party's theory, or, in the transactional setting, a change in the relevant market) may occur, which create conditions for the parties' return to the bargaining table. In some situations, then, you should consider a breakdown in bargaining as only the completion of one phase with the possibility of more stages to come.

§25.8 ADAPTING YOUR STRATEGY

The strategy that you initially develop should not be set in stone. As bargaining proceeds, the interests, rights, and power context of the negotiation may change; your client may modify her BATNA; speculation about the responses of the other party may simply be wrong; the information you gather during the negotiation may significantly affect your client's and your own perception of the situation; and the overall approach you have selected for the negotiation (adversarial or problem-solving) may turn out to be ineffective. Despite your valiant efforts to use a problem-solving approach to negotiation, for example, the other side might simply ignore your entreaties and bulldoze ahead with an adversarial approach. On the other hand, you may find that adversarial bargaining by both sides has worn both parties down to such a small bargaining range that a problem-solving approach helps to obtain a final agreement. "Competitive tactics early in the negotiation, perhaps ironically, sometimes increase the prospects for successful use of . . . problem solving tactics later in the negotiation."[20]

Accordingly, throughout the negotiation process, reevaluate your initial strategy and be open to adapting it to any changed circumstances. The analysis will be the same as the one you used in your initial planning: go back to your assessment of the parties' interests, rights, and power (Charts 24A, 24B, 24C, and 24D), have your client fine tune her BATNA, consider what additional information might be helpful, and reexamine the approach you have selected for addressing the different issues.

---

28. Joachim Hüffmeier & Guido Hertel, "Creativity in Negotiations" in *Negotiation Excellence: Successful Deal Making* 59, 77 (Michael Benoliel ed., 2d ed. 2014).
29. Folberg & Golann, *supra* note 19, at 35.

CHAPTER

26

STYLES AND RITUALS

§26.1 CREATING NEGOTIATING STYLES

In conducting any negotiation, you should select for yourself a negotiating style that will work well in the circumstances. You should also recognize any issues raised by cultural differences between you and the other side.

§26.1.1 SELECTING A STYLE FOR A PARTICULAR NEGOTIATION

As you have learned, negotiating, like most other lawyering skills, requires the ability to communicate. You may have developed the most creative and clever strategy possible, but you will fail unless you can communicate effectively with the other side. (See Chapter 5.) Your style is an important aspect of this ability to communicate. Style is the manner in which you personally relate to the other side—for example, your word choice, tone of voice, body language, and eye contact.

Strategy is the overall approach you have chosen to achieve your client's goals—adversarial, problem solving, or both. Style is the personal manner in which you execute this strategy: how you present your proposals, listen to the other side's proposals, and respond. Obviously, this distinction is a bit artificial (often your tone will reflect your strategy). But the distinction helps in understanding the conduct of a negotiation. Strategy is the content of your presentation to the other side (*what* you say). Style is the way you package this presentation (*how* you say it). Just as you select a strategy for a particular negotiation, you also select a style (or styles).

We do not suggest that you try to become someone who you are not. How you negotiate—as well as how you examine a witness, counsel a client, or argue to a judge—will grow out of who you are. You can change your negotiation style or modify it to meet the needs of a particular situation, but to some degree the ways you negotiate or try a case will be determined by your personality. If you are naturally abrasive and aggressive, for example, it will be difficult, if not impossible, for you to come across as a Milquetoast.

But you cannot ignore the fact that the style you use in your communications with your adversary may have an important effect on its outcome. Part of becoming an effective lawyer is learning how to act. As you become more experienced, try to develop a repertoire of negotiating masks that grow out of your personality but also communicate effectively in the particular situation. Indeed, this approach is applicable to all aspects of the lawyering process. Consider, for example, the cross-examination of witnesses in an assault case. The defense lawyer might very well wear a very different mask in her questioning of the eighty-year-old grandmother who allegedly witnessed the incident and the detective who obtained the confession from her client.

Two categories of negotiating style are *combative* and *cordial*. While a combative style is tough, dominating, forceful, aggressive, and attacking, a cordial style is personable, friendly, and tactful.[1] Obviously, there is a broad continuum between these two styles. And in any given negotiation, a lawyer might switch from one to another style depending upon the impact the lawyer wants to make on the other side. Moreover, since style depends in large part on the perception of the listener, the precise attributes of a particular style will depend significantly on the culture in which the negotiation is taking place. That perception might vary from one region of the country to another, and it might vary from one type of law practice to another. What is combative in a complex federal antitrust negotiation might be considered very tepid in high-volume urban eviction bargaining.

In choosing your negotiation style, consider a number of factors. Sometimes your selection will be based on the strategy you choose. If you are using an adversarial approach, if your client has a strong rights or power-based BATNA, and if she is willing to make few concessions, you may select a combative style to demonstrate to the other side your client's confidence in her position. On the other hand, if you are using a problem-solving strategy, if your client has a strong interest in maintaining good relations with the other side, and if she is open to a wide

1. See Gerald R. Williams, *Legal Negotiation and Settlement* 21, 23 (1983). Williams's definition of competitive and cooperative conflates both strategic and stylistic aspects of the negotiator. We focus solely on the stylistic considerations. We use "combative" and "cordial" because they clearly connote the tone, rather than the substance of the communication. The terms "competitive" and "cooperative," although used by other authors, are ambiguous because they could refer either to substance or tone. See Robert M. Bastress & Joseph D. Harbaugh, *Interviewing, Counseling, and Negotiating: Skills for Effective Representation* 390 (1990); Donald G. Gifford, *Legal Negotiation: Theory and Applications* 18 (1989). Actually, *all* negotiations are competitive in the sense that each side tries to satisfy its own interests. Problem-solving and adversarial approaches and combative and cordial tones are just different ways of accomplishing that.

variety of solutions to the issues, you might choose a cordial approach to encourage mutual brainstorming.

Other times, however, your selection of style will depend not so much on the strategic approach you have selected as on your attempt to respond to a position of your adversary.[2] Consider, for example, this exchange between the City Attorney and Cassini's lawyer during a negotiation in the group home case:

City Attorney: I'm sorry, Sara. May I call you Sara? But my bosses have told me that this case has to go to some type of disposition. I agree with you about the need for facilities for people with AIDS; one of my sister's friends is dying of AIDS. But there's a lot of political pressure on the city, and we can't ignore it. Now, if your client would be willing to close the home and pay a token fine, I'm sure we can work this out. I can tell you, both my bosses and I want your client to stay out of jail.

Cassini's Attorney: Come on now, Mr. Jackson, we all know that the case law supports our position, and that eventually your case will be thrown out. If you want, I can spend the whole day talking to you about the Supreme Court precedents in our favor. But I *don't* want to talk about the law. That's simply a waste of time . . .

City Attorney: Sara, I'm sorry, but . . .

Cassini's Attorney: *Just listen to me!* Think of the time you'll be wasting responding to all my papers! I think it's in both of our clients' interests—and in the interest of the neighbors of the home—to work out a mutually acceptable agreement. I know your client doesn't want this case going on forever, but my client will stand by her guns to maintain facilities for people with AIDS. Why don't we just try to find another location in the city . . .

City Attorney: I'm sorry, Sara, there's no way; I really wish we could do it . . .

Cassini's Attorney: [*standing up*] Please don't interrupt me. Just listen. Is it *really* in your interest to litigate this case?

City Attorney: Regrettably, I have to.

In this interchange, the City Attorney clearly has chosen an adversarial approach but has decided to be perceived as cordial. (In fact, he may feel contempt

---

2. See generally Robert J. Condlin, *Bargaining with a Hugger: The Weaknesses and Limitations of a Communitarian Conception of Legal Dispute Bargaining, or Why We Can't All Just Get Along*, 9 Cardozo J. Conflict Resol. 1, 80 (2007) (describing a negotiation in an employment discrimination case in which the plaintiff's attorneys successfully used an adversarial approach in response to the employer's unreasonably low offer but throughout were unfailingly polite and respectful).

for both Cassini and her lawyer, but he has selected this style to set a tone for the bargaining.) He knows that Cassini and her lawyer view this case as very significant, but uses a cordiality mask to try to open the door for a swift resolution of the case; the city gets rid of the house, and Cassini gets off with a light fine. Cassini's lawyer, on the other hand, wants to use a problem-solving approach, but feels frustrated in her inability to engage the City Attorney in this process. In response to the City Attorney's refusal to brainstorm, she becomes combative to try to get him to listen. She says, in essence, to the City Attorney, "If you want to focus solely on the criminal charges, we can litigate them to the hilt. But since we do have some mutual interests, let's work things out."

Still other times, your choice of style should be based on credibility factors. The effectiveness of your communication in a negotiation depends in large part on your own credibility. And style can have a significant effect on the way the other side and its lawyer perceive you. In a negotiation for the purchase of a $200,000 home, for example, where an issue arises about a $200 paint job, a combative approach most likely will be considered disproportionate to the circumstances and may damage the lawyer's credibility when more significant issues arise later in the negotiation. It might even lead to such mistrust that the deal will fall through.

One factor that should not affect your style is your client's or your own emotions about the other side or the other side's lawyer. As Fisher and Ury advise, you need to "separate the people from the problem."[3] While novice lawyers often select a combative approach against an experienced lawyer to show that "they know what they are doing," their bravado may not communicate effectively with the opposing lawyer, who will probably see through the mask and might even break off the negotiation. Other inexperienced lawyers, intimidated by their first negotiations, will mistakenly use a cordial approach because the other lawyer seems so "nice."

Communicate as effectively as possible. Your goal is not to score points or make friends.

§26.1.2 RECOGNIZING CROSS-CULTURAL DIFFERENCES

Although most legal negotiations occur between lawyers within the same local community, in recent years lawyers have become more involved in transactions and disputes with their counterparts from other cultures. Traditionally, such cross-cultural bargaining arose in the context of international diplomacy. Nowadays, however, it occurs regularly in negotiations between private lawyers and

---

3. Roger Fisher et al., *Getting to Yes: Negotiating Agreement Without Giving In* 11 (2d ed. 1991). For a different opinion on this issue, see Daniel L. Shapiro, *Emotions in Negotiations: Peril or Promise?* 87 Marq. L. Rev. 737, 745 (2004), in which the author observes

> While it is true that emotions can be a barrier to value-maximizing agreement, the common advice "to get rid of emotions" is infeasible and unwise. On the contrary, research suggests that negotiators can improve the efficiency and effectiveness of a negotiation by gaining an understanding of the information communicated by emotions, their own and those of others, and enlisting emotions into the negotiation.

official representatives of other nations, and in commercial transactions between companies in different countries.

Since styles of communication may vary significantly from culture to culture, consider the nature of the culture of the other side and its lawyer in selecting your negotiation style for effective cross-cultural bargaining. Even when negotiating with an attorney or party from another region of the country, you may want to think about the effect of cultural differences on negotiation style. Consider, for example, the characters of the soft-spoken Southern judge and abrasive New Yorker in the movie *My Cousin Vinnie*. Likewise, the gender of the participants may affect the style of the negotiation. Studies are inconclusive, however, on whether female and male lawyers behave significantly differently in negotiations.[4]

While it is beyond the scope of this text to discuss in depth methods for selecting a style in cross-cultural negotiation, it is helpful to identify some of the factors which should be considered (see also Chapter 6).[5]

*1. **Language.*** What you might consider standard norms of discourse in America may be viewed as abrasive and rude in another culture. In some negotiations, you will be communicating through an interpreter. You need to understand the limitations of translation and the effects of language structure on communication.

*2. **Environment.*** While in the United States, for example, the conference room or formal boardroom is the principal setting for bargaining, in other cultures, the real negotiations occur elsewhere: in hotel lobbies, dining rooms, or private homes.

*3. **Social organization and hierarchy.*** In crafting a style for a negotiation with someone from another culture, consider aspects of that culture's social hierarchy. In societies with strict vertical hierarchies, it is considered inappropriate to bargain with someone of a different status. This can cause problems for an American lawyer in countries where lawyers have a lower social rank than they do here.

*4. **Contexting.*** Social scientists distinguish between high context cultures in which the participants rely most heavily on how a statement is said rather than what is said and low context cultures in which the participants rely primarily on what is said.[6] In a high context culture, such as Japan or the Arab countries, the

---

4. See Lloyd Burton et al., *Feminist Theory, Professional Ethics, and Gender-Related Distinctions in Attorney Negotiating Styles*, 1991 J. Disp. Resol. 199; Thomas F. Guernsey, *A Practical Guide to Negotiation* 26–27 (1996).
5. See David A. Victor, *Cross-Cultural Awareness*, in *The ABA Guide to International Business Negotiations* 15 (James R. Silkenat & Jeffrey M. Aresty, eds. 1994); John Barkai, *Cultural Dimension Interests, the Dance of Negotiation, and Weather Forecasting: A Perspective on Cross-Cultural Negotiation and Dispute Resolution*, 8 Pepp. Disp. Resol. L.J. 403 (2008). See also Raymond Cohen, *Negotiating Across Cultures* 19–32 (1991); Geert Hofstede et al., *Cultures and Organizations: Software of the Mind* (3d ed. 2010) (describing authors' empirical studies of cross-cultural differences throughout the world during the past three decades).
6. Cohen, *supra* note 5, at 25. ("A high-context culture communicates allusively rather than directly.")

parties rely a great deal on nonverbal communication and pay less attention to detail. In lower context cultures, such as Germany and the United States, the focus is on the words and literal meaning of the communication.[7] Accordingly, while a direct, combative style may be effective in many American negotiations, it may not work, and in fact may be counterproductive, in dealings with negotiators from high context cultures.

5. ***Conceptions of time.*** Some cultures, such as the United States, understand time in a monochronic manner: time is inflexible, and schedules should be adhered to as closely as possible. In other cultures, time is understood polychronically: it is flexible, and schedules are not closely adhered to. When an American negotiates with someone from a culture with a polychronic conception of time, the American may become impatient with the delays inherent in such a context and may respond combatively. The American may need to adjust style to that of the other side's culture.

6. ***Individualism vs. collectivism.*** The vast majority of people in the world live in collectivist societies in which the interests of the group prevail over individual interests, and harmony and loyalty are valued more than honesty. Only a minority of people live in societies like the United States in which individual interests predominate, and everyone is expected to look after herself or her immediate family. When Americans negotiate with someone from a collectivist culture, they most likely will be considered suspiciously as outsiders and may encounter deceptive negotiation tactics used against persons who are not part of the group. In such a context, American negotiators will need to take the time to build stable relationships with their collectivist negotiating partners to become accepted as insiders.[8]

7. ***Gender roles.*** In some cultures, men are expected to be assertive, tough, competitive, and focused on material success, while women are expected to be modest, cooperative, and concerned with the quality of life. In other cultures, gender roles overlap, and both men and women are expected to act cooperatively. Unfortunately, when bargaining with a man from a culture with distinct gender roles, you may confront someone who expects ego-boosting treatment and who seeks to resolve conflicts with threats and displays of force. And when bargaining with persons from a culture with less distinct roles, your counterparts are more

---

7. Victor, *supra* note 5, at 20. See also Michael Slackman, *The Fine Art of Hiding What You Mean to Say*, N.Y. Times, Aug. 6, 2006, §4 (Week in Review) at 5, describing an interview with the publisher of a newspaper in Iran:

> [The publisher noted that] Iranians find Americans easy to deal with because they are straightforward. That, he implied, could give Iranians an advantage in any negotiations. But for Americans to understand Iranians, he said, they must recognize that with Iranians, "the mind thinks something, the heart feels something else, the tongue says something else, and manners do something else.
>
> "It doesn't mean people are lying," he said. "They are just dealing with you with a different character."

8. Hofstede et al., *supra* note 5, at 89–134, 400; Barkai *supra* note 5, at 412–414.

likely to resolve conflicts by cooperation and to strive for consensus. They may respond quite negatively to a domineering, assertive, loud demeanor.[9]

*8. **Uncertainty avoidance.*** In every culture, people to some extent fear uncertainty and ambiguity. But in some cultures, members feel especially threatened by unstructured and unknown situations. Accordingly, bargainers from cultures with high uncertainty avoidance will likely have a need for structure and ritual in the negotiation process. They also likely will prefer predictable solutions and shy away from the unconventional.[10]

Given these variables in cross-cultural communication, you should consider the sensibilities of the other participants before you embark on negotiations that cross profound cultural divides. Lawyers who have participated in similar negotiations can provide helpful assistance. And you may want to consult the significant body of literature that is being developed on bargaining with negotiators from particular regions or countries.[11]

§26.2 NEGOTIATION RITUALS

Negotiations often follow set patterns. In some fields these rituals have become so well established that they are entrenched social expectations. Some labor negotiations between unions and management, for example, often entail months of useless bargaining between low-level representatives until the principals sit down at the table on the eve of a strike deadline to work out a contract. And experienced plaintiff personal injury lawyers and insurance claims agents who know each other well engage in almost ritualistic exchanges of information and offers and counteroffers before agreeing on a deal. In some urban eviction practices, lawyers for both parties know that the real bargaining will only take place in the hallways between the first and second calls of the cases.

Some rituals can serve useful psychological functions such as building trust, maintaining comfort levels, and setting a tone. You should investigate any customs or conventions that local practitioners usually follow for the kind of bargaining you will conduct. Your client or more experienced lawyers who have engaged in similar negotiations may have this information.

On the other hand, some rituals serve no useful purpose for your client and can actually be harmful. Novice lawyers conducting dispute negotiations often engage in a ritual that goes something like this: Each lawyer brags about the quality of the lawyer's evidence ("we have three witnesses who say your client ran the red light") and the likelihood of prevailing at trial ("the jury will be upset about my client's injuries"), while insulting the other lawyer's evidence ("nobody's going to believe

---

9. Hofstede et al., *supra* note 5, at 135–185, 400; Barkai *supra* note 5, at 414–415.
10. Hofstede et al., *supra* note 5, at 187–234, 400; Barkai *supra* note 5, at 415–417.
11. For example, see Urs Martin Lauchli, *Cross-Cultural Negotiations, with a Special Focus on ADR with the Chinese,* 26 Wm. Mitchell L. Rev. 1045 (2000); Rona R. Mears, *Contracting in Mexico: A Legal and Practical Guide to Negotiating and Drafting,* 24 St. Mary's L.J. 737 (1993); Robert J. Walters, *"Now That I Ate the Sushi, Do We Have a Deal?"—The Lawyer As Negotiator in Japanese–U.S. Business Transactions,* 12 Int'l Bus. 335 (1991). An excellent website on which you can compare cultural factors between two countries is *www.geert-hofstede.com* (visited Aug. 25, 2014).

your pathologist") and the other party's chance at trial ("I think you're going to lose"). This goes on like a barroom argument, each lawyer trying to top the other and each getting angry at the other, until finally both realize that time is running out and their clients need a deal. Then, without much thought about why, the lawyers quickly come to an agreement that is about halfway between the positions they started with. This is not really negotiation at all. It is a prolonged threat display, followed by a quick splitting of the difference. Neither side has really influenced the other, and neither has thought about interests, rights, or power enough to plan a careful negotiation.

In your conduct of a negotiation, weigh the advantages and disadvantages of following established bargaining patterns. Examine the effect of these rituals on your overall negotiation strategy. If you decide to break with established local tradition, consider ways to handle the situation without jeopardizing the negotiation. In an environment where swift adversarial bargaining is the norm, for instance, and you want to engage in a problem-solving approach, you may want to begin the negotiations by acknowledging explicitly that you know the usual custom in the area is to have quick exchanges of offers, but that you think it is in the interest of both parties to spend at least a short while brainstorming mutually agreeable solutions.

Besides learning your area's negotiation customs, learn the local bargaining semantics. These coded signals send messages—either intentionally or unintentionally—about a particular side's position or attitude in the negotiation. They differ by geographic region, cultural environment, and practice area. For example, in some places the phrase "I think we can work this out" is just an opening pleasantry to the bargaining, while elsewhere it is a message that the parties are on the brink of a deal. Likewise, the outburst, "This is hopeless! We're going to trial!" in one locale can literally mean that there is deadlock while in another merely that the other party is frustrated and will quickly be back to the table. Sensitivity to these different signals can help you maneuver your way through the bargaining.

The best way to become familiar with these signals is to play the role of an anthropologist during your initial negotiations in a particular locale. Be sensitive to the signals used by various negotiators and the way others respond to them. Think about this not only during negotiation, but also afterward when you have an opportunity to reflect on the bargaining dynamics.

CHAPTER

27

FOLLOWING THROUGH ON YOUR PLAN

§27.1 ADVERSARIAL APPROACH

Remember that your goal in adversarial bargaining is to maximize your client's gain and minimize your loss (see §25.4). You need to communicate your offers and concessions in a way that persuades the other party to agree on terms most favorable to your client.

§27.1.1 MAKING INITIAL OFFERS

Should you make your initial offer before the other side makes theirs? Or should you wait to hear their initial offer before you make yours? Many lawyers feel that it is always a sign of weakness to be the first party to make an offer. Lawyers often engage in a ritual dance at the beginning of a negotiation, each lawyer trying to delay making an initial offer until the other side has done so first.

While some empirical research has shown no apparent correlation between those who make the first offer and the eventual outcome of the negotiation, recent research has shown that making first offers can improve the outcome through strategic use of "anchoring."[1] Researchers have found

> that how we perceive a particular offer's value is highly influenced by any relevant number that enters the negotiation environment. Because they pull judgments

---

1. Compare Robert M. Bastress & Joseph D. Harbaugh, *Interviewing, Counseling, and Negotiation: Skills for Effective Representation* 493 (1990) (concluding that no apparent correlation exists between first offers and outcomes) and Robert S. Adler, *Flawed Thinking: Addressing Decision Biases in Negotiation*, 20 Ohio St. J. on Disp. Resol. 683, 770 (2005) (observing that "first offers can markedly improve one's outcome"); Dan Orr & Chris Guthrie, *Anchoring, Expertise, and Negotiation: New Insights from Meta-Analysis*, 21 Ohio St. J. on Disp. Resol. 597, 621 (2006).

> toward themselves, these numerical values are known as *anchors*. In situations of great ambiguity and uncertainty, first offers have a strong *anchoring effect*—they exert a strong pull throughout the rest of the negotiation. Even when people know that a particular anchor should not influence their judgments, they are often incapable of resisting its influence.[2]

Accordingly, an aggressive, but not absurd, first offer can set the tone for further negotiation and may have a positive effect on the outcome. If, however, you have inadequate information about the value of the negotiated object or the relevant market, you may want the other side to make the first offer. From that offer, you can learn something about how much they think it is worth. In those circumstances, if you make the first offer, it might be too pessimistic and lead to a smaller return for your client.

Attorneys can avoid or minimize the impact of anchoring on negotiation by adopting certain de-biasing strategies. First, when confronted with an anchoring offer, you should consciously resist the urge to accept it. Stand back and evaluate it from both your own and your adversary's perspective rather than focusing solely on the amount of the offer. Second, rather than allowing yourself to be unduly influenced by the initial offer in your case, you should assess it based on an investigation of decisions in other similar cases or the handling of other transactions in your community. For example, consult with expert attorneys who have handled such cases or transactions or gather information from resources such as verdict reports on Lexis or Westlaw (see §20.3.1).[3]

§27.1.2 DECIDING HOW MUCH TO OFFER

To determine your initial offer, return to your assessment of interests, rights, and power (Charts 24A, 24B, 24C, and 24D). Then, try to predict the possible outcomes of the case—including your BATNA—by using the same methods you would use in preparing for client counseling (see §20.3.1).

Research does show a correlation between a forceful, but credible, initial offer and a better result for the party making the offer.[4] Apparently, such offers can convey the message that you are convinced of the strength of the case. The danger, of course, is that the other side will immediately reject it. If you stick to your guns, the other party might remain at the bargaining table—or might not. If the offer is rejected, you might have to make a quick concession that would send the exact opposite message—that you were really bluffing—unless you are committed to your offer and are willing to pursue your BATNA instead of negotiation. You

---

2. Adam D. Galinsky, *When to Make the First Offers in Negotiation*, Harvard Business School Working Knowledge for Business Leaders, at *http://hbswk.hbs.edu/archive/4302.html* (visited Aug. 25, 2014). Some scholars have questioned both the methodology of the research on the effect of anchoring on negotiation and the applicability of this research to legal bargaining. See, e.g., Robert J. Condlin, *Legal Bargaining Theory's New "Prospecting" Agenda: It May Be Social Science, But Is It News?*, 10 Pepp. Disp. Resol. L. J. 215 (2010) (observing that most of the anchoring research involved simulated negotiations with student subjects who were bargaining for the first time and simple problems lacking the information-rich context of most legal negotiation).
3. Orr & Guthrie, *supra* note 1, at 625–628.
4. Donald G. Gifford, *Legal Negotiation: Theory and Applications* 99 (1989); see generally Andrea Kupfer Schneider, *Aspirations in Negotiation*, 87 Marq. L. Rev. 675 (2004).

might decide instead to demonstrate the strength of your case through persuasive arguments rather than by inflating your initial offer.

Credibility problems can arise through "Boulwarism"—making only one offer, which you believe is reasonable and just, and telling the other side that you will settle on no other terms. Boulwarism is named after a former vice-president of General Electric who used this tactic in labor negotiations in the 1950s. Although his offers might be considered fair objectively, they generated controversy and friction and made settlement more diffucult. When the other side has hired someone—a union leader or a lawyer—to do the bargaining, one of the other side's interests may be to get enough out of the negotiation to make it appear the bargainer was worth hiring.

Most negotiators enter the bargaining process intending to give and take. Boulwarism, by challenging that basic notion, raises significant risks. Boulwarism can be effective only if three things are true: you have enough information to be reasonably certain that your one offer is better than the other side's BATNA; you can convince the other side of that; and you can convince the other side that you will not make any further concessions. If you try Boulwarism and it fails, you must either make a concession, losing credibility in the process, or stick to your initial offer and retreat to your own BATNA when it is rejected.

Generally, a good initial offer—a forceful, but credible one—is aimed further, but not too much further, than the best terms on which you think the other side might settle. Suppose you represent a plaintiff who is suing for $150,000, and you believe that the most the defendant might be willing to settle for is $85,000. Your initial offer should not be $85,000. If you offer that, the defendant will insist that you retreat—the process of give and take—and retreating would produce a settlement of less than $85,000. Instead, you offer to settle for more than that, but not so much more that you lose credibility. If you were to offer to settle for $150,000—the amount you sued for—the other side would laugh and ask you to get back in touch with them when you decide to negotiate. Instead, you offer to settle for the highest figure that does not hurt your credibility, perhaps $135,000.

§27.1.3 PRESENTING YOUR INITIAL OFFER

As with so much of lawyering, the way you communicate the initial offer is crucial to its effectiveness. You must convince the other side that your bottom line is high (even if your client has not set a bottom line).[5] The key to such a presentation is *credibility*. Unless the other party believes that you are committed to your position, you will not induce it to reassess its bargaining position.

Compare two versions of initial offers from Ransom's lawyer in *Ransom v. Dusak*:

> ***Initial Offer—Example 1***
> Unless repairs are made to Ransom's apartment within the next few weeks, we're going to take this case to trial. We also want $5,000 in damages. That's for the loss of use of her apartment for the last few months and for her medical bills. You know that because of the lack of heat in her apartment last winter her two-year-old

---

5. Bastress & Harbaugh, *supra* note 1, at 507.

and four-year-old came down with bronchitis, and my client had to pay the doctor bills. And there were other expenses resulting from the wretched conditions too. You know what they are; we've laid them out in the complaint. We also want punitive damages for her mental anguish. We are willing to waive some of those damages if the repairs are made as soon as possible.

Initial Offer—Example 2
We demand that the following repairs be made to my client's apartment by August 8: the roof must be repaired in the master bedroom by a licensed contractor; the entire apartment must be fumigated by a licensed exterminator; and the heating system must be repaired by a licensed plumber. By August 10, a representative from the Health Department will inspect to verify the fulfillment of these conditions. For breach of the warranty of habitability, we demand actual damages in the amount of $1,950—that's one-half of the rent paid from January to June. As I'm sure your client will acknowledge, the bedroom is one-half of the usable space in the apartment. Also, we want reimbursement for the $250 doctor bill my client paid because of the bronchitis caused by the lack of heat. Here's a copy of the bill. We'll also agree to only $250 in punitive damages if the repairs are made by August 8. As you know, Judge Lopez is hard on landlords who breach the warranty of habitability. Just last month, she assessed $2,000 in punitive damages against A & E Realty in a similar case.

These two examples illustrate the factors that most affect the credibility of initial offers: *specificity, justification,* and *consequence.*

Specificity reflects a firmness of the negotiator's commitment.[6] As you learned in §15.3.1, specific facts are more credible than mere conclusions because specific facts paint a clear and vivid picture while conclusions are ambiguous. Similarly, by presenting specific offers and demands in negotiation, you show your client's commitment to a position in clear terms. In Example 1, the lawyer ambiguously says that her client wants "repairs made . . . within the next few weeks," "damages for the loss of use of her apartment for the last few months," "other expenses," and "punitive damages." By not specifying the exact conditions her client wants repaired, the time deadline for the repairs, the amount of damages, and the precise basis for damages, she gives the impression that her client is ambivalent about her demands. Indeed, without an exact offer, the client appears to be unsure of her bottom line and open to making concessions.

The specificity in Example 2, on the other hand, demonstrates a strong commitment of the client to her particular positions: she knows when she wants the conditions remedied; what exact amount of damages she wants; and what the grounds are for her claims. And by specifying that she wants all the work performed by licensed contractors and to be confirmed by the representative from

---

6. Richard E. Walton & Robert B. McKersie, *A Behavioral Theory of Labor Negotiations* 93–94 (1965). Of course, if the offer is unrealistic, no degree of specificity will increase its credibility (see §27.1.2).

the Health Department, the lawyer tells the other side her client "means business" when she says she wants the work done properly.

Justification means clearly communicated reasons for your client's offer. Sound reasons give a ring of legitimacy to an offer. Your client did not arbitrarily pick this amount or take this position but instead has seriously considered it and is committed to it for the reasons you describe. And you rely on the logic of the justification to convince the other side that your offer is better than its BATNA. For this reason, the stronger the logic of your reasoning, the more credible is the specific justification.

Again, consider the two examples from *Ransom v. Dusak*. In Example 1, the lawyer gives no justification for her demand for damages for the loss of the use of her apartment. She vaguely refers to "other expenses resulting from the wretched conditions," does not explicitly point to any claims for relief in the complaint, and gives no reasons for the punitive damages except for a feeble reference to "mental anguish." The overall impact of this justification is weak. It appears that the lawyer has not done her homework, that neither she nor her client has seriously thought through the $5,000 demand, and that, therefore, her client is not firmly committed to the offer.

In contrast, the lawyer in Example 2 gives the legal basis for her claim, provides explicit arguments for the 50% abatement in rent, and even provides the other party's lawyer with evidence of damages. And by agreeing to only $250 in punitive damages if the repairs are made by August 8, she furnishes a credible rationale for the offer.

You develop your justifications from your assessments of interests, rights, and power (Charts 24A, 24B, 24C, and 24D). Sometimes, you can use a particular interest of your client—or of the other side—to establish the credibility of your offer. If, for example, Dusak worries about his reputation in the community, Ransom's lawyer might use that interest as a justification for an expedited schedule for work on the apartment. In other situations, you might want to visit the strengths and weaknesses portions of the rights assessment chart (Chart 24B on page 314) to develop a justification. And in still other situations, you may want to rely on power imbalances to "leverage" a deal. If, for example, Ransom is a member of a tenants group whose members are ready to withhold rent, she may have a very strong justification for requesting substantial damages.

Consequence means that the offer communicates the consequences that will ensue if the other side rejects it. Your statement of consequences will be credible only if the other side knows that you are willing and able to follow through with it. A strong commitment to the offer can be demonstrated by an explicit description of the consequences of its rejection. Often, but not always, the consequence is that you will pursue your BATNA rather than continue negotiating.

In Example 1 the lawyer vaguely refers to the consequences of "going to take this case to trial"—as though she is going through the motions of stating a consequence, rather than developing one persuasively. In Example 2, on the other hand, the lawyer specifically spells out the consequences: "As you know, Judge Lopez is hard on landlords who breach the warranty of habitability. Just last month, she assessed $2,000 in punitive damages against A & E Realty in a similar case." By providing a detailed account of the possible consequences, this lawyer communicates both her knowledge of the legal situation and her conviction as to the merits of her case. In framing your initial offer, always try to describe your BATNA in the most persuasive way possible.

§27.1.4 MAKING SUBSEQUENT DEMANDS AND CONCESSIONS

Unless the other side immediately accepts your initial offer, it might make counteroffers, and you will have to determine how to follow through with your strategy. One thing, however, is almost certain: you will not want to increase your demands. Although the law of professional responsibility does not prohibit such a tactic, it can cause you to lose a great deal of credibility and severely damage your relationship with the other side. If you have demonstrated a firm commitment to your initial offer, it seems illogical to be augmenting it. Moreover, the other party will most likely consider an increase in demand as an act of bad faith and mistrust your motives in any future bargaining. That tactic is warranted only when a surprising piece of important information appears and significantly changes the complexion of the case in your favor. If that happens, explain to the other side clearly and logically the reasons for your reverse in course.

Accordingly, after the initial offer and counteroffer, both sides will eventually have to make concessions of some kind. Indeed, in your planning for an adversarial negotiation, you identify various concession points between your initial offer and your bottom line (see §25.4). The fact that you identify these points in your preparation, however, does not mean that you automatically make a concession when your receive a counteroffer. Remember that your goal in adversarial bargaining is maximizing your gain. One of the ways of achieving this goal is to give the other side the impression that your client's bottom line is higher on the bargaining range than your client has actually placed it. Research has shown that a grudging approach to concessions pays off with better outcomes.[7] Rapid, and especially large, concessions, on the other hand, send the opposite message: after making an inflated initial offer, your client is willing to make substantial and continuing concessions. Similarly, if you make a series of concessions without receving any from the other side, you communicate a weak commitment to your positions.

Nevertheless, concessions will be required in certain circumstances.[8] First, concessions may be needed to prevent deadlocks. Lawyers generally understand that in adversarial bargaining a deal is possible within the two bargaining ranges only if each party makes at least some concessions. If you are not close to your client's bottom line, failure to make a concession when both parties dig in their heels will harm your client's interests unless your client's BATNA is better than any deal you foresee getting out of the negotiation.

The second reason for conceding something is to persuade the other side to make concessions, too. In some negotiations, the parties get stuck at a given point

---

7. Bastress & Harbaugh, *supra* note 1, at 520.
8. See generally *id.* at 516–518; Gifford, *supra* note 4, at 147–149.

and refuse to move. Even a slight concession shows some flexibility and may encourage some movement from the other side.

Third, concessions may be necessary to maintain a good working relationship with the other side. If your client and the other side plan to have an ongoing relationship after this particular negotiation, contentious scrabbling at each point in the bargaining can damage that relationship. Again, a flexible concession strategy may be needed.

Finally, concessions may be required when both parties face a deadline. Unless your client wants to abandon the negotiation and pursue her BATNA instead, you may need to make concessions as a deadline approaches. In the dispute context, this reason for concessions can be very important when a judge, hearing officer, or arbitrator is encouraging settlement. If the adjudicator views your intransigence as the reason for the negotiation's failure, you may enter the trial or hearing at a disadvantage.

Once you have decided to make a concession, think about how to package it in a way that will minimize an impression of weakness. Let us revisit the *Ransom v. Dusak* case and assume that Dusak's lawyer has responded to Ransom's initial offer by saying his client will only pay $100 nominal damages. Here are two possible ways of conceding:

> ***Concession—Example 3***
> All right, to move the negotiations along, my client will agree to damages of $1,550. But that's my client's bottom line. She won't move any further.

> ***Concession—Example 4***
> I think my client might agree to a slight decrease in damages just to get this case moving. We both know how long it takes to get a case on the trial calendar before Judge Lopez, and my client wants the money now to pay the medical bill. If you look at Judge Lopez's decision in the A & E Realty case, the smallest abatement she will give us is one-half. So to get this case settled now, we'll agree to a one-third abatement plus the $250 medical bill—that's $1,550. That's as generous as we can get. Under no circumstances is my client going to accept nominal damages of $100. Your client will have to get realistic.

In two ways, the concession in Example 4 is much stronger. First, it includes *a specific justification for the concession*. While the Example 3 lawyer gives no justification for her concession, the lawyer in Example 4 gives reasons: her client wants to pay the medical bill and does not have to wait for a trial. Just as in our analysis of the initial offers, a justification adds credibility to the position. Here, the concession does not come out of nowhere but instead reflects the interests of the conceding lawyer's client.

If you force yourself to give a specific justification for each concession, you impose a self-discipline that helps you resist the psychological pressure many novice lawyers feel to make concessions just to "get along" with the other side. If you and your client cannot identify a rationale for a concession, you should probably stand pat. As with initial offers, examine your assessment of interests, rights, and power to identify the bases for each concession.

Second, the lawyer in Example 4 *makes it clear that this concession will not inevitably lead to others*. She refers to Judge Lopez's decision in the A & E Realty case that allowed for a 50% abatement and argues that a one-third abatement is as generous as she can be. The message is clear: the consequence of a rejection of this offer will be trial, not further concessions. The Example 3 lawyer on the other hand merely makes the conclusory statement that her concession is her client's bottom line. By giving no explanation, she appears to be doing little more than bluffing.

The approach taken by the Example 3 lawyer can often lead to "splitting the difference" positional bargaining. By failing to provide Dusak's lawyer with any justification for her concession or explanation why she will not continue to concede, the lawyer in Example 3 opens the door to this kind of response: "All right, my client will only give $100; your client wants $1,550. Let's split the difference, say $725." Although that approach might be efficient near the end of a negotiation when the parties are very close to an agreement (see §28.4), it is dangerous at earlier stages because it focuses exclusively on the numbers rather than the reasons why the numbers exist: an analysis of your client's and the other party's interests, rights, and power. Splitting the difference is not negotiating. It is appropriate only when the parties are so close to settlement that it is no longer cost-efficient to argue about how to divide the last few inches.

The approach taken by the Example 4 lawyer also facilitates the negotiation process. By inviting Dusak's lawyer to make some concessions, she tries to engage in serious bargaining on the damages issue. She ends her concession by flatly rejecting a de minimis offer of damages and asks the other side to become more realistic. If Dusak's lawyer responds with an offer of $150 or $200, she will learn that—at least for now—there is little chance of any movement on the damages issue, and her client will have to decide whether to pursue her BATNA instead of negotiating. If Dusak's counteroffer is more substantial, Ransom's lawyer can decide whether to make further concessions.

§27.2 PROBLEM-SOLVING APPROACH

The biggest challenge for the problem-solving negotiator is to bring the other side into the problem-solving process.

§27.2.1 MAKING INITIAL OFFERS

Remember that, if you have chosen a problem-solving approach, your goal is to find solutions that will integrate the resources of both parties or increase resources to reach an agreement that will address both parties' interests. To achieve this goal, you want to engage in creative brainstorming with the lawyer for the other side. Fisher and Ury suggest that you try to persuade the other party to participate in an informal brainstorming session, separate from a negotiation meeting, where the parties can educate each other about their interests, and the participants can freely exchange ideas "off the record."[9] Although that might be worthwhile in settling international disputes or negotiations in complex, multi-party cases, in the day-to-day practice of law, it is usually not cost efficient.

Accordingly, in most situations, your initial offer is an invitation to problem-solving brainstorming within the negotiation itself. For this invitation to be effective, you need to accomplish four things: (1) establish explicitly that you want

---

9. Roger Fisher et al., *Getting to Yes: Negotiating Agreement Without Giving In* 63 (2d ed. 1991).

to take a problem-solving approach in the negotiation; (2) identify the interests both of your client and of the other side; (3) present a solution or range of solutions that addresses these interests; and (4) open the door to joint development of other options. For example, consider the following offer from Cassini's lawyer:

> Mr. Jackson, our job today is to try to settle this case. We both know that in typical plea bargaining of a case such as this, you would initially offer to recommend to the judge a sentence of a fine, in exchange for a plea to the charge and the closing of the house. I'd respond with a demand for dismissal of the case. We'd haggle back and forth about the relevant case law and argue about our predictions for decisions by the judge. At the end of the day, I would threaten to file motions to suppress and dismiss, and you'd demand a trial date from the judge.
>
> But I'd like to discuss whether we can work something out that will address the underlying interests of the city, my client, and the people in the community. I think my client and I have a pretty good idea of the city's position. The neighbors around my client's facility are very scared about the people who are living in the house. You and I know that most of those fears are unfounded; you cannot "catch" AIDS just by living next door to someone with the condition. But these neighbors are concerned about the value of their homes, the protection of their kids, and the overall quality of life in their community. And they are putting political pressure on the city. I understand the bind that you are in. But maybe the city can help them and the people living in the home.
>
> What if we arrange for an educational program at the local community center for the people in the neighborhood to inform them about the precautions Ms. Cassini has in place at the home to protect the community. And then perhaps the city could provide additional garbage pick-ups and city services in the area to tell the community that the existence of the facility actually is going to benefit the community. Ms. Cassini would then be able to maintain her homes, the neighbors would feel more at ease, and the pressure would be off your client. What do you think?

In this example, Cassini's lawyer opens the discussion by explicitly acknowledging the usual adversarial approach to plea bargaining but invites the City Attorney to think creatively about how the issues should be resolved.[10] In this way, she sends a clear message to the other side that she does not want to engage in hard bargaining but would like to work collaboratively to reach a solution. Be careful, however, not to look as if you are imposing a process on the other side. You want to signal your desire for joint problem solving.

Then, by specifically identifying the interests of both parties, Cassini's lawyer reinforces her message by communicating to the City Attorney that she understands the city's needs. "People listen better if they feel that you have understood them. They tend to think that those who understand them are intelligent and sympathetic people whose own opinions may be worth listening to. So if you want the other side to appreciate your interests, begin by demonstrating that you appreciate theirs."[11] Even if you are off the mark in your speculations about their

---

10. Robert H. Mnookin et al., *Beyond Winning: Negotiating to Create Value in Deals and Disputes* 207–209 (2000).
11. Fisher et al., *supra* note 9, at 51.

interests, the other side will appreciate your attempt to put yourself in their shoes. Statements like "I understand the bind you are in" invite the other side to look at your interests and engage in joint problem solving. Moreover, presentation of a possible solution or range of solutions suggests that you have a serious commitment to achieving a resolution that will address both parties' concerns. Just as a specific initial offer indicates a firm position in adversarial bargaining, concrete suggestions in the initial offer in problem-solving negotiation demonstrate that your recognition of the other party's interests is not mere lip service.

Be careful, however, not to become so detailed in your description of the proposed solution that you give the impression that you are wedded to it. You want your initial offer to open the door to joint problem solving, not to become the focus for positional bargaining. For that reason, it may be helpful to suggest one or two alternative options in your offer and ask the other side for its own proposals. In the Cassini negotiation, for example, the lawyer proposes a general education program and suggests additional garbage pick-up and "other services," and then asks the other side for its response. As the city becomes more explicit as to its interests and needs, Cassini's lawyer can work with the City Attorney to build on these proposals to develop a solution that will meet both parties' interests.

§27.2.2 HANDLING THE OTHER SIDE'S RELUCTANCE TO PROBLEM SOLVE

In many negotiations, after you have made your initial offer of a proposed solution, the other side's lawyer will answer with a classical adversarial response. In the Cassini case, for instance, the City Attorney might respond to the initial offer by saying: "I'm sorry, but the only solution the city will accept is the closing of these facilities. We're open to negotiation about a possible sentence for Ms. Cassini but nothing else." The natural tendency of many lawyers in this situation is to lecture the City Attorney about the advantages of agreeing to Cassini's proposals or to take the bait and change to an adversarial approach contesting the merits of the city's case. But, if you want to continue with a problem-solving approach, lectures and arguments will not help. Your goal is to convince the other side's lawyer that such a problem-solving approach will in fact satisfy their interests better than adversarial bargaining. To accomplish this goal, you need to get the other side talking about their interests, not just adversarial positions.

To reframe the discussion and focus on interests, respond to the other side's rigid positions with open-ended, problem-solving questions:

1. *Ask "why?"* Try to get the other side to identify the interests underlying their position. When the City Attorney responds that the issue of the closing of the facilities is nonnegotiable, ask directly for the basis for his client's position. If, for example, he says, "because of the political pressure from the neighbors," you may have an opening for brainstorming ways to address that concern.

2. *Ask "why not?"* Some lawyers simply will refuse to answer a direct question about their clients' interests but may be eager to criticize your proposals. So after the other side's lawyer rejects your proposal, ask what is wrong with it, and the other lawyer might start talking about the interests that lawyer is expected to protect. For instance, when the City Attorney rejects Cassini's proposal for

additional services because of the strains on the city's budget, her lawyer can start discussing ways to minimize increased costs or obtain funds from other sources.

3. Ask "what if?" Another technique for initiating joint problem solving is to probe specifics of solutions. After the City Attorney has rejected the educational program as ineffective, Cassini's lawyer could suggest alternatives: meetings with Cassini and Board of Health officials in neighbors' homes; visits by the neighbors to the facility; or participation by local clergy in the programs. Some lawyers will feel uncomfortable consistently saying "no" and may actually start brainstorming.

4. Ask for their advice. Most lawyers love to give advice to their adversaries, especially novice lawyers. By seeking counsel from the other side's lawyer, you may be able to get him to identify his client's interests and spark some problem-solving discussion. Cassini's lawyer perhaps could say to the City Attorney: "I know my client won't close the facilities. She is very committed to helping people with AIDS. What should I tell her?" Although the response might be a lecture on the necessity of obeying zoning laws, the City Attorney might start talking about the pressure from the neighbors and give you an opportunity to start a discussion on the issue.

5. Ask "what makes that fair?" Outright rejection of the other side's position often leads to adversarial bargaining about that position. To prevent that, you might ask the other lawyer why his client's position is fair. Try to get the other side to refocus from reliance on the rights or power that support its position to an explanation of why, from a practical standpoint, this position is reasonable. Suppose, for example, that Cassini's lawyer were to ask the City Attorney: "I know your interpretation of the zoning law and don't agree with it. But, putting that issue aside, how is displacing these people with AIDS fair and reasonable?" Again, if the City Attorney starts discussing the underpinnings of the city's decision to prosecute, you have an opening for joint problem solving.[12]

In many cases, the other side's lawyer will remain adamantly adversarial. The City Attorney, for instance, might consistently answer all these questions by saying: "I know your client's position, and it might be very reasonable. But the city is required to enforce the zoning laws, and Ms. Cassini broke them." Faced with such intransigency to the problem-solving approach, you might want to attempt to change the players in the game.[13] If you believe that the other side may be more open to problem solving than its attorney, you can write a letter to the opposing attorney presenting your appeal for problem solving and proposing solutions. Since the attorney usually must communicate this written offer to his client,[14] your letter might persuade the other side to instruct its lawyer to change his position. Or you may suggest to the opposing attorney the scheduling of a meeting of clients and attorneys. At that meeting, your direct appeals to the interests of the other party may be more effective than were your arguments to its attorney.

---

12. For an in-depth description of the use of these different questioning techniques, see William Ury, *Getting Past No: Negotiating Your Way from Confrontation to Cooperation* 78–89 (1993).
13. Mnookin et al., *supra* note 10, at 218–219.
14. Comment 2 to Model Rule of Professional Conduct 1.4(a)(1).

If all of these approaches fail, you have two choices: walk away from the bargaining table or join in adversarial bargaining. But try not to abandon prematurely your efforts to initiate problem-solving negotiation. Some lawyers do not instinctively problem solve, and it might take a while for the other lawyer to adjust to your approach. Moreover, even if you do switch to an adversarial approach, you might try to restart problem-solving efforts after you have demonstrated the strengths of your client's rights or power.

§27.2.3 PROBLEM SOLVING WITH THE OTHER PARTY

Even if the other lawyer agrees to join you in a problem-solving approach, your work is far from over. The fact that the other party will consider options addressing the interests of both parties does not mean that the solutions you have developed in your planning will be agreeable to the other side. In adversarial bargaining, after the initial offers, there is usually a give-and-take of concessions until an agreement is reached. In problem-solving negotiation, on the other hand, you need to work with the other lawyer to develop alternative solutions and fine tune them to try to reach a deal.

This process—referred to by William Ury as "building a golden bridge"[15] between your client and the other side—can be facilitated by several methods.

1. ***Keep focused on the parties' interests.*** For problem solving to work, the parties need to make their interests explicit and concentrate on developing solutions to meet these needs. If the parties become distracted and entangled in wrangles about rights and power, problem solving will fail. Assume, for instance, that the City Attorney in the Cassini case responds to her initial offer by saying: "I understand your interests, but you have to recognize where we are coming from. What if your client temporarily closes the homes, and we agree to look for other possible locations for the facilities?" If Cassini's lawyer replies, "My client has every right under the Fair Housing Act to keep these homes open," she has invited the City Attorney to return to adversarial bargaining. Rather than focusing on rights, she should explain to the City Attorney why his proposal does not meet her client's needs.

2. ***Engage in brainstorming.*** Often, especially where the relationship between the parties has been good or the lawyers both have adopted a cordial style, the two sides might want to engage in a brainstorming session as part of the negotiation. This process is quite simple: after identifying their respective interests, the parties can sit facing a large pad of paper or a whiteboard and generate different solutions to the problems; they star those options which seem most promising; and then, focusing on the interests of the parties, attempt to invent improvements in those options. The key to effective brainstorming with another party is separating the inventing of the options from evaluation of their merits.

---

15. Ury, *supra* note 12, at 105 (referring to a saying of Sun Tzu, "Build your opponent a golden bridge to retreat across").

> A brainstorming session is designed to produce as many ideas as possible to solve the problem at hand. The key ground rule is to postpone all criticism and evaluation of ideas. The group simply invents ideas without pausing to consider whether they are good or bad, realistic, or unrealistic. With those inhibitions removed, one idea should stimulate another, like firecrackers setting off one another.[16]

A neutral third party can even facilitate the discussion.

*3. **Try to develop ways to meet unmet needs.*** The major hang-up in problem-solving bargaining is usually that a proposed solution fails to meet the needs of a party. To address this problem, revisit the type of analysis you conducted in planning for problem-solving negotiation. Do not assume a fixed pie (one that cannot be made larger). Instead, think of ways to increase the available resources to meet that need.[17] If, for instance, the city worries that Cassini's proposal does not address the health needs of its sanitation workers, a possible option might be to obtain state funding to provide for equipment and training on the handling of HIV-infected materials.

Another way of dealing with unmet needs is to create conditional solutions. One of the parties in a negotiation might believe that a particular problem will arise in the future but the other disagrees. Instead of arguing over whether this contingency will occur, the parties can frame their agreement to address it. On the noise issue in the Cassini case, for example, if the neighbors fear increased traffic on their street in the evenings because of visitors to the group home, a possible solution might be a condition in the agreement that if the neighbors are bothered by noise in the evenings, Cassini will prohibit visitors to the facility after 8:00 p.m.

*4. **Engage in incorporation.*** In a problem-solving negotiation, if each party presents its own proposal, the parties might become so entrenched in their advocacy that the bargaining can quickly become adversarial in nature. To avoid this problem, try to incorporate elements of the other party's proposal into the modification of your own client's proposal. By recognizing some reasonableness in the other side's proposal, you continue to acknowledge its interests and keep the door open to further problem solving. Suppose you represent the landlord in the *Ransom v. Dusak* case, and the tenant's lawyer has proposed the completion of all the work in the apartment within one week, a completely independent counter-proposal might be greeted with the negative reaction that your client does not understand the terrible conditions in which Ransom lives. By agreeing to accept

---

16. Fisher et al., *supra* note 9, at 60. Recently one scholar has urged caution in the use of this type of brainstorming process. Chris Guthrie, *Panacea or Pandora's Box? The Costs of Options in Negotiation*, 88 Iowa L. Rev. 601 (2003). He argues that option generation in negotiation can have negative, as well as positive, consequences to the outcome of the bargaining. He contends, for example, that "negotiators may unwittingly devalue an option once it becomes part of a set of options because options that look attractive by themselves often look less attractive when compared to others" and may irrationally overvalue an earlier option once an inferior option is added to the mix. *Id.* at 608–625. To overcome these problems, he recommends that lawyers play an active role in the brainstorming process helping clients to make rational assessments of different options and to consider how to use option generation to their strategic advantage. *Id.* at 638–651.
17. See §25.5.1; Ury, *supra* note 12, at 118.

Ransom's repair list, but tinkering with particular work completion dates and the precise nature of the work, you might reach a deal.

*5. **Engage in logrolling.*** Do not assume that your counterpart's client values an issue in the same way your client values it. In many situations, parties prioritize particular issues differently from their counterparts. When parties engage in "logrolling," they make concessions on issues they do not value as strongly as their adversaries and, in return, receive concessions on issues they value more strongly than their counterparts. Rather than bargaining about each issue separately, logrolling recognizes the different priorities parties place on particular issues and, by addressing these issues at the same time, facilitates the development of outcomes acceptable to both parties.[18] In the Cassini case, for example, the City probably values the issue of adverse political fallout from a settlement stronger than Ms. Cassini. For her part, Ms. Cassini places a higher value on the issue of damages than the City. Instead of addressing each of these issues separately, the parties possibly could work out a deal under which Ms. Cassini would receive a token damages award from the City to compensate her for the emotional distress of the case, while the City would obtain an agreement from Ms. Cassini not to disclose the terms of the settlement to stave off possible adverse publicity.

*6. **Help the other side to save face.*** In many negotiations, the reputational and psychological needs of the parties are so important that any solution must address them. In such situations, think about ways to help the other side "save face" without compromising any of the priority interests of your own client. In the group home case, for example, the city is under significant political pressure from the neighbors. If the students representing Cassini can work out a deal in which the neighbors are satisfied, and if city officials will be able to hold a press conference trumpeting their concern both for the needs of the African-American community and for the protection of people with AIDS, city officials will certainly be satisfied with the deal.[19]

---

18. Joachim Hüffmeier & Guido Hertel, "Creativity in Negotiations" in *Negotiation Excellence: Successful Deal Making* 59, 63–64 (Michael Benoliel ed., 2d ed. 2014).

19. Apologies are another face-saving device. Research has shown that a full apology expressing responsibility for an alleged wrongdoing can increase the likelihood that a settlement offer will be accepted. A partial apology, however, expressing regret and sympathy, but not responsibility, does not affect the outcome and, in a case of severe injury, may actually increase the probability that the settlement offer will be rejected. Jennifer K. Robbennolt, *Apologies and Legal Settlement: An Empirical Examination*, 102 Mich. L. Rev. 460 (2003). As the lawyer for the party offering the apology, however, you should consider whether or not the apology might be admissible under the applicable evidentiary rules if a settlement is not reached. See Jay Folberg & Dwight Golann, *Lawyer Negotiation: Theory, Practice, and Law* 145–46 (2d ed. 2011).

CHAPTER
28

NEGOTIATION TACTICS

§28.1 INFORMATION BARGAINING

As we discussed in §25.6, whether you are bargaining adversarially or in problem-solving, you will engage in information bargaining. This section explains methods for gathering and concealing information.

§28.1.1 GATHERING INFORMATION

The techniques for gathering information during a negotiation are similar to those used in any other kind of fact retrieval: from client interviewing (Chapter 8) and witness interviewing (Chapter 9) to depositions. Your goal is to encourage a free flow of information, and your methods need to facilitate this process. While in a client interview, the client may be unwilling to provide needed facts because of embarrassment, mistrust, or psychological pressures, in a negotiation the other side's lawyer may be reluctant to share information for purely tactical reasons. In either case, you need to break down the barriers to communication.

1. Broad questions. As in client interviewing, the use of broad questions can facilitate information gathering in negotiation. Broad questions give the respondent some room to decide how much to discuss the topic (see §8.3.2). Many novice lawyers view negotiations primarily as a time to pontificate about the merits of their case, making confident statements to the other party's lawyer in hopes that the other side will capitulate. "Statements [however] generate resistance, whereas questions generate answers."[1] If you want needed information to evaluate your bargaining range in adversarial bargaining and to develop alternative solutions in problem-solving negotiation, the easiest method is broad questioning, not lecturing.

Consider, for instance, two approaches by Ransom's lawyer in the *Ransom v. Dusak* case for obtaining information about Dusak's assessment of the conditions in the apartment:

> *Example 1*
> My client has been living in those wretched conditions for months: rodents, falling ceiling, lack of heat. She's complained to Dusak, and he has done nothing. The Health Department has been out there—they verify the problems and are ready to take some action. What's your client going to do about it?
>
> *Example 2*
> What does your client think about the conditions in the apartment?

If Ransom's lawyer wants to get as much information as possible about the other side's evaluation of the conditions of the apartment, Example 1 does not accomplish it. By assuming in the question that the contested conditions exist and accusing Dusak of ignoring them, she puts the other lawyer on the defensive and closes the door on disclosure. The opposing lawyer's response will probably be an argument either contesting the particular conditions or whether the landlord failed to act.

The lawyer in Example 2, on the other hand, takes a nonjudgmental approach that invites as full a response as possible. In answering, Dusak's lawyer might divulge new facts—about the conditions in the apartment or about Dusak's conduct. Even if the lawyer asking the question is using an adversarial approach to the negotiation, the question still might help. Its purpose is to obtain information to aid in assessing Dusak's bargaining range—not to compel a concession. Throughout a negotiation, think carefully about the purpose of your communication with the other lawyer. The very same statement or question can be either beneficial or harmful depending upon its context. For example, in adversarial bargaining, Example 1, while it does not facilitate information bargaining, might help in arguing for a concession from Dusak.

After you ask broad questions, you can ask narrow ones to elicit further information (§8.3.2). If, for instance, Dusak's lawyer replies to the Example 2 question that his client knows about a heating problem, Ransom's lawyer might want to pose a series of "Anything else?" questions until she has exhausted the lawyer's knowledge. Then she might want to ask narrow questions exploring the specifics of Dusak's information on each condition. And finally, she might use leading questions to pin down the lawyer about particular facts, such as, "So Dusak knew that the exterminator was unable to get into the apartment?" The obvious danger with this approach is that the opposing lawyer may object that you

---

1. Roger Fisher et al., *Getting to Yes: Negotiating Agreement Without Giving In* 111 (2d ed. 1991).

are deposing rather than negotiating and refuse to answer the questions. Therefore, be selective in the areas in which you use this approach, and try to phrase the questions in noncombative ways that do not prejudge the issues or raise the ire of the other side.

2. Active listening. You have already learned about active listening in §8.1.2. In interviewing, the primary purpose of active listening is to establish rapport with the client. In information bargaining, it serves another objective as well: by expressing understanding of the other party's situation, you encourage full responses to questions. People feel that if you are willing to understand their point of view, they are comfortable telling you more about it.

Suppose you represent the seller in a negotiation for the sale of a house, and the inspection report has identified termite damage, a slight foundation problem under the bedroom, and some roof damage over the patio. Although all three of the problems can be remedied at a modest cost, the buyer's lawyer insists that the entire price has to be renegotiated. Despite your broad questioning, the other lawyer is evasive as to the reasons for his client's position. Your use of an active listening approach—especially with the buyer present—might prompt a more specific response: "I certainly understand your concerns. I remember when I was a first-time buyer. The inspection report upset me too, but I can assure you these problems can be easily remedied. What specifically disturbs you about them?" By acknowledging the feelings of the other side, you possibly stimulate a response.

3. Probing questions. In client interviewing, situations arise in which your client will simply say, "I just can't remember when it happened." At this point, you do not give up but ask probing questions to try to stimulate the client's memory: "Was it raining out that day?" or "Was it close to Christmas?" (See §7.6.) In information bargaining, there are times when the other lawyer will simply say, "I can't tell you." This failure to respond is usually caused not by a memory lapse but by the other lawyer's tactical need to keep the information from you. But the same probing technique that helps in interviewing can be beneficial here.

In information bargaining, probing entails giving the other lawyer an incentive to give a response. One technique is simply to ask your counterpart a direct question. Research shows that people are more inclined to lie by omission (not telling the whole truth) than by commission (falsely answering a direct question). By asking your counterpart to elaborate on an evasive answer, he may be reluctant to make a direct statement that is a lie and back away from the previous answer.[2] Another technique is to confront that lawyer with your knowledge of his evasiveness and to state that you assume the answer would be damaging to his client's case.[3] Consider, for example, this exchange in the *Ransom v. Dusak* case:

---

2. Peter Reilly, *Was Machiavelli Right? Lying in Negotiation and the Art of Defensive Self-Help*, 24 Ohio St. J. on Disp. Resol. 481, 528 (2009).
3. See Robert M. Bastress & Joseph D. Harbaugh, *Interviewing, Counseling, and Negotiating: Skills for Effective Representation* 415 (1990).

Ransom's Attorney:	How many times did your client try to send an exterminator to the apartment?
Dusak's Attorney:	I don't think this information is relevant to this case. If you want to negotiate, let's negotiate. If you want to try the case, let's go to trial.
Ransom's Attorney:	I'm sorry, but I do think this information is very relevant to our warranty of habitability claim. And regrettably I have to assume from your response that the exterminator only came once. That certainly strengthens our claim.

Although Dusak's lawyer can simply ignore the response, it might motivate him to become more forthcoming about the information requested. A related technique is to tell the other lawyer that the information is essential for your client's assessment of the case, and bargaining cannot continue without it.

*4. **Silence.*** A final technique for encouraging full responses is to respond to inadequate answers with silence. "If you have asked an honest question to which they have provided an insufficient answer, just wait. People tend to feel uncomfortable with silence, particularly if they have doubts about the merits of something they have said."[4] Using silence in this way may be hard given the tendency of most lawyers to talk more than they need to. But sometimes it can be the most effective technique. For instance, when Dusak's lawyer answered that the number of visits by the exterminator was irrelevant to the case, silence by Ransom's lawyer would have sent the message, "Come on now, let's get real! That's what this case is all about?" Without the combativeness of a verbal response, a long pause and expectant stare by Ransom's lawyer might embarrass Dusak's lawyer into a more acceptable response.

§28.1.2 CONCEALING INFORMATION

Part of your planning for information bargaining is deciding which facts you need to conceal. There are ethical constraints on your ability to hide information; you cannot lie, for example (see §23.5). But within those limitations, a number of techniques can help block disclosure of information.

*1. **Under-answering a question.*** Suppose you represent the defendant in a drug possession case and want to conceal your client's alcoholism. The prosecutor asks if your client has any addictions. The answer, "He does not use controlled substances" is honest, if incomplete.

*2. **Answer a question with a question.*** In the same drug possession case, the prosecutor asks whether your client has ever used controlled substances. If you

4. Fisher et al., *supra* note 1, at 112.

respond, "Was any drug paraphernalia found at the scene?" you might create a distraction that could divert the prosecutor into a different line of questions.

3. ***Answer a different question.*** Your client in the drug possession case has a record for possession that does not show up on the rap sheet, and the prosecutor asks you whether your client has any prior record for possession. "Look at what the rap sheet says" is not an untrue statement, but it is also not an answer to the question asked.

4. ***Ignore the question and shift to another topic.*** When the prosecutor asks whether your client has ever used a controlled substance, you might dodge the question by arguing that the lab reports are insufficient to show a controlled substance was even found on your client. By attacking the sufficiency of the case, you might divert the prosecutor's attention from your client's use of a controlled substance.

5. ***Explain why you will not answer the question.*** When the prosecutor asks for the maximum sentence your client will accept, the ethical rules suggest that you can misrepresent your client's position (see §23.5). Nevertheless, you might want to respond,

> You know, I don't find questions like that all that helpful, and here's why. If I asked *you* that, although I think you're a decent person, I'd be setting you up to deceive me. It's just a tough question to answer, and it's tempting to bend the truth. I'd have very little confidence in your answer, and so I'm not sure that the question itself would serve me very well. My suggestion is that we table that question.[5]

In this way, you cordially communicate to the other attorney that you understand his strategy, and it is not going to work.

All these techniques have disadvantages. Many experienced lawyers know about them and will persevere, trying to pin you down to an answer. In fact, if a cordial relationship with the other lawyer is important to your strategy, these techniques could actually be detrimental to your bargaining.

Moreover, since, in some instances, the other side will have access to other sources of proof for the requested information, your game-playing might have no effect other than to alienate the other lawyer. For this reason, in many cases where you have a strong need to conceal information, you may simply want to refuse to answer questions about that area and explain the reasons for your refusal. A forthright answer that "My client's prior use of controlled substances is irrelevant to this particular proceeding" may be far more effective than a dance around the issue.

---

5. Robert H. Mnookin et al., *Beyond Winning: Negotiating to Create Value in Deals and Disputes* 287 (2000).

§28.1.3 VERIFYING WHAT YOU THINK YOU KNOW

If your willingness to settle is predicated on certain facts, verify them. Do not make assumptions about facts you consider important. If *only* the other side can know whether those "facts" really are true (rather than assumptions on your part), do two things. First, ask them for proof. Second, ask them to represent and warrant in the written agreement produced by the negotiation (see §28.4.2) that the "facts" on which you rely are true.

If the other side lies to you about facts they represent and warrant to be true, the fraud is grounds for opening up the agreement and for getting damages. If the other side says something untrue through an honest mistake on their part, that might provide grounds for recision if your client later decides that the deal is undesirable. *Your goal is not only to get a good deal, but also to get a deal with escape hatches in case your client later needs to get out of it.* One way to do that is to insist that the other side take responsibility, to the extent possible, for facts on which you rely.

§28.2 COMMUNICATING ABOUT RIGHTS AND POWER

A party using an adversarial approach will usually use rights-based arguments and power-based threats or warnings in attempts to compel concessions by the other side. In problem-solving bargaining, even though the parties focus primarily on their mutual interests, they often use rights-based arguments to develop possible solutions. If, for example, parties in a sexual harassment dispute are trying to agree on standards for the employer's future policies, they may look to Equal Employment Opportunity Commission regulations for guidance and might argue about their meaning. Likewise, in the negotiation of a commercial contract, the parties may argue about the business norms in that industry in regard to a contested provision of the agreement. And to a lesser extent, problem-solving negotiators also use power-based tactics to accomplish their goals. They may assert their power in the first instance to try to force the other side into problem solving or, in the midst of the negotiation, power imbalances may set limits on the range of solutions available. If a tenants' group is negotiating with the landlord about problems in the building, for instance, as eager as both sides may be to work together to solve the problem, the landlord will probably not entertain an option that the tenants take over management of the building.

Negotiation is not just a series of offers, counteroffers, and concessions. Nor is it limited to the identification of interests, generation of options, and development of solutions. The energy that fuels both of these processes—what moves parties to concessions or mutual solutions—comes from communications about the parties' rights and power. The ability to communicate effectively about the parties' respective rights and power, therefore, is an essential skill in negotiation. (See Chapter 5.)

§28.2.1 ARGUING ABOUT RIGHTS

An argument is a group of ideas, arranged logically to convince somebody to do a particular thing or to adopt a particular belief. Lawyers argue about rights in a number of contexts—in motion practice in trial courts, in closing arguments before juries, in oral arguments in appellate courts, and in negotiations. Although all legal arguments have some similarities, argument in negotiation is unique. You are not trying to convince a neutral decision-maker but instead are trying to persuade somebody whose interests are at least initially in conflict with yours and your client's. This skill entails a number of important elements.[6]

*1. **Develop a detailed and organized argument.*** To be effective, all legal argument must be both well-developed and organized. That is especially true in a negotiation when you are trying to persuade someone who has the potential for being hostile to your argument. Detailed argumentation requires a crisp, explicit statement of the legal basis of the argument, a specific description of the facts supporting the application of the legal rule in this case, and a conclusion. This is the same kind of analysis as is used in the legal elements model for organizing facts (see Chapter 11).

Consider, for example, the persuasive impact of these different arguments of Ransom's lawyer in the *Ransom v. Dusak* case:

> *Example 3*
> My client is entitled to a $1,950 abatement of rent because your client has breached the warranty of habitability by failing to provide necessary services in Ransom's apartment.

> *Example 4*
> As I'm sure you know, under section 500 of the Property Code, your client had a duty to provide Ransom with an apartment fit for human habitation. Your client breached this duty when he failed to provide sufficient heat during last winter, to repair a leaking ceiling in the bedroom, and to spray the apartment for roaches. And, I'm also sure you know, under that same section of the Code, my client is entitled to actual and punitive damages for this violation. Here, she lost use of one-half of the apartment for six months, entitling her to a $1,950 abatement and $250 in punitive damages.

In Example 3, the lawyer merely states a conclusion without taking the listener through an analysis. (The late Judge Hubert L. Will of the U.S. District Court for the Northern District of Illinois used to call this type of argument "prayer balls to the gods": the lawyer throws out a legal rule and expects the judge or other listener to conduct the analysis herself.) The Example 4 lawyer does much better by

---

6. These elements were adapted from Robert J. Condlin, *Bargaining Without Law*, N.Y.L. School L. Rev. 281 (2011/2012) [hereinafter Condlin, *Bargaining Without Law*]; Robert J. Condlin, *"Cases on Both Sides": Patterns of Argument in Legal Dispute-Negotiation*, 44 Md. L. Rev. 65 (1985). Condlin calls this type of communication "conversational argument." In arguments of this sort, "it is inappropriate to make speeches, score debater's points, or rely on the mannerisms and maneuvers of public oratory to influence one another. . . . [Such argument] does not preach, impress, hector, or punish." Condlin, *Bargaining Without Law, supra*, at 311.

providing a step-by-step review of the rules, facts, and conclusion. He provides necessary details to support the argument (citation to the statutory authority, specific description of the conditions, explicit statement of damages) in a clear and tight format.

Obviously, this approach has limits. A lengthy discourse on the nuances of the law or an extensive review of the evidence, especially if both parties have a thorough understanding of the law and facts, can appear pedantic and turn the listener off. Sometimes, you need only mention the legal rules, focusing your presentation on the factual evidence. At other times, when the facts are not in dispute but the law is, you might need to concentrate on the case law supporting your interpretation of the rules. But beware of assuming that the other side's lawyer understands all the issues. Identify the important issues in dispute about the parties' rights and present a detailed and organized argument on those issues.

*2. **Engage in multi-dimensional reasoning.*** An argument can be based on any number of standards: legal rules; policies; common sense; tradition; business standards; professional judgment; or other norms. And often a number of items of evidence support the application of the standard in the case. The strength of your argument can be increased if you can expand the number of standards and/or facts upon which you rely. Your rights assessment in the case (Charts 24B and 24C) can provide you with these additional reasons.

Assume, for example, a lawyer represents a manufacturer that wants to build a small factory near a residential community. In negotiation with a community group, she can argue simply that the local zoning ordinance allows for the siting of the factory on this property. Alternatively, she can make the following argument:

> As I am sure that city officials have told you, the zoning ordinances allow us to build the factory here without the issuance of a permit or variance. Additionally, three similar factories have been built in other areas zoned I-A in the past five years without any city intervention. But most importantly, consider the jobs this factory will create for your community. The other two factories we operate each employs 50 people from the surrounding community. Finally, your fears about air pollution are unfounded. As our consultant's report shows, our environmental safety record is excellent.

While the first argument addresses solely the narrow issue of the zoning ordinance, the second argument raises not only that issue, but also policy reasons (the city's precedent with such projects) and factual support (increased employment and environmental safety). Whether the lawyer is using an adversarial or problem-solving approach, the second argument presents a more formidable presentation to the community group than the first.

*3. **Design a balanced argument.*** In any argument, balance can create an appearance of reasonableness. In negotiation, that is particularly important because the other side starts out with interests opposed to yours and thus treats you warily. By demonstrating that you understand the strengths and weaknesses on both sides of the case, you show that your assessment of rights is solid and that your reasoning is sound. The legitimacy of your argument will be significantly affected by your acknowledgment of any weaknesses in your case.

In the *Ransom* case, for example, if the landlord's lawyer makes the argument that no problems existed at the apartment, he will have little effect on Ransom's lawyer because the argument is unbalanced or one-sided. On the other hand, if the landlord's lawyer admits that some problems did exist, but that Ransom failed to give adequate notice and even refused entry to the exterminator, the landlord's lawyer increases the odds that Ransom's lawyer will hear and be influenced by the argument. In an adversarial context, this approach may result in a concession from Ransom, and, in a problem-solving setting, it may help to create an atmosphere for joint option generation.

4. Present facts persuasively. In some negotiations, the most contested issues will concern disputed facts. A dry and antiseptic presentation of the facts may have very little effect on the other side or its lawyer. On the other hand, a persuasive description of the facts may significantly enhance the force of your argument. In presenting your version of the facts to the other side, consider many of the same factors you do when you are preparing for a presentation of facts at a trial or hearing: the nature of your audience, the uncontested facts, a unifying theme, and persuasive images (see Chapter 13). Think of how you can tell a persuasive story that will have an emotional impact on the other lawyer.

In the Ransom case, for example, if you represent Ransom and know that the landlord's lawyer has small children, you may want to focus your presentation of the facts on the effect of the inadequate conditions on your client's children. Or in a criminal case, if you represent the defendant and are plea bargaining with a prosecutor who has an extremely heavy caseload, you may want to organize the facts around the theme of the multiple inconsistencies in the prosecution's case. In this way, you subtly send a message to the prosecutor that trial of this case will be too difficult to handle.

5. Ability to persist in face of rejection. While it is important in a negotiation to present a balanced argument to show your reasonableness, you can only be effective if you continue to press your principal points in the face of your adversary's rejection. Merely repeating the same points will not move your adversary. When met with resistance, you need to present your arguments in different ways—reframing them, offering new evidence, or probing for details about your opponent's objections, and modifying your positions only after being presented with arguments or information that provide a good basis for the change. Experienced bargainers expect arguments to be rejected, and you have to be ready to respond, not retreat.

6. Use unusual or unexpected arguments. Argument is most effective if it creates doubts your adversary cannot overcome within the negotiation time frame. If you rely solely on arguments that are obvious to your adversary, either because you have previously used them multiple times or because they are the boilerplate positions taken by parties in such cases, you will make little headway. Your goal, then, "is to tell the adversary something new about the issues in dispute, something he had not thought of on his own, and something that causes him to have second thoughts about what he believes to be true."[7]

§28.2.2 MAKING AND HANDLING THREATS

Making threats. A threat is a declaration by a negotiator of an intent to assert a right or power if the other party does not comply with a request or demand. While an argument is an attempt to persuade the other side logically of a client's rights in a dispute or transaction, a threat is an effort to use your client's rights or power to coerce the other side to agreement. Fisher and Ury say that "threats are one of the most abused tactics in negotiation."[8] They warn that threats can lead to counterthreats from the other party, create ill will between the parties, and even destroy relationships between the parties.

All of that is true. But there are times when logical arguments have no effect, and when the other party will not make any further concessions or agree to any alternative solutions. If your client has rights or powers that can be used to force the other party to budge, threats may be an effective tactic.

Threats work only if they are credible and will have a significant impact on the other side. If they lack credibility, the other party will just laugh them off. A threat by Ransom to stage a rent strike, for example, will have little effect if Dusak knows that no tenants organization exists and that Ransom has made no attempt to start one.

To determine whether you have potentially effective threats, consider your assessments of rights and power (Charts 24B, 24C, and 24D). Assess the strengths and weaknesses of your client's possible legal claims and power plays. Imagine what counterthreats could be raised against your client. Think about what steps the other side could take to shift the rights and power balances. Then ask yourself: "In light of these assessments, will a particular threat appear credible to the other side? And what impact will it have on them?"

Even if you can identify effective threats, think of ways of packaging them to lessen the potential for enmity, especially if the parties will have a continuing relationship after the negotiation. The most credible threats are not delivered with table pounding and insult. They are instead presented in the form of subtle suggestions that demonstrate the existence of the right or power without drama. The trick is to make a threat without being threatening.

Fisher and Ury suggest the use of warnings, rather than outright threats.[9] "A threat comes across as what you will do to them if they do not agree. A warning comes across as what will happen if agreement is not reached."[10] Contrast these threats from Ransom's lawyer:

---

7. Condlin, *Bargaining Without Law, supra* note 6, at 320.
8. Fisher et al., *supra* note 1, at 136.
9. *Id. at 137;* William Ury, *Getting Past No: Negotiating Your Way from Confrontation to Cooperation* 136 (1993).
10. Ury, *supra* note 9, at 137.

> *Example 5*
> If you don't agree to make the repairs in my client's apartment by June 15, she will get the tenants organization to start a rent strike and picket the building.

> *Example 6*
> If we can't reach an agreement to have the repairs made by June 15, it seems likely that we're not going to be able to control the tenants organization, and it may start a rent strike and picket the building.

Although both threats demonstrate Ransom's power, the second presents the consequences as though they were outside of the client's control. When Dusak's lawyer asks, "Are you threatening me?", Ransom's lawyer can reply, "I'm sorry, this is nothing personal. It's just my opinion as to how the tenants group will respond."[11]

Responding to threats. When you are confronted with a threat, you have several options. First, you can ignore the threat. If you believe that the claimed right or power underlying the threat is weak or that the other side will not carry it out, you might just write the threat off as ignorable bluster or venting by the other lawyer. If your client will not be significantly affected even if the threat is carried out, you might want to explain why it will have little impact and then continue the bargaining. There is a risk, however, that the other lawyer will try to divert you into a discussion of whether the threatened action will have the slight consequences you assert, and you may lose control of the agenda. If you consider the threat meaningless, cut this discussion off and get back to bargaining.

If the threat is credible and will have a significant impact on your client, you might explain to the other lawyer how you are able to equalize the rights or power imbalance. Outline the actions your client can take to neutralize the threat. You can identify these options from your rights and power assessments. For example, consider an employment discrimination dispute in which the plaintiff's lawyer threatens to seek class action certification if the employer does not agree to the plaintiff's offer. In response, the employer's lawyer might assert that the employer will extensively litigate the class certification motion, and if unsuccessful, will take an interlocutory appeal and tie up the case for years.

A third tactic is a counterthreat. From the arsenal of your own client's rights and powers, you can identify a threat that your client will carry out in retaliation if the other side follows through with its threat. In a negotiation for the sale of a house, for example, when the buyer threatens to purchase other property down the street instead, the seller can respond that it just received a call from another eager buyer. To work, this counterthreat has to be credible and has to have the potential for a significant impact on the other side—or it will be considered no more than bravado.

The danger with a counterthreat, however, is that it can lead to an escalation of tensions and a breakdown in bargaining. If your evaluation of your client's BATNA suggests that further negotiation would help, you may want to try to

---

11. For a discussion of the ethical issues raised by this reply, see §23.5.

soften your presentation of the counterthreat. When the buyer's lawyer threatens to buy another house instead, the seller's lawyer might say: "My client also received a call today from Dandy Realty with a serious prospect for a new buyer who wants to see the house tonight. But let's not be distracted by other buyers and sellers and get back to the terms of this deal."

§28.3 HANDLING SPECIAL PROBLEMS

§28.3.1 EXPRESSING ANGER

Anger, whether expressed quietly or volcanically, should be used only to make a point. If anger appears simply as an emotional reaction to the conduct or arguments of the other side, it can be detrimental to your client's interests. Like threats, anger can increase animosity between the parties, result in irrational decision-making, and lead to the premature termination of bargaining. Accordingly, if you feel that you cannot control your anger, distance yourself from the negotiation by taking a break to check in with your office for messages or go to the restroom. After you have calmed yourself and feel in control, return to the table.

On occasion, however, feigned anger, used purposefully, can be an effective communication tactic. If, for example, the other lawyer is insensitive to your client's interests, refuses to recognize any strength in a rights-based argument, summarily dismisses all your attempts to initiate problem-solving negotiation, makes outrageous demands, or engages in dishonest conduct, you may want to use anger as a means of getting that lawyer's attention. In these cases, your sole purpose is to communicate the seriousness of your displeasure to the other party, not to vent your frustrations. For this reason, express the anger in a controlled, lucid, and pointed way—not in an outburst. Once the other side has shown that it has received your message, you should return to your usual style.

Overuse of this tactic can be especially counterproductive if the anger is expressed with intense emotion. A lawyer who consistently uses angry outbursts to interrupt the other side's arguments will gain a reputation for hot-headedness. Other lawyers will simply ignore the behavior, and it will have no effect.

§28.3.2 HANDLING THE DIFFICULT ADVERSARY

Sometimes, you will face an obstreperous adversary who will try to control the negotiation by attacking you or your client. Or you will meet the dishonest lawyer who will try to prevail with phony or confusing data.

If you respond to these tactics with anger, your adversary will have accomplished something: you will lose control and be distracted from your strategy. When confronted with these tactics, you should stay focused on moving the negotiations in the direction you originally planned. In the words of William Ury, you want to "reframe" the attacks or dishonest tricks into facilitators of discussion.[12]

12. Ury, *supra* note 9, at 91–94.

There are several ways to reframe attacks from an obstreperous lawyer. First, you can ignore an attack and continue with your argument or proposal. Once the other side understands that you will not take the bait, it may abandon its attempts to distract you.

Second, you may want to reframe a personal attack into an argument on an issue. Suppose that in the Ransom case Dusak's lawyer shouts at Ransom's lawyer, "You legal aid lawyers! You get paid by the government and then file volumes of frivolous claims!" If Ransom's lawyer starts defending herself and her office, she accomplishes nothing, but if she pointedly asks Dusak's lawyer to point out the parts of her papers that are frivolous, she brings the discussion back to the issues in the case.

Third, you might want to recast personal attacks regarding past wrongs into options for the future. If Ransom's lawyer attacks Dusak as "a typical slum landlord who has consistently ignored the problems faced by my client," Dusak's lawyer can respond, "Let's stop dwelling on the past and try to develop a solution that will assist both of our clients."

As to dishonest tricks, you can challenge them immediately and directly. There is a risk, however. If you are wrong and the adversary is not actually being dishonest, you might find yourself accused of dishonesty. And even if you have not erred, you may just antagonize the other lawyer and damage the possibility of further bargaining. Accordingly, before you present a direct challenge, ask clarifying questions. If the other lawyer relies on certain data or evidence, ask for the specifics, for a copy of the document or records, or for substantiating facts. Use the misrepresentation as a vehicle for discovery. If that approach does not work, you may want to call your opponent's bluff. If in the negotiations for the sale of a house, for example, the seller insists that the house was exterminated for termites less than a year ago, the buyer's lawyer can respond, "So I'm sure you would have no objection to a provision in the contract that if you cannot provide a copy of an invoice for such an inspection within two weeks, you will pay for a new extermination."

§28.4 CLOSING THE DEAL

Wrapping up the deal includes concluding the negotiation discussions with the other side, discussing the final agreement with your client, and drafting the agreement or stipulation of settlement.

§28.4.1 CONCLUDING THE NEGOTIATION AND DISCUSSING IT WITH YOUR CLIENT

Sometimes, toward the end of a negotiation, the parties will reach an impasse. They will be close to settlement, but neither party will make the final concession or agree to compromise a particular interest. At that point, a formulaic approach such as "splitting the difference," might be very helpful. Although splitting the difference is inappropriate earlier in a negotiation (see §27.1.4), at the end when the parties are close to settlement principled negotiation may not be as important as a simple nudge to agreement. At this point even in adversarial negotiations, you want to help the other side save face and make it feel it won (see §27.2.3).

After the parties have reached an agreement, you should review in detail the terms with the other lawyer, confirming all the essential components. You want to make sure there are no misunderstandings.

Then contact your client immediately. If your client did not pre-authorize the exact agreement you reached (see §24.5), the agreement is tentative and does not become real until your client approves (and until the other lawyer's client approves, too, if the other lawyer did not have authority). If your client had pre-authorized the terms of this agreement, at least you want to share the news.

§28.4.2 DRAFTING THE AGREEMENT OR STIPULATION OF SETTLEMENT

The agreement should be memorialized in writing. If the parties have not been litigating against each other, the writing will usually include the word "Agreement" or "Contract" or the equivalent in big letters at the top of the first page. If the negotiation resolves litigation, the writing is a stipulation of settlement. A stipulation is an agreement between the parties to a lawsuit. If consideration flows in both directions, it's a contract even though it isn't called one. In some litigation settings, the stipulation is recited orally "on the record" in open court, and the transcript is the writing, even though not signed by the parties.

In any event, the precise wording of the agreement is crucial because afterward the parties will be governed by the words and not by your memory of what was agreed to. If possible, write the initial draft of the agreement yourself to assure precision on the provisions that are most important to your client. In certain settings, practitioners start from—but are not limited to—form contracts or stipulations. But even in those situations, make sure that the language conforms to the agreement you have actually reached. If it doesn't, write new language that does. When another lawyer tells you that "we don't need to deal with that particular issue in writing," you probably *do* need to put it in writing. Nothing protects your client better than a written agreement that spells out the deal exactly as you understand it. If there's a later dispute about what was agreed to, you are at a severe disadvantage without a signed agreement drafted to your satisfaction.

The paragraphs that follow are an introduction to—and not a full explanation of—agreement drafting. To learn how to do this well, read Tina L. Stark, *Contract Drafting* (2014). You really should learn how to draft well. Everything you've gained through negotiation can be lost if you make mistakes in drafting the agreement. (A stipulation of settlement in litigation is a contract between the parties and should be drafted like one, even if it begins with a litigation caption.) Here are a few foundational concepts of agreement drafting:

1. Use words that express precisely the agreement you have obtained from the other side. The Angels are a baseball team in Anaheim, California, which is near but not in Los Angeles. For several decades, they called themselves the California Angels. Many people in Anaheim feel that the team should not be ashamed of where it plays and should call itself the Anaheim Angels. The City of Anaheim owns the stadium used by the team. In 1996, the city and team negotiated a new lease, which included this language:

> Tenant [the Angels] will change the name of the Team to include the name "Anaheim" therein, such change to be effective no later than the commencement of the 1997 Season.

From 1997 to 2005, the team called itself the Anaheim Angels. In 2005, the team decided that it could make more money with a different name, and it began calling itself the Los Angeles Angels of Anaheim. The city thought it had a deal that the team would be called the Anaheim Angels. The team argued that it satisfied the language in the lease if the word Anaheim appeared *anywhere* in the team's name. The city sued and lost. If you look at a sports web site or a newspaper's sports section, you'll now see the team identified as the Los Angeles Angels or the L.A. Angels, which is also what you'll hear announcers say on television and radio. The media aren't required to give the full name of an organization they discuss.

What words in the lease might have prevented this? Try the following:

> The Tenant shall change the name of the Team to Anaheim Angels no later than the commencement of the 1997 Season and shall use that name for the Team and no other name throughout the remainder of the Lease Term.

Use words that express *precisely* the agreement you have obtained from the other side.

2. ***For each issue which you and the other side have settled, choose the appropriate ingredients of an agreement and draft accordingly.*** Agreements are made up of covenants, discretionary authority, conditions, representations, warranties, and declarations.

A *covenant* is a promise to do something ("Smith *shall* paint the house") or not to do something ("Smith *shall not* paint the house"). Those promises represent obligations and are the heart of most agreements. To express a covenant, begin with the name or designation of the party who has made the promise, add the word *shall*, and then add the thing the party has promised to do or not to do:

> Smith shall paint the house.
> Smith shall not paint the house.

Never—never—use the word *shall* in any other way. *Shall* means "has a legally enforceable duty to." "Smith shall paint the house" means that Smith has a legally enforceable duty to paint the house created by the contract. Therefore, *shall* should always be preceded by the person or organization that has the duty ("Smith"). And it should always be followed by language that precisely states what the duty is ("paint the house"). You will see countless agreements and statutes where this rule is violated. Every one of them, as a result, is harder to read and understand. And many of them are ambiguous as well. An agreement that does not state duties clearly and unambiguously creates the risk of later disputes and litigation because each side will interpret the vaguenesses and ambiguities to suit its own interest. In addition, an agreement can impose a duty *only* on a person or organization who is a party to it. "Any lawsuit to enforce this Agreement shall be commenced in the courts of the state of New Mexico" is wrong. A lawsuit cannot have a duty; only a party can.

Discretionary authority is permission to do something ("Smith *may* paint the house"). To express discretionary authority, begin with the party who has the authority, add the word *may*, and then add the thing the party has discretion to do or refrain from doing. A party with discretionary authority is not required to exercise it. It is discretionary. If it were required, it would be a covenant.

A *condition* limits a covenant or discretionary authority to a condition that must be satisfied before the covenant or discretionary authority is effective. Where the condition can be expressed in the same sentence as the covenant or discretionary authority, use an "if" clause to express the condition.

> If the outside temperature is 60.0°F or more at 9:00 A.M. on March 15, Smith shall paint the house on that day [a *covenant*].

> If the outside temperature is greater than 45.0°F and less than 60.0°F at 9:00 A.M. on May 15, Smith may paint the house on that day [*discretionary authority*].

A condition that functions as an exception can be expressed in an "except" or "unless" clause. Where a covenant or discretionary authority is subject to several conditions, a single sentence may be inadequate, and you may have to use some other construction.

A *representation* is a statement of fact intended to induce reliance. If a party misrepresents facts about the present or the past (not about the future)[13] and intends his assertion to induce the other party to enter into contract, the other party has remedies for misrepresentation. Unlike a representation, a *warranty* does not require inducement. And the warranteed statement can be about the present, the past, or (unlike a representation) the future. A representation or a warranty is made by one party to the other. If in negotiation the other side has made a statement of fact on which you or your client rely or otherwise want to be true, draft the agreement so that the other side represents and warrants that statement ("Jones represents and warrants that she has sole fee simple title, without encumbrances, to the house").

Make the other side *both* represent *and* warrant because in a later lawsuit growing out of the agreement, a misrepresentation and a breach of warranty require different burdens of proof and yield different remedies. Having both theories available gives you the maximum flexibility later. (If the statement is about the future, it can be only a warranty because representations are limited to the present and the past.) Even if the other side has not volunteered a statement on which you want to rely, you can negotiate for it, for example, by asking the other

---

13. Under some limited circumstances a promise about future events can be the basis for a claim of misrepresentation. "[A] promise or a prediction of future events may by implication involve an assertion that facts exist from which the promised or predicted consequences will follow, which may be a misrepresentation as to those facts. Thus, from a statement that a particular machine will attain a specified level of performance when it is used, it may be inferred that its present design and condition make it capable of such a level. Such an inference may be drawn even if the statement is not legally binding as a promise." Restatement (Second) of Contracts §159, cmt. c (1981).

lawyer, "Is your client willing to represent and warrant that she has sole and clear title to the house?" If the point is important to your client, a negative answer to a question like that is a danger sign.

A *declaration* is a statement made by both parties jointly ("This agreement is governed by the law of New Mexico").

While you're negotiating, remember that what you're working toward is a written agreement made up of the ingredients explained above. As you and the other side resolve each issue in the negotiation, develop in your own mind an approximate sense of how you will express the resolution of that issue in the written agreement. Often, you and the other side will negotiate the words that will appear in the agreement—either as you negotiate the deal itself or as you draft and find yourself negotiating again over the details expressed in words.

Especially in a deal in which performance is required by a party over a period of time, you should include remedies provisions addressing the issue of nonperformance of the terms of the contract. You might want to consider methods for increasing the costs to the other side for noncompliance, such as the forfeiting of funds deposited in an escrow account. If you're settling litigation, the agreement should provide procedures for bringing the case back to court and perhaps sanctions against the offending party. If the tenant in an eviction action, for example, promises to pay back rent on a payment schedule, the landlord's lawyer may request a provision allowing for the issuance of an eviction order upon her default. In response, the tenant's lawyer might request a grace period for payment and the right to notice and hearing before the granting of such an order. And in a transaction, consider possible penalties against the nonperforming party, such as the imposition of liquidated damages.

INDEX